WORLD WRECKER

To Chris
Best Wishes
Rich Gombert

ABOUT THE AUTHOR

Richard W. Gombert lives with his wife, two beautiful daughters and a dog along the north coast in Ohio. By day he works as a computer systems administrator for a large manufacturing company.

An avid reader, Rich counts his true conversion to science fiction as starting when he read “Galaxy Mission” by Edmond Hamilton in the sixth grade.

Rich attends conventions and conferences, both SF and gaming, and is the archivist for the Science Fiction Poetry Association. He is also an owner, moderator, or member of various online book groups as well as a member of a local SF/F/H book group.

Rich can be found online at various times (too many) and locations including Facebook, Yahoo groups, LinkedIn, Plaxo, and many other (sorry no Twitter yet).

Among his many activities he enjoys reading, brewing and drinking beer, gaming, music, genealogy, history, and traveling with his family.

You can email him at:

rgombert@yahoo.com

WORLD WRECKER

An Annotated Bibliography of

Edmond Hamilton

by

Richard W. Gombert

With an Introduction by Jack Williamson

THE BORGO PRESS

An Imprint of Wildside Press LLC

MMIX

BIBLIOGRAPHIES OF MODERN AUTHORS

ISSN 0749-470X

Number Twenty-Two

www.wildsidebooks.com

FIRST EDITION

CONTENTS

INTRODUCTION

by Jack Williamson

By way of review, I have just reread Leigh Brackett's introduction to *The Best of Edmond Hamilton* and Ed's own afterword. Taken together, they might make a better introduction to this volume than I can write. Certainly, they bring a fresh life to my own recollections of the remarkable man I first met more than sixty years ago.

Edmond Hamilton was a good deal more complex and more interesting than anyone might guess from reading his early fiction. He had a caustic wit and a sardonic view of the world, especially of women—that was long before he met Leigh. He was a biblomaniac who haunted bookstores, read voraciously, and never forgot anything he read. He explored odd corners of history. He recited forgotten poets. He loved good talk. He was an inveterate punster; he and his younger sister, Betty, used to enjoy duels of puns.

Fanzines and cons were still to come when American science fiction was new, back in the 1920s, but the back pages of the magazines were full of letters from readers, in tiny print but exciting to fans like me, still intoxicated with those wondrous worlds of the liberated imagination. The editors must have liked them because they were free. Complete with names and addresses, they put us in touch with one another and gave me my first friends in the field. Miles J. Breuer was a busy Nebraska physician who knew more about writing than I did. He took me on as a sort of journeyman apprentice; we published a short story and then a novel in collaboration.

Jerome Seigel gave me Ed's address—still a raw beginner then, Jerry was later one of the creators of *Superman.* I had read Ed's "Comet Doom" in *Amazing*. I wrote him, and we discovered a shared interest in Mark Twain and the Mississippi. In the summer of 1931 we met in Minneapolis, planning to buy a houseboat and take it down the river.

A crazy dream. Neither of us had ever been in even a rowboat. But we bought an outboard motor boat and camping equipment and set out for New Orleans, learning as we went. In spite of a few rough moments with the river and once or twice with each other, we got there, camping on sand bars along the scenic upper river and staying in the YMCA when the scenery had given way to willows along the levies.

In the long days that might have been boring, he would tell me about all the great works of imagination I had never read.

His chief fiction market at the time was *Weird Tales*. He sold Farnsworth Wright forty stories without a rejection, and still sent return postage with every new story. Wright was himself a fascinating and almost heroic figure. Half disabled with Parkinson's disease and handicapped by starvation budgets, he made *WT* truly "the unique magazine," a pioneer fantasy publication back when fantasy was poison to most readers. The stories he could buy for a penny a word were often pretty bad, but there were a gifted few who wrote fine fantasy for the love of it. The best of the magazine was unforgettable.

Most of Ed's stories were what Wright called "weird scientific." His tales of the Interstellar Patrol were heroic adventure in the far-off future without much science. A little band of veteran warriors from a mix of galactic races fought desperately to defeat malignant aliens and save civilization. Written with scant concern for style or character, they featured hectic action and Ed's own emotion. He hammered them out on a little portable typewriter with such conviction that the "o"s were punching round holes in the pages before he came to the end. Those early epics paved the way for all the better-known space operas still to come from E. E. Smith and a hundred others.

In New Orleans we looked up E. Hoffmann Price, who was working for Union Carbide to support a wife and infant son, and already a *WT* regular. He was a West Pointer, a veteran of World War II, an astrologer, an Orientalist who smoked a hookah, collected Persian rugs, and cultivated Turkish and Arab friends. His remarkable vitality enabled him to entertain us with his salty talk and exotic drinks through most of the nights without any apparent danger to the job. A man of the world, as I saw him then, and a retired soldier of fortune. I named the hero of my next novel for him.

He and Ed were my introduction to Farnsworth Wright and his little clan of regular contributors. Living on an isolated New Mexico ranch, I never got to know many of them, but they were a fascinating group, devoted to fantasy and what was still the mysterious East. Later in Chicago I met Otis Adelbert Kline and Wright himself. Still later in California, Ed drove Price and me to Auburn, to call on Clark Ashton Smith, maybe a genius and certainly a singular recluse, whose name in the clan had been Klar

Kash Ton. Wright was the first great fantasy editor. Generous to me, he bought a good many of my stories.

Ed and I were friends as long as he lived. Though our homes were far apart we saw a good deal of each other through the years before we married. In the fall of 1933, I spent a few weeks with him at his home in New Castle, Pennsylvania, about twenty miles from Youngstown. His mother was Pennsylvania Dutch, a small, vigorous, sharp-tongued woman, and I think the real head of the family. His father, Scott Hamilton, struck me as an easy-going type, glad enough to leave responsibility to her. Esther, an older sister, was on the *Youngstown Telegram* and I think a power in the steel city. Ed regarded her with some awe; he once told me that the scar on his nose came from a knife she had thrown. Betty, the younger sister, was more amiable and closer to him.

In her introduction, Leigh says he had been a child prodigy. Certainly he had a fine mind. Born in 1904, he entered college at fourteen and left at seventeen, I suppose because of boredom and impatience with any sort of discipline. He held down a railroad job for a time before he began writing, but I think his chief interest had been tracking down and reading the fantasy and science fiction classics that were still in those days hard to find. He had what seemed to me an enviable existence. Living in New Castle with his parents until he married, he was more or less immune to the financial uncertainties of writing for the pulps. I have pleasant recollections of hiking with him in the hills near his home and driving downtown at night for ice cream and the *New York Times*.

At the end of that 1933 visit, I drove with him down to Key West. The depression had driven the town officially bankrupt. The big resort hotel had shut down. We rented a house with our own tropical orchard for eight or ten dollars a month. It was near Ernest Hemingway's mansion, but he was away, hunting lions in Africa. More enterprising than I, Ed got to know a lot of the local characters. He got the use of a boat for putting a mast and sail on it, and did a good bit of fishing.

A summer or two later, he and Betty stopped to visit me in New Mexico and get a taste of ranch life. He came back several times through the years. I saw him again in New Castle. In 1937 we drove from there to New York. I enjoyed my glimpse of the city and meeting more writers and editors.

And we both kept writing. The pulps had been slow to feel the depression, I suppose because they were still affordable entertainment, but radio had begun offering still cheaper fare. Some of the pulps endured, including Standard Magazines edited by Leo

Margulies, with Mort Weisinger as an able assistant. Under various pen names, Ed was selling to *Thrilling Detective*, *Thrilling Wonder*, and *Startling*. Under his own name and the house name, Brett Sterling, he wrote nearly all the Captain Future novels.

When Weisinger moved over to the comics in 1949, Ed went with him and soon became a staff writer for *Superman*. None of this output had much appeal to literary critics. If that bothered him he never said much about it, though he used to grumble about his slavery to the comics. We were staying alive as science fiction writers before it was easy—if it ever was. We wrote what we could sell.

If he spent little time on style or character in his early work, nobody cared. He wrote great tales and wrote them fast, with little need for revision. When standards changed, he was able to change with them. Some of his stories had always been memorable. I think he learned from Leigh Brackett after they were married, as I think she learned from him.

He had always been a master of plot. Her early stories were well-written interplanetary adventures with more color than his, and characters more strikingly drawn. Much of her later work was done for TV and for Howard Hawks and other film producers. The last thing she wrote was the script for *The Empire Strikes Back*. Though they never claimed to be collaborating, I'm sure they influenced each other. Leigh's last novels were space operas he admired, and certainly his own craftsmanship continued to improve.

In their later years, they divided their time between Los Angeles and an old farmhouse near Youngstown, which they bought and restored. They traveled extensively. And, being writers, they kept on writing. When conventions began to honor writers, they were duly honored. Ed's work had always been popular. I recall his pleasure on discovering a Captain Future Club in Sweden. Though he never wrote to please the critics, he earned more attentions than he has ever received. I'm happy to see this book appearing.

An Edmond Hamilton Chronology

1904	Edmond Moore Hamilton was born on October 21st in Youngstown, Ohio to Scott B. Hamilton, a cartoonist, and Maude Whinery, a school teacher. He grew up in the Youngstown - Pittsburgh, PA region and was a bright and gifted child.
1919	He entered Westminster College at age 15, studying Physics.
1922	He took a job as a clerk for the Pennsylvania Railroad.
1926	His first story, "The Monster-God of Mamurth" was published in the August issue of Weird Tales. His next 39 stories were accepted for publication.
1928	The first of the Interstellar Patrol stories, "The Crashing Suns" was published. The hardback collection of Mr. Hamilton's **The Horror on the Asteroid and Other Tales of Planetary Horror** was published.
1932	The first of the Stuart Merrick stories was published "Kaldar, World of Antares."
1936	The first of Mr. Hamilton mysteries **Murder in the Grave**, was published.
1939	The Ethan Drew stories were published.
1940	The first of the Captain Future stories were published. He married Leigh Bracket on 31 December. A successful writer in her own right, she wrote mostly for the movies ("Return of the Jedi"), and she also wrote some Mysteries and Science Fiction.
1946	The stories **The Star Kings** and the **Star of Life** were published. **The Star Kings** would later be printed as a paperback and become Mr. Hamilton's most popular book. **City at World's End** was published.
1956	**Battle for the Stars**, originally credited to the pseudonym of Alexander Blade, was published.
1960	The novel **The Haunted Stars** was published.
1962	The story "Requiem" was published.
1964	Mr. Hamilton and his wife were joint Guests of Honor at the 1964 World Science Fiction convention in Oakland, CA (Pacificon). The story "The Pro" was published Mr. Hamilton had 1 other story published.
1965	The story "What's It Like Out There" was published. Mr. Hamilton had 1 other story published.

1966	The novels **Doomstar** and **The Weapon From Beyond** were published. **The Weapon From Beyond** was the first of the "Starwolf" books. Mr. Hamilton had 1 other story published.
1969	Mr. Hamilton was invited to watch the launch of Apollo 12 on 14 November from the VIP box at Cape Kennedy. Mr. Hamilton had 2 stories published.
1977	Mr. Hamilton died February 1st in Lancaster, CA of complications following kidney surgery. The book **The Best of Edmond Hamilton** came out this year.

Ed and Leigh spent the summers in rural northeastern Ohio and the winters in California.

About the Format of each Entry

Basic Book Entry

Title of Book (coauthor if any) (Series if any), City: Publisher, Publication date, number of pages (p.). Size (in cm.). ill. (if illustrated). (Additional information if any). ISBN or other identifying number. Cover and/or interior artist. Type of binding if known. [Language if not English]

REPRINTS:

Number (information)), City: Publisher, Publication date, number of pages (p.). Size (in cm.). ill. (if illustrated). Additional information if any). ISBN or other identifying number. Cover and/or interior artist. Type of binding if known. [Language if not English]

CHAPTERS or CONTENTS: If the book is a novel the number of chapters or chapter titles. If the book is an anthology or collection the contents will be listed.

REVIEWS:

Reviewer. Publication. Volume:issue, number (Publication date): Page (Pg.) or pages (pp.).

Synopsis of the story.

Basic Magazine Entry

Story Title (coauthor if any) (Series if any), City: Publisher, Publication date, number of pages (p.). Size (in cm.). ill. (if illustrated). (Additional information if any). ISBN or other identifying number. Cover and/or interior artist. Type of binding if known. [Language if not English]

REPRINTS:

Number (information)), City: Publisher, Publication date, number of Pages (p.). Size (in cm.). ill. (if illustrated).

Additional information if any). ISBN or other identifying number. Cover and/or interior artist. Type of binding if known. [Language if not English]

CHAPTERS: number of chapters or chapter titles if available.

REVIEWS:

Reviewer. Publication. Volume:issue, number (Publication date): Page (Pg.) or pages (p.).

Notes

Bolded entries are book titles.
Underlined items are serial publications (magazines).
"Quoted" items are titles of short fiction or articles.

Page notations:

Pg. _	Starts on indicated page.
_ p.	item has this many pages
pp. _	item runs from first listed page to the last listed page.

Type of binding may be chap, cloth, paperback (mass market), trade paper.

Publication date is the publication or copyright date indicated in the book, unless a different, actual release date is known.

_: <publisher unknown> City unknown: Publisher is not known.

? p.	Unknown number of pages.
<year>	Publish year unknown

If there is no ill. cm. that means that this information was not available.

A
They Would Become Books

A1 "The Metal Giants" in Weird Tales, 8:6 (December 1926) Pg. 724.
Illustrator: Joseph Dustin[i].

REPRINTS:

b as **The Metal Giants**. Washburn, ND: Swanson Book Co. 1932, 35 p. (Science Fiction Reprint #1). paper. [collection]

c in **The Gernsback Awards. 1.: 1926**. Edited by Forrest J. Ackerman, Los Angeles, CA: Triton, 1982, pp. 59-81. Illustrator: Joseph Dustin. [collection]

A2 "Crashing Suns." in Weird Tales, 12:2 (August 1928) Pg. 193.
Illustrator: Hugh Rankin.;
Part Two in Weird Tales, 12:3 (September 1928) Pg. 375.
Illustrator: Hr. (Hugh Rankin).

REPRINTS:

b as **Patrulha Interstellar**. Lisboa: Livros do Brasil. 1950, p. (No. 133) Translation by Eurico da Fonseca. [collection] [Brazilian]

c **Crashing Suns**. New York, NY: Ace Books, 1965, 192 p. paper [F-319] Cover: Ed Valigursky. Interior: Jack Gaughan. [collection]

ba as **Patrulha Interstellar**. Lisboa: Livros do Brasil. 1968, p. (No. 133) Translation by Eurico da Fonseca. [collection] [Brazilian]

d as **O Polemos ton Ilion**. Athens: Sympan/Lynari, 1968, p. Translated by N. Chochlakis. [collection] [Greek]

da as **O Polemos ton Ilion**. Athens: Sympan/Lynari, 1980, p. Translated by N. Chochlakis. [collection] [Greek]

e Riverdale, NY: Baen Books. August 1, 2008. SKU: 1401403190.

CONTENTS:

"Crashing Suns" [See A2]
"The Star Stealers" [See B10]

“Within the Nebula” [See B13]
“The Comet Drivers” [See B7]
“The Cosmic Cloud” [See B32]

A3 “Outside the Universe.” in Weird Tales, 14:1 (July 1929) Pg. 49. Illustrator: C. C. Senf.;
Part Two - Weird Tales, 14:2 (August 1929) Pg. 219. Illustrator: C. C. Senf.;
Part Three - Weird Tales, 14:3 (September 1929) Pg. 374. Illustrator: C. C. Senf.;
Part Four - Weird Tales, 14:4 (October 1929) Pg. 517. Illustrator: C.C. Senf.

REPRINTS:

b as **Hors de l’univers & Les voleurs d’etoiles**. _: editions Opta. 1957, 457 p. 21 cm. (with **Les Voleurs d-etoiles (The Star Stealers**). (Club du livre d’anticipation; 56) [collection] [French]

c as **Outside the Universe**. New York, NY: Ace Books. 1964, 173 p. paper (F-271). Cover: Ed Valigursky. Interior: Jack Gaughan. [collection]

d as **Luta Inter-galactica**. Lisboa: Livros do Brasil. 1964, p. Tranlator: Jorge Fonseca. (No. 92). [collection] [Brazilian]

e as **L’invasione della Galassia**. Piacenza: Casa Editrice La Tribuna. 1964, 181 p. 19cm. (Gallassia No. 115) Traslator: Maurizio Cesari. [collection] [Italian]

ea as **L’invasione della Galassia**. Piacenza: Casa Editrice La Tribuna. 1970, 181 p. Traslator: Maurizio Cesari. (with **Corridoi del tempo** by Andre Norton). [collection] [Italian]

f Tokyo: Hayakawa Publishing, Inc. 1971, 248 p. (SF15). Translator: Masahiro Noda. [Japanese]

g as **Hors de l’univers**. Paris: editions Opta, 1975, 457 p. (Club du Livre #56). ISBN: 2-7201-0018-8. Translator: Bruno Martin. [French]

h as **Hors de l’univers & Les voleurs d’etoiles**. Paris: editions Opta, 1975, p. (Club du Livre d’Anticipation – Limited to 5120 numbered copies). Translator: Bruno Martin. [collection] [French]

fa Tokyo: Hayakawa Publishing, Inc. 1978, 161 p. B6(TM-25). Translator: Masahiro Noda. [Japanese]

i as **Les voleurs d’etoiles**. _: publisher ubknown? <year>, p. [collection] [French]

j Riverdale, NY: Baen Books. August 1, 2008. SKU: 0241002710.

CHAPTERS:

SUMMARY:

The interstellar patrol intercepts a large fleet of ships coming into the galaxy. They amass all their forces and fight a pitched battle, but lose and the invaders gain a foothold in the cancer cluster. The galactic government deciphers some of the aliens' story and find that they are fleeing the collapse of their own galaxy. They had originally tried to invade the Andromeda galaxy but were repulsed by its inhabitants. The galactic council sends a small squadron of ships to the Andromeda galaxy to, try and convince its inhabitants to help defend our Milky Way.

REVIEWS:

P. Miller. Analog 76(1) (September 1965) Pp. 150-151.

A4 "The Murder In the Clinic" in Scientific Detective Mysteries, (May 1930) Pg. 390.

REPRINTS:

b as collection.**Murder in the Clinic**[ii]. London: Utopian Publishers, 1946, 36 p. paper. [collection]

c in **The Invisible Master**. Bloomington, IL: Black Dog Press, 2000, p. Pg. 76. chap [collection]

CHAPTERS:

I: Murder
In the Clinic
Dr. Braller
Who is Ransome?
The Telephone
By Door or Window?
II: Dr. Jackson Arrives
Ransome Again
Facial Surgery
A Scientific Criminal
III: The Quarrel
Accused
Misty Statements
IV: False Evidence
Reconstruction
The Letter
Was it A Forgery?
V: The Secret Worker
The Face-Moulder
Behind the Scenes
Untangling the Web

A5 "Horror on the Asteroid" in Weird Tales, 22:3 (September, 1933): Pg. 298. Illustrator: Jayem Wilcox.

REPRINTS:

b as collection. London[iii]: Philip Allan, 1936, 256 p.[iv] 20 cm. cloth. [collection]

c as collection. Boston, MA: Gregg Press, 1975, p. (75-5745) Pg. 59. Introduction by Gerry de la Ree. cloth. [collection]

CONTENTS:

"The Horror on the Asteroid"	p. 9 - 58	[See A5]
"The Accursed Galaxy"	p. 59 - 98	[See B69]
"The Man Who Saw Everything"	p. 99 - 126	[See ?]
"The Earth-Brain"	p. 127 - 184	[See B45]
"The Monster-God of Mamurth"	p. 185 - 218	[See B1]
"The Man Who Evolved"	p. 219 -	[See B35]

REVIEWS:

4* *WORLD WRECKER*, BY RICHARD W. GOMBERT

D. Mullen. SF Studies 2(3). (November) Pg. 278.
C. Brown. Locus 182:4. (17 December 1975) Pg.
B. Rapoport. SF Review Monthly 11:17. (January 1976) Pg. 18.

A6 "The Lake of Life" in Weird Tales, 30:3 (September 1937) Pg. 258;
Part Two - Weird Tales, 30:4 (October 1937) Pg. 459;
Part Three - Weird Tales, 30:5 (November 1937) Pg. 596;
Illustrator: Virgil Finlay.

REPRINTS:

b as **The Lake of Life**. Chicago: R. Weinberg. c1978, 80 p. ill. 21 cm. (Series Title: Lost Fantasies #8). chap
Note: This is bound with "The Hunch" by G. Lyle and "The Inn" by R. Ernest.

A7 "The Great Illusion" in Thrilling Wonder, 11:3 (June 1938) Pg.
Note: With Jack Williamson, Raymond Z. Gallun and John Russell Fearn.

REPRINTS:

b as "La grande illusion" in **Univers 04**. _: editions J'Ai lu, <year>, p.
c in **The Great Illusion**. by Eando Binder. Wallsend.: Philip Harbottle, c1973, p. ill. photos ; 22 cm. Pg. 12. paper. (Fantasy Booklet #4).
d in **Spider Island: The Collected Stories of Jack Williamson, Volume Four**, Jack Williamson, Royal Oak, MI: Haffner Press, 2002, p. [collection]

A8 "The Prisoner of Mars" in Startling Stories, (May 1939) Pg. 14.
Illustrator: H. W. Wesso.

REPRINTS:

b as **Tharkol, Lord of the Unknown**. Manchester: Sydney Pemberton, 1950, p.
c _: World Distributors; WFC. 1950. 160 p. paper.

CHAPTERS: 24

While on an expedition in Northern Quebec to search out the mystery of his father, Philip Crain and friends find a wrecked craft in the woods. They explore the craft and two of them are inadvertently sent to Mars.

A9 "Captain Future and the Space Emperor." Captain Future Magazine.1:1 (Winter 1940) Pg. 12. Illustrator: Wesso.

REPRINTS:

b as **Captain Future and the Space Emperor**. New York, NY: Popular Library, 1967, 128 p. 18cm. paper (60-2457).

c as <unknown> _: <publisher unknown> 1969, [Greek]

d as <unknown> Hayakawa Publishing, Inc. 31 May 1974, 279 p. Translator: Masahiro Noda. [Japanese]

e as **Captain Future en de Keizer van het Heelal**. Rotterdam: Ridderhof, 1975, 195 p. 18cm. ISBN: 90.308.0215.4. (Science Fiction series No. 24).[v] Translator: Iskraa Bundels. [Dutch]

f adapted into an animated television program in four parts. _: Toei Doga, 1978-79, [Japanese]
Note: This is available in Video, DVD, Video CD and in some cases LaserDISC in English, French, German, Italian, Japanese and Spanish. [vi]

g as **Kapten Frank och rymdkejsaren**[vii]. in Kapten Frank Rymdens Hjalte Malmo: Pulp Press, 1980, 112 p. paper. Translator: Bertil Falk. ISBN: 91-86086-00-6. [Swedish]

h as **Die lebende Legende**. Bergisch Gladbach: <publisher unknown>, 1981, (BSF 25001). Translator: Marcel Bieger. [German]

i as **The Sombre Emperor**. Athens: Sympan/Lyhnari, 1989, p. Translated by Geni Mistraki. [Greek]

A10 "Calling Captain Future." in Captain Future Magazine, 1:2 (Spring 1940) Pg. 12. Illustrator: H. Wesso.

REPRINTS:

b as **Panik Im Kosmos**. Rastatt: <publisher unknown> 1962, p. (U 311). Translator: M.F. Arnmann. [German]

c **Calling Captain Future**. New York, NY. Popular Library, 1967, 144 p. 18 m. paper. (60-2421).

d Tokyo: Hayakawa Publishing, Inc. 30 November 1971, p. Translator: Masahiro Noda. [Japanese]

d _: <publisher unknown> February 1973, p. (SF Bungaku Zenshu #18). Translator: Chikashi Uchida. [Japanese]

e as **Panik Im Kosmos**. _: Utopia, 1974, p. [German]

f as <unknown>. _: SF, 1977, p. [Korea]

g adapted into an animated television program in four parts[viii]. _: Toei Doga, 1978-79, [Japanese]
Note: This is available in Video, DVD, Video CD and in somecases LaserDISC in French, German, Italian, Japanese and Spanish.

h as **Kollisionsziel Erde**. Bergisch Gladbach: <publisher unknown>, 1981, p. (BSF 25002). Translator: Marcel Bieger. [German]

i in <unknown>. _: <publisher unknown> 1993, 336 p. [Russian]
Note : This is a collection contains: **Calling Captain Future**, **Captain Future's Challenge** and **Quest Beyond the Stars**.

j Tokyo: Hayakawa Publishing, Inc. March 1995, p. [Japanese]

k in <unknown>. _: <publisher unknown> 1993, 394 p. [Russian]
Note : This is a collection contains: **Outlaw World**, **Calling Captain Future**, **Outlaws of the Moon**.

l in <unknown>. _: <publisher unknown> 1998, 401 p. [Russian]
Note : This is a collection contains: **Captain Future's Challenge**, **Calling Captain Future**, and **Quest Beyond the Stars**.

CHAPTERS:

The Menace from Space
The Futuremen
On Desert Mars
Flight into Peril
Trail to Pluto
Graveyard of Space
Encounter in Space
On the Artic World
Coming of Doctor Zarro
The Marching Mountains
In the Ice City
Interplanetary Prison
Street of Hunters
Cobalt Clue
Monster Trap
World of Illusion
Hall of Enemies
Dark Star Secret
In Outer Space
Trail in the Stars

Captain Future answers a summons from the President of the Solar System.

A11 "Captain Future's Challenge." in Captain Future Magazine, 1:3 (Summer 1940) Pg. 14. Illustrator: H. W. Wesso.

REPRINTS:

b New York, NY: Popular Library, 1967, p. paper.

c as **Kampf Um Gravium**. Rastatt: <publisher unknown> 1961, p. (UGB 147). Translator: Heinz Zwack. [German]

d as **Kampf Um Gravium**. _: Utopia, 1971, p. [German]

e Tokyo: Hayakawa Publishing, Inc. 31 July 1971, 307 p. Translator: Masahiro Noda. [Japanese]

f adapted into an animated television program in four parts.[ix] _: Toei Doga, 1978-79, p. [Japanese]
Note: This is available in Video, DVD, Video CD and in some cases LaserDISC in English, French, German, Italian, Japanese and Spanish.

g as **Die Gravium Sabotage**. Bergisch Gladbach: <publisher unknown> 1982, 154 p. (BSF 25003). Translator: Richard Bellinghausen. [German]

h in <unknown>. _: <publisher unknown> 1993, 336 p. [Russian]
Note : This is a collection contains: Calling Captain Future, Captain Future's Challenge and Quest Beyond the Stars.

i Tokyo: Hayakawa Publishing, Inc. March 1995, p. [Japanese]

j in <unknown>. _: <publisher unknown> 1994, 475 p. [Russian]
Note : This is a collection contains: **Captain Future's Challenge**, **Calling Captain Future**, and **Quest Beyond the Stars**.

k in <unknown>. _: <publisher unknown> 1998, 402 p. [Russian]
Note : This is a collection contains: **Captain Future's Challenge**, **Calling Captain Future**, and **Quest Beyond the Stars**.

A12 "Triumph of Captain Future." in Captain Future Magazine, 2:1 (Fall 1940) Pg. 14. Illustrator: H. W. Wesso.

REPRINTS:

b as "Kapten Franks triumf." serialized in Jules Verne Magasinet. 32/1941- 43/1941 (12 Parts). [Swedish]

c as **Captain Zunkunft Greift Ein**. Rastatt: <publisher unknown> 1961, p. (UGB 142). Translator: Lothar Heinecke. [German]

d as **Galaxy Mission**. New York, Popular Library, 1967, 128 p. 18 cm. paper. (60-2437).

da as **Galaxy Mission**. New York, NY: Popular Library, 1969, p. paper. (60-2437).

e as **Captain Zunkunft Greift Ein**. _: Utopia, 1975, p. [German]

f Tokyo: Hayakawa Publishing, Inc. 31 May 1975, p. Translator: Masahiro Noda. [Japanese]

g adapted into an animated television program in four parts.[x] _: Toei Doga, 1978-79. [Japanese]
Note: This is available in Video, DVD, Video CD and in some cases LaserDISC in French, German, Italian, Japanese and Spanish.

h as **Der Lebenslord**. Bergisch Gladbach: <publisher unknown> 1982, p. (BSF 25004). Translator: Ralph Tegtmeier. [German]

i in <unknown>. _: <publisher unknown> 1994, 475 p. [Russian]
Note : This is a collection contains: Captain Future's Challenge, Calling Captain Future, and Quest Beyond the Stars.

A13 "A Yank at Valhalla." in Startling Stories, (January 1941) Pg. 14.

REPRINTS:

b New York, NY: Ace Books, 1940, 128 p. paper.

c as "En Yankee Far Till Valhall." Serialized in Jules Verne Magasinet 19/1943 - 33/1943, (15 Parts). [Swedish]

d as **The Monsters of Juntonheim: A Complete Book-length Novel of Amazing Adventure**. Manchester: Sydney Pemberton, 1950, 160 p. [British]

e as **The Monsters of Juntonheim**. _: World Distributors, 1950, p.

f in Fantastic Story Magazine. 5:1 (January 1958) Pg. 10.

g as **Unternehmen Walhalla**. Rastatt: <publisher unknown> 1958, p. (UG: 75). [German]

h New York, NY: Ace Books. March 1973, p.
NOTE: This is an Ace Double with **The Sun Destroyer** by Ross Rocklynne.

i _: PageTurner, Published in Digital (Microsoft Reader).

j as " The Monsters of Juntonheim" in **The Two Worlds of Edmond Hamilton**. _: Wildside Press. May 14, 2008. (8.8 x 5.9 x 0.3 in) ISBN-10: 1434468208; ISBN-13: 978-1434468208.
With "The Stars, My Brothers."

k _: Renaissance E Books/Page Turner, March 17, 2003. Kindle. 236 Kb. \ ASIN: B000FA66KS.

l Riverdale, NY: Baen Books. February 1, 2008. SKU: 1588731675.

CHAPTERS:

The Rune Key
Mystery Land
Jotun and Aesir
Odin Speaks
Shadow of Loki
Ancient Science
Ambush!
World of Gnomes
Loki's Prison
Captives in Jotunheim
The Arch-Fiend Alive
The Master Scientist's Laboratory
Flight and Death
Thor's Oath
Down to the Fire World
Creatures of the Flame
Battle of Science
Battle for Asgard
Flank Attack
Ragnarok Comes
Epilogue

A scientific mission to the Artic circle dredges up an ancient rune key. One of their members is off on the adventure of his life.

REVIEWS:

D. D'Ammassa. Son of WSFA Journal 90:3. (May 1973) Pg. <unknown>
http://authors.booksunderreview.com/H/Hamilton,_Edmond/

A14 "Captain Future and the Seven Space Stones." in Captain Future Magazine, 2:2. (Winter 1941) Pg. 14. Illustrator: H. Wesso.

REPRINTS:

b as "Kapten Frank och de sju magiska stenarna." in Jules Verne Magasinet #10 - #25 (16 Parts): 1942, Pg. 25. [Swedish]
c as **Diamanten der Macht**. Rastatt: <publisher unknown> 1960, p.

(UGB 151). Translator: Heinz Zwack. [German]

d as **Captain Future and the Seven Space Stones**. Tokyo: Hayakawa Publishing, Inc. 28 February 1966, p. Translator: Masahiro Noda. [Japanese]

e as **Diamanten der Macht**. _: Utopia, 1972, p. [German]

f Tokyo: Hayakawa Publishing, Inc. 31 March 1972, 202 p. Translator: Masahiro Noda. [Japanese]

g Tokyo: Hayakawa Publishing, Inc. 1974, p. [Japanese]

h adapted into an animated television program in four parts.[xi] _: Toei Doga, 1978-79, p. [Japanese]
Note: This is available in Video, DVD, Video CD and in somecases LaserDISC in French, German, Italian, Japanese and Spanish.

ca as **Diamanten der Macht**. Bergisch Gladbach: <publisher unknown> 1982, 171 p. (BSF 25005). Translator: Richard Bellinghausen. [German]

g Tokyo: Hayakawa Publishing, Inc. 1995, p. [Japanese]

Captain Future enters into a battle of wits with Ul Quorn, a nefarious part martian scientist forced to run a freak show in a traveling circus. He is looking for the Seven Space Stoneswhich contain the records of an ancient martian scientist.

A15 "Star Trail To Glory." in Captain Future Magazine, 2:3 (Spring 1941) Pg. 14. Illustrator: H. W. Wesso.

REPRINTS:

b as "Kapten Frank och posträнarna." Sweden: Jules Verne Magasinet #26 - #41 (16 Parts): 1942, Pg. 41. [Swedish]

c as **Star Trail to Glory**. Tokyo: Hayakawa Publishing, Inc. 31 July 1966, 178 p. Translator: Masahiro Noda.

d _: <publisher unknown> February, 1968, p. (SF Mesaku Series # 14). [Japanese]

d Tokyo: Hayakawa Publishing, Inc. 31 May 1972, 260 p. Translator: Masahiro Noda. [Japanese]

e as **Sternstrasse zum Ruhm**. Bergisch Gladbach: <publisher unknown> 1982, 158 p. (BSF 25006). Translator: Ralph Tegtmeier. [German]

f _: Kaiseisha, <year>,p.cm. Translator: Masahiro Noda. [Jpanese]

g adapted into an animated movie.[xii] _: Ben J. Productions, 1989.
Note: This is available in Video, DVD, in French.

h Tokyo: Hayakawa Publishing, Inc. September 1995, p. [Japanese]

A16 "The Magician of Mars." Captain Future Magazine. 3:1 (Summer 1941) Pg. 14.

REPRINTS:

b as **The Magician of Mars**. _: Hayakawa, 1941, p. [Japanese]

c as "Kapten Frank och trollkarten från Mars." serialized in Jules Verne Magasinet. 46/1941 - 6/1942, p. [Swedish]

d New York, NY: Popular Library. 1968, 128 p. paper (60-2450).

e Tokyo: Hayakawa Publishing, Inc. 31 December 1970, 302 p. Translated by Masahiro Noda. [Japanese]

f _: Gemini, November 1977, p. (Editions Solaris). [Italian]

g adapted into an animated television program in four parts. [xiii] _: Toei Doga, 1978-79, p. [Japanese]
Note: This is available in Video, DVD, Video CD and in somecases LaserDISC in French, German, Italian, Japanese and Spanish.

h as **Der Marsmagier**. Bergisch Gladbach: <publisher unknown> 1982, 156 p. (BSF 25007). Translated by Ralph Tegtmeier. [German]

i in <unknown>. _: <publisher unknown> 1994, 475 p. [Russian]
Note : This is a collection contains: Captain Future's Challenge, Calling Captain Future, and Quest Beyond the Stars.

j Tokyo: Hayakawa Publishing, Inc. March 1995, p. [Japanese]

k in <unknown>. _: <publisher unknown> 1998, 472 p. [Russian]
Note : This is a collection contains: The Magician of Mars, Outlaws of the Moon, Outlaw World, and Quest Beyond the Stars.

REVIEWS:

D. Paskow. Luna Monthly 19:22. (December 1970) Pg.

A17 "The Lost World of Time." in Captain Future Magazine, 3:2. (Fall1941) Pg. 14. Illustrator: H. Wesso.

REPRINTS:

b as "Kapten Frank i en försvunnen värld." in Jules Verne Magasinet #5 - #18 (14 Parts): 1943, Pg 18. [Swedish]

c as **Im Zeitstrom verschollen**. Rastatt: <publisher unknown> 1961, p. (UGB 144). Translator: Heinz Zwack. [German]

d Tokyo: Hayakawa Publishing, Inc. 15 January 1967, 192 p. Translator: Masahiro Noda. [Japanese]

e as **Im Zeitstrom verschollen**. _: Utopia, 1972, p. [German]

f Tokyo: Hayakawa Publishing, Inc. 30 September 1972, 274 p. Translator:

Masahiro Noda. [Japanese]

g as <unknown>. _: SF, 1975, p. [Korea]

h _: <publisher unknown> December 1978, p. (SF Kodomo Toshokan # 26). Translator: Masami Fukushima. [Japanese]

i adapted into an animated television program in four parts.[xiv] _: Toei Doga, 1978-79, [Japanese]
Note: This is available in Video, DVD, Video CD and in some cases LaserDISC in English, French, German, Italian, Japanese and Spanish.

ca as **Im Zeitstrom verschollen**. Bergisch Gladbach: <publisher unknown> 1982, 155 p. (BSF 25008). Translator: Ralph Tegtmeier. [German]

CHAPTERS:

Mystery Asteroid
Citadel of Science
The Cry from the Past
The Second Moon
Futuremen in the Past
Unexpected Company
Star Worshipers
Planets of the Past
On the Rocket Trail
A Conjurer on Mars
The Way Out
A World can Die
Zikal's Spy
Death Under Yugra
Disaster
Castaways Before Creation
Birth of a New System
Darwin's Mistake
The Plot Against a World
Planet's End

A group of meteor miners land on a small asteroid. Captain Future discovers a message and decides to help Damur, an ancient scientist. After preparations, the Futuremen head back 100,000,000 years into the past. Damur explains that the Katain's coming conjunction with Jupiter will destroy Katain.

The Futuremen succeed in saving the inhabitants of Katain even though one of the members attempts to sabotage the mission.

A18 "The Quest Beyond The Stars" in Captain Future Magazine, 3:3 (Winter 1942) Pg. 15. Illustrator: Orban.

REPRINTS:

b as **Quest Beyond the Stars**. New York, NY: Popular Library, 1941, p. paper.

c as "Kapten Frank och de kosmiska strälarna," serialized in Jules Verne Magasinet 28/1943 - 40/1943 (13 Parts). 1943, Pg. 40. [Swedish]

ba New York, NY: Popular Library, 1960, 128 p. paper.

d as **Gefahr aus dem Kosmos**. Rastatt: <publisher unknown> 1961, p. (UGB 153). Translated by Heinz Zwack. [German]

bb New York, NY: Popular Library, 1969, 142 p. paper (60-2389).

e as **Gefahr aus dem Kosmos**. _: Utopia, 1973, p. [German]

f Tokyo: Hayakawa Publishing, Inc. 31 May 1973, 263 p. Translated by Masahiro Noda. [Japanese]

g as **Komisk Fara**, Stokholm: Bokforlaget Regal. 1975, 152 p. ISBN: 91-85048-53-4. paper. (#18 of Science Fiction-serien). Translator: Bertil Falk. [Swedish]

h adapted into an animated television program in four parts.[xv] _: Toei Doga, 1978-79, p. [Japanese]
Note: This is available in Video, DVD, Video CD and in somecases LaserDISC in French, German, Italian, Japanese and Spanish.

i as **Die Matariequelle**. Bergisch Gladbach: 1983, 157 p. (BSF 25009). Translated by Richard Bellinghausen. [German]

j as **I Metanastes ton Astron**. Athens: Sympan/Lynari. 1989, p. Translator: Anna Papadimtriou.

k in <unknown>. _: <publisher unknown> 1993, 336 p. [Russian]
Note : This is a collection contains: Calling Captain Future, Captain Future's Challenge and Quest Beyond the Stars.

l in <unknown>. _: <publisher unknown> 1994, 475 p. [Russian]
Note : This is a collection contains: Captain Future's Challenge, Calling Captain Future, and Quest Beyond the Stars.

m in <unknown>. _: <publisher unknown> 1998, 402 p. [Russian]
Note : This is a collection contains: Captain Future's Challenge, Calling Captain Future, and Quest Beyond the Stars.

n in <unknown>. _: <publisher unknown> 1998, 472 p. [Russian]
Note : This is a collection contains: The Magician of Mars, Outlaws of the Moon, Outlaw World, and Quest Beyond the Stars.

CHAPTERS:

Warning World

Cosmic Secret
Nebula Danger
Dark Mystery
Castaways of the Stars
City Beneath the Ice
Into the Cosmic Cloud
World of the Green Sun
In the Palace Dungeon
Feast in Ko
The Fight in the Palace
Into the Mystery
Epic of the Past
Struggle of Worlds
World of the Watchers
Star Trails

Mercury is a dying world. Promising to try and save the planet, Curtis and the Futuremen travel outside of the Solar sytem to look for the Birthplace of Creation at the center of the Galaxy. Meeting up with survivors from other such missions, they manage to penetrate the protective dust cloud around the center of the galaxy. Once within the center of this cloud, they become embroiled in a struggle between two worlds. The world of Kor attacks Thruun and Captain Future has to race to the Birthplace to save it from the Korian ruler's plans.

REVIEWS:

D. Paskow. Luna Monthly 1:31. (June 1969) Pg.
R. Goulart. Venture Science Fiction 3(2):123-124. (August 1969): Pg.

A19 "Outlaws of The Moon." in Captain Future Magazine, 4:1 (Spring 1942) Pg. 14. Illustrator: Orban.

REPRINTS:

a as "Kapten Frank och radiumkriget." serialized in Jules Verne Magasinet 1/1942 - 2/1943, (14 Parts). p. [Swedish]
b New York, NY: Popular Library, 1960, p.
ba New York, NY: Popular Library, 1969, 128 p. paper. (60-2399).
c Tokyo: Hayakawa Publishing, Inc. 30 June 1980, 260 p. Translator: Masahiro Noda [Japanese]

d as **Das Erbe der Lunarier**. _: publisher unknown ? 1983, 160 p. (Bd. 25010). [German]

e as **Captain Future: Outlaws of the Moon**. _: <publisher unknown> 1997, p.

f in <unknown>. _: <publisher unknown> 1993, 394 p. [Russian]
Note : This is a collection contains: Outlaw World, Calling Captain Future, Outlaws of the Moon.

g in <unknown>. _: <publisher unknown> 1998, 472 p. [Russian]
Note : This is a collection contains: The Magician of Mars, Outlaws of the Moon, Outlaw World, and Quest Beyond the Stars.

CHAPTERS:

Lunar Secret
Star Rover's Return
Tragedy on Earth
Outlawed Futuremen
Slow Motion World
Alien City
Moon Dog Gorge
Lunar Caves
Shapes in the Dark
Grag's Stratagem
Moon Men
Mountains of Light
Battle in the Moon
Marsh of Monsters
World without Power
Epilog

An enterprising scientist decides to explore the moon for Captain Future's home. He discovers a hidden deposit of radium, the power source of the Solar System. He enters a partnership with a powerful mining magnate and they launch a smear campaign against Captain Future and the Futuremen. They succeed in winning a government concession to mine the radium on the moon. When the futuremen return and discover this, they go to the president to convince him to revoke the license. While Curt is meeting with the president, the president is killed. Curt and the Futuremen are branded outlaws and they escape the Planetary Patrol to prove their innocence.

REVIEWS:

J. Schaumburger. Luna Monthly 9:25. (February 1970) Pg.
<unknown> Vision of Tomorrow 1(5):19-20. (February 1970) Pg.

A20 "The Comet Kings." in Captain Future Magazine, 4:2 (Summer 1942) Pg. 11. Illustrator: H. W. Wesso.

REPRINTS:

b The Comet Kings. _: Hayakawa. 1942, p. [Japanese]

c as "Kapten Frank och kometkungarna." serialized in Jules Verne Magasinet 51/1943 - 16/1944 (16 Parts), p.[Swedish]

d New York, NY: Popular Library. 1960, 127 p. paper.

e as **Im schatten der allus**. Rastatt: <publisher unknown> 1962, p. (U 349). [German]

da New York, NY: Popular Library. 1969, p. paper. (60-2407).

f as **Im schatten der allus**. _: Utopia, 1978, p. [German]

ba Tokyo: Hayakawa Publishing, Inc. 31 March 1978, 246 p. Translator: Masahiro Noda [Japanese]

g adapted into an animated television program in four parts.[xvi] _: Toei Doga, 1978-79, p. [Japanese]
Note: This is available in Video, DVD, Video CD and in somecases LaserDISC in French, German, Italian, Japanese and Spanish.

ea as **Im schatten der allus**. _: Bastei Lhubbe. 1983, p. Translator: Horst Mayer. [German]

db as **Im schatten der allus**. Bergisch Gladbach: <publisher unknown> 1983, 155 p. (BSF 25011). Translator: Ralph Tegtmeier. [German]

CHAPTERS:

I	Vanishing Spaceships
II	Riddle of the World
III	On the Comet World
IV	The Cometae
V	Shadow of the Allus
VI	The Throne Room
VII	Desperate Research
VIII	The Lightning Feast
IX	Dark Triumph
X	Road to Mystery
XI	The Allus
XII	Mental Duel
XIII	Secret of the Invaders
XIV	Curt's Way
XV	The Door Outside

XVI Lost Paradise

Ships are disapearing from the space lanes. When Joan Randall and Ezra Gurney go missing, Captain Future and the Futuremen investigate. They discover that the ships were drawn into Halley's comet where a previously unknown world exists. The inhabitants of this world, the Cometae, are being led by a mysterous race known as the Allus. Curt and the Futuremen discover the true nature of the Allus and foil their nefarious plans.

A21 "Planets In Peril.[xvii]" in Captain Future Magazine, 4:3 (Fall 1942): Pg. 13. Illustrator: Morey.

REPRINTS:

b as "Kapten Frank - nationalhjälten." in Jules Verne Magasinet. #39 1944 - #32 1945 (16 Parts), p. [Swedish]

c as **Planets in Peril**. New York: Popular Library, 1960, p. paper.

d as **Held der Sage**. Rastatt: <publisher unknown> 1962, p. (U 351). Translator: Horst Mayer. [German]

ca New York, NY: Popular Library, 1969, 128 p. paper. (60-2416).

e as **Held der Sage**. _: Utopia, 1978, p. [German]

f Tokyo: Hayakawa Publishing, Inc. 31 July 1978, 290 p. Translator: Masahiro Noda.

g adapted into an animated television program in four parts.[xviii] _: Toei Doga, 1978-79, [Japanese]
Note: This is available in Video, DVD, Video CD and in somecases LaserDISC in French, German, Italian, Japanese and Spanish.

h as **Held der Vergangenheit**. _: Bergisch Gladbach, 1983, 156 p. (BSF 25009). Translator: Richard Bellinghausen. [German]

CHAPTERS:

People from Beyond
The Futuremen
National Hero
Into Infinity
Dusk of Empire
Under the Red Moon
On a Dead World
Trail to Danger
Discovery
Disaster

Checkmate
The Unbodied
Phantom Prisoners
Into the Darkness
Graveyard of Suns
World of Dread
In the Citadel
Escape
Deadly Secret
Revelation

Tharko Thrin, the Martian scientist, adapts some equipment left by the Allus and succeeds in contacting another universe. This universe sends two representatives to Thrin's laboratory to meet with Thrin and the Futuremen. Their universe is approaching the end of its entropic life. They seek help in defending their race from the 'Cold Ones' and to convince their people that their universe will be reborn. Captain Future and the Futuremen travel to this distant universe to aid them.

A22 "Face of The Deep." in Captain Future Magazine, 5:1 (Winter 1943) Pg. 15. Illustrator: Orban.

REPRINTS:

b as **The Face of The Deep**. Tokyo: Hayakawa, 1943, p. [Japanese]

c as "Kapten Frank och fångtransparten," serialized in Jules Verne Magasinet 13/1943 - 16/1943 (14 Parts) Pg. 26. [Swedish]

d Tokyo: Hayakawa Publishing, Inc. 31 August 1973, 290 p. Translator: Masahiro Noda. [Japanese]

e adapted into an animated television program in four parts.[xix] _: Toei Doga, 1978-79, [Japanese]
Note: This is available in Video, DVD, Video CD and in some cases LaserDISC in French, German, Italian, Japanese and Spanish.

f as **Planetoid des Todes**. : <publisher unknown> 1983, 158 p. (BSF 25013). Translator: Ralph Tegtmeier. [German]

A23 "Star of Dread.[xx]" in Captain Future Magazine, 5:3 (Summer 1943): Pg. 13. Illustrator: Orban. Cover: Earle K. Bergey.

REPRINTS:

b	as **Verrat Auf Titan**. Rastatt: <publisher unknown> 1962, p. (U 309). Translator: Horst Mayer. [German]

c	as **Verrat Auf Titan**. _: Utopia, 1978, p. [German]

d	Tokyo: Hayakawa Publishing, Inc. 30 November 1978, 263 p. Translator: Masahiro Noda. [Japanese]

e	adapted into an animated television program in four parts.[xxi] _: Toei Doga, 1978-79. [Japanese]
Note: This is available in Video, DVD, Video CD and in somecases LaserDISC in French, German, Italian, Japanese and Spanish.

f	as **Stern des Grauens**. Bergisch Glacbach: <publisher unknown> 1984, 158 p. (BSF 25015). Translator: Ralph Tegtmeier. [German]

A24 "Magic Moon.[xxii]" in Captain Future Magazine, 6:1 (Winter 1944): Pg. 15. Illustrator: Orban.

REPRINTS:

b	as "Den magiska mänen." in Jules Verne Magasinet #33, 1945, Pg. 45. [Swedish]

c	as **Magic Moon**. Tokyo: Hayakawa Publishing, Inc. 31 August 1974, p. Translator: Masahiro Noda. [Japanese]

d	adapted into an animated television program in four parts.[xxiii] _: Toei Doga, 1978-79. [Japanese]
Note: This is available in Video, DVD, Video CD and in some cases LaserDISC in French, German, Italian, Japanese and Spanish.

e	as **Captain Future: Magic Moon**. _: <publisher unknown> 1987, p.

A25 "Red Sun of Danger.[xxiv]" in Startling Stories, 12:1 (Spring 1945): Pg. 11. Illustrator: Thomas. Cover: Earle Bergey.

REPRINTS:

b	as **Danger Planet**. New York, NY: Popular Library, 1968, p. mass market paperback.

c	as **Danger Planet**. Tokyo: Hayakawa Publishing, Inc. 15 March 1981, p. Translator: Masahiro Noda. [Japanese]

d	as **Die Krypta Der Kangas**. _: Utopia, 1981, p. [German]

e	as **Die Krypta Der Kangas**. Rastatt: <publisher unknown> <year>, p. [U 305]. Translator: Heinz Zwack. [German]

A26 Tiger Girl[xxv]. London: Utopian Publishers. 1945, 36 p. [British]

A27 "Outlaw World." in Startling Stories, 13:1. (Winter 1946) Pg. 11.
Illustrator: Orban. Cover: Earle Bergey.

REPRINTS:

aa "Outlaw World." in Startling Stories, (Winter 1946) Pg. 11. Illustrator: Orban. Cover: Earle Bergey. [British]

ab "Outlaw World." in Startling Stories, (June 1949) Pg. 11. Illustrator: Orban. Cover: Earle Bergey. [Canadian]

b **Outlaw World**. New York: Popular Library,. 1960, p.

c as **Die Radium Falle**. _: <publisher unknown> 1961, p. [German]

ca as **Die Radium Falle**. Rastatt: <publisher unknown> 1962, p. (U 354). Translator: Werner Eppelsheim. [German]

ba New York, NY: Popular Library. 1969, 126 p. paper. (60-2376).

d _: Gemini, September 1978, p. (Editions Solaris). [Italian]

e as **Die Radium Falle**. _: Utopia, 1982, p. [German]

f Tokyo: Hayakawa Publishing, Inc. 30 June 1982, 258 p. Translator: Masahiro Noda. [Japanese]

g as <unknown>. _: <publisher unknown> 1992, 352 p. [Russian]

h as <unknown>. _: <publisher unknown> 1993, 512 p. [Russian]
Note: This is a collection containing: Pardon my Iron Nerves, Outlaw World and Children of the Sun.

i as **Captain Future: Outlaw World**. _: <publisher unknown> 1996, p.

j in <unknown>. _: <publisher unknown> 1993, 394 p. [Russian]
Note : This is a collection contains: Outlaw World, Calling Captain Future, Outlaws of the Moon.

k in <unknown>. _: <publisher unknown> 1998, 472 p. [Russian]
Note : This is a collection contains: The Magician of Mars, Outlaws of the Moon, Outlaw World, and Quest Beyond the Stars.

CHAPTERS:

Radium Raiders
Warning From Space
Into Dreams
Suprise Attack
Space Trail to Danger
In the Moon Forest
On the Pirate Asteroid

Disastrous Discovery
World of the Cave-Apes
Planetoid Trap
Catastrophe from the Sky
The Face in the Void
In the Meteor Swarm
Secret of Mars
Into Fiery Peril
Outlaw World
In the Solar Satellite
Citadel of Evil
Defeat
Dark Battle

A mysterious new band of pirates is stealing all the radium in the Solar System. This band is terrorizing the solar system and the Planet Patrol can not find their secret base. Setting out to solve this mystery, Curt Newton joins a band of Pirates and travels to the pirate asteroid. After re-joining with the Futuremen, they track the radium raiders to the fiery world of Vulcan, where they confront and vanquish the raiders.

REVIEWS:

L. del Rey. Worlds of If 19(8):147. (October 1969) Pg.
C. Brandon. Science Fiction Review 35:38. (February 1970) Pg.

A28 "The Star of Life" in Startling Stories, 14:3. (January, 1947) Pg. 13. Cover: Earle Bergey.

REPRINTS:

b **The Star of Life**. New York: Torquil (Dodd, Mead), 1959, 193 p. cloth. (59-6638).
c Toronto: Dodd, Mead, April 1959, p. 2 printings. [Canadian]
d Doubleday, Science Fiction Book Club, 1959, p.
e Greenwich, CT.: Fawcett Publisher (Crest), 1959, 187 p. paper (s329). Illustrator: Powers.
f as **Das Gestirn des Lebens (2 Bande)**. Munchen: <publisher unknown> 1965, p. (T 374/375). Translator: Heinz F. Kliem. [German]
g as "**La stella della vita**." Verona: Arnoldo Mondadori Editore, 1960, 236 p. I Roman di (Urania 236). [Italian]
h as "**L'Astre de Vie**." Paris: Editions Albin Michel, 1973, 249 p.(Science Fiction, 2nd serie #20). Translator: Jean Guillemin. [French]

i in **Space Opera**. Edited by Brian W. Aldiss. _: Futura, 1974, p.
j in **The Eighty-Minute Hour**. Edited by Brian W. Aldiss. _: Cape, 1974, p.
ja in **The Eighty-Minute Hour**. Edited by Brian W. Aldiss. _: Doubleday, 1974, p.
ia in **Space Opera**. Edited by Brian W. Aldiss, _: Weidenfeld Nicolson, 1974[xxvi], p.
jb in **The Eighty-Minute Hour**. Edited by Brian W. Aldiss. _: Pan Books, 1974, p.
ib in **Space Opera**. Edited by Brian W. Aldiss, _: Doubleday, 1975, p.
ic in **Space Opera**. Edited by Brian W. Aldiss, _: Avon, 1975, p.
jc in **The Eighty-Minute Hour**. Edited by Brian W. Aldiss. _: Triad/Panther, 1974, p.
ga as "**La Stella della vita**." Verona: Arnoldo Mondadori Editore, 8 maggio 1977, p. (Urania 722). [Italian]
k as "Az élet csillaga," Galaktika #32, szerk. Kuczka Péter, Kozmosz, 1978, p. frod. Gömöri Péter. [?]
l as "Az élet csillaga," Galaktika (June 1987) Pg. ford. M. Nagy Péter.
m as "To Asteri tis Zois" in **Anthologia Epistimonikis Fantasias - Opera tou Diastimatos, Vol. 3**. edited by Makis Panorios. Athens: Komits, 1990, p 139-61. Translator: George Ntoumas. [Greek]
n _:King Features[xxvii], <year>, p.
o as "De Levensster" in **Kleine Science Fiction-Omnibus 4**. _: publisher unknown? <year>, p. [Dutch]
p Riverdale, NY: Baen Books. September 1, 2008. SKU: 0245232265

CHAPTERS: 20

DEDICATION: To Leigh.

REVIEWS:

P. Miller. Analog 64(4):152. (December 1959) Pg.
David Pringle. **The Ultimate Guide to Science Fiction**. Pharos Books, 1990.

A29 "The Star Kings" in Amazing Stories, (September 1947) Pg. 8.

REPRINTS:

aa in Amazing Stories Quarterly. : (September 1947) Pg.
b The **Star Kings**. New York, NY: Frederick Fell, 1949, 262 p. cloth (49-11802).

c as **Beyond the Moon**. New York, NY: New American Library, 1949,[xxviii]
p.
paper.
d as **Beyond The Moon**. Toronto: McLeod, 1949, p. [Canadian]
e as **Beyond The Moon**. _: Signet, September 1950, 167 p. paper (812).
f in Planet Stories.[xxix] : () Pg.
g in Two Complete Science-Adventure Books. 1:2 (Spring 1951) Pg. 4.
ea as **Beyond The Moon**. _: Signet, 1951, p paper (812 2nd).
h London: Museum Press, 1951, 85p.
as <unknown>[xxx]. _: <publisher unknown> <year>, p. [Norwegian]
i as "Stjernefyrstens sønn." Oslo: Begendahs Forlag, 1951, p. Translator: Ivar Widerø Tomtum. [Norwegian]
j presented as a dramatized production by the Salem High School, Salem Oregon[xxxi]. <year>.
k as **Les Rois des Etoiles**. _: Hachette-Gallimard. 1951, p. (Rayon Fantastique #2). [French]
l as **Les Rois des Etoiles**. _: Editions J'ai Lu, 1952, p. 432 p. Translator: Giles Malar. Illustrator: Tibor Csernus. [French]
m as **Herrscher im Weltraum: 200,000 Jarhe Spater**. Berlin: Gebruder Weiss Verlag, 1952, 284 p. Translator: Margaret Auer. [German]
n as **Guerra nella galassia**. Verona: Arnoldo Mondadori Editore, 1953, p. (Urania 14). [Italian]
o as **Los reyes de las estrellas**. _: Nebula 1953. p.(14). [Spanish]
ia London: Museum Press, <year>, 219p. 19 cm. [British]
p serialized as "Bortom mänen." Stockholms-Tidningen: in Jules Verne Magasinet. July 8 - September 15 1954, p.
[Swedish]
q as **Beyond the Moon**. Serialized in The Bombay Chronicle, Bombay: Begining Wed. October 27 1954, Pg. 5. [Indian]
oa as **Los reyes de las estrellas**. _: Nebula, 1955, p. (14). [Spanish]
r _: <publisher unknown> 1957, p. (24) [Japan]
s as **Herrscher im Weltraum (2 Bande)**. Munchen: Gebruder Weiss. 1965, p. (418/419). Translator: Nachdruck. [German]
t as **Les Rois des Etoiles et Retour Aux Etoiles [The Star Kings and Return to the Stars]**. Paris: Club du Livre D'Anticipation, 1967, 391 p. (Ed. Opta 'Classique SF:12'). Translators: Gilles Malar & Frank Straschitz.
Introduction by Sam Moskowitz. [French]
u New York, NY: Paperback Library, First printing August 1967, 190 p. paper. (53-538). Illustrator: Gaughan.
v _: <publisher unknown> 1967, 178 p. (SF 3). [Japan]
w New York: Warner Books, Inc. First printing - August 1967, 190 p. paper (76-942).

ta as **Les Roiles des Etoiles/Retour aux Etoiles**. _: OPTA, 1968, p. (Club du Livre d'Anticipation #12 - Limited to 4150 numbered copies, including bibliography). [French]

x _: Hayakwa Publishing, Inc. 1969, 251 p. (SF H P 3217). Translator: Tetsu Yano. [Japanese]

y Tokyo: SogenShinsha, 1969, 315 p. (SF 637-1). Translator: Kazuo Inoue. [Japanese]

va _: <publisher unknown> <year>, 219 p. (SF 5) [Japan]

ub New York, NY: Paperback Library, 1970, p. paper. (64-472 2nd).

wa New York, NY: Warner Books, Inc. Second printing November 1970, 190 p. paper (76-942).

ta New York, NY: Paperback Library, November 1970, 190 p. paper (64-472).

z as **Les Rois des Etoiles**. _: editions J'ai Lu SF, 1972, 306p. (#432) Translator: Gilles Martin. [French]

sa as **Herrscher im Weltraum (2 Bande)**. Munchen: Gebruder Weiss, 1973, 158 p. (TTB[xxxii] 221). Translator: Nachdruck. [German]

wb New York, NY: Warner Books, Inc. Third printing September 1975, 190 p. paper (76-492). Illustrator: FMA.

1 as **Die Sternenkonige**. Munchen: Heyne-Buch, 1980, 221 p. (HSF 3774). Translator: Margaret Auer. With an afterwards by Thomas LeBlanc. [German]

wc New York, NY: Warner Books, Inc. Third printing September 1981, 190 p. paper (76-492). Illustrator: FMA.

2 _: Kaiseisha, 1985, 195 p. (SF 9).[Japanese]

3 in The Chronicles of the Star Kings. _: Time Warner Books, UK. April 17, 1986. Venture Science Fiction. 400 p. ISBN-10: 0099478609; ISBN-13: 978-0099478607 [British]
With **Return to the Stars**.

4 Riverdale, NY: Baen Books. February 1, 2008. SKU: 1419183435. ISBN-13: 978-1-4191-8343-0; ISBN-10: 1-4191-8343-5
Cover: Doug Chaffee.

5 _: Renaissance eBooks, <year>, p. Published in Digital (Adobe).

6 _: Amazon Digital Services, <year> Kindle. 406 Kb. ASIN: B00124XF68.

CHAPTERS:

John Gordon
Future Universe
Mystery Raiders
Magic Planet
Weird Masquerade
The Feast of Moons
Star Princess
The Spy From the Cloud

In the Palace Prison
Flight into the Void
Galactic Plot
In the Cosmic Cloud
Master of the Cloud
Dark-World Menace
Mystery of the Galaxy
Sabotage in Space
Wrecked in the Nebula
Monster Men
World of Horror
Doom off the Pleiades
Mutiny in the Void
Galatic Crisis
The Secret of the Empire
Storm over Throon
The Star Kings Decide
Battle Between the Stars
The Disruptor
Star-Rovers Return

Twentieth Century Earthman John Gordon is propelled into the far future, while his counterpart travels back to the past do some research. While in the far future, events happen that prevent John Gordon from returning as planned. He is forced to take Zarth Arns place as prince of the galactic empire and defend it against Shorr Kahn and his forces. After using the Mythical weapon and saving the day, John Gordon finally returns home.

REVIEWS:

P. Miller. Analog 46(4):98-99. (December 1950) Pg.
<unknown>. Authentic Science Fiction No. 19:112. (March 1952): Pg.
<unknown> The Birmingham Post. "Travellers All." 18 (September 1951) Pg. E3.
<unknown> Catholic Herald. (21 September 1951) Pg.
L. F. New Worlds No. 11:95. (Fall 1951) Pg.
<unknown> Our Best Trade List. 1949-50 (Fall & Winter), Frederick Fell. Advertisement. p. 6.
Rex Lardner. "Seven Novels of Varied Interest - Mid-Galactic: The Star Kings" in The New York Times - Book Review. (18 December 1949) Pg. 16.
S. Merwin. Thrilling Wonder Stories 36(1):156. (April 1950).

F. Pohl. Super Science Stories 6(3):98. (March 1950) Pg.
B. Tucker. Science Fiction Newsletter #17:2. (October 1950) Pg.
F. Patten. Delap's Fantasy & Science Fiction Review 7:25-26. (October 1975) Pg.
David Pringle. **The Ultimate Guide to Science Fiction**. Pharos Books, 1990.
Estep, Larry. Edmond Hamilton's Star Kings. http://pulpgen.com/pulp/edmond_hamilton/star_kings.html.

as **Beyond the Moon**:
R. Lowndes. Future Science Fiction 2(1):98. (May 1951) Pg.
<unknown> http://authors.booksunderreview.com/H/Hamilton,_Edmond/

A30 "The Valley of Creation." in Startling Stories, (July 1948) Pg. 9. Illustrator: Virgil Finlay.

REPRINTS:

b The **Valley of Creation**. Lancer Books, Inc. 1954, 159 p. (72-721).
c New York, NY: Lodestone Publishing, Inc. 1964, p. paper (B-5006). Illustrator: Emsh.
d as **La Valle Della Creazione**. _: La tribune Editore, 1965, p. (Galassia #60). [Italian]
e as **Das Tal der Schoepfung**. Munchen: <publisher unknown> 1966, p. (T: 436). Translator: Birgit Bohusch. [German]
ba New York, NY: Lancer Books, Inc. 1967, p. (73-577). Illustrator: Emsh.
f as **Les Vallee Magique.** Paris: OPTA, 1971, 253 p. (Galaxie Bis #19). Translator: Bruno Martin. [French]
g as **La Vallee Magique**. Paris: Librarie des Champes-Elysees, 1974, 251 p. 17 cm. [Le Masque Science Fiction #10] . Translator: Bruno Martin. [French]
h _: <publisher unknown> 1975, 230 p. (Q-Tbooks SF). [Japan]
i as **La Vallee Magique** Geneva: Edito-Service, 1976, 261 p. ill. 21 cm. (Les Chefs-d'Oeuvre de la Science Fiction #16). Translator: Bruno Martin. Illustrator: Hienz Stieger. [Swiss]
j as **O Vale Da Criacao**. Lisboa: Edicao <Livros do Brasil>, <year>, p. (N. 232. da Coleccao Argonauta). Translation: Maria Emilia Ferros Moura. [Brazilian]
k _: Renaissance E Books/Page Turner, August 8, 2004 Kindle. 284 Kb. ASIN: B000FC1VYC.
l Riverdale, NY: Baen Books. September 1, 2008. SKU: 1437735770.
m _: Wildside Press. <year> paper. ISBN-13: 978-1434498519.

hardback. ISBN-13: 978-1434498526

CHAPTERS:

Alien Dream
Strange Beasts
Into Mystery
Hidden Land
Wolf Hatred
Daring Plan
Secret Mission
Weird City
Judgement of the Guardian
Dread Metamorphosis
Forest Danger
Death in Anshan
The Flight in the Palace
Return to Doom
The Wrath of the Clans
The Cavern of Creation
The Day of the Brotherhood

Eric Nelson and his small band of mercenaries, trapped in a Chinese frontier town, conditionally accept a job in a remote valley of China. There, they have to fight an alien race to clear the pass and fight a 'weird' army before reaching the town of Anshan. There they learn their enemies are an alliance of men and beast called the Brotherhood. Having captured one of the Brotherhood's members, they attempt to sneak in and capture the leader. They fail and Eric Nelson is punished by having his conciousness is transferred into the body of a wolf. To be released must travel to the rebel village (Anshan) and free a captive. The other mercenaries plan to burn the valley so they can get to the platinium. Eric makes his last stand against his old comrades and barely wins the day.

REVIEWS:

P. Miller. Analog 74(6):90. February 1965, Pg.
D. Pringle. **The Ultimate Guide to Science Fiction**. Pharos Books, 1990.

A31 "City at World's End." **in** Startling Stories, (July 1950): Pg. 11.

REPRINTS:

b as **City at World's End**. New York: Frederick Fell, 1951, 239 p. 20 cm. cloth (51-10074).

c New York, NY: Galaxy Publishing Co. 1951, 128 p. 18 cm. digest [Galaxy SF Novel #18]

d Toronto: McLeod, 1951, p.

e London: Museum Press, September 1952, 192 p. [British]

ea London: Science Fiction Book Club, 1952, 192p. 20 cm. [British]

f as **SOS, die Erde erkaltet**. Berlin[xxxiii]: Weiss, 1952, 262 p. (T:211). Translator: Margaret Auer. [German]

g as **Ville Sous Globe [City under Glass Globe]**. _: Hachette-Gallimard, 1952, p. (Rayon Fantastique #13). [French]

h _: <publisher unknown> 1953, 126 p. (Galaxy Novel #18). Illustrator: Emsh.

i as **Agonia della Terra**. Verona: Arnoldo Mondanori Editore, 1953, p. (Urania #23). [Italian]

j as **Agonia della Terra**. _: Corgi, 1954, 221 p. (T58). [Italian]

k London: Transworld, 1954, 221 p. 17 cm. [British]

l Greenwich, CT: Fawcett Crest Publishing, 1956, p. paper (s184).

fa as **SOS, die Erde erkaltet**. Berlin: Weiss, <year>, 207 p. (TB. 1956). Translator: Margaret Auer. [German]

m as **City at World's End: A Chillingly Prophetic Novel of Science Fiction**. Greenwich, CT: Fawcett Crest Publishing, 1957, p. paper (s184).

fb as **SOS, die Erde erkaltet**. _:Weiss, 1957, p. (T:211). [German]

la Greenwich, CT: Fawcett Crest Publishing,[xxxiv] 1961, p. paper. (s494).

fc as **SOS, die Erde erkaltet**. Munchen: Weiss, 1962, p. (T:211). Translator: Nachdruck. [German]

lb Greenwich, CT: Fawcett Crest Publishing, 1964, p. (L758).

n as **Agonia Della terra**. Verona: Arnoldo Mondanori Editore, 1965, p. (I Romanzi di Urania #386). [Italian]

o _: Koudansha, 25 August 1965, 238 p. (9). Translator: Masahiro Noda.[Japanese]

p _: <publisher unknown> 1969, 172 p. (SF 18). [Japanese]

fd as **SOS, die Erde erkaltet**. Berlin-Munchen: Gebruder Weiss Verlag, 1973, p. (TB 213). Translator: Nachdruck. [German]

lc Greenwich, CT: Fawcett Crest Publishing, 1974 (c1957), 160 p. 18 cm. (M2026) (H2026).

q as **Les Ville Sous Globe**. Paris: Librarie des Champs-Elysees, 1974, 252 p. 17 cm. [Le Masque Science Fiction #12]. [French]

r _: <publisher unknown> 1976, 428 p. (SF 11) [Japanese]

s Ballantine Books (Del Rey 30987), July 1983, p. paper. Cover: Rick

Sternbach. ISBN: 0-345-30987-1. [xxxv]

t _: Arthur's Classic Novels. May 30, 2004. HTML. http://arthursclassicnovels.com/arthurs/various/citywe10.html.

u _: Many Books.net.. December 4, 2005. Kindle. 232 Kb. ASIN: B0014NKQ2E

v _: Page Turner. 2004. ISBN: 5551361918.

ua _: Evergreen Review, Inc. September 8, 2007. Kindle. 620 Kb. ASIN: B000VUNXJ4.

w _: Brownstone Books. September 1, 2007. 160 pg. (8.4 x 5.4 x .06 in.) ISBN-10: 1434485668; ISBN-13 978-1424485663.

x _: Books-On-Line. <year> HTML. http://www.books-on-line.com/bol/BookDisplay.cfm?BookNum=31861

y Riverdale, NY: Baen Books. September 1, 2008. SKU: 0345309871.

ub _: Amazon Digital Services. February 6, 2009. Kindle. 235 Kb. ASIN: B0001RTS2XK.

CHAPTERS:

cataclysm
the incredible
dying planet
dead city
in the red dawn
caravan into tomorrow
under the dome
middletown calling!
out of the silence
from the stars
revelation
crisis
embattled city
last appeal
mission for earth
at vega
judgement of the stars
fateful return
middletown decides
appointment with destiny
waking world

The first bomb to drop in a new war throws the city of Middletown, Ohio 400,000 years into the future. The inhabitants, led by a team of scientists from a secret research facility, struggle to survive on a barren liveless earth. A ship from the galactic federation lands and involves the inhabitants in the politics of that future civilization.

REVIEWS:

L. de Camp. Analog 47(6):142-143, (August 1951) Pg.
G. Conklin. Galaxy 3(6):83. (March 1952) Pg.
L. Flood. New Worlds No. 18:96. (November 1952) Pg.
Boucher & McComas. The Magazine of Fantasy & Science Fiction 2(4):83-84. (August 1951) Pg.
David Pringle. **The Ultimate Guide to Science Fiction**. Pharos Books, 1990.
<unknown> http://authors.booksunderreview.com/H/Hamilton,_Edmond/

A32 "Starman Come Home!" in Universe Science Fiction, (September 1954) Pg. Illustrator: H.W. McCauley. Cover: H.W. McCauley.

REPRINTS:

b as **The Sun Smasher**. New York, NY: Ace Books, 1959, 110 p. (D-351). Note: Published with "Starhaven" by Ivar Jorgenson.

c as **Im Banne der Vergangenheit**. Rastatt(Baden): Erich Pabel Verlag, 1960, 128 p. (Utopia Zukunfts Roman). Translator: M.F. Arnemann. [German]

ca as **Im Banne der Vergangenheit**. Muchen: <publisher unknown> 1966, p. (TE: 118). Translator: Nachdruck. [German]

d as **Die Macht der Valkan**. Berlin: <publisher unknown> 1978, p. (UTB 3434). Translator: Nachdruck. [German]

e as **The Sun Smasher**. _: <publisher unknown> 1978, 262 p. 19 cm. [Japanese]

f as **The Sun Smasher**._: Renaissance E Books/Page Turner, April 14, 2009 Kindle. 210 Kb. ASIN: B0026LTM9Q.

g as **The Sun Smasher**. Riverdale, NY: Baen Books. September 1, 2008. SKU: 1437735770.

REVIEWS:

P. Miller. Analog 64(3):153. (November 1959) Pg.

A33 "Battle for the Stars.[xxxvi]" in Imagination, 7:3 (June 1956) Pg.

Cover: Malcolm Smith.

EXPANDED AND REPRINTED[xxxvii]:

b Battle for the Stars. New York: A Torquil Book (Dodd, Mead), 1961, 206 p. 22 cm. cloth (61-15300).

c _: Doubleday Science Fiction Book Club, 1961, p.

d London: Mayflower Paperback, 1963, 131 p. [0480]

e New York, NY: Paperback Library, (1st) August, 1964, 159 p. 18 cm. paper (52-311).

f as **Die Gestirn der Ahen**. _: <publisher unknown> 1964, p. [German]

g as **Die Heimat der Astronauten**. Munchen: Wilhelm Hey ne Verlag.. 1964, p. Translator: Wulf H. Bergner. (Heyne-Buch Nr. 3032). [German]

h as **La Spedizione della V Flotta**. Verona: Arnoldo Monadori Editore, April. 1965, 142 p. 19cm. (I Romanzi di Urania, no. 381). Illustrated. Translator: Bianca Russ. [Italian]

ea New York, NY: Paperback Library, (2nd) December, 1967 (c1961), 159 p. 18 cm. paper. (52-609).

ga as **Die Heimat der Astronauten**. Munchen: Wilhelm Heyne Verlag, 1969, p. (Heyne-Buch Nr. 3167). Translator: Wulf H. Bergner. [German]

ha as **La Spedizione della Quinta Flotta**. Milano: Arnoldo Mondadori Editore, 1976, p. (Oscar Ragazzi; 42). Tranlator: Bianca Russo. [Italian]

i _: Kuboshoten, July 1979, 247 p. Translator: Jyunko Yoshikawa. (SF) [JP80016972] [Japanese]

j as **La Spedizione Della V Flotta**. Verona: Arnoldo Monadori Editore, 1982. (Classici Uranoa #103). [Italian]

k New York, NY: Tor Books, May 1989, p. paper. (55960-6).
Note: Bound with **Nemisis From Terra** By Leigh Brackett.

l Riverdale, NY: Baen Books. August 1, 2008. SKU: 0812559606.

CHAPTERS: 22

Star Captain Jay Birrel becomes involved in a plot between the various star kingdoms to conquer the earth. The earth is now a minor player in galactic politics, but remains independent from the great star kingdoms.

REVIEWS:

http://authors.booksunderreview.com/H/Hamilton,_Edmond/

A34 "Thunder World." in Imaginative Tales, 3:4 (July 1956) Pg. 6.

Cover: Lloyd N. Rognan.

REPRINTS:

b as **In Den Klauen Jupiters**. Rastatt (Baden): Erich Pabel Verlag. 1956, p. [German]

c as **In Den Klauen Jupiters**. Rastatt (Baden): Erich Pabel Verlag. 1966, p. (Utopia Zukunfts Roman 489). Translator: Thomas Schluck. [German]

Farrel Baird vows to seek vengence on those responsible for the death of his father. He joins the Outer Planets Bureau and is shipped out to Ganyemede. He joins a team to travel to Jupiter and prepare for a major assault. He discovers that his body is built for the Outer Planets. While on Jupiter, he confronts the man involved with his father's death. He needs proof to confront the head of the Outer Planets Bureau for having his fathe killed. Eventually he confronts the killer in front of Sherriff, the head of the Outer Planets Bureau. Farrel then leads the Jupiter crew on a journey across the planet to find a more stable area for the first colony.

A35 "Fugitive of the Stars." Imagination, 8:6 #58 (December 1957): Pg. 6. Cover: Malcolm Smith.

EXPANDED AND REPRINTED[xxxviii]:

b as **Fugitive of the Stars**. New York, NY: Ace Books, 1965, 116 p. (M-111). Illustrator: Jack Gaughan.
Note: This is an Ace Double with **Land Beyond the Map** by Kenneth Bulmer.

c as **Fluchtling der Randwelten**. Munchen: Terra Astra - SF Ramane aus der Perry-Rhodan-Redaktion #27, 1972, p. Translator: Birgit Ress-Bohusch. [German]

ca as **Fluchtling der Randwelten**. _: Moewig-Verlag, 1975, p. [German]

d Riverdale, NY: Baen Books. September 1, 2008. SKU: 1602823987.

CHAPTERS: 27

After being convicted of negligence Jim Horne is on the planet Skereth looking for Ardic, his junior pilot on the ill-fated final voyage of the Vega Queen. He joins forces with the political opposition party, they discover that the Vega Queen was sabotaged to destroy the leader of the Vellae's rival party, who was on board. The group is building an illegal and dangerous project.

A36 The Haunted Stars. New York: Torquil (Dodd,Mead). March 1960, 192 p. cloth. (59-15721).

REPRINTS:

a Toronto: Dodd. 1960.
b Doubleday Science Fiction Book Club, 1960, 192 p. (2 printings).
c : King Features Syndicate. 1961, p. Illustrator: T. Nowodzinski.
d New York, NY: Pyramid Books. February 1962, 159 p. paper (F-698). Illustrator: Kandinsky.
e as **Das Gestirn der Ahnen**. Munchen: <publisher unknown> 1964, p. (TS 84). Translator: Wulf H. Bergner. [German]
f Tokyo: Hayakawa Shobo Publishing, Inc. Sept. 1964 (c1960), 224 p. 19 cm. (SF HPB3217). Translator: Syokichi Kawaguchi. [Japanese]
g as **Gli Incappucciati d'ombre**. Milano: Arnoldo Monadori Editore. 5 April 1964, 166 p. 19cm. (I Ramanzi di Urania, no. 331). Illustrated. Translator: Bianca Russo. [Itailian]
h London: Herbert Jenkins, 1965, 174 p.[xxxix] 20 cm. [British]
i as **Les Mondes Interdits**. _: Champs Elysees, 1978, p. (SF 70).
j _: <publisher unknown> 1981, 22 p. 16 cm. (SF 459). [Japanese]
ga as **Gli In cappucciati D'ombre**. Milano: Arnoldo Monadori Editore, 1982, p. (Classici Urania 065). [Italian]
h Riverdale, NY: Baen Books. September 1, 2008. SKU: 1515006980.

CHAPTERS: 25

DEDICATION: To Jack Williamson, who knows the starways!

A dedicated, young philologist has been asked to help decipher what he thinks are some old texts for the Smithsonian museum. He discovers it was a ruse to get him to the U.S. Space program base in New Mexico. There he finds several of his most esteemed colleagues have also been recruited. They discover that the U.S. base on the moon has found the remains of an ancient installation. This team of lingusts has been assembled to crack the alien language. They journey to the Van Ryn home world where they discover that for many centuries the Van Ryn had also conquered space only to be repulsed by another race.

REVIEWS:

S. Cotts. Amazing Stories 34(7):137. (July 1960).
P. Miller. Analog 66(3):167-168. (November 1960).
F. Gale. Galaxy 21(4):156-157. (April 1963).
H.H. Holmes. Herald Tribune Book Review 13 May 1960.
David Pringle. **The Ultimate Guide to Science Fiction**. Pharos Books, 1990.

A37 Return to the Stars[xl]. New York, NY.: Lancer Books. 1964, p.

REPRINTS:

b Tokyo: Sogensha Co. Ltd. 1964, p. [Japanese]
c as **Le retour aux etoiles**. Paris: Editions J'ai Lu. 1967, 310p. 17 cm. Translator: Frank Straschitz. [French]
d in **Les rois des etoiles & Retour aux etoiles**[xli][xlii]. _: Ed. Opta. 1968, p. (Classique SF: 12). [French]
aa New York, NY.: Lancer Books. 1969, 207 p. paper.
e _: Prestige Books. 1969.
ab New York, NY.: Lancer. 1970, 207 p. paper. (74612). Illustrator: Steranko.
ca as **Les Retour aux Etoiles**. _: J'ai Lu SF, 1972, 310 p. 17x11 cm. (SF Fantasy: 432). Translator: Frank Straschitz. [French]
cb as **Les Retour aux Etoiles**. _: J'ai Lu SF, 1973, 310 p. (#490). Translator: Frank Straschitz.[French]
f _: <publisher unknown> February 1973, 260 p. (SF 637-2). [Japanese]
g as **Ihre Heimat sind die Sterne**. Rastatt/Baden: Erich Pabel Verlag, May 1976, p. [German]
h as **Regresso Aos Ceus**. Lisboa: Edicao <livros do Brasil>, <year>, p. (N 237). Translator: Eurico Fonseca. [Brazilian]
i as **Rucker zu den Sternen**. Munchen: Heyne-Buch, 1981, 203 p. [HSF 3781] Translator: Thomas LeBlanc. [German]
cc as **Les Retour aux Etoiles**. _: J'ai Lu SF. 1991, 310 p. 17x11 cm. (SF Fantasy: 432). Translator: Frank Straschitz. [French]
cd as **Les Retour aux Etoiles**. _: J'ai Lu SF. 1998, p. Translator: Frank Straschitz.[French]
j in The Chronicles of the Star Kings. _: Time Warner Books, UK. April 17, 1986. Venture Science Fiction. 400 p. ISBN-10: 0099478609; ISBN-13: 978-0099478607 [British]
With **The Star Kings**.
k Riverdale, NY: Baen Books. September 1, 2008. SKU: 4477461275.

CONTENTS:

"The Kingdom of the Stars"	[See B231]
"The Shores of Infinity"	[See B253]
"The Broken Stars"	[See B235]
"The Horror From the Magellanic"	[See B236]

John Gordon, having returned to the twentieth century from the far distant future, seeks psychiatric help for these wild fantasies. Just on the verge of recovery, Zarth Arn contacts him from the future. This time Zarth brings him physically across the gulf of time. He meets up with his love, a princess of Formalhaut, and is embroiled again in a galactic conflict to save the galaxy against invaders from the Megallanic clouds.

REVIEWS:

D. Malcolm. Vision of Tomorrow 1(10):53-54. (July 1970).
L. del Rey. Worlds of If 20(6):150-151. (July/August 1970).
D. Paskow. Luna Monthly 22:25. (March 1971).
T. Pauls. Science Fiction Review 42:32. (January 1971).
David Pringle. **The Ultimate Guide to Science Fiction**. Pharos Books, 1990.

A38 Doomstar. New York, NY: Belmont. 1966, 158 p. 18cm. paper (B50-657).

REPRINTS:

b New York, NY: Belmont. 1969,p. paper (B50-857).
ba New York, NY: Belmont Tower. 1978, p. paper. (51336). Illustrator: Attila Hujja.
c _: Kuboshoten. September 1981, 255 p. Translator: Sanpei Kamata. [Japanese]
d Riverdale, NY: Baen Books. September 1, 2008. SKU: 0505513366.

CHAPTERS: 25

REVIEWS:

<unknown>
http://authors.booksunderreview.com/H/Hamilton,_Edmond/

A39 The Weapon from Beyond (Starwolf #1).[xliii] Ace Book,

1967, 158 p. paper (G-639). Illustrator: Jack Gaughan.

REPRINTS:

b as **Arma do Alben**. Lisbon: Editorial Panorama. 1967, p.[Portugese]

c as **Il lupo dei Cieli**. Milano: Arnoldo Mondadori Editore. 11 February 1968, 162 p. 19cm. (I Romanzi di Urania, no. 481). Illustrated. Translator: Mario Galli. [Italian]

d as **Der Sternwolf**. Munchen: <publisher unknown> 1969. p. (TN 80). Translator: Birgit Ress -Bohusch. [German]

e as **Vapnet från det okända**[xliv]. Stockholm: Lindqvist. 1970, 159 p. paper. Translator: Carl Henner. [Swedish]

f Tokyo: Hayakawa Publishing, Inc. 1970, 240 p. Translator: Masahiro Noda. [Japanese]

g as **Les Loups des Étoiles**. Paris: editions Opta. 1971, 467 p. (Club du Livre d'Anticipation #31 - Limited to 6150 numbered copies). Illustrated. Translation: Richard Chomet. [French]

h as **L'Arme de Nulle Part**. Paris: Librairie des Champs-Elysees, 1977, 253p. (Le Masque Science Fiction #62). ISBN: 2-7024-0651-3. Translator: Richard Chomet. [French]

i _: Hamlyn. May 1978. 464 p. (40030-8).[British]

ba as **Arma do Alben**. Lisboa: Emp. Tip. Casa Protuguesa, Sucrs, Lda. <year>, p. Translation: Maria Roque Casimiro. [Brazilian]

j in **Starwolf: The Classic Space Adventure Trilogy**. New York, NY: Ace Books, October 1982, 456p. paper.

ja New York, NY: Ace Books. June 1986, 456 p. paper. (Sixth Printing)

k as **L'Arme de Mulle Part**. Paris: A. Michel, 1987, 190p. (Albin'Pche #11). Translator: Richard Chomet. [French]

l adapted into two low-budget live-action Japanese movies titled "Fugitive Alien" and "Fugitive Alien II."

m _: __. March 1994, 249 p. (SF 4-1).

n as **Die Waffe der Vhollaner**. Bastei-Lübbe, <year>, p. (TB 23165). [German]

o in **Les Loups des Étoiles**. _: Gallimard , <year>, p. (Folio SF #135). [French]

p in **Les Loups des Étoiles**. _: Denoel, <year>, p. (Lunes d'Encre #6). [French]

q Riverdale, NY: Baen Books. August 1, 2008. SKU: 1299450172.

CHAPTERS: 20

REVIEWS:

David Pringle. **The Ultimate Guide to Science Fiction**. Pharos

Books, 1990.
Eric Vial in Galaxies, No. 16 (March 2000): [French]
Roland C. Wagner in Bifrost No. 18 (May 2000): [French]
Valérie Frances in Khimaira No. 20 (September 2003): [French]
Jean-François Thomas in Galaxies No. 30 (September 2003): [French]

A40 An den Ufern der Unendlichkeit.[xlv] Rasttat: Hubert Strassl. 1968, p. (U 571). [collection] [German]

CONTENTS:

"Konigreich der Sterne" (Kingdom of the Stars) [See B231]
"An den Ufern der Unendlichkeit" (The Shores of Infinity) [See B237]

A41 The Closed Worlds (Starwolf #2). New York: Ace Books. 1968, 156 p. 18cm. paper (G-701). Illustrator: Jack Gaughan.

REPRINTS:

b as **Todesschranke um Allubane**. Munchen: <publisher unknown> 1969, p. (TN 83). Translator: Birgit Res-Bousch. [German]
c Tokyo: Hayakawa Publishing, Inc. 30 June 1971, 266 p. Translator: Masahiro Noda. [Japanese]
d as **Morgan Chane, Il Lupo dei Cieli**. _: Libra, 1978, p.. (Classici #29).
e as **Les Monde Interdits**. Paris: Librairie des Champs-Elysees, 1977, 249p. (Le Masque Science Fiction #70). [French]
f in **Starwolf: The Classic Space Adventure Trilogy**. New York, NY: Ace Books, October 1982, 456p. paper.
fa New York, NY: Ace Books, June 1986, 456p. paper. (Sixth Printing)
g as **Die verbotenen Welten**. _: Bastei-Lübbe, <year>, p. (TB 23168). [German]
h Riverdale, NY: Baen Books. August 1, 2008. SKU: 0021077010.

CHAPTERS: 20

REVIEWS:

David Pringle. **The Ultimate Guide to Science Fiction**. Pharos Books, 1990.

A42 Kinder der Sonne[xlvi]. Munchen: Moewig, 1968. 64 p.

(Terra Utopische Romane Science Fiction; 545). [German] [Collection]

CONTENTS:

"Der grüne Komet" (The Comet Doom) [See A36]
"Kinder der Sonne" (Sunfire!) [See A36]
"Die Stadt am Himmel" (Babylon in the Sky) [See A36]
"Die Degenerierten" (Devolution) [See A36]

A43 World of Starwolves (Starwolf #3). New York: Ace Books, 1968, 158 p. paper. Illustrator: Jack Gaughan.

REPRINTS:

b as **Die Singenden Sonnen**. Munchen: 1969, p. (TN 87). Translator: Birgit Ress-Bohusch. [German]

c _Tokyo: Hayakawa Publishing, Inc. 31 December 1971, 259 p.Translator: Masahiro Noda. [Japanese]

d as **Le Planete des Loups [Wolve's Planet]**. Paris: Librairie des Champs-Elysees, 1978, p. (Le Masque Science Fiction #79). ISBN: 2-7024-0771-4. Translation: Richard Chomet. [French]

e in **Starwolf: The Classic Space Adventure Trilogy**. New York, NY: Ace Books. October 1982, 456 p. paper.

ea New York, NY: Ace Books. June 1986, 456 p. paper. (Sixth Printing).

f _: __. April 1994, 252 p. (SF46; SF 4-3). [Japanese]

g as **Die Welt der Sternwölfe**. Bastei-Lübbe, <year>, p. (TB 23170). [German]

h Riverdale, NY: Baen Books. August 1, 2008. SKU: 0020077661.

CHAPTERS: 21

The Singing Suns have been stolen by the Starwolves. Morgan Chane convinces John Dillulo to mount an expedition to retrieve them. They travel to the place where the stones were broken up and sold. They contact the first buyer. Morgan and John discover that all the other buyers were merely agents for anotehr race. These beings live in a secret and well protected system known as the Closed Worlds. This buyer holds the mercenaries captive while John and Chane attempt to recover the Singing Suns. This attempt fails. Morgan Chane escapes to the Starwolves home world were he convinces the Starwolves to raid this hidden system. The Starwolves succeed and Morgan returns the Singing Suns and wins the freedom of the other mercenaries.

REVIEWS:

P. Miller. Analog 85(1):168. (March 1970)
J. Cawthorn. New Worlds No. 191:62. (June 1969)
L. del Rey. Worlds of If 19(8):147-148. (October 1969)
D. Halterman. Son of WSFA Journal 17:3-4. (March 1971)
David Pringle. **The Ultimate Guide to Science Fiction**. Pharos Books, 1990.

A44 What's it Like Out There? and Other Stories.[xlvii] New York: Ace Books, 1974, 320 p. paper. (8065). [collection]

REPRINTS:

b as **Godenschemering en Andere Verhalen**. Rotterdam: Scala. 1975, 311 p. 18cm. ISBN: 90.6221.031.7. (Scala science fiction reeks No. 4)[xlviii] Translator: Iskraa Bundels [Dutch]
c as **Waechter der Zeiten**. _: <publisher unknown> 1980, p. [German]
d as Como i Aquilo por la? _: <publisher unknown> 1984, p. (Mensagens do Futuro). Translator: Eurico da Fonseca. [Brazilian]
e as Ex?lio, Espa?o 5. 1984, p. Translator: de A. de Paes Salva??o.

CONTENTS:

What's It Like Out There?	7	[See B206]
The King of Shadows	33	[See B188]
Castaway	57	[See B234]
Serpent Princess	66	[See B191]
The Stars, My Brothers	97	[See B227]
Dreamer's World	144	[See B161]
Twilight of the Gods	184	[See B195]
Sunfire!	227	[See B228]
The Inn Outside the World	245	[See B178]
The Watcher of the Ages	262	[See B196]
Transuranic	280	[See B192]
The Isle of the Sleeper	304	[See B121]

REVIEWS:

<unknown> Bestsellers, September 1974, p. 26.
<unknown> Locus 166:5. (23 October 1974)
<unknown> Publishers Weekly 205(25):62. (24 June 1974)

David Pringle. **The Ultimate Guide to Science Fiction**. Pharos Books, 1990.

A45 **La Valle degli Dei**. Piacenza: La Tribuna, 1977, 148 p. (Galassia; 225). Translator: R. Rambelli. [Italian]

CONTENTS:

La Valle degli Dei(The Valley of the Gods)
Il Crepuscolo degli Dei (Twilight of the Gods)
Ritorno al Sabba (Return to the Sabbath) - Robert Bloch
Il Nuovo Seme (Novo Sjeme) - Damir Mikulicic

A46 The Best of Leigh Brackett. Edited with an introduction by Edmond Hamilton. Garden City, NY: Nelson Doubleday in arrangement with Ballantine/Del Rey a division of Random House, 1977, xvii, 334 p. 22 cm. cloth. Cover Sleve: Jack Wollhiser. [Collection]
Note: This is a collection of Leigh Bracketts' stories (Mr. Hamilton's wife).

REPRINTS:

b Garden City, New York: Garland Pub. 1983, p.

CONTENTS:

"Story-Teller of Many Worlds" - E. Hamilton	vii.
"The Jewel of Bas"	1
"The Vanishing Venusians"	46
"The Veil of Astellar"	73
"The Moon that Vanished"	99
"Enchantress of Venus"	141
"The Woman from Altair"	201
"The Last Days of Shandakor"	231
"Shannach-the Last"	259
"The Tweener"	308
"The Queer Ones"	324
"Afterward"	359

A47 The Best of Edmond Hamilton. Edited with an introduction by

Leigh Brackett. New York, NY: Ballantine/Del Rey. 1977, xviii, 381 p. 22 cm. cloth. (77-574). LCCN: 77-155163. Cover: Don Maitz. [Collection]

REPRINTS:

b NY: Ballantine/Del Rey, 1977, xviii, 381 p. 18 cm. paper. (259000). LCCN: 77-574. ISBN: 0-345-259000-9. Cover: Van Dongen.

c Garden City, New York: Nelson Doubleday, XVII, July 1977, 334 p. 22 cm. (1561).

ca Garden City, NY: Garland Publishing, 1983, Xviii, 381 p. LCCN: 81-47372.

d as **Die besten Stories**. Munchen: Moewig, 1980, 400 p. 18 cm – (Playboy Science Fiction; 6701 ISBN: 3-8118-7036-X). Cover: Oliveiero Berni. [German]

CONTENTS:

REVIEWS:

L. del Rey. Analog 97(8):170-172. (August 1977)

D. Schweitzer. Science Fiction Review 23:76-77. (November

1977)
<unknown> Publishers Weekly 212(1):74. (4 July 1977)
A. Budrys. The Magazine of Fantasy & Science Fiction 53(5): 18-20. (November 1977)
D. Miller. Booklist 74(5):462. (1 November 1977)
R. B. Kliatt Paperback Book Guide 12(1):13. (Winter 1978)
M. Wooster. Son of WSFA Journal 90:R7-R10. (May 1978)
David Pringle. **The Ultimate Guide to Science Fiction**. Pharos Books, 1990.
<unknown>
http://authors.booksunderreview.com/H/Hamilton,_Edmond/

A48 Starwolf: The Classic Space Adventure Trilogy. New York, NY: Ace Books. October 1982, 456p. 18 cm. paper. [Collection]

REPRINTS:

b New York, NY: Ace Books. June 1986, 456 p. paper. (Sixth Printing).
c as **Les loups des Etoiles, l'int_grale**. Paris: Deno_l, 2000, 523p. 21 cm. ISBN: 2-207024958-6. Translation: Richard Chomet.

CONTENTS:

Weapon From Beyond	[See A39]
Closed Worlds	[See A41]
World of the Starwolves	[See A43]

REVIEWS:

J. Cawthorn. New Worlds No. 176:64. (October 1967)
http://authors.booksunderreview.com/H/Hamilton,_Edmond/

A49 Starwars of the Galaxy [3BE3_HbIE __TBbI GAJIAKT_K]. _: Library Stars, 1991, p. [collection] [cloth]

CONTENTS:

The Island of Unreason	3	[See B54]
Mysterious World	21	[See ?]
Outside the Galaxy	142	[See ?]
The Valley of Invisible Men	209	[See B133]
Life Stars	271	[See ?]

A50 Kaldar, World of Antares. Edited by Stephen haffner. Royal Oak, Michigan: Haffner Press. 1998, p. Illustrator: Job Arfstrom. Note: This collects the three Stuart Merrick stories in one volume.

CONTENTS:

A51 The Vampire Master. Edited by Stephen Haffner. Royal Oak, Michigan: Haffner Press, 1998, p. Illustrator: Job Arfstrom. Introduction by Hugh B. Cave

This collects the four stories in one volume. These originally appeared in <u>Weird Tales</u> under the pseudonym of Hugh Davidson.

CONTENTS:

A52 The Invisible Master. Bloomington, IL: Black Dog Press, 2000, 76 p. chap [collection]

CONTENTS:

A53 Stark and the Star Kings. Edited by Stephen Haffner. Royal Oak, Michigan: Haffner Press. 2005, 648 p. (9.3 x 6.2 x 1.7 in.) Trade Edition: ISBN: 1-893887-2. 100-copy Slipcased Limited Edition (signed by Jakes & Ebel): ISBN: 1-893887-17-0; ISBN-10: 1893887162.; ISBN-13: 978-1893887169 Illustrated by Ax Ebel. Introduction by John Jakes.

CONTENTS:

Introduction	
The Star Kings	[See A29]
Queen of the Martian Catacombs	
Enchantress of Venus	
Black Amazon of Mars	
Return to the Stars	[See A37]
Stark and the Star Kings	[See B238]

A54 The Metal Giants and Others, The Collected Edmond Hamilton, Volume One[xlix]. Edited by Stephen Haffner. Royal Oak, Michigan: Haffner Press. 1 July 2009, 648 p. Hardback. Introduction by Robert Weinberg. Illustrated by Hugh Rankin. ISBN-10: 1893887316; ISBN-13: 978-1893887312

CONTENTS:

Introduction by Robert Weinberg	
"The Monster-God of Mamurth"	[See B1]
"Across Space"	[See B2]
"The Metal Giants"	[See A1]
"The Atomic Conquerors"	[See B3]
"Evolution Island"	[See B4]
"The Moon Menace"	[See B5]
"The Time-Raider"	[See B6]
"The Comet Doom"	[See B7]
"The Dimension Terror"	[See B8]
"The Polar Doom"	[See B9]
"The Sea Horror"	[See B12]
"Locked Worlds"	[See B11]

“The Abysmal Invaders” [See B14]

A55 The Star-Stealers: The Complete Adventures of The Interstellar Patrol, The Collected Edmond Hamilton, Volume Two[l]. Edited by Stephen Haffner. Royal Oak, Michigan: Haffner Press. 1 July 2009, 648 p. Hardback. Introduction by Walter Jon Williams. Illustrated by C. Barker Petrie, Jr. ISBN-10 1893887316; ISBN-13 97818938871312

CONTENTS:

Introduction by Walter Jon Williams
“Crashing Suns” [See A2]
“The Star-Stealers” [See B10]
“Within the Nebula” [See B13]
“Outside the Universe” [See A3]
“The Comet-Drivers” [See B19]
“The Sun People” [See B24]
“The Cosmic Cloud” [See B32]
“Corsairs of the Cosmos” [See B63]
“The Hidden World” [See B16]

A56 The Collected Captain Future, Volume One: Captain Future and the Space Emperor[li]. Edited by Stephen Haffner. Royal Oak, Michigan: Haffner Press. 1 July 2009, 648 p. Hardback. Introduction by Walter Jon Williams. Illustrated by Hugh Rankin. ISBN-10 1893887332; ISBN-13 97818938871336.

CONTENTS:

Introduction by ?
Original Magazine Editorial
“Captain Future & the Space Emperor” [See A9]
“Calling Captain Future” [See A10]
“Captain Future’s Challenge” [See A11]
“The Triumph of Captain Future” [See A12]
“The Future of Captain Future”
Artwork Gallery

Other Foreign Editions - Unknown Stories

O vale da criawc ao. _: Edipceao Livros do. 1954. [Brazilian]
Trevas nas Estrelas. _: Edipcao Livros do. 1960. [Brazilian]
Luta Intergbalactica. _: Edipcao Livros do. 1965. [Brazilian]
Yhu Sho kuai j^en Sai-lo po shih ti pi mi. _: Ta Chung Shu Chhu. 1977. [Chinese]

Review of the Captain Future Series

R. Weston. Son of WSFA Journal 21:7. (May 1971)

The following sales statistics were compiled from the royalty statements held in the collection and are included for the curious.

Torquil		
The Star of Life	American	2542
	Canadian	124
The Haunted Stars	American	2354
	Canadian	112
The Battle for the Stars	American	1654
	Canadian	148
Frederick Fell		
City at World's End		2737
Horror On the Asteroid	England	458
	Colonies	88

This is not meant to be an accurate reflection of sales. There is no information available for paperback sales. It is unclear as to whether or not all the royalty statements are in evidence.

B
Stories Published in Periodicals

B1 "The Monster-God of Mamurth" in Weird Tales, 8:2 (August, 1926) Pg. 307. Illustrator: G. Olinick[lii].

REPRINTS:

b in **Beware After Dark!** Edited by T. Everett Harre. _:Macaulay, 1929, p. [collection]

bb in **Beware After Dark!** Edited by T. Everett Harre. _: Gold Label, 1931, p. [collection]

ab in Weird Tales, 26:3 (September, 1935) Pg. 381.

c in **The Horror on the Asteroid and Other Tales of Planetary Horror**. London: Philip Allan. 1936. cloth. p. 59. [collection]

bc in **Beware After Dark!** Edited by T. Everett Harre. _: Emerson, 1942, p. [collection]

bd in **Beware After Dark!** Edited by T. Everett Harre. _: Emerson, 1942, p. [collection]

d in Magazine of Horror, #14 (Winter, 1966-7) Pg.

ca in **The Horror on the Asteroid and Other Tales of Planetary Horror**. _: Gregg Press, 1975. cloth. (75-5745). p. 59. [collection]

e in **The Best of Edmond Hamilton**. Edited by Leigh Brackett. Garden City, NY.: Nelson Doubleday, 1977. cloth. [collection]

ea in **The Best of Edmond Hamilton**. Edited by Leigh Brackett. _: Ballentine, 1977. paper. [collection]

eb as "Der Monster-Gott Von Mamurth." in **Die Besten Stories**. 1980. (PSF 6701). [collection] [German]

f as **Le Dieu monstrueux de Mamurth**. Paris: Nouvelles Editions Oswald, 1986.(Fatastique, Science-Fiction, adventure; 176). 202 p. 21 cm.[French]

g as "Le Dieu monstrueux de Mamurth," **in Les meilleurs recits de Weird Tales 1**. Paris: Oswald, ?. [collection] [French]

h in Black Gate, 1:2, #2 (Summer 2001) Pg.

A disheveled archeologist wanders into camp from out of the depths of the desert. He is near death and relates the story of his adventure. He tells of finding a stone outside a caravan stop. He translated the markings on the stone and discovered directions to a forbidden city and a warning message. He supplies himself and tries to hire guides and porters, but they refuse. Alone, he arrives at Mamurth and begins to explore. To his horror he finds a menacing sevret. He barely escapes with his life.

B2 "Across Space" serialized in Weird Tales, 8:3 (September, 1926): Pg. 307. Part Two: 8:4 (October 1926) Pg. 520. Conclusion: 8:5 (November 1926) Pg. 690. Illustrator: G. Olinick[liii].

B3 "The Atomic Conquerors" in Weird Tales, 9:2 (February, 1927) Pg. 168. Illustrator: G. Olinick.

B4 "Evolution Island" in Weird Tales, 9:3 (March, 1927) Pg. Illustrator: G. Olinick

REPRINTS:

b in **Weird Tales: Thirty-Two Unearthed Treasures**. Edited by Robert Weinberg, Stefan R. Dziemiasowic and Martin H. Greeberg. _: Outlet Books, 1988. p. [collection]

B5 "The Moon Menace" in Weird Tales, 10:3 (September, 1927): Pg. 311. Illustrator: H.R. (Hugh Rankin).

REPRINTS:

b in Famous Science Fiction, #2 (Spring, 1967) Pg.

B6 "The Time Raider" serialized in Weird Tales, 10:4 (October, 1927) Pg. 459. Part Two: 10:5 (November, 1927): 639. Part Three: 10:6 (December, 1927) Pg. 832. Conclusion: 11:1 January, 1928) Pg. 105. Illustrator: H.R. (Hugh Rankin).

B7 "The Comet Doom" in Amazing Stories, (January, 1928): Pg. 926. Illustrator: Frank R. Paul.

REPRINTS:

b in Tales of Wonder, #4 (August, 1930) Pg. Illustrator: Harry E. Turner.

Cover: Nick (aka John) Nicholson. [British]

bb in Tales of Wonder, #8 (Autumn, 1939) Pg. Illustrator: Harry E. Turner. [British]

c in Amazing Stories, 40:3 (December, 1965) Pg. 64. Illustrator: Frank R. Paul.

d as "Der grune Komet" in **Kinder der Sonne**. Munchen: <publisher unknown>, 1968, p. (TTB 545). [German]

e in **Isaac Asimov's Wonderful Worlds of Science Fiction #4: Comets**. Edited by Isaac Asimov, Martin H. Greenberg & Charles G. Waugh. _: NAL/Signet, 1986, p. [collection]

They discover that a strange green comet is passing through the solar system, and it will pass close to the earth. Leaving his home in Ontario, Marlin is walking around Lake Erie when he stops at Grayton, Ohio. From there he catches a fishing boat ride across the lake. On the way past a small island, the boat is destroyed by a strange ray. He swims to the island where he meets Walter Coburn. Coburn, on vacation, tells a very strange story. The pair attempt to prevent the destruction of the Earth, but the fail. Coburn's former partner Hanley saves the earth in the end.

B8 "The Dimension Terror" in Weird Tales, 11:6 (June, 1928): Pg. 769. Illustrator: Hugh Rankin.

B9 "The Polar Doom" in Weird Tales, 12:3 (September, 1928): Pg. Illustrator: Hugh Rankin.

B10 "The Star-Stealers" in Weird Tales, 13:2 (February, 1929) Pg. 149. Illustrator: H.R.[liv] (Hugh Rankin). Cover: Hugh Rankin.

REPRINTS:

b in **Avon Fantasy Reader No. 6**. _: Avon Books, 1951 (c1948), p. Pg. 65. [collection]

c in **Patrulha Interstellar**. Lisboa: Livros do Brasil, 1950, p. Translation by Eurico da Fonseca. (No. 133). [collection] [Brazillian]

d in **Crashing Suns**. New York: Ace Books, 1965, 192 p. (F-319) [collection]

e as "I Kleftes ton Asterion" in **O Polemos ton Ilion**. Athens: Sympan/Lynari, 1968, p. Tranlstor: N. Hohlakis. [collection]

[Greek]

ea as "I Kleftes ton Asterion" in **O Polemos ton Ilion**. Athens: Sympan/Lynari, 1980, p. Tranlstor: N. Hohlakis. [collection] [Greek]

B11 "Locked Worlds" in Amazing Stories Quarterly, (Spring, 1929): Pg. 222. Illustrator: Frank R. Paul.

REPRINTS:

b in Amazing Stories, (July 1968) Pg. 39.

B12 "The Sea Horror" in Weird Tales, 13:3 (March, 1929) Pg. 351. Illustrator: C. C. Senf.

REPRINTS:

b in Tales of Wonder. () Pg.

B13 "Within The Nebula" in Weird Tales, 13:5 (May, 1929) Pg. 597. Illustrator: Boak. (aka Hugh Rankin).

REPRINTS:

b in **Patrulha Interstellar**. Lisboa: Livros do Brasil, 1950. (No. 133), p. Translation by Eurico da Fonseca. [collection] [Brazilian]

c in **Crashing Suns**. New York, NY: Ace Books, 1965, 192 p. paper. (F-319)

d as "Mesa sto Nefeloma" in **O Polemos ton Ilion**. Athens: Sympan/Lynari, 1968, p. Tranlstor: N. Hohlakis. [collection] [Greek]

da as " Mesa sto Nefeloma " in **O Polemos ton Ilion**. Athens: Sympan/Lynari, 1980, p. Tranlstor: N. Hohlakis. [collection] [Greek]

B14 "The Abysmal Invaders" in Weird Tales, 13:6 (June, 1929): Pg. 741. Illustrator: H.R. (Hugh Rankin).

B15 "The Other Side of the Moon" in Amazing Stories Quarterly, (Fall 1929) Pg. 516. Illustrator: H. W. "Wesso" Wessolowski. Cover: H. W. "Wesso" Wessolowski.

REPRINTS:

b Science Fiction Adventure Classics, #8 (Winter, 1969) Pg. 4. Illustrator: H. W. "Wesso" Wessolowski.

CHAPTERS:

The Howland Sensation
The Moon Raiders
Out to the Moon
The Cylinder Starts
The Other Side of the Moon
The Battle of the Flying-Circles
Through Strange Perils
Howland's Story
A Saga of Worlds
To Crash Down Man Forever!
A Fight for Freedom
Up The Wall
Howland's Way
Epilogue

The lone survivor of a scientific mission to Yucatan returns to his midwestern university. He informs his friends that their dear friend and colleague, Dr. Howland, has not perished, but is alive on the moon This galvanizes the three friends to try and rescue Dr. Howland from the creatures that have taken him captive. They mount a small expedition to the Yucatan and manage to find their way to the Moon.

B16 "Hidden World" in Science Wonder Quarterly, #1 (Fall, 1929): Pg. 84. Illustrator: Frank R. Paul. Cover: Earle K. Bergey.

REPRINTS:

b in Fantastic Story Quarterly, 1:1 (Spring, 1950) Pg. 11. Illustrator: Virgil Finlay.

c in **The Star-Stealers: The Complete Adventures of The Interstellar Patrol, The Collected Edmond Hamilton, Volume Two**. Royal Oak, Michigan: Haffner Press. 1 July 2009.

d serialized on the Haffner Press web page:
http://www.haffnerpress.com/hid00.html
Note: This is the 1950 version. Two new chapters posted each week.

B17 "Cities in the Air" serialized in Air Wonder Stories, (November, 1929) Pg. 390. Conclusion - Air Wonder Stories, (Winter 1930) Pg.

B18 "The Life Masters" in Weird Tales, 15:1 (January, 1930) Pg. 59. Illustrator: H.R. (Hugh Rankin).

B19 "The Comet Drivers" in Weird Tales, 15:2 (February, 1930): 172. Illustrator: H.R. (Hugh Rankin).

REPRINTS:

b in **Crashing Suns**. New York: Ace Books, 1965, paper. 192 p. (F-319) [collection]

c in **Patrulha Interstellar**. Lisboa: Livros do Brasil, 1950 (No. 133), p. Translation by Eurico da Fonseca. [collection] [Brazilian]

d as "I Odigi tou Komiti" in **O Polemos ton Ilion**. Athens: Sympan/Lynari, 1968, p. Translator: N. Hohlakis. [collection] [Greek]

da as " I Odigi tou Komiti" in **O Polemos ton Ilion**. Athens: Sympan/Lynari, 1980, p. Translator: N. Hohlakis. [collection] [Greek]

B20 "The Space Visitors" in Air Wonder Stories, (March, 1930): Pg. 804.

REPRINTS:

b in Startling Stories, (September, 1939) Pg. 110.

c in Tales of Wonder. () Pg.

B21 "Evans of the Earth Guard" in Air Wonder Stoires, (April, 1930) Pg. 902.

B22 “The Invisible Master” in Scientific Detective Monthly, (April, 1930) Pg. 300. Illustrator: Ruger.

REPRINTS:

b in **The Invisible Master**. Bloomington, IL: Black Dog Press, 2000. 76 p. chap [collection]

B23 “The Plant Revolt” in Weird Tales, 15:4 (April, 1930) Pg. 487. Illustrator: H.R.

b in **The Earth in Peril**. Edited by Donald A. Wollheim. _: <publisher unknown> <year>, 1957, p. [collection]

B24 “The Sun People” in Weird Tales, 15:5 (May, 1930) Pg. 606. Illustrator: C. C. Senf.

B25 “The Universe Wreckers” serialized in Amazing Stories, (May, 1930) Pg. 102. Part Two - Amazing Stories, (June, 1930): 254. Part Three - Amazing Stories, (July, 1930) Pg. 346. Illustrator: Wesso.

B26 “The Death Lord” in Weird Tales, 16:1 (July, 1930) Pg. 83.

B27 “World Atavism” in Amazing Stories, (August, 1930) Pg. 428. Illustrator: Frank R. Paul.

REPRINTS:

b in Science Fiction Adventure Classics, (Winter, 1967) Pg. 27.

B28 “The Second Satellite” in Astounding Stories, 3:2 (#8) (August, 1930) Pg. 175. Illustrator: A. Fleming Gould.

B29 "Pigmy Island" in Weird Tales, 16:2 (August, 1930) Pg. 175.
Illustrator: H.R.

REPRINTS:

b in **Switch on the Night**. edited by Christine Campbell Thompson. London: Selwyn & Blount, 1931, p. [collection] [British]

c in **Not at Night Omnibus**. Edited by Christine Campbell Thompson. London: Selwyn & Blount. 1937, p. 145-170.[lv] [collection] [British]

ca in **Not at Night**. Edited by Christine Campbell Thompson. _: Arrow, 1960, p. [collection]

d in Man From U.N.C.L.E. (October, 1967) Pg.

B30 "The Man Who Saw the Future" in Amazing Stories, (October 1930) Pg. 600. Illustrator: Morey.

REPRINTS:

b in **The Horror on the Asteroid and Other Tales of Planetary Horror**. London: Philip Allan, 1936. p. cloth. Pg. 59. [collection]

c in Tales of Wonder, (#11). (Summer, 1940) Pg. 24.

d in Amazing Stories, (February, 1961) Pg. 85. Illustrator: Morey.

e in **Strange Signposts**. Edited by Sam Moskowitz and Roger Elwood. New York, NY: Holt, Rinehart and Winston, 1966. p. cloth. pp 194-207. [collection]

f in **Other Worlds, Other Times**. Edited by Sam Moskowitz and Roger Elwood. _: MacFaddan-Bartell, 1969, p. paper. [collection]

g as "L'uomu Che Vide Il Futuro" in **Il Pianeta Degli Angeli**. _: Editrice Libra, 1975, p. (Nova SF #32) [collection] [Italian]

h in **The Fantastic Pulps.** Edited by Peter Haining. New York, NY: St. Martin's Press, Inc. 1975, p. cloth. pp. 244-259. [collection]

ha in **The Fantastic Pulps.** Edited by Peter Haining. _: Gollancz, 1975, p. [collection]

hb in **The Fantastic Pulps.** Edited by Peter Haining. _: Vintage, 1975, p. [collection]

I as "O Anthropos pou Ezise tin Wxelixi" in Enigmata tou Sibantos, issue #26-27 (July-August 1977) Pg. Translator: Ntinos Garoufalias. [Greek]

j in **Amazing Science Fiction Anthology: The Wonder Years: 1926-1935**. Edited by Martin H. Greenberg. Lake Geneva, WI.: TSR, Inc. 1987, p. paper. [collection]

k as "O Anthropos pou Ezise tin Wxelixi" in **O Zoferos Autokratoras**.

Athens: Siban/Lichnari, 1989, p. Translator: Jenny Mistraki. [collection] [Greek]

l in **14 Amazing Science Fiction Stories from the 30's to the 60's**. _: Amazon Digital Servies.. <year> 21 Kb. ASIN B001TH8L72..

m _: Amazon Digital Servies.. <year> 896 Kb. Pg. 130. ASIN B002DMKYS6.

n _: Project Gutenberg February 13, 2009. EPUB, MOBI, Plucker, HTML and Plain Text fomats. 18-90 Kb. EText-No. 28062. http://www.gutenberg.org/etext/28062.

B31 "The Mind-Master"[lvi] in Weird Tales, 16:4 (October, 1930) Pg. 489. Illustrator: P.E.H.

B32 "The Cosmic Cloud" in Weird Tales, 16:5 (November, 1930): Pg. 631. Illustrator: C. C. Senf.

REPRINTS:

b in **Patrulha Interstellar**. Lisboa: Livros do Brasil, 1950, p. (No. 133). Translation by Eurico da Fonseca. [collection]

c in **Crashing Suns**. New York: Ace Books, 1965, 192 p. paper. (F-319) [collection]

d as "To Cosmiko Sinefo" in **O Polemos ton Ilion**. Athens: Sympan/Lynari, 1968, p. Translator: N. Chochlakis. [collection] [Greek]

da as " To Cosmiko Sinefo" in **O Polemos ton Ilion**. Athens: Sympan/Lynari, 1980, p. Translator: N. Chochlakis. [collection] [Greek]

B33 "The Horror City" in Weird Tales, 17:2 (February - March, 1931): Pg. 192

B34 "Monsters of Mars" in Astounding Stories, 6:1 (#16). (April, 1931) Pg. 4. Illustrator: Gould.

B35 "The Man Who Evolved" in Wonder Stories, (April, 1931) Pg. 1266. Illustrator: Frank R. Paul.

REPRINTS:

b in **The Horror on the Asteroid and Other Tales of Planetary Horror**. London: Philip Allan. 1936, p. cloth. Pg. 59. [collection]

c in Startling Stories, (November, 1940) Pg. 110.

d in **From Off This World**. Edited by Leo Margulies and Oscar J. Friend. Merlin Press, 1949,[lvii] p. paper. [collection]

e in **Before the Golden Age**. Edited by Isaac Asimov. Garden City, NY.: Nelson Doubleday, 1974, p.cloth. [collection]

ea in **Before the Golden Age**. Edited by Isaac Asimov. _: Robson, 1974, p. cloth. [collection]

ba in **The Horror on the Asteroid and Other Tales of Planetary Horror**. _: Gregg Press, 1975, p. cloth. Pg. 59. (75-5745) [collection]

eb in **Before the Golden Age Book 1**. Edited by Isaac Asimov. _: Fawcett Crest, 1975, p. paper. [collection]

f in **The Best of Edmond Hamilton**. Edited by Leigh Brackett. Garden City, NY.: Nelson Doubleday, 1977, p. cloth. [collection]

fa in **The Best of Edmond Hamilton**. Edited by Leigh Brackett. : Ballentine, 1977, p. paper. [collection]

g as "The Man Who Lived the Evolution." in Enigmas of the Universe #26, 59-65 pp. and #27, 122-23 pp. (July and August, 1977): Translator: Dinos Garoufalias.

h as "Der Mann, Der Sich Entwickelte." in **Die Besten Stories**. _: <publisher unknown> <year>, 1980, p. (PSF 6701) [collection]

ec in **Before the Golden Age**. Edited by Isaac Asimov. _: Black Cat, 1974, p. [collection]

i as "The Man Who Lived the Evolution." in **The Sombre Emperor**. Athens: Sympan/Lyhnari, 1989, p. Translator: Geni Mistraki. [collection]

J as "O Anthopos pou Exelichtike" in Apagorevmenos Planitis, #7 (November-December, 1997) Pg. Translator: Vaso Hounou. [collection] [Greek]

CHAPTERS:

1:
2: A Mad Scheme
3: The Man Who Evolved
4: The Brain Monster
5: The Last Mutation

Dr. Pollard has discovered a way to accelerate evolution. He asks two old college mates to assist him with the experiment.

B36 "Ten Million Years Ahead" in Weird Tales, 17:3 (April – May, 1931) Pg. 304.

B37 "The Earth-Owners" in Weird Tales, 18:1 (August, 1931) Pg. 22. Illustrator: Wesso.

B38 "The Sargasso of Space" in Astounding Stories, 7:3 (#21). (September, 1931) Pg. 390. Illustrator: H. W. Wesso. Cover[lviii].

REPRINTS:

b in **Astounding Science Fiction Stories: The 60th Anniversary Collection Red Volume**. Edited by James Gunn. _: Easton Press, 1990, p. cloth. Pg 3. [collection]

c _: Project Gutenberg. May 16, 2009. EPUB, MOBI, Plucker, HTML and Plain Text fomats.26-203 Kb. EText-No. 28832. http://www.gutenberg.org/etext/28832.

d in The Sargasso of Space and Two Others. _: Wildside Press. June 1, 2009. 170 pp. (8.8 x 5.9 x 0.6 in.) ISBN-10: 1434405060; ISBN-13: 978-1434405067.
With "The Copper-Clad World" by harl Vincent.

e _: Amazon Digital Services. <year> 134 Kb. ASIN: B002D48LQ6.

ea _: Amazon Digital Services. <year> 39 Kb. ASIN: B002AQT7N8

f _: Many Books.net. <year> Multiple electronic formats. 9783 words..

B39 "The Shot from Saturn" in Weird Tales, 18:3 (October, 1931): Pg. 343.

B40 "Creatures of the Comet" in Weird Tales, 18:5 (December, 1931) Pg. 630.

B41 "The Reign of the Robots" in Wonder Stories, (December, 1931) Pg.848.

REPRINTS:

b in **Strange Love Stories**. Anonymous. _: Utopian, 1946, p. [collection]

B42 "Dead Legs" in Strange Tales of Mystery and Terror, (January 1932) Pg.299.

REPRINTS:

b in Weird Terror Tales, #1 (Winter 1970) Pg.

c in **Strange Tales**. Edited by William H. Desmond, Diane Howard, John Howard & Robert K. Weiner. _: Odyssey Publications, 1976, p. [collection]

d in **The Vampire Master and Other Tales of Terror**, Royal Oak, MI: Haffner Press, 2000, p. cloth. [collection]

B43 "A Conquest of Two Worlds" in Wonder Stories, 16:3 (February 1932) Pg. 1046.

b in Startling Stories, (January, 1948) Pg. 70.[lix]

c in **Every Boy's Book of Science Fiction**. Edited by Donald A. Wollheim. : Frederick Fell. 1951, p. cloth. Pg. 143. (Introduction). [collection]

c in **Every Boy's Book of Science Fiction**. Edited by Donald A. Wollheim. _: McLeod, 1951, p. [collection]

d in **The Best of Edmond Hamilton**. Edited by Leigh Brackett. Garden City, NY: Nelson Doubleday, 1977, p. cloth. [collection]

da in **The Best of Edmond Hamilton**. Edited by Leigh Brackett. : Ballentine, 1977, p. paper. [collection]

e as "Die Eroberung Zweier Welten." in **Die Besten Stories.** _: <publisher unknown> <year>, p. (PSF 6701) [collection]

CHAPTERS:

1:
2: The Conquest of Mars
3: Jupiter Next!
4: The Renegade

Three college friends join the space forces to open the new frontiers of Mars and Jupiter. Over the years they advance through the ranks. After the brutal conflicts with the Martians, one defects and becomes a traitor.

B44 "The Three from the Tomb"[lx] in Weird Tales, 19:2 (February, 1932) Pg. 178. Illustrator: Joseph Dustin[3].

REPRINTS:

b in Startling Mystery Stories. #8 (Spring, 1968) Pg.

B45 "The Earth Brain" in Weird Tales, 19:4 (April, 1932) Pg. 466.

REPRINTS:

ba in **The Horror on the Asteroid and Other Tales of Planetary Horror**. London: Philip Allan. 1936. P. cloth. Pg. 59. [collection] [British]

bb in **The Horror on the Asteroid and Other Tales of Planetary Horror**. Gregg Press, 1975, p. cloth. Pg. 59. (75-5745). [collection]

c in **Acolytes of Cthulhu**. Edited by Robert M. Price, _: Fedogan & Bremmer, 2001, p. [collection]

B46 "The Terror Planet" in Weird Tales, 19:5 (May. 1932) Pg. 611.

B47 "The Space Rocket Murders" in Amazing Stories, (October, 1932) Pg. 582. Illustrator: Morey.

REPRINTS:

b in Science Fiction Adventure Classics, (Fall, 1968) Pg. 5.

B48 "The Dogs of Dr. Dwann" in Weird Tales, 20:4 (October, 1932) Pg. 491. Illustrator: Nelson.

REPRINTS:

b in Startling Mystery Stories, (Winter, 1969) Pg.

c in **Satan's Pets**. Edited by Vic Ghildalia. New York, NY.: Manor Books, 1972, p. [collection]

B49 "Vampire Village"[lxi] in Weird Tales. 20:5 (November, 1932) Pg.

REPRINTS:

b in **Weird Vampire Tales**. Edited by Robert Weinberg, Stefan R. Dziemianowicz and Martin H. Greenberg. New York, NY: Gramercy Books, 1992, p. cloth. pp. 117-127. [collection]

B50 "The Man Who Conquered Age"[lxii] in Weird Tales, 20:6 (December, 1932) Pg. 749. Illustrator: M.W.

B51 "Snake-Man"[lxiii] in Weird Tales. 21:1 (January, 1933) Pg.

B52 "Kaldar, World of Antares" in Magic Carpet, (April, 1933): Pg. 221. Illustrator: Jayem Wilcox.

REPRINTS:

b in **Swordsmen In the Sky**. Edited by Donald A. Wollheim. New York, NY.: Ace Books, 1964, p. paper. [collection]

c in **Kaldar, World of Antares**. Royal Oak, MI: Haffner Press, 1998, p. cloth. [collection]

CHAPTERS:

I: The Start
II: Kaldar, World of Antares
III: Chan of Corla
IV: Spider-Men and Poison-Spray
V: Over the Fungus Forest
VI: In the Cosp City
VII: Flight and Battle
VIII: Epilog

B53 "The Star-Roamers" in Weird Tales, 21:4 (April, 1933) Pg. 461. Illustrator: Jayem Wilcox.

B54 “The Island of Unreason”[lxiv] in Wonder Stories, 12:1 (May, 1933) Pg. 970.

REPRINTS:

b in Startling Stories, (Spring, 1945) Pg. 90.

c in **Murder in the Clinic**. _: Utopian, 1946, p. [collection] [British]

d in **The History of Science Fiction Magazines: 1926-1935**. Edited by Michael Ashley[lxv]. Chicago, IL.: Henry Regnery, 1974, p. cloth. Pg. 154. [collection]

e in **The Best of Edmond Hamilton**. Edited by Leigh Brackett. Garden City, NY.: Nelson Doubleday, 1977, p. cloth. [collection]

ea in **The Best of Edmond Hamilton**. Edited by Leigh Brackett. : Ballentine, 1977, p. paper. [collection]

f as “Die Insel Der Unvernunft.” in **Die Besten Stories**. 1980 (PSF 6701) [collection]

g as “Nisi ton Paralogon” in **O Zoferos Autokratoras**. _: <publisher unknown>, 1988, p. Translator: Jenny Mistraki. [collection] [Greek]

ga as “Nisi ton Paralogon” in **O Zoferos Autokratoras**. Athens: Sympan/Lyhnare, 1989, p. Translator: Jenny Mistraki. [collection] [Greek]

h as “L’ile de deraison” in **Les meilleurs recits de Wonder stories**. Edited by Jacques Sadoul. _: editions J’ai lu, <year>, p. [collection] [French]

I as “Lisola degli irragionevoli.” _: <publisher unknown> <year>, p. Racconto Sp. 1. (1933?)

B55 “The Fire Creatures” in Weird Tales, 22:1 (July, 1933) Pg. 26. Illustrator: Jayem Wilcox.

B57 “Vampire Master.”[lxvi] serialized in Weird Tales, 22:4 (October, 1933) Pg.
Part Two - 22:5 (November, 1933) Pg.
Part Three - 22:6 (December, 1933):
Conclusion - 23:1 (January, 1934) Pg.

REPRINTS:

b in **The Vampire Master and Other Tales of Terror**, Royal Oak, MI: Haffner Press, 2000, p. cloth. [collection]

CHAPTERS:

1:
2: Henderson's Story
3: A Vigil for a Vampire
4: Gerritt Geisert
5: The Bodies that Walked
6: Geisert Manor
7: The Master of the Dead-Alive
8: At the Wilsey House
9: A Lover from the Dead
10: What Olivia Told
11: The Quest in the Hills
12: Stake and Steel
13: Called Forth
14: The Struggle

B58 "Snake-Men of Kaldar" in Magic Carpet, (October, 1933) Pg. 473. Illustrator: Jayem Wilcox.

REPRINTS:

b in **The Magic Carpet Magazine**. Edited by William H. Desmond, Diane M. Howard, John R. Howard & Robert K. Wiener. _: Odyssey Publications, 1998, p. [collection]

c in **Kaldar, World of Antares**. Royal Oak: MI: Haffner Press, 1998, p. cloth. [collection]

CHAPTERS:

I: Back to Kaldar
II: The Wall of Glowing Death
III: The Land of the Gurs
IV: Through the Snake-men's City
V: Battle's End
VI: Merrick, Chan of Corla

B59 "The War of the Sexes" in Weird Tales, 22:5 (November, 1933) Pg. 551.

REPRINTS:

b in **Avon Science Fiction Reader No. 1**. Avon Books, 1951, p. Pg.3.

Cover:[lxvii] [collection]

B60 "The Man with X-Ray Eyes"[lxviii] in Wonder Stories, (November, 1933) Pg. 386. Illustrator: Winter.

REPRINTS:

b in **The Sex Serum**. Edited by Dickson. _: Utopia, 1945, p. [collection]

b in Startling Stories, 14:1 (Summer, 1946) Pg. 62.[lxix] Illustrator:[lxx]

B61 "The Man Who Returned" in Weird Tales, 23:2 (February, 1934) Pg. 219. Illustrator: Jayem Wilcox.

REPRINTS:

b in **Weird Tales: Stories of Fantasy**. Edited by Leo Margulies. New York, NY: Pyramid Books, 1964, p. [collection]

c as "Der Mann, Der Zuruckkehrte." in **Ullstein Kriminalmagazin 10**. Edited by Leo Margulies. _: publisher unknown? 1976, p. (UTB 1163). [German]

d in **Weird Tales**. [1]. Edited by Peter Haining. _: Neville Spearman, 1976. p. cloth. Pg. 21. [British]

e in **The Best of Edmond Hamilton**. Edited by Leigh Brackett. Garden City, NY.: Nelson Doubleday, 1977, p.cloth. [collection]

ea in **The Best of Edmond Hamilton**. Edited by Leigh Brackett. _: Ballentine, 1977, p. paper. [collection]

da in **Weird Tales**. [2][lxxi]. Edited by Peter Haining. _: Sphere, 1978, p. cloth. [collection] [British]

ba in **Weird Tales: Stories of Fantasy**. Edited by Leo Margulies. : Jove, 1979, p. [collection]

f as "Der Mann, Der Zuruckkehrte." in **Die Besten Stories**. 1980, p. (VPSF 6701). [collection] [German]

g in **Fear! Fear! Fear!** Selected by Helen Hoke. New York, NY: Franklin Watts, Lmtd. 1981, p. cloth. p 113- 130. Illustrated by Sean Eckett. [collection]

db in **Weird Tales**. [1]. Edited by Peter Haining. _: Carroll & Graf, 1990, p. [collection]

dc in **Weird Tales**. [1]. Edited by Peter Haining. _: Xanadu, 1991, p. [collection]

B62 "Thundering Worlds" in Weird Tales, 23:3 (March, 1934) Pg. 331. Illustrator: Harold Hammond[lxxii]

REPRINTS:

b in **The Best of Edmond Hamilton**. Edited by Leigh Brackett. Garden City, NY.: Nelson Doubleday, 1977, p. cloth. [collection]

ba in **The Best of Edmond Hamilton**. Edited by Leigh Brackett. _: Ballentine, 1977, p. paper. [collection]

c as "Donnernde Welten." in **Die Besten Stories**. _: publisher unknown? 1980, p. (PSF 6701) [collection]

B63 "Corsairs of the Cosmos" in Weird Tales, 23:4 (April, 1934): Pg. 449. Illustrator: H. R. Hammond.

B64 "Cosmos End"[lxxiii] in Fantasy Magazine, (December, 1934) Pg.

REPRINTS:

b serialized in **Perry Rhodan #59** Edited by Forrest J. Akerman. New York: Ace Books, Inc. <year>, p,; Part Two - **Perry Rhodan #60** Edited by Forrest J. Akerman. New York: Ace Books, Inc. <year>, p.

B65 "Master of Genes"[lxxiv] in Wonder Stories, (January, 1935) Pg. 958. Illustrator: Paul.

REPRINTS:

b in Thrilling Stories. #1. (1946) Pg. [British]

B66 "Murder in the Grave" in Weird Tales, 25:2 (February, 1935): Pg.199.

B67 "The Truth Gas" in Wonder Stories, (February, 1935) Pg. 1060. Illustrator: Paul.

B68 "The Eternal Cycle" in Wonder Stories, (March, 1935) Pg. 60. Illustrator: Saaty. Cover: Paul.[lxxv]

REPRINTS:

b in **Gosh! Wow! (Sense of Wonder)**. Edited by Forrest J. Akerman. _: Bantam, 1981, p. Illustrator: E. J. Gold. [collection]

ba in **Gosh! Wow! (Sense of Wonder)**. Edited by Forrest J. Akerman. Nevada City, California: Sirius SF, 1993, p. [collection]

B68 "Murder At Weed Key" in Thrilling Detective, (May, 1935): Pg.

B69 "The Accursed Galaxy"[lxxvi] in Astounding Stories, 15:5 (#56). (July, 1935) Pg. 64. Illustrator: Elliot Dold, Jr.

REPRINTS:

b in **The Horror on the Asteroid and Other Tales of Planetary Horror**. London: Philip Allan, 1936, p. cloth. Pg. 59. [collection]

c in **Before the Golden Age**. Edited by Isaac Asimov. Garden City, NY.: Nelson Doubleday, 1974, p. cloth. [collection]

ca in **Before the Golden Age**. Edited by Isaac Asimov. _: Robson, 1974, p. cloth. [collection] [British]

d in **The Horror on the Asteroid and Other Tales of Planetary Horror**. Gregg Press. 1975, p. cloth. Pg. 59. (75-5745) [collection]

cb in **Before the Golden Age, Book 3**. Edited by Isaac Asimov. : Fawcett Crest, 1975, p. paper. [collection]

e in **The Best of Edmond Hamilton**. Edited by Leigh Brackett. Garden City, NY.: Nelson Doubleday, 1977, p. cloth. [collection]

ea in **The Best of Edmond Hamilton**. Edited by Leigh Brackett. : Ballentine, 1977, p. paper. [collection]

f as "Die Verfluchte Galaxis" in **Die Besten Stories**. _: <publisher unknown> 1980, p. (PSF 6701).

cd in **Before the Golden Age**. Edited by Isaac Asimov. : Black Cat, 1988, p. cloth. [British]

g as "La galaxia Maldita" in **Antes dela Edad de Oro 2 (Before the Golden Age 2)**. _: Ediciones Martines Roca. 1989, p. Relatos (ortos de amtores varios) [collection]

B70 "The Avenger from Atlantis" in Weird Tales, 26:1 (July,

1935) Pg. 2. Illustrator: Jack Binder. Cover: M. Brundage.

REPRINTS:

b as "The Vengence of Ulios" in **The Magic of Atlantis**. Edited by Lin Carter. _: <publisher unknown>, 1970, p. [collection]

c as "The Vengence of Ulios" in **Isaac Asimov's Magical Worlds of Fantasy #9: Atlantis**. Edited by Isaac Asimov, Martin H. Greenberg and Charles Waugh. New York, NY: Signet, 1988, p. paper. [collection]

B71 "The Six Sleepers" in Weird Tales, 26:4 (October, 1935): Pg. 402. Cover: M. Brundage.

REPRINTS:

aa in Weird Tales, (October 1935) Pg.[Canadian]

B72 "The Cosmic Pantograph" in Wonder Stories, (October, 1935): Pg. 554. Illustrator: Paul.

REPRINTS:

b in 30 Thrilling Tales.[lxxvii] ._: publisher unknown? <year> Pg.

c in Fantastic Story Magazine, 3:1 (Fall, 1951) Pg. 101.

d as "Kosmisches Schauspiel." in Utopia Magazin, Nr. 26 (1959) Pg.. [German]

e as "Flucht Aus Dem Kosmos." in **Science Fiction Stories 34**. Edited by Walter Spiegl._: publisher unknown? 1973, p. (UTB 3029). [collection] [German]

B73 "The Great Brain of Kaldar" in Weird Tales, 26:6 (December, 1935) Pg. 707.

REPRINTS:

aa in Weird Tales, (December, 1935) Pg. [Canadian]

b in **To the Star and Beyond**. Edited by Sheldon Jaffrey. Marcel Island: Starmont House, 1989, p. 370 (Facsimile Fiction Series #5). ISBN: 1-55742-137-4. cloth. [collection]

ba in **To the Star and Beyond**. Edited by Sheldon Jaffrey. Marcel Island:

Starmont House, 1989, p. 370 (Facsimile Fiction Series #5). ISBN: 1-55742-136-6. paper. [collection]

c in Pulp Valt, #6 (November, 1989) Pg.

d in **Kaldar, World of Antares**. Royal Oak, MI: Haffner Press, 1998, p. [collection]

CHAPTERS:

I: On A Far World
II: Unseen Men
III: The City of Invisibility
IV: Creatures of the Brian
V: In the Brain Chamber

B74 "The Ramrod Key Killings" in Popular Detective, (February, 1936) Pg.

B75 "Leopard's Paw" in Popular Detective. 6:2. (March, 1936) Pg.

B76 "In the World's Dusk" in Weird Tales, 27:3 (March, 1936) Pg. 345. Illustrator: Virgil Finlay.

REPRINTS:

b in Weird Tales, 27:3 (March, 1936) Pg. Illustrator: Virgil Finlay. [Canadian]

c in **The End of the World**. Edited by Donald A. Wollheim. New York, NY.: Ace Books, 1956, p. paper. [collection]

d as "Der Letzte Mensch".in **DerLetzte Mensch**. Edited by Donald A. Wollheim. _: <publisher unknown> 1963, p. (T 271). [collection] [German]

e as Le crépuscule du monde in Fiction No. 191 (November 1969) Pg. Translation: Michel Deutsch. [French]

f as "Welt im Dammerlicht" in **Science Fiction Stories 28**. Edited by Donald A. Wollheim. _: publisher unknown? 1973, p. (UTB 2980). [German]

g in **The Best of Edmond Hamilton**. Edited by Leigh Brackett. Garden City, NY.: Nelson Doubleday, 1977, p. cloth. [collection]

ga in **The Best of Edmond Hamilton**. Edited by Leigh Brackett. : Ballentine, 1977, p. paper. [collection]

h as "Welt im Dammerlicht." in **Die Besten Stories**. _: <publisher

unknown> 1980, p. (PSF 6701). [German]

i in **The Last Man On Earth**. Edited by Isaac Asimov, Martin H. Greenberg and Charles G. Waugh. New York, NY: Fawcett Crest Books, March 1982, p. paper. [collection]

j as “Welt im Dammerlicht.” in **Der Letzte Mensch Auf Erden**. Edited By Isaac Asimov, Charles G. Waugh and Martin H. Greenberg. _: <publisher unknown> 1984, p. (HSF 4076). [collection] [German]

k as “To Iliovasilema tou Cosmou” in **Anthologia Epistimonikis Fantasias – Taxidia sto Choro ke ton Chrono. Vol. 2.** _: Komitis. 1990, p. pp 61-62. Translator: Gorge Ntoumas. [collection] [Greek]

l as “At the Worlds Dusk” in **The Best from SF Magazine No. 1**. _Tokyo: Hayakawa Publishing, Inc. <year>, p. [collection] [Japanese]

m as “In de Wereldschemering” in **Kleine Science Fiction Omnibus**. _: <publisher unknown> <year>, p. [collection] [Dutch]

B77 “Intelligence Undying” in Amazing Stories, (April, 1936): Pg. 13.

REPRINTS:

b in Amazing Stories, (April, 1966) Pg. 45. Illustrator: Morey.

c in Fantastic, (April, 1979) Pg.

B78 “Murder Mountain” in Popular Detective, (April, 1936) Pg.

CHAPTERS:

I: House of Death
II: ‘Kill them All’
III: The Madman
IV: Nemesis’ End

B79 “The Earth Dwellers” in Thrilling Mystery. 2:3 (April, 1936): Pg. 48.

b in **The Vampire Master and Other Tales of Terror**, Royal Oak, MI: Haffner Press. 2000, p. cloth.

B80 “Murder in the King Family” in Thrilling Detective, (April, 1936) Pg.

B81 “Carter Makes A Squeal” in Popular Detective, (May, 1936): Pg.

B82 “Crimson Gold” in Popular Detective. 7:1. (May, 1936) Pg.

B83 “Copper Proof” in Thrilling Detective, (May, 1936) Pg.

B84 “Beasts that Once were Men” in Thrilling Mystery, (May, 1936) Pg.

b in **The Vampire Master and Other Tales of Terror**, Royal Oak, MI: Haffner Press. 2000, p. cloth. [collection]

B85 “Child of the Winds” in Weird Tales, 27:5 (May, 1936) Pg. 597. Illustrator: Virgil Finlay.

REPRINTS:

b in Weird Tales, 27:5 (May, 1936) Pg. 597. Illustrator: Virgil Finlay. [Canadian]

c in **Boris Karloff Horror Anthology**. Edited by Boris Karloff. _: Souvenier, 1965, p.

ca in **Boris Karloff's Favorite Horror Stories**. Edited by Boris Karloff. _: Avon, 1965, p.

d in **The Best of Edmond Hamilton**. Edited by Leigh Brackett. Garden City, NY.: Nelson Doubleday, 1977, p. cloth. [collection]

da in **The Best of Edmond Hamilton**. Edited by Leigh Brackett. : Ballentine, 1977, p. paper. [collection]

e as “Das Kind Der Winde.” in **Die Besten Stories**. _: <publisher unknown> 1980, p. (PSF 6701). [collection] [German]

B86 "Hell Train" in G-Men, (June, 1936) Pg.

B87 "The House of the Evil Eye"[lxxviii] in Weird Tales, 27:6 (June, 1936) Pg.

REPRINTS:

aa in Weird Tales, (June, 1935) Pg. [Canadian]

b in **The Vampire Master and Other Tales of Terror**, Royal Oak, MI: Haffner Press. 2000, p. cloth. [collection]

B88 "When The World Slept" in Weird Tales, 28:1 (July, 1936): Pg. 36. Illustrator: M.S.[lxxix]

REPRINTS:

aa in Weird Tales, (July, 1936) Pg. [Canadian]

B89 "Crooked Cop" in Popular Detective, (August, 1936) Pg.

B90 "The Crime Crusader" in Thrilling Detective, (August, 1936): Pg.

B91 "The Door Into Infinity" in Weird Tales, 28:2 (August-September, 1936) Pg. 130. Cover:[lxxx]

B92 "Snow Clue" in Popular Detective, (September, 1936) Pg.

B93 "Children of Terror" in Thrilling Mystery. 4:2. (September, 1936) Pg.

b in **The Vampire Master and Other Tales of Terror**, Royal Oak, MI: Haffner Press. 2000, p. cloth. [collection]

B94 "Last Bequest" in Popular Detective, (October, 1936) Pg.

B95 "Cosmic Quest" in Thrilling Wonder, (October, 1936) Pg. 33.

B96 "Devolution"[lxxxi] in Amazing Stories, (December 1936) Pg. 90.

REPRINTS:

b in Amazing Stories, (April 1961) Pg. 25. Illustrator: Morey.

c as "Die Degenerierten" in **Kinder der Sonne**. Munchen: <publisher unknown> 1968, p. (TTB 545). [collection] [German]

d in Science Fiction Classics Annual, New York, NY: Ultimate Publishing Co. 1970, p. pp.37-52. Illustrator: Morley.

e in **Before the Golden Age**. Edited by Isaac Asimov. Garden City, NY.: Nelson Doubleday, 1974, p. cloth. [collection]

ea in **Before the Golden Age**. Edited by Isaac Asimov. _: <publisher unknown>, 1974, p. [collection] [British]

eb in **Before the Golden Age Book 3**. Edited by Isaac Asimov. _: Fawcett Crest, 1975, p. paper. [collection]

f in Amazing Stories, 52:3 (May, 1979) Pp. 32-48. Illustrator: S. Mavor.

g in **Friendly Aliens**. Edited by John Robert Colombo. _: <publisher unknown> <year>, p. [collection]

h in **Amazing Science Fiction Anthology: The War Years 1936-1945**. Edited by Martin H. Greenberg. Lake Geneva, WI.: TSR, Inc. 1987, p. paper. [collection]

ec in **Before the Golden Age**. Edited by Isaac Asimov. _: Black Cat, 1988, p. [collection] [British]

i in **The Best from SF Magazine No. 3**. _Tokyo: Hayakawa Publishing, Inc. <year>, p. [collection] [Japanese]

j as "Involicion" in **Antes dela Edad de Oro 2 (Before the Golden Age 2)**. _: Ediciones Martines Roca, 1989, Relatos (ortos de amtores varios). [collection]

k in **Masterpieces: The Best Science Fiction of the Century**. Edited by Orson Scott Card. _: Ace, 2001, p. [collection]

A brilliant scientist creates a device to reverse evolution.

B97 "Face to Face" in Popular Detective, (December, 1936) Pg.

B98 "Sea Murder" in Thrilling Detective, (December, 1936) Pg.

B99 "Mutiny on Europa" in Thrilling Wonder Stories, (December, 1936) Pg. 64.

CHAPTERS:

I: On the Prison Moon
II: Revolt in the Dark
III: Hemmed In
IV: When the Wall Failed

B100 "Murder Press" in Popular Detective, (January, 1937) Pg.

B101 "Ball Bearing Death" in Popular Detective, (February, 1937) Pg.

B102 "Kid Stuff" in The Phantom Detective. 18:2 (March, 1937) Pg.

B103 "The Seeds from Outside" in Weird Tales, 29:3 (March, 1937): Pg. 361.

REPRINTS:

b in **The Best of Edmond Hamilton**. Edited by Leigh Brackett. Garden City, NY.: Nelson Doubleday, 1977, p. cloth. [collection]

ba in **The Best of Edmond Hamilton**. Edited by Leigh Brackett. _: Ballentine, 1977, p. paper. [collection]

c as "Die Saat Aus Dem All" in **Die Besten Stories**. 1980. _: <publisher unknown> p. (PSF 6701). [collection]

d in **100 Creepy Little Creature Stories**. Edited by Stefan R. Dziemianowicz, Robert Weinberg and Martin H. Greenberg, _: Barnes & Noble, 1994, p. [collection]

e in **100 Wild Little Weird Tales**. Edited by Robert Weinberg, Stefan R. Dziemianowicz and Martin H. Greenberg, _: Barnes & Noble, 1994, p. [collection]

f as "Les graines d'ailleurs" in **Les meilleurs recits de Weird Tales 2**.

Edited by Jacques Sadoul. _: Editions J'ai lu, <year>, p. [collection] [French]

B104 "The Corpse Died Twice" in Popular Detective, (April, 1937): Pg.

B105 "A Million Years Ahead" in Thrilling Wonder Stories, (April, 1937) Pg. 92.

B106 "Fessenden's Worlds"[lxxxii] in Weird Tales, 29:4 (April, 1937) Pg.
413.

REPRINTS:

b in **Beyond Space and Time**. Edited by August Derlith. _: Pellegrini Cudahy, 1950, p. [collection]

ba in **Beyond Space and Time**. Edited by August Derlith. _: Berkley Publishing, 1958, p. [collection]

c as "Avite aarum seshichilla" in **Selected Science Fiction Stories**. Trichur: Amina Book Stall, 1963, p. [collection] [Indian]

d as "Bala Methavi. Itara Sastra Vignana Kathalu." Science Fiction Stories. Madras: Vijaya Publications, 1964, p.[collection] [Indian]

e in **The Best of Edmond Hamilton**. Edited by Leigh Brackett. Garden City, NY.: Nelson Doubleday, 1977, p. cloth. [collection]

ea in **The Best of Edmond Hamilton**. Edited by Leigh Brackett._: Ballentine, 1977, p. paper. [collection]

f in **Science Fiction: The Best of Yesterday**. Edited by Dr. Arthur Liebman. _: Richards Rosen. 1980, p. [collection]

g as "Fessendes Welten" in **Die Besten Stories**. _: <publisher unknown> 1980, p. (PSF 6701) [collection]

h in **The Best from SF Magazine No. 2**. _Tokyo: Hayakawa Publishing, Inc. <year>, p. [collection] [Japanese]

B107 "Death Dolls" in Thrilling Detective, (May, 1937) Pg. 78.

B108 "His Sworn Duty" in The Phantom Detective. 18:3. (July, 1937): Pg.

B109 "Space Mirror" in Thrilling Wonder Stories, (August, 1937) Pg. 43.

B110 "World Of The Dark Dwellers" in Weird Tales, 30:2 (August, 1937) Pg. 179.

B111 "Death Comes in Glass" in Thrilling Detective, (September, 1937) Pg. 54. Illustrator: T.G.

B112 "(Prize Title Contest Story)" in The Phantom Detective. 20:3. (October, 1937) Pg.

B113 "Holmes' Folly" in Thrilling Wonder Stories, (October, 1937): Pg. 59.

B114 "When Space Burst" in Thrilling Wonder Stories, (December, 1937) Pg. 90.

B115 "Child Of Atlantis" in Weird Tales, 30:6 (December, 1937): Pg. 708. Illustrator: Virgil Finlay.

B116 "The Space Beings" in Tales of Wonder, #5 (Winter, 1938): Pg. 39.

B117 "The House of Living Music" in Weird Tales, 31:1 (January, 1938) Pg. 21. Illustrator: Virgil Finlay.

B118 "Power Pit 13" in Thrilling Adventure, (February, 1938) Pg.

B119 "The Conqueror's Voice"[lxxxiii] in Science Fiction Stories, (March, 1938) Pg. 34.

B120 "Easy Money"[lxxxiv] in Thrilling Wonder Stories, (April, 1938): Pg. 55.

REPRINTS:

b in **The Best of Edmond Hamilton**. Edited by Leigh Brackett. Garden City, NY.: Nelson Doubleday, 1977, p. cloth. [collection]

ba in **The Best of Edmond Hamilton**. Edited by Leigh Brackett. : Ballentine, 1977, p. paper. [collection]

c as "Leichtverdientes Geld" in **Die Besten Stories**. _: <publisher unknown> 1980, p. (PSF 6701) [collection]

B121 "The Isle of The Sleeper" in Weird Tales, 31:5 (May, 1938): Pg. 588. Illustrator: Virgil Finlay.

REPRINTS:

b in Weird Tales, 43:4 (May, 1951) Pg. 42.

c in **The Ghoul Keepers**. Edited by Leo Margulies. New York, NY.: Pyramid Books, 1965, p. paper. [collection]

d in **What's It Like Out There?** Edmond Hamilton. New York, NY.: Ace Books, 1974, p. mass market paper [collection]

e as "Het Eiland van de Slaper" in Godenschemering en Andere Verhalen. Rotterdam: Scala. 1975, p. 311. 18cm. ISBN: 90.6221.031.7. (Scala science fiction reeks No. 4).[lxxxv] Translator: Iskraa Bundels [Dutch]

f in **To Sleep, Perchance to Dream...Nightmare**. Edited by Stefan R. Dziemianowicz, Robert Weinberg and Martin H. Greenberg. _ : Barnes & Noble, 1993, p. [collection]

B122 "Murder in the Void" Thrilling Wonder Stories, 11:3. (June, 1938) Pg. 14.

B123" Horror in the Telescope" in Tales of Wonder, #3 (Summer, 1938) Pg. 33.

B124 "He that Hath Wings" in <u>Weird Tales</u>, 32:1 (July, 1938) Pg. 70.

REPRINTS:

b in <u>Fantastic Stories of Imagination</u>. 12:7 (July, 1963) Pg. 22. Illustrator: Virgil Finlay.

c in **Worlds of Weird**. Edited by Leo Margulies. New York, NY: Jove, 1965, p. 103, paper. [collection]

d as "L'uoma Aato" in **L'uoma Aato**. _: Editrice Libra, 1975, p. (Nova S.F. #29). [collection] [Italian]

d in **The Best of Edmond Hamilton**. Edited by Leigh Brackett Garden City, NY.: Nelson Doubleday, 1977, p. cloth. [collection]

ea in **The Best of Edmond Hamilton**. Edited by Leigh Brackett. _: Ballentine, 1977, p. paper. [collection]

e in **Weird Legacies**. Edited by Mike Ashley. _: Star, 1977, p. [collection] [British]

f as "Der mann, Der Flugel Hatte." in **Die Besten Stories**. _: <publisher unknown> 1980, p. (PSF 6701). [collection]

g in **Young Mutants**. Edited by Isaac Asimov, Martin H. Greenberg and Charles Waugh. New York, NY: Harper & Row, 1984, p. pp. 85-121, cloth. [collection]

ga in **Young Mutants**. Edited by Isaac Asimov. :_ Dragon, 1986, p.[collection] [British]

B125 "The Sea Terror" in <u>Tales of Wonder</u>, (August, 1938) Pg. 72.

B126 "The Fire Princess" serialized in <u>Weird Tales</u>, 32:2 (August, 1938) Pg. 167. Part Two - 32:3 (September, 1938) Pg. 325. Conclusion - 32:4 (October, 1938) Pg. 455. Illustrator: Virgil Finlay.

B127 "Woman From the Ice" in <u>Thrilling Mystery</u>, (September, 1938): Pg. 35.

b in **The Vampire Master and Other Tales of Terror**, Royal Oak, MI: Haffner Press, 2000, p. cloth.

B128 "The Man Who Lived Twice" in Amazing Stories, (November 1938) Pg. 76. Illustrator: Robert A. Fuqua.

REPRINTS:

b in Science Fiction Adventure Classics, (Winter, 1967) Pg. 88.

B129 "The Ephemerae" in Astounding Stories, 22:4 (December, 1938): Pg. 50. Illustrator: Binder.

B130 "The Cosmic Hiss" in Thrilling Wonder Stories, (#97). (December, 1938) Pg. 90.

B131 "Bride of the Lightning" in Weird Tales, 33:1 (January, 1939): Pg. 61. Illustrator: Virgil Finlay.

B132 "Under the White Star" in Science Fiction, 1:1. (March, 1939): Pg. 6.

REPRINTS:

b in **To the Star and Beyond**. Edited by Sheldon Jaffrey. Marcel Island: Starmont House, 1989, 370 p. (Facsimile Fiction Series #5). ISBN: 1-55742-137-4. cloth. [collection]

ba in **To the Star and Beyond**. Edited by Sheldon Jaffrey. Marcel Island: Starmont House, 1989, 370 p. (Facsimile Fiction Series #5). ISBN: 1-55742-136-6. paper. [collection]

B133 "Valley of Invisible Men" in Amazing Stories, (March, 1939): Pg. 22. Illustrator: R. Fuqua.

REPRINTS:

b as "Osynlighetens dal" serialized in Jules Verne-Magasinet (18/1941): Pg. and (19/1941) Pg.

c in Science Fiction Adventure Classics, (November, 1972) Pp. 30-72. Illustrator: R. Fuqua.

CHAPTERS:

I	The Hidden Land
II	Daughter of the Korlu
III	The Games of the Full Moon
IV	The Fight on the Lake
V	The Chambers of the God
VI	Phantoms in the Night
VII	The City of Peril
VIII	Power of the God
IX	Epilogue

B134 "Comrades of Time" in Weird Tales, 33:3 (March, 1939) Pg. 102. Illustrator: Virgil Finlay.

REPRINTS:

b in Lost Fantasies, No. 5 (1977) Pp. 5-26.

B135 "The Fear Neutralizer" in Startling Stories, (March, 1939) Pg. 108. Illustrator:[lxxxvi]

REPRINTS:

b in **Science Fiction Yearbook #2**. Edited by Helen Tono. New York, NY: Popular Library, Inc. 1968, p. Pg.. 4.

B136 "Armies of the Past" in Weird Tales, 33:4 (April, 1939) Pg. 61.

b in **Lost Fantasies**, No. 5 (1977) Pg.

B137 "Short-Wave Madness"[lxxxvii] in Science Fiction Stories, (June, 1939) Pg. 57.

B138 "The Man Who Solved Death" in Science Fiction, 1:3. (August, 1939) Pg. 32.

B139 "Debtor at Eight" in Detective Short Stories, (September, 1939): Pg.

B140 "Horror Out of Carthage" in Fantastic Adventure, (September, 1939) Pp. 6-23.

REPRINTS:

b in Fantastic, 17:6 (August, 1968) Pp. 22-50. Illustrator: Jay Jackson.

B141 "Dweller in the Darkness" in Science Fiction, (October, 1939): Pg. 56.

REPRINTS:

aa in Science Fiction, (October, 1939) Pg. [Brtish]
b in Thrilling Wonder Stories, (February, 1940) Pg.

B142 "The Three Planeteers" in Startling Stories, (January, 1940): Pg. 12. Illustrator: Virgil Finlay.

b _: Renaissance E Books/PageTurner. September 23, 2005. 346 Kb. ASIN: B000FCKF1W.

CHAPTERS:

I: Comrades of Peril
II: Cold-World Menace
III: Into the Zone
IV: Pirate Princes
V: Secret Enemy
VI: The Trap
VII: Shadow of the League
VIII: Out of the Past
IX: Imprisoned Planeteers
X: Under Saturn's Rings
XI: Secret Police
XII: Citadel of Fear
XIII: Dictator of Worlds
XIV: Under the Psychophone
XV: Through the Tempest
XVI: Forbidden World

XVII: In the Shining Waters
XVIII: Damned Souls of Erebus
XIX: Cheerly's Cunning
XX: At Uranus' Orbit
XXI: The Fight on the Moon
XXII: Blaine's Weapon
XXIII: Epilogue

B143 "Doom Over Venus" in Thrilling Wonder Stories, (May, 1940): pp. 85-110. Illustrator: Frank R. Paul.

CHAPTERS:
I: The Solar Station
II: In the Dream-House
III: The Friends of Venus
IV: Three Spies
V: Perilous Plan
VI: Incredible Impersonation
VII: The Horror at the Ball
VIII: Citadel of Fear
IX: Scientist's Secret
X: Metamorphosis Reversed
XI: Mystery's End

B144 "Interplanetary Graveyard" in Future Fiction, (March, 1940): Pg. 56. Illustrator: Lindsay Robert Streeter.

REPRINTS:
b in **To the Star and Beyond**. Edited by Sheldon Jaffrey. Marcel Island: Starmont House, 1989, 370 p. (Facsimile Fiction Series #5). ISBN: 1-55742-137-4. cloth. [collection]
ba in **To the Star and Beyond**. Edited by Sheldon Jaffrey. Marcel Island: Starmont House, 1989,. 370 p. (Facsimile Fiction Series #5). ISBN: 1-55742-136-6. paper. [collection]

B145 "Lilene, the Moon Girl" in Amazing Stories, (May, 1940): Pg. 66.

REPRINTS:

b in Science Fiction Adventure Classics, (Spring, 1971) Pg. 75.

B146 "Dictators of Creation" in Thrilling Wonder Stories, (May, 1940) Pg. 50. Illustrator: Frank R. Paul.

B147 "City From The Sea" in Weird Tales, 35:3 (May, 1940) Pg. 14. Cover: Hannes Bok[lxxxviii].

B148 "World Without Sex"[lxxxix] in Marvel Science Stories, (May, 1940) Pg. 41.

REPRINTS:

b in **Sensous SF from the Weird & Spicy Pulps**. Edited by Sheldon Jaffrey. Bowling Green, Ohio: Bowling Green University Press, 1984, p. [collection]

B149 "The Isle of Changing Life" in Thrilling Wonder Stories, (June, 1940) Pg. 33.

B150 "Lost Treasure of Mars" in Amazing Stories, 14:8 (August, 1940) Pg. 68.

REPRINTS:

b in Amazing Stories, 43:3 (September, 1969) Pg. 84. Illustrator: Julian S. Krupa.

Gareth Crane, an archeologist, and his venusian aide, Bugeys, have discovered the lost treasure of Kau-ta-lah. Jean Edwards and two disreputable guides are, also, after the treasure. Crane tells them of the inscription he found telling of an even greater treasure held by the king of Ushtu. He convinces the greedy guides to go after it. Once in Ushtu, they locate that which they are seeking. This discovery leads to the death of the two guides and almost kills Crane and Ms. Edwards. They are saved by the natural talents of Crane's Venusian aid.

B151 "The Night the World Ended" in Thrilling Wonder Stories,
(September, 1940) Pg. 82.

REPRINTS:

b as "När Jorden gick under" in Jules Verne-Magasinet #6 (1940) Pg.

B152 "Sea Born" in Weird Tales, 35:5 (September, 1940) Pg. 76.

aa in Weird Tales, (February, 1942) Pg. [British]

B153 "Murder Asteroid" in Thrilling Wonder Stories, (October, 1940): Pg. 80. Illustrator: Frank R. Paul.

REPRINTS:

b as "Mordet på asteroiden" in Jules Verne-Magasinet (18/1942) Pg. [Swedish]

c _: Utopian, 1946, p.

B154 "The Revolt on the Tenth World" in Amazing Stories, (November, 1940) Pg. 60. Illustrator: Krupa.

REPRINTS:

b as "Revolt på tionde Varlden" in Jules Verne-Magasinet (42/1946) Pg. [Swedish]

c in Science Fiction Adventure Classics, (Winter, 1967) Pg. 103. Illustrator: Julian S. Krupa.

While drinking in a bar on Mars, Jim Crane is recruited as a pilot for Jan Vliet, a questionable umbron miner on Umbriel. As he has lost his pilot's license, he accepts the position to fly again. On Umbriel, he meets the other pilots and Jan Vliet. He plots to steal Jan Vliet's treasure but Crane has another objective as well. The other pilot sets up a diversion that works a little too well. Crane, with the help of Jean Ellis, defeats the locals and wins the girl.

B155 "Gift from the Stars" in Thrilling Wonder Stories, (December, 1940) Pg. 91.

REPRINTS:

b serialized as "Stjärnornas gåva" in Jules Verne-Magasinet (26/1941) Pg. Part Two in Jules Verne-Magasinet (27/1941) Pg.

B156 "A Brother To Him" in Thrilling Detective, (December 1940): Pg.

B157 "Mystery Moon" in Amazing Stories, 15:1 (January 1941) Pg. 72. Illustrator: Fuqua.

CHAPTERS:

1:
2: Tragic Mystery
3: Lunar Prison
4: Pirate Moon
5: Space Duel
6: World of Enigma
7: Power of the Rheans

Young Eric Rand discovers a secret about his father and mother. Sentenced to the Lunar prison for the killing of his uncle, Eric escapes and leads a pirate crew in an attempt to clear his name.

B158 "The Horse that Talked" in Fantastic Adventure, (January, 1941) Pg. 108. Illustrator: Jay Jackson.

REPRINTS:

b serialized as "Den talande hästen" in Jules Verne-Magasinet (38/1941): Pg.; Part Two in Jules Verne-Magasinet (39/1941) Pg.

B159 "Son of Two Worlds" in Thrilling Wonder Stories, (August,

1941) Pg. 14. Illustrator: Virgil Finlay.

REPRINTS:

b serialized as "Son av två världar" in Jules Verne Magasinet (6/1947)Pg.; Part Two - in Jules Verne Magasinet (7/1947) Pg.; Conclusion – in Jules Verne Magasinet (8/1947) Pg.

c in **3 From Out There**. Edited by Leo Margulies. New York: Pyramid Books, 1959, 123 p. paper. [collection]

ca in **3 From Out There**. Edited by Leo Margulies. London: Panther, 1960 (c 1959), 190 p, 18 cm. Pg. 123. [collection] [British]

cb in **3 From Out There**. Edited by Leo Margulies. New York: Pyramid Books, 1965, p. 123, paper. [collection]

B160 "Day of the Micro-Men" in Science Fiction, (September, 1941): Pg. 50.

REPRINTS:

b in **To the Star and Beyond**. Edited by Sheldon Jaffrey. Marcel Island: Starmont House, 1989, 370 p (Facsimile Fiction Series #5). ISBN: 1-55742-137-4. cloth. [collection]

ba in **To the Star and Beyond**. Edited by Sheldon Jaffrey. Marcel Island: Starmont House, 1989, 370 p. (Facsimile Fiction Series #5). ISBN: 1-55742-136-6. paper. [collection]

B161 "Dreamer's Worlds" in Weird Tales, 36:2 (November 1941): Pg. 6. Illustrator: Dolgov.

REPRINTS:

b in **What's It Like Out There?** Edmond Hamilton. New York, NY.: Ace Books, 1974, p. mass market paper [collection]

c as "De Wereld van een Dromer" in **Godenschemering en Andere**. Verhalen. Rotterdam: Scala, 1975,. 311 p. 18cm. ISBN: 90.6221.031.7. (Scala science fiction reeks No. 4).[xc] Translator: Iskraa Bundels [Dutch]

B162 "Wacky World" in Amazing Stories, (March, 1942) Pg.198. Illustrator: Rod Ruth.

REPRINTS:

b in Amazing Stories, (April 1956) Pg. 60.
c in Science Fiction Adventure Classics, #8 (Fall, 1969) Pp.16-39.

B163 "Treasure on Thunder Moon" in Amazing Stories, (April, 1942) Pg. 198. Illustrator: Malcolm Smith.

B164 "The Quest in Time" in Fantastic Adventure, 4:6 (June, 1942): Pg.150. Illustrator: Jay Jackson.

REPRINTS:

b in Science Fiction Yearbook, (Winter, 1967) Pg.

CHAPTERS:

1:
2: Into Past Ages
3: The Conquistadors
4: In Montezuma's Palace
5: The Abduction
6: The Fight at the Temple
7: Lo Noche Triste
8: Epiloge

Dr. Madison sends a message asking Nick Clark to come to an isolated Mexican town where Madison's daughter Kay and an assistant are conducting experiments. When he gets there Nick discovers that both the assistant and, Kay, are trapped in the past. Nick is cast back in time to try and rescue them.

B165 "The Daughter of Thor" in Fantastic Adventure, (August, 1942): Pg. 10.

B166 "Through Invisible Barriers" in Thrilling Wonder Stories, (October, 1942) Pg. 15.

REPRINTS:

b as "Professor Wilson råkar illa ut" in Jules Verne-Magasinet 37/1943 – 43/1943 (7 Parts). [Swedish]

B167 "The World with a Thousand Moons" in Amazing Stories, (December, 1942) Pg. 64. Illustrator: Ned Hadley.

REPRINTS:

b serialized as "De tusen meteorernas värld." Jules Verne Magasinet, #13 – #17, 1944, (5 Parts). [Swedish]

c in **To the Star and Beyond**. Edited by Sheldon Jaffrey. Marcel Island: Starmont House, 1989, 370 p. (Facsimile Fiction Series #5). ISBN: 1-55742-137-4. cloth. [collection]

ca in **To the Star and Beyond**. Edited by Sheldon Jaffrey. Marcel Island: Starmont House, 1989, 370 p. (Facsimile Fiction Series #5). ISBN: 1-55742-136-6. paper. [collection]

B168 "Lost City of Burma" in Fantastic Adventure, (December, 1942): Pg. 38.

CHAPTERS:

I:
II: Jungle Mystery
III: Land of the Gods
IV: Golden City
V: Shadow of Horror
VI: Citadel of the Nagas
VII: The Flame of Life

B169 "No-Man's-Land of Time" in Science Fiction Stories, (April, 1943) Pg. 45. Illustrator: Lillis.

B170 "Exile"[xci] in Super Science Stories, (May, 1943) Pg. 88.

REPRINTS:

b in Super Science Stories, (April, 1944) Pg. [Canadian]

c in **Looking Forward**. Edited by Milton Lesser. _: Beechurst Press, 1953, p. [collection] c in **Looking Forward**. Edited by Milton Lesser. _: Cassell, 1955, p. [collection]

d as "Két világban éltem, Univerzum #163 (September, 1970) Pg. ford. ___. [?]

e in **The Best of Edmond Hamilton**. Edited by Leigh Brackett. Garden City, NY.: Nelson Doubleday, 1977, p. cloth. [collection]

ea in **The Best of Edmond Hamilton**. Edited by Leigh Brackett. _: Ballentine, 1977, p. paper. [collection]

f as "Exil" in **Die Besten Stories**. _: <publisher unknown> 1980, p. (PSF 6701) [collection]

g in **Isaac Asimov Presents the Greatest Science Fiction Stories 5: 1943**. Edited by Isaac Asimov and Martin H. Greenberg. New York, NY: DAW, 1981, p. [collection]

h in **Peter Davidson's Book of Alien Monsters**. Edited by Perter Davidson, _: Hutchinson, 1982, p. [collection] [British]

ha in **Peter Davidson's Book of Alien Monsters**. Edited by Perter Davidson, _: Sparrow, 1983, p. [collection]

i in **The Golden Years of Science Fiction: Third Series**. Edited by Isaac Asimov & Martin H. Greenberg. _: Crown/Bonanza. 1984, p. [collection]

j in **101 Science Fiction Stories**. Edited by Robert Weinberg, Stefan R. Dziemianowicz & Martin H. Greenberg. _: Barnes & Noble. 1986, p. [collection]

k as "A számkivetett" in Metagalaktika 9, szerk. Luczka Péter, Móra, 1986, p. Ford. Békés András.

l in **100 Astounding Little Alien Stories**. Edited by Robert Weinberg, Stefan R. Dziemianowicz and Martin H. Greenberg. _: Barnes & Noble, 1996, p. [collection]

B171 "The Valley Of The Assassins" in Weird Tales, 37:2 (November, 1943) Pg. 8. Illustrator: A.R. Tilburne.

REPRINTS:

b in **Ghouls and Ghosts**. Edited by Singer. _ : W. H. Allen, 1972, p. [collection] [British]

c as "Das Tal Der Assassinen." in **Horror IV**. _: <publisher unknown> 1974, p. (HTB 5096). [collection] [German]

d in **Shriek**. Edited by Singer. _: Eclipse books, 1974, p. [Australian] [collection]

e in **Fear! Fear! Fear!** Selected by Helen Hoke. New York, NY: Franklin Watts, Ltd. 1981, pp. 113-130, cloth. Illustrated by Sean Eckett. [collection]

B172 "The Free-Lance of Space" in Amazing Stories, 18:3 (May, 1944) Pg. 122. Illustrator: Julian S Krupa.

REPRINTS:

b as "Rymdens Fribytare" in Jules Verne-Magasinet. #13 (1946) Pg.. [Swedish]

c in Science Fiction Adventures, (May 1974) Pg.

B173 "The Shadow Folk" in Weird Tales, 38:1 (September, 1944): Pg. 6.

B174 "Priestess of the Labyrinth" in Weird Tales, 38:3 (January, 1945) Pg. 8. Illustrator: M. Brundage. Cover: M. Brundage.

B175 "The Shining Land" in Weird Tales, 38:5 (May, 1945) Pg. 30. Cover: Pete Kuhlhoff.

B176 "Invaders from the Monster World" in Amazing Stories, (June, 1945) Pg. 68.

B177 "The Deconventionalizers" in Thrilling Wonder Stories, (Summer, 1945) Pg. 59.

B178 "The Inn Outside the World"[xcii] in Weird Tales, 38:6 (July, 1945) Pg. 64. Cover: Lee Brown Coye.

REPRINTS:

b in **My Best Science Fiction Story**. Edited by Leo Margulies. _: Pocket Books,[xciii] 1949, p. [collection]

ba in **My Best Science Fiction Story**. [12 of 25]. Edited by Leo Margulies and Oscar J. Friend. New York, NY.: Pocket Books - Merlin Press, May 1954, p. Pg. 81. [collection]

c [Japan]

d in Most Thrilling Science Fiction, (Fall, 1969) Pg.

e as "L'auberge hors du temps" in Fiction 185 (May 1969) Pg. Translation: Michel Deutsch. [French]

f in **Science Fact/Fiction**. Edited by Edmund J. Farrell, Thomas E. Gage, John P Fordreshen, Raymond J. Rodrigus. Glenview, IL.: Scott, Foresmann & Company, 1974, p. [collection]

g in **What's It Like Out There?** Edmond Hamilton. New York, NY.: Ace Books, 1974, p. [collection]

h as "De Herberg Buiten de Wereld" in **Godenschemering en Andere**. Verhalen. Rotterdam: Scala, 1975, 311 p. 18cm. ISBN: 90.6221.031.7. (Scala science fiction reeks No. 4).[xciv] Translator: Iskraa Bundels [collection] [Dutch]

B179 "Lost Elysium" in Weird Tales, 39:2 (November, 1945) Pg. 10.

B180 "Trouble on Titan" in Startling Stories, (Fall, 1945) Pg. 75.

B181 "The Man Who Saved The Earth" in **The Best of Science Fiction**. Edited by Groff Cronklin. _: <publisher unknown> 1946, p.

B182 "Forgotten World" in Thrilling Wonder Stories, 28: 1 (Winter, 1946) Pg. 13.

REPRINTS:

b in Fantanstic Story Magazine, 7:3 (Fall, 1954) Pg. 10. Illustrator: Virgil Finlay.

c in **The Giant Anthology of Science Fiction**. Edited by Leo Margulies. _: Merlin Press. 1954,[xcv] p. cloth. [collection]

d in Fanastid Story Magazine, (Fall, 1954) Pg.

e in **Race to the Stars**. Edited by Leo Margulies and Oscar J. Friend. New York, NY: Fawcett Crest Publications, Inc. First Printing October 1958, p. (s245) [collection]

f as "L'eva Dell'Infinito" in **L'eva Dell'Infinito**. _: Editrice Libra. 1973, p. (Nova S.F. #22.). [collection] [Italian]

CHAPTERS:

Stranger From the Stars

Ancient Town
Old Planet
Mystery Machine
Desperate Play
"You Owe A Chance to Earth"
Last Frontier
Solar Struggle
An Earthman Comes Home

A space-engineer is ordered to Earth for treatment of a psychological disorder. He dreads going back to the now forgotten backwater planet.

B183 "The Valley of The Gods" in Weird Tales, 39:5 (May, 1946): Pg. 8. Illustrator: Ronald Clyne.

REPRINTS:

b in **Weird Tales of the Supernatural**. Edited by Kurt Singer. _: W.H. Allen, 1966, p. [collection]

c in **Supernatural**. Edited by Kurt Singer. _: Eclipse Books, 1974, p. [collection]

d in **Weird Tales of the Supernatural**. Edited by Kurt Singer. _: White Lion, 1975, p. [collection] [British]

e as "Il Piancta Morta" In **Il Leone Di Comarre**. _: Editrice Libra. 1974, p. (Nova S.F. #28). [collection] [Italian]

B184 "The Dead Planet" in Startling Stories, (Spring, 1946) Pg. 84.

REPRINTS:

b in **Worlds of Tomorrow**. Edited by August Derlith. _ : Pellegrini Cudahy. 1953, p. [collection]

ba in **Worlds of Tomorrow**. Edited by August Derlith. New York: Berkely Books. 1953, p. Pg. 5.[xcvi] [collection]

bb in **Worlds of Tomorrow**. Edited by August Derlith. _ : Weidenfeld Nicolson 1955, p. [collection]

bc in **Worlds of Tomorrow**. Edited by August Derlith. _ : Berkely Books. 1958, p. [collection]

c in **Exploring Other Worlds**. Edited by Sam Moskowitz. __: <publisher unknown> 1963, p. [collection]

bd in **Worlds of Tomorrow**. Edited by August Derlith. _ : For Square

Books, 1963, p. [collection]
d in **Ghosts, Castles, and Victims**. Edited by Wolf/Wolf. _ : Fawcett Crest, 1974, p. [collection]
e in "A halott bolygo," Galaktika, (June, 1990) Pg. ford. Kaposi Tamás.
f in **Space Stories**. Edited by Mike Ashley. _ : Robinson Children's Books, 1996, p. [collection]
g as "La planete morte" in **Histoires de planetes**. _: editions Livre de poche, <year>, p. [collection] [French]
h as "De Dode Planeet" in **Science Fiction Verhalen**. [collection] [Dutch]

B185 "The Indestructible Man" in Thrilling Wonder Stories, (Spring, 1946) Pg. 32. Illustrator: John Norman.

CHAPTERS:

I: The Cat that Couldn't be Killed
II: Bullet Proof
III: Strange Doom
IV: Drowned Man's Return

B186 "Day of Judgement" in Weird Tales, 39:7 (September, 1946): Pg. 20. Cover: Pee Kuhlhoff.

REPRINTS:

b in **The Best of Edmond Hamilton**. Edited by Leigh Brackett. Garden City, NY.: Nelson Doubleday, 1977, p. cloth. [collection]
c in **The Last Man On Earth**. Edited by Isaac Asimov, Martin H. Greenberg and Charles G. Waugh. New York, NY: Fawcett Crest Books, March 1982, p. paper. [collection]
d as "Tag Des Gerichts." in **Die Besten Stories**. _: <publisher unknown> 1980, p. (PSF 6701.) [collection]
e as "Tag Des Gerichts." **in Der Letzte Mensch Auf Erden**. Edited By Isaac Asimov, Charles G. Waugh and Martin H. Greenberg. _: <publisher unknown> 1984, p. (HSF 4076) [collection]

B187 "Never the Twain Shall Meet" in Thrilling Wonder, (Fall, 1946) Pg. 60.

B188 "The King of Shadows" in Weird Tales, 39:9 (January, 1947):

Pg. 38.

REPRINTS:

b in **What's It Like Out There?** Edmond Hamilton. New York, NY.: Ace Books, 1974, p. paper. [collection]

c as "De Konig der Schaduwen" in **Godenschemering en Andere**. Verhalen. Rotterdam: Scala, 1975, 311 p. 18cm. ISBN: 90.6221.031.7. (Scala science fiction reeks No. 4).[xcvii] Translator: Iskraa Bundels [collection] [Dutch]

B189 "Come Home From Earth" in Thrilling Wonder, (February, 1947) Pg. 91.

B190 "Proxy Planeteers" in Startling Stories, 15:3 (July, 1947) Pg. 88.

B191 "Serpent Princess" in Weird Tales, 40:2 (January, 1948) Pg. 6.

REPRINTS:

b in **Man Called Poe**, _: <publisher unknown> 1968, p. [collection]

c in **What's It Like Out There?** Edmond Hamilton. New York, NY.: Ace Books, 1974, p. paper. [collection]

d as "Slangenprinses" in **Godenschemering en Andere.** Verhalen. Rotterdam: Scala. 1975, 311 p. 18cm. ISBN: 90.6221.031.7. (Scala science fiction reeks No. 4).[xcviii] Translator: Iskraa Bundels [collection] [Dutch]

Hugh Macklin and associates find an ancient temple dedicated to the serpent goddess - Tiamat. It was sealed with a curse against awakening the goddess. That night, Hugh dreamt about the goddess. In his dream he had gone into the sea, found a city and saw her sleeping. She spoke to him telepathically and told him to ring the bell in the temple. When he woke, he found himself standing outside the now opened temple. Jan Roos had the same dream. Inside they found the bell which Jan Roos rang. That night, Roos ran into the ocean to answer the call of the evil but beautiful Tiamat. Later, Thorpe rang the bell and also ran into the ocean. Macklin donned a diving suit to follow the two men. He saw Tiamat, agreed that he could love her but did not want to end up like the others, who now worshipped her but were pseudo-living. Although their bodies were there, they no longer breathed. Hugh had brought the Sceptre of Marduk, a sistrum, and rang it. Tiamat and her people froze.

B192 "Transuranic" in Thrilling Wonder Stories, (February, 1948) Pg. 72.

REPRINTS:

b in **What's It Like Out There?** Edmond Hamilton. New York, NY.: Ace Books, 1974, p. mass market paper [collection]

c as "Transuranic" in Godenschemering en Andere Verhalen. Rotterdam: Scala. 1975, 311 p. 18cm. ISBN: 90.6221.031.7. (Scala science fiction reeks No. 4).[xcix] Translator: Iskraa Bundels [collection] [Dutch]

d as "Element 144." in **Wachter Der Zeiten**. _: <publisher unknown> 1980, p. [UC 17] [Collection]

B193 "The Might-Have-Been" in Weird Tales, (March, 1948) Pg.

B194 "The Knowledge Machine"[c] in Thrilling Wonder Stories, (June, 1948) Pg. 109.

REPRINTS:

b in Science Fiction Yearbook, #1. (1967) Pg.

B195 "Twilight of the Gods" in Weird Tales, 40:5 (July, 1948) Pg. 4. Illustrator: Humiston. Cover:

REPRINTS:

b in **Weird Tales of the Supernatural**. Edited by Kurt Singer. _: W.H. Allen, 1966, p. [collection]

c in **What's It Like Out There?** Edmond Hamilton. New York, NY.: Ace Books, 1974, p. paper. [collection]

d as "Godenschemering" in **Godenschemering en Andere**. Verhalen. Rotterdam: Scala. 1975, 311 p. 18cm. ISBN: 90.6221.031.7. (Scala science fiction reeks No. 4).[ci] Translator: Iskraa Bundels [collection] [Dutch]

e in **Supernatural**. Edited by Kurt Singer. _: Eclipse Books, 1974, p. [Australian] [collection]

f in **Weird Tales of the Supernatural**. Edited by Kurt Singer. _: White Lion, 1975, p. [collection] [British]

g as “Gotterdammerung” in **Wachter Der Zeiten**. _: <publisher unknown> 1980, p. (UC 17) [collection]

B196 “The Watcher of Ages”[cii] in Weird Tales, 40:6 (September, 1948):Pg. 68. Illustrator: Humiston.

REPRINTS:

b in **What’s It Like Out There?** Edmond Hamilton. New York, NY.: Ace Books, 1974, p. paper. [collection]

c as “De Wachter der Tijden” in **Godenschemering en Andere**. Verhalen. Rotterdam: Scala. 1975, 311 p. 18cm. ISBN: 90.6221.031.7. (Scala science fiction reeks No. 4).[ciii] Translator: Iskraa Bundels [collection] [Dutch]

d as “Wachter Der Zeiten” in **Wachter Der Zeiten**[civ]. _: <publisher unknown> 1980, p. (UC 17) [collection]

B197 “Alien Earth”[cv] in Thrilling Wonder Stories, 34:1. (April, 1949): Pg. 54.

REPRINTS:

b in **Alien Earth & Other Stories**. Edited by Roger Elwood and Sam Moskowitz. New York, NY: MacFadden-Bartell, 1969, p.paper. [collection]

c in **The Best of Edmond Hamilton**. Edited by Leigh Brackett. Garden City, NY.: Nelson Doubleday, 1977, p. cloth. [collection]

d in **The Best of Edmond Hamilton**. Edited by Leigh Brackett. _: Ballentine, 1977, p. paper. [collection]

e as “Fremde Erde” in **Die Besten Stories**. _: <publisher unknown> 1980, p. (PSF 6701) [collection]

f in **Caught in the Organ Draft**. Edited by Isaac Asimov, Martin H. Greenberg and Charles G. Waugh. March 1983, p. paper. (FSG) [collection]

g in **Isaac Asimov Presents the Greatest Science Fiction Stories 11: 1949**. Edited by Isaac Asimov and Martin H. Greenberg. New York, NY: DAW, 1984, p. paper. [collection]

h in **Isaac Asimov Presents the Golden Years of Science Fiction**. Edited by Isaac Asimov and Martin H. Greenberg. _: Cron/Bonanza, 1988, p. [collection]

B198 "Return of Captain Future" in Startling Stories. 20:3. (January, 1950) Pg. 94. Illustrator: Astarita. Cover:.

REPRINTS:

b in Startling Stories. (January, 1950) Pg. [Canadian]

c as "Kapten Franks Återkomst." in Jules Verne Magasinet #4. (1970) Pg. [Swedish]

d in **Captain Future Handbook**. Edited by unknown. _: <publisher unknown> July 1983, p. [collection] [Japanese]

e as **Il Ritorno di Capitain Futuro**. _: Nova SF, May 2002, p. (Nova SF # 54). [collection] [Italian]

CHAPTERS:

In the Moon-Laboratory
Futuremen's Return
Alien Enemy
Last Weapon

Joan Randall and Ezra Gurney travel to the moon to save the Futuremen's equipment from the certain destruction by government's impending actions. There, they find Captain Future and the Futuremen have returned, but have kept quiet because they brought something very dangerous back with them.

B199 "Children of The Sun" in Startling Stories, 21:2 (May, 1950): Pg. 98. Illustrator: Orban.

REPRINTS:

b in **Captain Future Handbook**. Edited by unknown. _: <publisher unknown> July 1983, p. [Japanese]

c as <unknown>. _: <publisher unknown> 1990, 256 p.[Russian]
Note: This is a collection containing: "Pardon my Iron Nerves" and "Children of the Sun."

d as <unknown>. _: <publisher unknown> 1993, 512 p. [Russian]
Note: This is a collection containing: "Pardon my Iron Nervers," **Outlaw World** and "Children of the Sun."

e	in Thrilling Novels, No. 39 (1996) Pg.

CHAPTERS:

Quest of the Futuremen
Citadel of Mystery
Dread Metamorphosis
The Bright Ones

B200 "Harpers of Titan" in Startling Stories, 22:1 (September, 1950): Pg. 96. Illustrator: Orban.

REPRINTS:

aa	in Startling Stories, (September, 1950) Pg. [Canadian]
ab	in Startling Stories, (September, 1950) Pg. [British]
b	in **Worlds of Weird**. Edited by Leo Margulies. _: <publisher unknown> <year>, p. paper.
c	included with **Dr. Cyclops**. by Henry Kuttner. New York: Popular Library. 1967, p. paper. Note: Includes "Too Late for Eternity" by Bryce Walton.
d	as **Les Harpistes de Titan**. _: J'ai Lu, April 1977, p. [French]
e	in SF. #8 (August 1977) Pg. [Japanese]
f	in **Captain Future Handbook**. Edited by unknown. _: <publisher unknown> July 1983, p. [collection] [Japanese]
g	as "Les Harpistes de Titan" in **Les meilleurs recits de startling stories**. Edited by Jacques Sadoul. _: editiosn J'ai lu, <year>, p. [collection] [French]

CHAPTERS:

Shadowed Moon
Unearthly Stratagem
Once Born of Flesh
The Harpers

Captain Future and the Futuremen travel to Titan to prevent an uprising among the natives. The local earthman contact is killed and the Brain becomes "Human" again to try to prevent the impending revolt.

B201 "Pardon My Iron Nerves" in Startling Stories, 22:2 (November,

1950) Pg. 78. Illustrator: Orban.

REPRINTS:

aa in Startling Stories, (November, 1950) Pg. [British]
b in SF. (August 1966) Pg. [Japanese]
c _: <publisher unknown> Feberuary 1972, p. (Space Opera Meisaku-sen #1). [Japanese]
d in **Captain Future Handbook**. Edited by unknown. _: <publisher unknown> July 1983, p. [collection] [Japanese]
e as <unknown>. _: <publisher unknown> 1990, 256 p. [Russian]
Note: This is a collection containing: Pardon my Iron Nerves and Children of the Sun.
f as <unknown>. _: <publisher unknown> 1993, 512 p. [Russian]
Note: This is a collection containing: Pardon my Iron Nerves, Outlaw World and Children of the Sun.
g in Thrilling Novels, No. 49 (1996) Pg.

CHAPTERS:

Metal man
Mission to Pluto
The Machs
Crazy moon

B202 "Moon of The Unforgotten" in Startling Stories, 22:3 (January, 1951) Pg. 118. Illustrator: Orban.

REPRINTS:

aa in Startling Stories, (January, 1951) Pg. [Canadian]
b in **Captain Future Handbook**. Edited by unknown. _: <publisher unknown> July 1983, p. [Japanese]
c in Thrilling Novels, No. 39 (1996) Pg.
d as **La Luna degli Eterni Ricordi**. _: Nova SF, August 2001, p. (Nova SF # 50). [Italian]

B203 "Earthmen No More" in Startling Stories, 23:1 (March, 1951): Pg. 76. Illustrator: Orban.

REPRINTS:

b in **Captain Future Handbook**. Edited by unknown. _: <publisher unknown> July 1983, p. [collection] [Japanese] c in Thrilling Novels, No. 39 (1996) Pg.

CHAPTERS:

The Awakening
Return from Space
Men of Earth
Earthman No More

Captain Future and the Futuremen revive John Carey, a space-frozen old explorer. He is taken to Earth and discovers he no longer fits in.

B204 "Birthplace of Creation" in Startling Stories, 23:2 (May, 1951): Pg. 120. Illustrator: Orban.

REPRINTS:

aa in Startling Stories, (August, 1952) Pg. [British]
b in Starwind: Science Fiction & Fantasy, 2:1 (Fall, 1976) Pg. 46. Illustrator: Michael Jones. Introduction: Gary Hoppenstand.
c in **Captain Future Handbook**. Edited by unknown. _: <publisher unknown> July 1983, p. [Japanese]
d in Thrilling Novels, No. 39 (1996) Pg.

CHAPTERS:

Citadel of the Futuremen
Cosmic Secret
The Birthplace
Powers of the Watchers

B205 "Lords of the Morning" in Thrilling Wonder Stories, 40:3 (August, 1952) Pg. 12. Illustrator: Alex Schomberg.

Edward Martin suffers from a strange affliction which causes him to mentally travel back in time. While on an archeological expedition to some Mayan ruins in Mexico, he finds himself inhabiting the body of a Spaniard 400 years ago. As this spaniard, he discovers earth has been visited from space.

B206 "What's It Like Out There"[cvi] in Thrilling Wonder Stories, (December, 1952) Pg. 66. Illustrator: Orban.

REPRINTS:

b in **The Best From Startling Stories**. Edited by Samuel Mines. New York: Henry Holt, 1953, p. cloth. [collection]

c in **Startling Stories**. Edited by Samuel Mines. _: Henry Holt, 1953, p. [collection]

ca in **Startling Stories**. Edited by Samuel Mines. _: Cassell, 1954, p. [collection]

d as "A quoi ga ressemble lá-haut?." a Radio Geneve dramatization for the winter 1960-61 season.[cvii] Translated & Adapted by Pierre Versins and Martiene Thomé.

e in **A Century of Science Fiction**. Edited by Damon Knight. New York: Simon & Schuster, 1962, p. Pg. 80.[collection]

f in Treasury of Great Science Fiction Stories. #12. _: publisher unknown? 1965, p. [collection]

ea in **A Century of Science Fiction**. Edited by Damon Knight. _: Gollancz. 1963, p. [collection]

g in **Science Fiction for People Who Hate Science Fiction**. _: publisher unknown? 1966, p.cloth. [collection]

h as "Wie Ist Es Dort Draussen?" in **Die Superwaffe**. Edited by Terry Carr. _: <publisher unknown> 1968, p. (GSF 095). [collection] [German]

i in **What's It Like Out There?** Edmond Hamilton. New York, NY.: Ace Books, 1974, p. paper. [collection]

j as "Hoe is het Daar?" in Godenschemering en Andere Verhalen. Rotterdam: Scala, 1975, 311 p. 18cm. ISBN: 90.6221.031.7. (Scala science fiction reeks No. 4)[cviii] Translator: Iskraa Bundels [Dutch]

k in **Godenschemering**. Rotterdam: Scala Science Fiction Reeks, 1975, 311p, 18cm. [collection] [Dutch]

l in **Explorers of Space**. Edited by Robert Silverberg. _: Thomas Nelson 1975, p. paper. [collection] [British]

la in **Explorers of Space**. Edited by Robert Silverberg. _: Thomas Nelson 1975, p. paper. [collection]

m in **The Best of Edmond Hamilton**. Edited by Leigh Brackett. _: Ballantine, 1977, p. [collection]

ma in **The Best of Edmond Hamilton**. Edited by Leigh Brackett. Garden City, NY.: Nelson Doubleday, 1977, p. cloth. [collection]

n in **The Road to Science Fiction #2: From Wells to Heinlein**. Edited by James E. Gunn. New York, NY: New American Library, February 1979, p. paper. [collection]

o in **Wide-Angle Lens**. Edited by Phyllis R. Fenner. _: William Morrow,

1980, p. [collection]

p in **The Future in Question**. Edited by Isaac Asimov. _: Fawcett. 1980, p. paper. [collection]

q as "Wie Ist Es Da Oben?" in **Die Besten Stories**. _: <publisher unknown> 1980, p. (PSF 6710). [collection] [German]

r in **Waechter der Zeiten**. _: <publisher unknown> 1980, p. [collection] [German]

s in **Isaac Asimov's Science Fiction Treasury**. Edited by Isaac Asimov, Martin H. Greenberg and Joseph D. Olander, 1980, p. paper. (BNZ) [collection]

t as "Wie Ist Es Da Oben?" in **Piloten Aus Zeit Und Raum**. Edited by Ronald M. Hahn. Ensslin. _: publisher unknown? 1982, p. [collection] [German]

u as "Hur är det där ute?" Stockholm: Nova Science Fiction, 4:3 (December, 1984) Pp. 25-39. Translator: Bertil Mårtensson. Illustrator: Annika Roos. [Swedish]
Note: With introduction.

v in **Isaac Asimov Presents the Great Science Fiction #14**. Edited by Isaac Asimov, Martin H. Greenberg and Charles G. Waugh. New York, NY: DAW, 1986, p. 308. paper. [collection]

na in **The Road to Science Fiction #2: From Wells to Heinlein**. Edited by James E. Gunn. _: Rowman & Littlefield Pub Inc. October 2002, 328 p. ISBN: 0810844397. paper. [collection]

B207 "The Unforgiven" in Startling Stories, 31:1 (October, 1953): Pg. 76.

REPRINTS:

b in Science Fiction Yearbook, (1969) PG.

B208 "Sacrifice Hit" in The Magazine of Fantasy & Science Fiction, (November, 1954) Pg. 100.

REPRINTS:

b as Matérial humain in UfictionU, No. 22 (September 1955) Pg. Translation: Translator unknown. [French]

B209 "The Legion of Lazarus" in Imagination, 7:2 (#48). (April, 1956) Pg. 6.

Hyrst wakes up from "Humane Penalty" and finds himself with new powers. He is telepathically contacted and receives help in being released. He had been found guilty of murdering MacDonald, his partner. Hyrst finds himself 50 years in his future and involved in a fight for MacDonald's hidden Titanite. The "Lazurites" want the Titanite for the starship they had built. The opposition is led by Bellaver, the grandson of Hyrst's old boss. Hyrst just wants find out who really killed MacDonald and force a confession. Hyrst eventually finds the killer and the Titanite. He convinces Bellaver to exchange in the killer for the Starship. The Lazurites rescue Hyrst before Bellaver can seek his revenge.

B210 "Citadel of the Star Lords" in Imagination, 7:5 (#51) (October, 1956) Pg. 8. Cover: Lloyd N. Rognan.

Price is flying his beechcraft unlit and low across the Nevada landscape. He is trying to avoid detection by US officials for illegally transporting Arnolfo Ruiz across the US-Mexico border. He ends up in the center of the blast from a new type of Hydrogen bomb which transports him from 1979 to 2039. He finally lands by the Mississippi river near Missouri. He is taken prisoner by a hunting party, and taken to Sawyer, the chief of the Missouris. Price tells them he comes from the west to deliver the plane to the chief.

B211 "The Cosmic Kings"[cix] in Imaginative Tales, 3:6 (November, 1956) Pg. 8. Cover: Lloyd Rognan.

B212 "The Starcombers" in Science Fiction Adventure, (December, 1956) Pg. 5. Illustrator: Bowman. Cover: Ed Emsh.

REPRINTS:

b in Science Fiction Adventure, (November, 1958) Pg. [British]

c in **Great Science Fiction Adventures**. Edited by Larry T. Shaw. New York, NY.: Lancer Books, 1963, p. [collection]

d as "I Cercatori Della Stelle" in **La Nave Della Ombre**. _: Editrice Libra. 1972, p. (Nova S.F. #19). [collection] [Italian]

B213 "The Tattooed Man"[cx] in Imaginative Tales, 4:2 (March, 1957): Pg. 6. Cover: Malcolm Smith.

B214 "The Sinister Invasion"[cxi] in Imagination Science Fiction, 8:3 (June, 1957) Pg. 9. Cover: Lloyd Rognan.

B215 "World of Never-Men" in Imaginative Tales, 4:4 (July, 1957): Pg. 6. Cover: Malcolm Smith.

Colin Baker, out to find the killer of his remshi, joins a band of outlaws looking for the legendary Martian city of Cherlorne. Crossing the desert of the Bitter Sea, they run out of water. A group of androids appear in thier midst. The outlaws are given water and told to return. They decide to break camp and follow the androids, but Baker is left to die. He escapes stumbles upon the village of Llorn. Catching up to the others, a dust storm hits. In the storm, he finds a cave with the lost city of Cherlorne.

B216 "The Ship From Infinity" in Imaginative Tales, 4:6 (November, 1957) Pg. 6. Cover: Lloyd N. Rognan.

Ross Farrel wakes up in a Martian prison cell and manages to escape. He receives a message from Victor through Tolti, the daughter of a mutual Martian friend. Farrel retrieves the "peeper." Farrel and Tolti manage to make it to Ceres where they meet up with Victor. Then they meet up with old Croy again narrowly avoiding capture. The salvage ships meet up and start to salvage the Ship from Infinity when Whitmer and Leach show up with Benson. The two sides battle for the ship.

B217 "No Earthman I" in Venture Science Fiction. 1:6 (#6). (November, 1957) Pg. 85. Illustrator: John Giunta.

REPRINTS:

b in Venture Science Fiction, (June, 1964) Pg. [British]

B218 "Last Call for Doomsday"[cxii] in Imagination Science Fiction, 8:6 (#58) (December, 1957) Pg.

B219 "The Cosmic Looters"[cxiii] in Imagination Science Fiction, (February, 1958) Pg.

B220 "Men of the Morning Star" in Imaginative Tales, 5:2 (March, 1958) Pp. 6-59. Illustrator: Becker. Cover: Lloyd Rognan.

B221 "Corridor of the Suns" in Imagination, 9:2 (April, 1958) Pg. 6. Illustrator: D. Bruce Berry. Cover: Malcom Smith.

Eric Lindeman creates an illegal space-ship. He convinces V. Evers and J. Straw to go to the Andromeda Galaxy with him. They discover a horrible secret and decide to return to tell the Galactic Council. Since they are wanted, they attempt to contact a friend. Joined by a beautiful red-headed Valloan, they are followed by the G.C. cruisers. They sneak into Shuyler's compound until the Galactic Council arrives and Shuyler is taken into custody.

B222 "The Dark Backward" in Venture Science Fiction, 2:3 (#9). (May, 1958) Pg. 6. Illustrator: Giunta & Schoenherr.

b in Venture Science Fiction, (February, 1965) Pg. [British]

c as "Dans l'abîme du passé" in Fiction, No. 135 (February 1965) Pg. Translation: Gersaint. [French]

B223 "Planet of Exile" in Space Travel, (July, 1958) Pg. 30. Illustrator: D. Bruce Berry.

B224 "The Star Hunter" in Space Travel, 5:5 (September, 1958) Pg. 30.

A scientist working for the King of Orion has a discovered a terrible new weapon. Mason, an Agent of Terran Intelligence, is sent to try and find the scientist. He manages to avoid the Navy of the Orion Kingdom and infiltrates the outlaw organization of the Marches. He works with the leader of the outlaws to find the scientist and the weapon, Mason destroys it just before the Orion Navy can get it.

B225 "The Godmen" in Space Travel, (November, 1958) Pg. 6[cxiv]. Illustrator: D. Bruce Berry.

B226 "Requiem" in Amazing Stories, (April, 1962) Pg. 48. Illustrator: Summers.

REPRINTS:

b in Fiction Spécial, No. 11 (1967) Pg. Translation: Frank Straschitz. [French]

c in **Modern Masterpieces of Science Fiction**. Edited by Sam Moskowitz. _: World, 1965, p. [collection]

d in Most Thrilling Science Fiction Ever Told, (Winter, 1967) Pg. 28. Illustrator: Summers.

e in **The Vortex Blasters**. Edited by Sam Moskowitz. New York, NY: MacFadden Books, 1968, pp. 27-43. [collection]

f in **The Learning Maze & Other Stories**. Edited by Roger Elwood. _: <publisher unknown> 1974, p. [collection]

ea in **The Vortex Blasters**. Edited by Sam Moskowitz. _ : Hyperion, 1974, p. [collection]

g as "Requiem Per La terra" in **La Danzatrice Di Ganimede**. _: Editrice Libra. 1975, p. (Nova S.F.) [collection] [Italian]

h in **The Best of Edmond Hamilton**. Edited by Leigh Brackett. Garden City, NY.: Nelson Doubleday, 1977, p. cloth. [collection]

ha in **The Best of Edmond Hamilton**. Edited by Leigh Brackett. _: Ballentine, 1977, p. paper. [collection]

i as "Requiem." in **Die Besten Stories**. _: <publisher unknown> 1980, p. (PSF 6701) [collection]

j in **Catastrophies!** Edited by Isaac Asimov, Martin H. Greenberg and Charles G. Waugh. New York, NY: Fawcett Crest Books, July 1981, p. [collection]

k in **Amazing Stories: 60 Years of the Best Science Fiction**. Edited by Isaac Asimov and Martin H. Greenberg. Lake Geneva, WI:

TSR, Inc. July 1985, pp. 103-114, trade paper. [collection]

l as “Requiem” in **Faszination Der Science Fiction**. Edited by Isaac Asimov, Charles G. Waugh, Martin H. Greenberg. _: <publisher unknown> 1985, p. (BSFSp 24068) [collection]

m as “Requiem” in **Histoires de catastropes**. _: editions Livre de poche, <year>, p.[collection] [French]

B227” The Stars, My Brothers” in <u>Amazing Stories</u>, (May, 1962) Pg. 6. Illustrator: Virgil Finlay.

REPRINTS:

b in <u>The Most Thrilling Science Fiction Ever Told</u>, (#8). (Spring, 1968): Pg. 4. Illustrator: Virgil Finlay.

c in **Alien Worlds**. Edited by Roger Elwood. New York, NY.: Paperback Library, 1964, p. [collection]

d in **What’s It Like Out There?** Edmond Hamilton. New York, NY.: Ace Books, 1974, p. paper. [collection]

e as “De Sterren, mijn Broeders” in Godenschemering en Andere Verhalen. Rotterdam: Scala, 1975, 311 p. 18cm. ISBN: 90.6221.031.7. (Scala science fiction reeks No. 4).[cxv] Translator: Iskraa Bundels [Dutch]

f as “Meine Bruder Sind Die Sterne” in **Wachter Der Zeiten**. _: <publisher unknown> 1980, p. (UC 17). [collection]

g in **Amazing Stories: Vision of Other Worlds**. Edited by Martin H. Greenberg. _ : TSR, 1986, p. [collection]

h _: Project Gutenberg. March 18, 2008. Multiple electronic formats. 39-360 Kb. EText-No: 24870 http://www.gutenberg.org/etext/24870

i in **14 Amazing Science Fiction Stories from the 30’s to the 60’s**. _: Amazon Digital Servies.. <year> 896 Kb. Pg. 36. ASIN B002DMKYS6.

j in **The Two Worlds of Edmond Hamilton**. _: Wildside Press. May 14, 2008. (8.8 x 5.9 x 0.3 in) ISBN-10: 1434468208; ISBN-13: 978-1434468208.
With “The Monsters of Jontonheim.”

k _: Wilder Publications. April 9, 2009. 72 pp. (7.9 x 4.9 x 0.3 in.) ISBN-10: 1604596635; ISBN-13: 978-1604596632.

B228 “Sunfire!” in <u>Amazing Stories</u>, (September, 1962) Pg. 6. Illustrator: Virgil Finlay.

REPRINTS:

b in **The Best of Amazing**. Edited by Joseph Ross. _: Doubleday, 1967, p. [collection]

c as "Kinder der Sonne" in **Kinder der Sonne**. Munchen, Germany:. _: <publisher unknown> 1968, p. (TTB 545) [collection]

d in **The Best of Amazing**. _: Belmont, 1969, p. [collection]

e in The Most Thrilling Science Fiction Ever Told, (February, 1973) Pg.

f in **What's It Like Out There?** Edmond Hamilton. New York, NY.: Ace Books, 1974, p. paper. [collection]

g as "Sonnenfeuer" in **Wachter Der Zeiten**. _: <publisher unknown> 1980, p. (UC 17) [collection]

B229 "Babylon in the Sky" in Amazing Stories, (March, 1963) Pg. 6. Illustrator: Lloyd Birmingham.

REPRINTS:

b as "Die Stadt am Himmel" in **Kinder der Sonne**. Munchen, Germany: <publisher unknown> 1968, p. (TTB 545) [collection]

c in Great Science Fiction, #8 (Fall, 1967).

B230 "After a Judgement Day" in Fantastic Stories, 12:12 (December, 1963): 6. Illustrator: Virgil Finlay.

REPRINTS:

b in The Most Thrilling Science Fiction Ever Told, (October, 1972) Pg.

c in **The Best of Edmond Hamilton**. Edited by Leigh Brackett. Garden City, NY.: Nelson Doubleday, 1977, p.cloth. [collection]

d in **The Best of Edmond Hamilton**. Edited by Leigh Brackett. _: Ballentine, 1977, p. paper. [collection]

e as "Nach Einem Gerichstag" in **Die Besten Stories**. _: <publisher unknown> 1980, p. (PSF 6701) [collection]

B231 "Kingdom of the Stars"[cxvi] in Amazing Stories. 39:4 (September, 1964) Pg. 6. [See A32]. Illustrator: Robert Adragana. Cover: Robert Adragana.

REPRINTS:

b in _: Tokyo Sogensha Co. Ltd. 1964, p. [Japanese]

c as **Le retour aux etoiles**. _: Editions J'ai Lu. 1967, p. Translator: Frank Straschitz. [French]

d in **Les rois des etoiles & Retour aux etoiles**. : _: Ed. Opta, 1968, p. ['Classique SF: 12'] [French]

e as "Konigreich Der Sterne" in **An Den Ufern Der Unendlichkiet**. Rastatt: Hubert Strassl, 1968, p. (U 571). [collection] [German]

f as "Lianna Di Formalhaut" in **Terra, Acqua, Fucco, Aria**. _: Editrice Libra, 1968, p. (Nova S.F. #6). [collection] [Italian]

g in Science Fiction Greats, (Fall, 1970) Pg.

h in **Return To the Stars**. New York, NY.: Lancer, 1970, 207 p. paper. (74612)

i in **Return To the Stars**. _: Prestige Books, 1970, 207p, paper.

j in **Planets of Wonder**. Edited by Terry Carr. New York, NY: Thomas Nelson, Inc. 1976, pp.137-189. 21cm.

k in **Ihre Heimat sind die Sterne**. Rastatt/Baden: Erich Pabel Verlag, May 1976, p. (TTB 274). [German]

l as "Die Sternenkonigreiche" In **Ruckkehr Zu Den Sternen**. _: <publisher unknown> 1980, p.[HSF 3781] [collection] [German]

m in **Regresso Aos Ceus**. Lisboa: Edicao <Livros do Brasil>, <year>, p. (N 237). Translator: Eurico Fonseca. [Brazillian]

B232 "The Pro"[cxvii] in The Magazine of Fantasy & Science Fiction, 27:4 (#161) (October, 1964) Pg. 21.
Note: There is an introduction that begins on page 21. The story starts on page 22.

REPRINTS:

b as "Der Profit." In **F & SF 12 - Expedition nach Chronos**. edited by Walter Ernsting. _: publisher unknown? 1965, p. (HSF 3065) [collection]

c as "Quand on est de metier" in Ficiton 134 (January 1965) Pg. Translatore: Paul Alpérine. [French]

d in **Great Science Fiction Stories about the Moon**. Edited by Thomas M. Dikty. _: <publisher unknown> 1967, p. [collection]

e in **The Best of Edmond Hamilton**. Edited by Leigh Brackett. Garden City, NY.: Nelson Doubleday, 1977, p. cloth. [collection]

ea in **The Best of Edmond Hamilton**. Edited by Leigh Brackett. : Ballentine, 1977, p. paper.[collection]

f as "Der Profit" in **Die Besten Stories**. _: <publisher unknown> 1980, p.

(PSF 6701). [collection]

g in **Inside the Funhouse**. Edited by Mike Resnick. _ : AvoNova, 1992, p.

B233 "The Shores of Infinity" in Amazing Stories, (April, 1965) Pg. 7. Illustrator: Schelling. Cover: Paula McLane.

REPRINTS:

b in _: Tokyo Sogensha Co. Ltd. 1964, p. [Japanese]

c as **Le retour aux etoiles**. _: Editions J'ai Lu. 1967, p. Translator: Frank Straschitz. [French]

d in **Les rois des etoiles & Retour aux etoiles**. _: Ed. Opta, 1968, p. [Classique SF: 12] [French]

e as "Konigreich Der Sterne" in **An Den Ufern Der Unendlichkiet**. Rastatt: Hubert Strassl, 1968, p. (U 571). [collection] [German]

f as "Le Rive Dell'Infinito" in **Le Rive Dell'Infinito**. _: Editrice Libra, 1968, p. (Nova S.F. #7). [collection] [Italian]

g in **Return To the Stars**. New York, NY.: Lancer, 1970, 207p, paper. (74612)

h in **Return To the Stars**. Prestige Books, 1969, p. paper.

i in The Most Thrilling Science Fiction Ever Told, (August, 1973) Pg.

j in **Ihre Heimat sind die Sterne**. Rastatt/Baden: Erich Pabel Verlag, May 1976, p. (TTB 274). [German]

k as "Die Sternenkonigreiche." In **Ruckkehr Zu Den Sternen**. _: <publisher unknown> 1980, p. (HSF 3781). [German]

l in **Regresso Aos Ceus**. Lisboa: Edicao <Livros do Brasil>, <year>, p. (N 237). Translator: Eurico Fonseca. [Brazillian]

B234 "Castaway" in **The Man Called Poe**. Edited by Sam Moskowitz. Garden City, NY: Doubleday, 1968, p. [collection]

REPRINTS:

b in **The Man Called Poe**. Edited by Sam Moskowitz. _: Gollancz, 1970, p. [collection] [British]

c in **What's It Like Out There?** Edmond Hamilton. New York, NY.: Ace Books, 1974, p. [collection]

d as "Uitgestoten" in Godenschemering en Andere Verhalen. Rotterdam: Scala. 1975, 311 p. 18cm. ISBN: 90.6221.031.7. (Scala science fiction reeks No. 4).[cxviii] Translator: Iskraa Bundels [Dutch]

e in **The Best of Edmond Hamilton**. Edited by Leigh Brackett. Garden City, NY.: Nelson Doubleday, 1977, p. cloth. [collection]

ea in **The Best of Edmond Hamilton**. Edited by Leigh Brackett. : Ballentine, 1977, p. paper. [collection]

f as "Ein Ausgetossner" in **Die Besten Stories**. _: <publisher unknown> 1980, p. (PSF 6701).

B235 "The Broken Stars" as **Le retour aux etoiles**. _: Editions J'ai Lu. 1967, p. Translator: Frank Straschitz. [French]

REPRINTS:

b in **Les rois des etoiles & Retour aux etoiles**. _: Ed. Opta, 1968, p. [Classique SF: 12] [French]

c as "Konigreich Der Sterne" in **An Den Ufern Der Unendlichkiet**. Rastt: Hubert Strassl, 1968, p. (U571). [German]

d in **Return To the Stars**. New York, NY.: Lancer, 1970, p. 207 paper. (74612).

e in **Return To the Stars**. Prestige Books, 1969, p. paper.

f in **Ihre Heimat sind die Sterne**. Rastatt/Baden: Erich Pabel Verlag, May 1976, p. (TTB 274). [German]

g as "Die Sternenkonigreiche" in **Ruckkehr Zu Den Sternen**. 1980, p. (HSF 3781). [German]

h in **Regresso Aos Ceus**. Lisboa: Edicao <Livros do Brasil>, <year>, p. (N 237). Translator: Eurico Fonseca. [Brazillian]

i in <u>Fantastic</u>, 18:2 (December, 1968): 6-36. Illustrator: Dan Adkins.

B236 "Horror From the Magellanic" as **Le retour aux etoiles**. _: Editions J'ai Lu. 1967, p. Translator: Frank Straschitz. [French]

REPRINTS:

c in **Les rois des etoiles & Retour aux etoiles**. _: Ed. Opta, 1968, p. [Classique SF: 12] [French]

d as "Konigreich Der Sterne" in **An Den Ufern Der Unendlichkiet**. Rastatt: Hubert Strassl, 1968, p. (U571). [collection] [German]

e in **Return To the Stars**. New York, NY.: Lancer, 1970, p. 207 paper. (74612).

f in **Return To the Stars**. Prestige Books, 1969, p. paper.

g in **Ihre Heimat sind die Sterne**. Rastatt/Baden: Erich Pabel Verlag, May 1976. (TTB 274). [German]

h as "Die Sternenkonigreiche" in **Ruckkehr Zu Den Sternen**. _: <publisher unknown> 1980, p. (HSF 3781). [collection] [German]

i in **Regresso Aos Ceus**. Lisboa: Edicao <Livros do Brasil>, <year>, p.

(N237). Translator: Eurico Fonseca. [Brazillian]

B237 "Iron One" in **Signs & Wonder**. Edited by Roger Elwood. _: Revell, 1972, p.

B238 "Stark and the Star Kings"[cxix] with Leigh Brackett, in **The Last Dangerous Visions**. Edited by Harlan Ellison, Unpublished.

REPRINTS:

b in **Stark and the Star Kings**, Edited by Stephen Haffner. Royal Oak, Michigan: Haffner Press. 2005, 648 p. (9.3 x 6.2 x 1.7 in.) Trade Edition: ISBN: 1-893887-2. 100-copy Slipcased Limited Edition (signed by Jakes & Ebel): ISBN: 1-893887-17-0; ISBN-10: 1893887162.; ISBN-13: 978-1893887169 Illustrated by Ax Ebel. Introduction by John Jakes.

c Riverdale, NY: Baen Books. February 1, 2008. SKU: 1893887162.

For more information on pseudonyms please see Appendix B - Pseudonyms

---

The following stories are referred to in correspondence housed in the Jack Williamson collection at Golden Library of the Eastern New Mexico Universty. However no publication information has been found on any of them.

"The Friction Killer"

This is mentioned in a letter from Charles D. Horning (Wonder Stories) dated 8 February, 1935. Apparently Mr. Hamilton turned down the offer to write this story. Mr. Gatter's synopsis was turned over to Dr. Keller, presumedly he then wrote the story.

"The Three Trolls"

This was the first story of Mr. Hamilton's that Farnsworth Wright turned down for publication. From a letter by Mr. Wright (Weird Tales) was dated 24 October 1932.

“The Four Immortals”

This was possibly published elsewhere under a different title. It was referred to in a letter by Farnsworth Wright (Weird Tales) dated 12 February 1935.

“The Hole in Time”

This was referred to in a letter from Farnsworth Wright (Weird Tales) dated 7 July 1936.

“Ghost Planet”

This is from a letter dated 23 February 1945 by Leo Margulies. Possibly a story intended for the comics. This was probably retitled “The Dead Planet.”

“Electro-Education Unlimited”

From a letter dated 22 March 1946 by Leo Margulies. This was probably retitled “The Knowledge Machine.” In the story there is a company named Electron Education Unlimited.

“The End of the World was Long Ago”

This is from a letter dated 21 March 1959 by Leo Margulies. This possibly was a story for the comics.

“The Man Who Missed the Moon”

This is from a letter dated 26 June 1959 by Leo Margulies. This possibly was a story for the comics.

“The House of the Nine Worlds”

This is from a letter by 22 June 1945 by Sam Merwin.

“Power Loot From Mars”

This is from a letter dated 10 October 1945 by Sam Merwin.

“Dying Fingers Point”

This is from a blurb underneath the title/author of “Face to Face.” It says: “From the same authors as Dying Fingers Point and .”

“Matériel humain,” in Fiction 22 [French]

C
Correspondence

All dates are as written or typed on the letter itself by the correspondent. In the few instances where there was no date the date was taken from the postmark if possible. These are indicated by the word postmark in the Notes column.

Letters to Edmond Hamilton, or both Edmond & Leigh - By Date

Date	From	Reference	Notes
	?	H1 M687a	Pub. Report for "Horror on the Asteroid"
	Albert P. Blaustein	H1 B645	Re: "The Invisible Matter" April 30 Science Detect.
	Albert P. Blaustein	H1 B645	
	Ray Bradbury	H1 B798	
	Avram Davidson	H1 B753	
	BG Davis	H1 A489	Bulletin to Contibutors (2 copies)
	T.E. Dikty	H1 D576	"What's It Like Out There?" Reprint permission
	Helen McCloy Dresser	H1 M331	
	K.G. Dunn	H1 M678b	
	First Fandom	H1 M678c	
	Oscar J. Friend	H1 F865	
	Oscar J. Friend	H1 F865	
	John H Guidry	H1 M678c	New Orleans SF Assoc.
	John Jakes	H1 M6	
	David Jones	H1 M678b	
	Indian S.L.B.T report	H1 N535	
	Schuyler Miller	H1 M651	
	Samuel Mines	H1 M576	
	Henry Moskowitz	H1 M678c	
	Evelyn Paige	H1 M678e	
	Raymond A Palmer	H1 A489	Notice to Contributors
	Raymond A Palmer	H1 A489	Notice to Contributors
	Penguin Press	H1 M687a	Announcement

Date	From	Refernce	Notes
	E. Hoffman Price	H1 P946	
	The Pub. Fiscal Corp	H1 M687a	Announcement (2 copies)
	Danny Rowe	H1 M678e	
	The Sci-Fi Forum	H1 M678c	
	Scwartz & Weisinger	H1 M687a	
	Sidney Soloman	H1 F317	(Frederick Fell, Inc.)
	Charles S. Strong	H1 M576	
	Tom Swicegood	H1 S976	
	Tom Swicegood	H1 S976	
	Tom Swicegood	H1 S976	
	David Vern	H1 A489	
	Mort Weisinger	H1 W428	
	Mort Weisinger	H1 W428	
	Farnsworth Wright	H1 W949	
V-J Day	Mort Weisinger	H1 W428	
Tues Morn	Manly Wade Wellman	H1 W452	
Wed. Noon 1944	Jack Williamson	H1 W731	
2/25/1925	Farnsworth Wright	H1 W949	
2/1/1926	Farnsworth Wright	H1 W949	
2/9/1926	Farnsworth Wright	H1 W949	
3/22/1926	Farnsworth Wright	H1 W949	
3/22/1926	Farnsworth Wright	H1 W949	
3/26/1926	Farnsworth Wright	H1 W949	
3/29/1926	Charles Fort	H1 F736	
5/14/1926	Farnsworth Wright	H1 W949	
5/18/1926	Farnsworth Wright	H1 W949	
5/27/1926	Charles Fort	H1 F736	
7/12/1926	Farnsworth Wright	H1 W949	
7/15/1926	Farnsworth Wright	H1 W949	
8/31/1926	William R. Sprenger	H1 S768	
9/11/1926	Farnsworth Wright	H1 W949	
10/25/1926	Charles Fort	H1 F736	
11/29/1926	William R. Sprenger	H1 S768	
12/16/1926	William R. Sprenger	H1 S768	
1/8/1927	Farnsworth Wright	H1 W949	
2/23/1927	Farnsworth Wright	H1 W949	
6/13/1927	Farnsworth Wright	H1 W949	
8/29/1927	Miriam Bourne	H1 A489	
9/3/1927	H. Gernsback	H1 A489	"The Comet Doom" Acceptable

Date	From	Refernce	Notes
9/28/1927	Miriam Bourne	H1 A489	
1/21/1928	Farnsworth Wright	H1 W949	
3/17/1928	Farnsworth Wright	H1 W949	
10/26/1928	H. Gernsback	H1 A489	
10/30/1928	T. Everett Harre	H1 H296	
11/28/1928	H. Gernsback	H1 A489	"Locked Worlds" Acceptable
12/8/1928	T. Everett Harre	H1 H296	
1/19/1929	Farnsworth Wright	H1 W949	
3/2/1929	Miriam Bourne	H1 A489	
3/6/1929	Miriam Bourne	H1 A489	
3/5/1929	H. Gernsback	H1 G376	
3/11/1929	H. Gernsback	H1 G376	
4/5/1929	H. Gernsback	H1 G376	
5/10/1929	Miriam Bourne	H1 A489	"The Other Side of the Moon" Acceptable
8/7/1929	T. Everett Harre	H1 H296	
8/12/1929	H. Gernsback	H1 G376	
8/14/1929	T. Everett Harre	H1 H296	
8/29/1929	T. Everett Harre	H1 H296	
11/12/1929	Miriam Bourne	H1 A489	"The Universe Wreckers" Acceptable
11/13/1929	H. Gernsback	H1 G376	
11/16/1929	David Lasser	H1 L347	
12/12/1929	H. Gernsback	H1 G376	
1/7/1930	H. Gernsback	H1 G376	
1/10/1930	Astounding	H1 M687a	Re: "Monsters of Mars"
1/14/1930	Miriam Bourne	H1 A489	
1/18/1930	Harry Bates	H1 B329	
2/25/1930	H. Gernsback	H1 G376	
3/11/1930	David Lasser	H1 L347	
3/14/1930	Astounding	H1 M687a	Re: "The Second Satellite"
3/17/1930	David Lasser	H1 L347	
4/30/1930	Farnsworth Wright	H1 W949	
6/4/1930	David Lasser	H1 L347	
7/3/1930	David Lasser	H1 L347	
8/15/1930	Miriam Bourne	H1 A489	"The Meteor Man"
11/26/1930	Miriam Bourne	H1 A489	

Date	From	Refernce	Notes
2/17/1931	Charles Fort	H1 F736	
3/3/1931	Astounding	H1 M687a	Re: "The Sargasso of Space"
5/6/1931	S. J.	H1 M687a	Re: "Dead Legs"
6/8/1931	Farnsworth Wright	H1 W949	
6/24/1931	William R. Sprenger	H1 S768	
9/7/1931	Abraham Merritt	H1 M572	
11/19/1931	David Lasser	H1 L347	
12/4/1931	David Lasser	H1 L347	
12/9/1931	Farnsworth Wright	H1 W949	
2/24/1932	H. Gernsback	H1 G376	
2/24/1932	J. Harvey Haggard	H1 M678e	
3/25/1932	Abraham Merritt	H1 M572	
4/28/1932	Harry Bates	H1 B329	
10/20/1932	Florence C. Bothmer	H1 A489	"Vanishing Iron" for ASQ
10/24/1932	Farnsworth Wright	H1 W949	
10/28/1932	Harry Bates	H1 B329	
2/14/1933	Farnsworth Wright	H1 W949	
3/7/1933	Farnsworth Wright	H1 W949	
6/15/1933	Farnsworth Wright	H1 W949	
8/28/1933	Farnsworth Wright	H1 W949	
9/28/1933	Farnsworth Wright	H1 W949	
11/1/1933	William Crawford	H1 M687a	
11/24/1933	William R. Sprenger	H1 S768	
12/18/1933	Russ Hodgkins	H1 H688	
12/19/1933	T. O'Conor Sloane Ph	H1 A489	Re: "Vanishing Iron"
12/27/1933	William R. Sprenger	H1 S768	
1/4/1934	Russ Hodgkins	H1 H688	
1/30/1934	William R. Sprenger	H1 S768	
2/5/1934	H. Gernsback	H1 G376	
2/15/1934	Florence C. Bothmer	H1 A489	"Colonists of Mars" Aceptable
3/31/1934	Farnsworth Wright	H1 W949	
5/16/1934	Farnsworth Wright	H1 W949	
5/25/1934	Julius Schwartz	H1 S411	
5/31/1934	Mort Weisinger	H1 W428	
8/13/1934	William R. Sprenger	H1 S768	
10/24/1934	Mort Weisinger	H1 W428	
11/3/1934	Mort Weisinger	H1 W428	

Date	From	Refernce	Notes
1/31/1935	William R. Sprenger	H1 S768	
2/8/1935	Russ Hodgkins	H1 H688	
2/13/1935	Farnsworth Wright	H1 W949	
2/16/1935	Farnsworth Wright	H1 W949	
5/2/1935	Farnsworth Wright	H1 W949	
8/30/1935	T. O'Conor Sloane Ph	H1 A489	Re: "Vanishing Iron"
10/16/1935	Doone Burks	H1 M687a	
2/7/1936	Russ Hodgkins	H1 H688	
2/21/1936	Leo Margulies	H1 M331	
7/7/1936	Farnsworth Wright	H1 W949	
1/25/1937	Farnsworth Wright	H1 W949	
2/6/1937	William R. Sprenger	H1 S768	
2/13/1937	Charles Fort	H1 F736	
4/16/1937	Farnsworth Wright	H1 W949	
10/26/1937	Farnsworth Wright	H1 W949	
12/22/1937	William R. Sprenger	H1 S768	
1/26/1938	BG Davis	H1 A489	
2/16/1938	Farnsworth Wright	H1 W949	
3/11/1938	Raymond A palmer	H1 A489	
6/6/1938	John W. Campbell Jr.	H1 C188	
7/21/1938	Farnsworth Wright	H1 W949	
10/10/1938	Raymond A Palmer	H1 A489	Notice to Contributors
10/27/1938	John W. Campbell Jr.	H1 C188	
11/28/1938	Walter H. Gillinger	H1 G481	
2/17/1939	Farnsworth Wright	H1 W949	
6/13/1939	Mort Weisinger	H1 W428	
10/9/39	Julius Schwartz	H1 S411	
10/20/1939	Farnsworth Wright	H1 W949	
12/11/1939	Farnsworth Wright	H1 W949	
1/29/1940	Farnsworth Wright	H1 W949	
4/12/1940	David Vern	H1 A489	Re: "The Incredible Three"
5/7/1940	Walter H. Gillinger	H1 G481	
5/22/1940	David Vern	H1 A489	
6/25/1940	David Vern	H1 A489	
7/15/1940	Walter H. Gillinger	H1 G481	
8/13/1940	Monte	H1 M678e	

Date	From	Refernce	Notes
9/9/1941	Walter H. Gillinger	H1 G481	
10/10/1941	Leo Margulies	H1 M331	
2/27/1942	Oscar J. Friend	H1 F865	
4/9/1942	Ray Palmer	H1 M678d	
4/14/1942	Leo Margulies	H1 M331	
4/21/1942	Leo Margulies	H1 M331	
5/7/1942	Oscar J. Friend	H1 F865	
5/22/1942	Leo Margulies	H1 M331	
6/9/1942	Oscar J. Friend	H1 F865	
8/28/1942	Leo Margulies	H1 M331	
12/9/1942	Oscar J. Friend	H1 F865	
3/22/1943	Oscar J. Friend	H1 F865	
5/7/1943	Leo Margulies	H1 M331	
6/3/1943	Oscar J. Friend	H1 F865	
8/10/1943	Julius Schwartz	H1 S411	
8/20/1943	Leo Margulies	H1 M331	
10/1/1943	Oscar J. Friend	H1 F865	
10/7/1943	Ray Bradbury	H1 B798	
11/17/1943	Julius Schwartz	H1 S411	
12/10/1943	Julius Schwartz	H1 S411	
12/17/1943	Jack Williamson	H1 W731	
1/19/1944	Oscar J. Friend	H1 F865	
1/21/1944	Leo Margulies	H1 M331	
1/24/1944	Oscar J. Friend	H1 F865	
1/25/1944	Walter H. Gillinger	H1 G481	
1/26/1944	Oscar J. Friend	H1 F865	
1/31/1944	Oscar J. Friend	H1 F865	
1/31/1944	Julius Schwartz	H1 S411	
2/7/1944	Julius Schwartz	H1 S411	
2/9/1944	Oscar J. Friend	H1 F865	
2/18/1944	Jack Williamson	H1 W731	
3/4/1944	Julius Schwartz	H1 S411	
5/4/1944	Jack Williamson	H1 W731	
5/9/1944	Leo Margulies	H1 M331	
5/17/1944	Leo Margulies	H1 M331	
5/17/1944	Julius Schwartz	H1 S411	
5/23/1944	Lamont Buchanan	H1 B919	Eyrie Letter
6/10/1944	Julius Schwartz	H1 S411	
6/16/1944	Leo Margulies	H1 M331	
7/4/1944	Julius Schwartz	H1 S411	

Date	From	Refernce	Notes
7/10/1944	Jack Williamson	H1 W731	
7/21/1944	Leo Margulies	H1 M331	
8/24/1944	Ray Bradbury	H1 B798	Postmark Date
9/2/1944	Julius Schwartz	H1 S411	
9/8/1944	Lamont Buchanan	H1 B919	Re: Eyrie Notes for "Priestess of the Labrynth"
9/25/1944	Leo Margulies	H1 M331	
10/23/1944	Jack Williamson	H1 W731	
11/2/1944	Jack Williamson	H1 W731	
11/10/1944	Lamont Buchanan	H1 B919	Re: "The Inn Outside the World"
12/15/1944	Leo Margulies	H1 M331	
12/18/1944	Jack Williamson	H1 W731	
12/20/1944	Leo Margulies	H1 M331	
1/2/1945	Lamont Buchanan	H1 B919	
1/5/1945	Leo Margulies	H1 M331	
2/23/1945	Leo Margulies	H1 M331	
3/15/1945	Lamont Buchanan	H1 B919	Request Eyrie for "The Inn Outside the World"
3/18/1945	S.A. McElfresh	H1 M678b	
3/21/1945	Leo Margulies	H1 M331	
3/27/1945	Lamont Buchanan	H1 B919	Thanks Eyrie "The Inn Outside the World"
3/30/1945	S.A. McElfresh	H1 M678b	
4/11/1945	Jack Williamson	H1 W731	
5/4/1945	Thos. O. Mabott	H1 M678b	
5/20/1945	Jack Williamson	H1 W731	
6/1/1945	Lamont Buchanan	H1 B919	Re: "Lost Elysium"
6/9/1945	Julius Schwartz	H1 S411	
6/21/1945	Walter H. Gillinger	H1 G481	
6/22/1945	Sam Merwin Jr.	H1 M576	
7/2/1945	Lamont Buchanan	H1 B919	Re: "Lost Elysium"
7/2/1945	Sam Merwin Jr.	H1 M576	
7/2/1945	Jack Williamson	H1 W731	
7/9/1945	Mort Weisinger	H1 W428	
8/3/1945	Sam Merwin Jr.	H1 M576	
8/10/1945	Charles S. Strong	H1 M576	
8/23/1945	Mort Weisinger	H1 W428	
9/27/1945	Jack Williamson	H1 W731	
10/1/1945	Mort Weisinger	H1 W428	

Date	From	Refernce	Notes
10/3/1945	Walter H. Gillinger	H1 G481	
10/8/1945	Raymond A. Palmer	H1 A489	Re: "The Star Kings"
10/10/1945	Samuel Mines	H1 M576	
10/16/1945	Mort Weisinger	H1 W428	
10/30/1945	Bernard Breslaner	H1 B842	From Detective Comics Inc. Re: Batman Story
11/23/1945	Sam Merwin Jr.	H1 M576	
11/29/1945	Walter H. Gillinger	H1 G481	
11/30/1945	Lamont Buchanan	H1 M678d	
1/2/1946	Lamont Buchanan	H1 M678d	
1/18/1946	Leo Margulies	H1 M331	
1/24/1946	R. G. (Bob) Jones	H1 M678d	
1/28/1946	Walter H. Gillinger	H1 G481	
2/7/1946	Lamont Buchanan	H1 B919	Re: "Day of Judgement"
2/10/1946	Jack Williamson	H1 W731	
2/21/1946	Leo Margulies	H1 M331	
3/1/1946	Lamont Buchanan	H1 B919	Re: " Day of Judgement"
3/1/1946	Leo Margulies	H1 M331	
3/5/1946	Lamont Buchanan	H1 B919	
3/15/1946	Leo Margulies	H1 M331	
3/16/1946	Walter H. Gillinger	H1 G481	
3/20/1946	Raymond A Palmer	H1 A489	
3/22/1946	Leo Margulies	H1 M331	
4/26/1946	Leo Margulies	H1 M331	
5/6/1946	Walter H. Gillinger	H1 G481	
7/1/1946	Lamont Buchanan	H1 B919	Re: "The King of Shadows"
7/12/1946	Mort Weisinger	H1 W428	
11/1/1946	Leo Margulies	H1 M331	
11/9/1946	Walter H. Gillinger	H1 G481	
12/14/1946	Robert E. Briney	H1 M678e	
12/30/1946	Sam Merwin Jr.	H1 M576	
3/20/1947	Lamont Buchanan	H1 B919	
4/22/1947	Sam Merwin Jr.	H1 M576	
4/22/1947	Donald A. Wollheim	H1 W864	
6/2/1947	Russ Hodgkins	H1 H688	
7/1/1947	Russ Hodgkins	H1 H688	
7/18/1947	Lamont Buchanan	H1 B919	
8/8/1947	Sam Merwin Jr.	H1 M576	
8/20/1947	Russ Hodgkins	H1 H688	

Date	From	Refernce	Notes
9/2/1947	Lamont Buchanan	H1 B919	Re: "The Might-Have-Been"
9/23/1947	Joseph Green	H1 M576	
10/4/1947	Donald B. Day	H1 M678c	
10/24/1947	Leo Margulies	H1 M331	
12/12/1947	Sam Merwin Jr.	H1 M576	
2/6/1948	Lamont Buchanan	H1 M678d	
4/9/1948	Sam Merwin Jr.	H1 M576	
4/30/1948	Lamont Buchanan	H1 B919	Re: "The Watcher of the Ages"
8/5/1948	Drayton S. Haff	H1 M687a	
8/16/1948	William L. Hamling	H1 H223	
11/11/1948	Oscar J. Friend	H1 F865	
11/24/1948	Frederik Pohl	H1 P748	
12/1/1948	Oscar J. Friend	H1 F865	
1/28/1949	Oscar J. Friend	H1 F865	
2/14/1949	Frederik Pohl	H1 P748	
2/28/1949	Oscar J. Friend	H1 F865	
3/2/1949	Oscar J. Friend	H1 F865	
3/23/1949	Sam Merwin Jr.	H1 M576	
3/29/1949	Samuel Mines	H1 M576	
6/8/1949	Ray Bradbury	H1 B798	
6/8/1949	Jack Williamson	H1 W731	
6/10/1949	Sam Merwin Jr.	H1 M576	
6/14/1949	Henry Kuttner	H1 K97	
6/16/1949	Henry Kuttner	H1 K97	
7/2/1949	Ray Bradbury	H1 B798	
7/6/1949	Henry Kuttner	H1 K97	
7/21/1949	Dorthy McIlwraith	H1 B919	
7/22/1949	Oscar J. Friend	H1 F865	
7/26/1949	August Derleth	H1 D431	
7/28/1949	Oscar J. Friend	H1 F865	
8/1/1949	A. Derleth	H1 D431	
8/3/1949	Ray Bradbury	H1 B798	
8/19/1949	Sam Merwin Jr.	H1 M576	
9/12/1949	Ray Bradbury	H1 B798	
9/17/1949	A. Derleth	H1 D431	
9/22/1949	Sam Merwin Jr.	H1 M576	
9/24/1949	A. Derleth	H1 D431	
9/26/1949	L. Sprague DeCamp	H1 D291	
10/4/1949	Oscar J. Friend	H1 F865	

Date	From	Refernce	Notes
10/8/1949	Oscar J. Friend	H1 F865	
10/26/1949	Ray Bradbury	H1 B798	
11/7/1949	Ray Bradbury	H1 B798	
11/7/1949	Ray Bradbury	H1 B798	Postmark Date
11/17/1949	Henry Kuttner	H1 K97	
11/18/1949	Oscar J. Friend	H1 F865	
11/30/1949	Ray Bradbury	H1 B798	
12/1/1949	Oscar J. Friend	H1 F865	
12/16/1949	Sam Merwin Jr.	H1 M576	
12/17/1949	Oscar J. Friend	H1 F865	
12/30/1949	Sam Merwin Jr.	H1 M576	
1/2/1950	Mort Weisinger	H1 W428	
1/6/1950	Ruth Amslow (F. Fell)	H1 F317	
1/13/1950	Ray Bradbury	H1 B798	
1/20/1950	Ray Bradbury	H1 B798	
1/29/1950	E. Hoffman Price	H1 P946	
2/15/1950	Oscar J. Friend	H1 F865	
3/3/1950	Leo Margulies	H1 M331	
3/7/1950	Ray Bradbury	H1 B798	
3/8/1950	Oscar J. Friend	H1 F865	
3/16/1950	L. Sprague DeCamp	H1 D291	
4/1/1950	Oscar J. Friend	H1 F865	
4/7/1950	Ray Bradbury	H1 B798	
4/11/1950	Oscar J. Friend	H1 F865	
4/12/1950	Henry Kuttner	H1 K97	
4/19/1950	Oscar J. Friend	H1 F865	
4/24/1950	Oscar J. Friend	H1 F865	
5/12/1950	Sam Merwin Jr.	H1 M576	
5/17/1950	Ned Brown	H1 M687a	
5/23/1950	Oscar J. Friend	H1 F865	
6/8/1950	Ray Bradbury	H1 B798	
6/28/1950	Sam Merwin Jr.	H1 M576	
6/29/1950	F.J. Ackerman	H1 A182	
7/10/1950	Sam Merwin Jr.	H1 M576	
7/12/1950	Oscar J. Friend	H1 F865	
7/12/1950	Oscar J. Friend	H1 F865	
7/18/1950	Oscar J. Friend	H1 F865	
7/28/1950	F.J. Ackerman	H1 A182	
7/28/1950	Sam Merwin Jr.	H1 M576	
8/8/1950	Ray Bradbury	H1 B798	
8/17/1950	Oscar J. Friend	H1 F865	
8/24/1950	Oscar J. Friend	H1 F865	

Date	From	Refernce	Notes
8/29/1950	Ray Bradbury	H1 B798	Postmark Date
9/19/1950	Ray Bradbury	H1 B798	Postmark Date
9/23/1950	Oscar J. Friend	H1 F865	
10/6/1950	Sam Merwin Jr.	H1 M576	
10/7/1950	Mr. Gene Garretson	H1 M678c	
10/8/1950	Ray Bradbury	H1 B798	
10/24/1950	Miss Betty Steward	H1 M678c	
10/25/1950	Oscar J. Friend	H1 F865	
10/30/1950	Oscar J. Friend	H1 F865	
11/1/1950	Oscar J. Friend	H1 F865	
11/30/1950	Oscar J. Friend	H1 F865	Change of Address Notice; Postmark Date
11/30/1950	James J. Klinikowski	H1 M678c	
12/6/1950	Oscar J. Friend	H1 F865	
12/13/1950	Oscar J. Friend	H1 F865	
12/28/1950	Ray Bradbury	H1 B798	
1/10/1951	Oscar J. Friend	H1 F865	
1/12/1951	E. Hoffman Price	H1 P946	
1/15/1951	Sidney Soloman (F. Fell)	H1 F317	
2/23/1951	Sam Merwin Jr.	H1 M576	
2/28/1951	Ernest O Stout	H1 M678b	
3/3/1951	Oscar J. Friend	H1 F865	
3/6/1951	Sam Merwin Jr.	H1 M576	
3/22/1951	Ray Bradbury	H1 B798	
3/30/1951	Ray Bradbury	H1 B798	
4/18/1951	Oscar J. Friend	H1 F865	
4/26/1951	Oscar J. Friend	H1 F865	
6/25/1951	Ray Bradbury	H1 B798	
8/3/1951	Samuel Mines	H1 M576	
8/21/1951	Oscar J. Friend	H1 F865	
9/3/1951	Henry Kuttner	H1 K97	
10/18/1951	F. Fell	H1 F317	
10/25/1951	Avgust Petrisic	H1 F865	
11/1/1951	Ray Bradbury	H1 B798	
11/23/1951	F. Fell Inc. w/O. Kiln	H1 F317	Royalty Statement "The Star Kings"
11/23/1951	F. Fell Inc. w/O. Kiln	H1 F317	Royalty Statement "City at World's End"
11/26/1951	Wayne DaMetz (F. Fell)	H1 F317	
11/27/1951	Samuel Mines	H1 M576	
11/28/1951	Oscar J. Friend	H1 F865	

Date	From	Refernce	Notes
12/3/1951	L. Sprague DeCamp	H1 D291	
12/5/1951	Oscar J. Friend	H1 F865	
12/28/1951	Amaryllis Sponagle	H1 M678b	
1/5/1952	Oscar J. Friend	H1 F865	
1/15/1952	Thos. Taylor	H1 M678b	
1/29/1952	A. Derleth	H1 D431	
3/5/1952	Oscar J. Friend	H1 F865	
3/6/1952	E. Hoffman Price	H1 P946	
3/27/1952	Samuel Mines	H1 M576	
4/3/1952	Oscar J. Friend	H1 F865	
5/20/1952	E. Hoffman Price	H1 P946	
5/23/1952	F. Fell Inc. w/O. Kiln	H1 F317	Royalty Statement "City at World's End"
5/24/1952	Thos. Taylor	H1 M678b	
6/6/1952	Samuel Mines	H1 M576	
6/10/1952	Oscar J. Friend	H1 F865	
6/23/1952	Arthur Brandwein	H1 M678b	
6/25/1952	Samuel Mines	H1 M576	
7/5/1952	Oscar J. Friend	H1 F865	Change of Address Notice; Postmark Date
7/21/1952	Oscar J. Friend	H1 F865	
8/2/1952	Merle I. Franklin	H1 M678e	
8/9/1952	L. Sprague DeCamp	H1 D291	
8/19/1952	L. Sprague DeCamp	H1 D291	
9/5/1952	Oscar J. Friend	H1 F865	
9/10/1952	L. Sprague DeCamp	H1 D291	
9/14/1952	Henry Kuttner	H1 K97	
9/22/1952	Oscar J. Friend	H1 F865	
10/17/1952	L. Sprague DeCamp	H1 D291	
11/13/1952	L. Sprague DeCamp	H1 D291	
11/14/1952	L. Sprague DeCamp	H1 D291	
11/24/1952	F..Fell Inc. w/O. Kiln	H1 F317	Combined Royalty "The Star Kings" & "City at World's End"
11/24/1952	F. Fell Inc. w/O. Kiln	H1 F317	Royalty Stateme "The Star Kings"
11/24/1952	F. Fell Inc. w/O. Kiln	H1 F317	Royalty Statement "City at World's End"
11/26/1952	Robert W. Pratt	H1 M678b	
11/28/1952	Samuel Mines	H1 M576	
12/17/1952	Oscar J. Friend	H1 F865	

Date	From	Refernce	Notes
2/6/1953	L. Sprague DeCamp	H1 D291	
2/25/1953	William L. Hamling	H1 H223	
3/6/1953	Samuel Mines	H1 M576	
3/10/1953	Samuel Mines	H1 M576	
4/9/1953	Fanny Ellsworth	H1 M576	
4/14/1953	Ray Palmer	H1 M678d	
4/29/1953	Fanny Ellsworth	H1 M576	
5/5/1953	F. Fell Inc. w/O. Kiln	H1 F317	Royalty Statement “City at World’s End”
5/5/1953	William L. Hamling	H1 H223	
5/7/1953	Oscar J. Friend	H1 F865	
8/23/1953	Ray Bradbury	H1 B798	
9/4/1953	L. Sprague DeCamp	H1 D291	
9/17/1953	Ray Bradbury	H1 B798	
9/17/1953	L. Sprague DeCamp	H1 D291	
9/28/1953	Anthony Boucher	H1 B753	
10/8/1953	Oscar J. Friend	H1 F865	
10/9/1953	L. Sprague DeCamp	H1 D291	
10/12/1953	Ruth Stark	H1 M687a	
10/14/1953	Ray Bradbury	H1 B798	
11/25/1953	Bea Mahaffey	H1 M687a	
12/3/1953	Bea Mahaffey	H1 A489	
12/10/1953	F. Fell Inc. w/O. Kiln	H1 F317	Royalty Statement “The Star Kings”
12/10/1953	F. Fell Inc. w/O. Kiln	H1 F317	Royalty Statement “City at World’s End”
12/15/1953	Robert N. Rolfe	H1 R747	
1/23/1954	Mick McCowas	H1 B753	Re: “They Went into Space”
2/26/1954	Oscar J. Friend	H1 F865	
3/23/1954	Cylvia Klieinman	H1 M331	
3/28/1954	A. Boucher	H1 B753	
4/1/1954	Robert P. Mills	H1 M657	
4/22/1954	John Keipp	H1 M678b	
5/7/1954	Ray	H1 M687a	
5/10/1954	Jahn Keipp	H1 M678b	
5/27/1954	T.E. Dikty	H1 D576	
6/4/1954	Basil Wells	H1 W453	
6/6/1954	Andre Norton	H1 N882	
6/10/1954	Samuel Mines	H1 M576	
6/10/1954	Basil Wells	H1 W453	

Date	From	Refernce	Notes
6/19/1954	Oscar J. Friend	H1 F865	
6/28/1954	T.E. Dikty	H1 D576	
7/9/1954	Samuel Mines	H1 M576	
7/12/1954	Jack Williamson	H1 W731	
7/23/1954	F. Fell	H1 F317	
7/26/1954	Edward E. Smith	H1 S646	
8/2/1954	F. Fell Inc. w/O. Kiln	H1 F317	Royalty Statement "City at World's End"
8/6/1954	Edward E. Smith	H1 S646	
8/26/1954	Oscar J. Friend	H1 F865	
9/29/1954	Oscar J. Friend	H1 F865	
11/3/1954	L. Sprague DeCamp	H1 D291	
1/22/1955	E. Hoffman Price	H1 P946	
3/7/1955	Robert H. Searcy	H1 M678b	
4/2/1955	A. Derleth	H1 D431	
4/7/1955	Robert H. Searcy	H1 M678b	
4/21/1955	Art Nyman	H1 M678b	
4/28/1955	Robert H Searcy	H1 M678b	
9/20/1955	Gerald J. Pollinger	H1 F865	
9/30/1955	Edward E. Smith	H1 S646	
10/12/1955	William L. Hamling	H1 H223	
10/27/1955	William L. Hamling	H1 H223	
11/5/1955	William L. Hamling	H1 H223	
11/6/1955	Larry Farsace	H1 M678c	
11/30/1955	William L. Hamling	H1 H223	
12/10/1955	William L. Hamling	H1 H223	
1/10/1956	Alberta Leek	H1 M678b	
1/20/1956	Basil Wells	H1 W453	
2/3/1956	William L. Hamling	H1 H223	
2/26/1956	William L. Hamling	H1 H223	
3/1/1956	Julius Schwartz	H1 S411	
3/5/1956	William L. Hamling	H1 H223	
3/15/1956	Paul W. Fairman	H1 A489	
3/31/1956	Miss R.(oberta) Wild	H1 M678b	
4/4/1956	William L. Hamling	H1 H223	
4/11/1956	Oscar J. Friend	H1 F865	
4/30/1956	Julius Schwartz	H1 S411	
5/22/1956	Julius Schwartz	H1 S411	
5/27/1956	E. Hoffman Price	H1 P946	
5/29/1956	William L. Hamling	H1 H223	
6/8/1956	F.J. Ackerman	H1 A182	
6/11/1956	E. Hoffman Price	H1 P946	

Date	From	Refernce	Notes
6/20/1956	F.J. Ackerman	H1 A182	
6/24/1956	E. Hoffman Price	H1 P946	
6/28/1956	F.J. Ackerman	H1 A182	
7/7/1956	William L. Hamling	H1 H223	
7/9/1956	Oscar J. Friend	H1 F865	
7/9/1956	Larry Shaw	H1 S535	
7/12/1956	Basil Wells	H1 W453	
7/13/1956	Larry Shaw	H1 S535	
7/31/1956	Larry Shaw	H1 S535	
8/4/1956	F.J. Ackerman	H1 A182	
8/20/1956	William L. Hamling	H1 H223	
8/21/1956	L. Sprague DeCamp	H1 D291	
8/23/1956	Oscar J. Friend	H1 F865	
8/23/1956	Larry Shaw	H1 S535	
8/26/1956	Larry Shaw	H1 S535	
9/14/1956	Otto Binder	H1 B613	
9/29/1956	Otto Binder	H1 B613	
10/1/1956	F. Fell	H1 F317	
10/12/1956	Oswald Train	H1 M678b	
10/16/1956	William L. Hamling	H1 H223	
10/22/1956	Oscar J. Friend	H1 F865	
10/29/1956	F.J. Ackerman	H1 A182	
10/30/1956	William L. Hamling	H1 H223	
11/27/1956	William L. Hamling	H1 H223	
12/7/1956	Mort Weisinger	H1 W428	
12/21/1956	F.J. Ackerman	H1 A182	
12/26/1956	Larry Shaw	H1 S535	
12/27/1956	William L. Hamling	H1 H223	
12/31/1956	Stephen F. Schulthei	H1 S387	
1/3/1957	Basil Wells	H1 W453	
1/12/1957	F.J. Ackerman	H1 A182	
1/23/1957	F.J. Ackerman	H1 A182	
1/27/1957	Robert Wild	H1 M678c	15th World SF Con London '57
2/8/1957	Jim Hendryx, Jr	H1 M576	
3/4/1957	William L. Hamling	H1 H223	
3/9/1957	William L. Hamling	H1 H223	
3/14/1957	C.L. Barrett, M.D.	H1 S646	
3/18/1957	James E. Gunn	H1 G976	
4/6/1957	Allan Howard	H1 M678c	
4/11/1957	Jim Hendryx, Jr.	H1 M576	

Date	From	Refernce	Notes
4/29/1957	William L. Hamling	H1 H223	
5/15/1957	E. Hoffman Price	H1 P946	
5/22/1957	William L. Hamling	H1 H223	
6/20/1957	Isabelle Taylor	H1 M687a	
6/22/1957	Edward E. Smith	H1 S646	
7/2/1957	William L. Hamling	H1 H223	
7/2/1957	William L. Hamling	H1 H223	
7/8/1957		H1 M657	
9/19/1957	Oscar J. Friend	H1 F865	
9/27/1957	William L. Hamling	H1 H223	
9/30/1957	F. Fell Inc. w/O. Kiln	H1 F317	Royalty Statement "City at World's End"
10/2/1957	Larry Shaw	H1 S535	
10/23/1957	F. Fell	H1 F317	
12/20/1957	Oscar J. Friend	H1 F865	
12/20/1957	William L. Hamling	H1 H223	
12/31/1957	William L. Hamling	H1 H223	
1/10/1958	Sondra Mandell	H1 M657	
2/4/1958	William L. Hamling	H1 H223	
2/18/1958	F. V. Fell	H1 F317	
2/28/1958	William L. Hamling	H1 H223	
3/1/1958	MI SF Society	H1 M678c	
3/17/1958	Oscar J. Friend	H1 F865	Change of Address Notice
3/26/1958	William L. Hamling	H1 H223	
3/28/1958	Winifred Glass	H1 F317	Reprint Permision "Forgotten World"
3/30/1958	Ray Bradbury	H1 B798	
4/28/1958	Julius Schwartz	H1 S411	
5/7/1958	William L. Hamling	H1 H223	
5/14/1958	Leo Margulies	H1 M331	
5/20/1958	Leo Margulies	H1 M331	
5/23/1958	F.V. Fell	H1 F317	
5/24/1958	L. Sprague DeCamp	H1 D291	
5/29/1958	Oscar J. Friend	H1 F865	
5/29/1958	Leo Margulies	H1 M331	
5/31/1958	F. Fell Inc. w/O. Kiln	H1 F317	Royalty Statement "City at World's End"
6/23/1958	F.V. Fell	H1 F317	
6/24/1958	Leo Margulies	H1 M331	
6/27/1958	Leo Margulies	H1 M331	
7/8/1958	Leo Margulies	H1 M331	

Date	From	Refernce	Notes
7/21/1958	Leo Margulies	H1 M331	
7/23/1958	Mort Weisinger	H1 W428	
7/31/1958	Jim Hendryx, Jr.	H1 M576	
8/6/1958	Leo Margulies	H1 M331	
8/13/1958	Leo Margulies	H1 M331	
8/16/1958	V.R. Emanual	H1 E58	
8/25/1958	Leo Margulies	H1 M331	
9/3/1958	V.R. Emanual	H1 E58	
9/9/1958	Leo Margulies	H1 M331	
9/12/1958	V.R. Emanual	H1 E58	
10/3/1958	Leo Margulies	H1 M331	
10/10/1958	A. Derleth	H1 D431	
10/10/1958	Leo Margulies	H1 M331	
10/20/1958	Marty Greenberg	H1 M687a	
12/5/1958	Donald A. Wollheim	H1 W864	
12/11/1958	Donald A. Wollheim	H1 W864	
12/16/1958	Leo Margulies	H1 M331	
1/7/1959	Leo Margulies	H1 M331	
1/7/1959	Manfred Alex	H1 M678b	
1/19/1959	Leo Margulies	H1 M331	
2/7/1959	William L. Hamling	H1 H223	
2/12/1959	Leo Margulies	H1 M331	
3/12/1959	Donald A. Wollheim	H1 W864	
3/21/1959	Leo Margulies	H1 M331	
4/19/1959	Oscar J. Friend	H1 F865	
5/14/1959	Cylvia K. Margulies	H1 M331	
6/26/1959	Leo Margulies	H1 M331	
7/6/1959	E. Hoffman Price	H1 P946	
7/15/1959	Leo Margulies	H1 M331	
7/21/1959	Cylvia K. Margulies	H1 M331	
7/29/1959	Cylvia K. Margulies	H1 M331	
8/7/1959	Eleanor Newburger	H1 N535	
8/8/1959	Eleanor Newburger	H1 N535	
8/19/1959	Leo Margulies	H1 M331	
9/15/1959	Indian S.L.B.T. report	H1 N535	
9/17/1959	Cylvia K. Margulies	H1 M331	
10/10/1959	E. Hoffman Price	H1 P946	
10/15/1959	Leo Margulies	H1 M331	
10/27/1959	Schuyler Miller	H1 M651	
10/29/1959	Jack Williamson	H1 W731	
11/4/1959	Leo Margulies	H1 M331	

Date	From	Refernce	Notes
12/20/1959	Tec Carnell	H1 M687a	
12/28/1959	L. Sprague DeCamp	H1 D291	
12/31/1959	Eleanor Newburger	H1 N535	
3/11/1960	Basil Wells	H1 W453	
3/16/1960	Jack Williamson	H1 W731	
3/18/1960	Damon Knight	H1 K71	
3/18/1960	Donald A. Wollheim	H1 W864	
5/5/1960	L. Sprague DeCamp	H1 D291	
5/18/1960	Ann Stern	H1 M331	
6/14/1960	Leo Margulies	H1 M331	
6/18/1960	William L. Hamling	H1 H223	
7/21/1960	Harry Jacobson	H1 M687a	
8/8/1960	Pierre Versins	H1 M687a	Note: Date on letter 29/60
9/19/1960	Ann Stern	H1 M331	
10/17/1960	Charles Beaumont	H1 B378	
10/30/1960	Charles Beaumont	H1 B378	
11/1/1960	Torquil & Co, Inc.	H1 M331	Royalty Report on "The Haunted Stars"
11/14/1960	Cele Goldsmith	H1 A489	
11/28/1960	Julius Schwartz	H1 S411	
12/2/1960	F.J. Ackerman	H1 A182	
2/8/1961	James R. Sieger	H1 S571	
2/20/1961	Cylvia K. Margulies	H1 M331	
2/27/1961	Cylvia K. Margulies	H1 M331	
4/17/1961	Donald A. Wollheim	H1 W864	
4/29/1961	Bob Silverberg	H1 S587	
5/2/1961	Pierre Versins	H1 M687a	
5/8/1961	Leo Margulies	H1 M331	
5/9/1961	Donald A. Wollheim	H1 W864	
5/19/1961	Helen McCloy Dresser	H1 M331	
5/27/1961	L. Sprague DeCamp	H1 D291	
6/27/1961	Mrs. Saima Heckmeyer	H1 M331	
6/28/1961	Cele Goldsmith	H1 M678d	
8/26/1961	Ingrid Fritzsch	H1 M678b	
8/31/1961	Helen McCloy Dresser	H1 M331	
9/25/1961	Helen McCloy Dresser	H1 M331	
10/5/1961	Damon Knight	H1 K71	
11/21/1961	Lin Carter	H1 M687a	
11/25/1961	E. Hoffman Price	H1 P946	
11/28/1961	Lin Carter	H1 C323	
12/21/1961	Leo Margulies	H1 M331	

Date	From	Refernce	Notes
12/24/1961	Helen McCloy Dresser	H1 M331	
1/6/1962	Brett Halliday	H1 M331	
2/16/1962	Robert Jennings	H1 J54	
3/5/1962	Charles Beaumont	H1 B378	
3/13/1962	Cylvia K. Margulies	H1 M331	
3/27/1962	Cele Goldsmith	H1 A489	
5/1/1962	Torquil & Co, Inc.	H1 M331	Royalties on "The HauntedStars," "Star of Life" & "Battle for the Stars"
5/8/1962	Cele Goldsmith	H1 A489	Pub. Rights "Sunfire"
5/12/1962	Robert Jennings	H1 J54	
5/12/1962	Douglas Mackey	H1 M678e	
6/3/1962	E. Hoffman Price	H1 P946	
6/17/1962	Sam Moskowitz	H1 M912	
6/24/1962	Stephen F. Schultheis	H1 S387	
6/26/1962	E. Hoffman Price	H1 P946	
8/20/1962	Douglas Taylor	H1 M678e	
8/22/1962	Cylvia K. Margulies	H1 M331	
9/6/1962	Cele Goldsmith	H1 A489	
9/19/1962	Douglas Taylor	H1 M678e	
10/29/1962	Robert G. Shively	H1 M678b	
11/1/1962	Cele Goldsmith	H1 A489	Decided on "Babylon in the Sky" as title
11/1/1962	Cele Goldsmith	H1 A489	Pub. Rights "Babylon in the Sky"
11/6/1962	Torquil & Co, Inc.	H1 M331	Royalties on "The Haunted Stars," "Star of Life" & "Battle for the Stars"
11/28/1962	Edward E. Smith	H1 S646	
12/17/1962	Leo Margulies	H1 M331	
2/17/1963	Brett Halliday	H1 M331	
2/21/1963	Donald A. Wollheim	H1 W864	
3/4/1963	John Brunner	H1 B897	Postmark Date
5/1/1963	Torquil & Co, Inc.	H1 M331	Royalties on "The Haunted Stars," "Battle for the Stars"
11/1/1963	Bill Allen	H1 M678b	

Date	From	Refernce	Notes
11/6/1963	Torquil & Co, Inc.	H1 M331	Royalties on “Star of Life,” “Battle for the Stars”
12/7/1963	E. Hoffman Price	H1 P946	
1/14/1964	Cele Goldsmith	H1 M678d	
1/20/1964	Cele Goldsmith	H1 M678d	
2/19/1964	Harry Harrison	H1 H318	
3/18/1964	E. Hoffman Price	H1 P946	
4/1/1964	AH Mercer (BSFA)	H1 M678c	
4/24/1964	Eric Frank Russell	H1 R961	
5/27/1964	Mike Moorcock	H1 M819	
9/27/1964	Alva Rogers	H1 M678e	
10/2/1964	Cele G. Lalli	H1 A489	
10/8/1964	Owen C Girley	H1 M678b	
10/12/1964	Eric Frank Russell	H1 R961	
11/18/1964	Edward E. Smith	H1 S646	
12/21/1964	E.J. Frost	H1 M678e	
12/22/1964	Steve Perrin	H1 M678c	
1/11/1965	E.J. Frost	H1 M678b	
1/29/1965	Sam Moskowitz	H1 M912	
3/23/1965	Terry Lowry	H1 M678e	
3/29/1965	Cele G. Lalli	H1 A489	
4/27/1965	Roger G. Peyton	H1 M678c	Article in Vector latest issue to letter date
9/1/1965	C.L. Barrett, M.D.	H1 S646	
7/8/1967	Bengt-Olaf Ringberg	H1 R581	
9/12/1967	Jacques Sadoul	H1 M687a	
12/10/1967	Bengt-Olaf Ringberg	H1 R581	
1/31/1968	Jacques Sadoul	H1 M687a	
2/3/1968	Blane Smith	H1 M678b	
3/14/1968	A. Bertram Chandler	H1 C455	
4/10/1968	E. Hoffman Price	H1 P946	
4/16/1968	Jannick Storm	H1 S885	
5/2/1968	Lawrence Cruikshank	H1 C955	
5/4/1968	Jannick Storm	H1 S885	
6/19/1968	E. Hoffman Price	H1 P946	
6/27/1968	Jas. P. Young	H1 M678b	
8/23/1968	E. Hoffman Price	H1 P946	
9/10/1968	Bengt-Olaf Ringberg	H1 R581	

Date	From	Refernce	Notes
9/24/1968	John H Guidry	H1 M678c	
10/14/1968	Sabastian Martinez	H1 M687a	
12/1/1968	Bengt-Olaf Ringberg	H1 R581	
1969	John J. Piera	H1 M678e	
2/4/1969	Bengt-Olaf Ringberg	H1 R581	
4/11/1969	Iwan Hedman	H1 M678c	
5/5/1969	Dan Followell	H1 M678b	
6/2/1969	Joanne Burger	H1 M678b	
6/14/1969	Dan Followell	H1 M678b	
7/21/1969	Theodore Quock	H1 M678b	
10/8/1969	Michel Demuth	H1 D389	
12/1/1969	Jeffrey Rothenberg	H1 M678b	
1/6/1975	David ?	H1 D251	

Letters From Edmond Hamilton - By Date

Date	To	Refernce	Notes
7/5/1930	David Lasser	H1 L347	
6/11/1942	Raymond Palmer	H1 A489	Response on Bottom
2/3/1944	Julius Schwartz	H1 S411	
5/19/1944	Raymond A. Palmer	H1 A489	Response on Bottom
3/28/1945	Raymond A Palmer	H1 A489	Response on Bottom
8/21/1945	Mort (M. Weisinger)	H1 S411	
1/6/1947	E. Hoffman Price	H1 P946	
2/13/1947	E. Hoffman Price	H1 P946	
7/7/1947	Russ Hodgkins	H1 H688	
11/6/1947	E. Hoffman Price	H1 P946	
12/3/1949	Oscar J. Friend	H1 F865	
7/15/1950	Oscar J. Friend	H1 F865	
4/16/1951	Mr. N.L. Pines	H1 M576	
6/14/1954	Ray(mond A . Palmer)	H1 A489	Response on Bottom
8/2/1954	Ray(mond A . Palmer)	H1 A489	Response on Bottom
2/17/1956	F.J. Ackerman	H1 A182	
2/17/1956	F.J. Ackerman	H1 A182	Rights Authorization
6/23/1956	F.J. Ackerman	H1 A182	
6/30/1956	F.J. Ackerman	H1 A182	
6/30/1956	W. J. Delaney	H1 A182	
6/30/1956	Selwyn & Blount, Ltd	H1 A182	
9/24/1956	Frederick V. Fel	H1 F317	
10/11/1956	William K. Friedman	H1 A182	
10/25/1956	F.J. Ackerman	H1 A182	
10/25/1956	William K. Friedman	H1 A182	
2/26/1957	Oscar J. Friend	H1 F865	
3/15/1957	F.J. Ackerman	H1 A182	
3/15/1957	F.J. Ackerman	H1 A182	
8/10/1957	Oscar J. Friend	H1 F865	
10/16/1957	Frederick V. Fel	H1 F317	

Date	To	Refernce	Notes
11/5/1957	Frederick V. Fel	H1 F317	
2/6/1958	Frederick V. Fel	H1 F317	
5/19/1958	Frederick V. Fel	H1 F317	
5/19/1958	Leo Margulies	H1 M331	
5/24/1958	Leo Margulies	H1 M331	
5/27/1958	Leo Margulies	H1 M331	
6/26/1958	Leo Margulies	H1 M331	
8/9/1058	Leo Margulies	H1 M331	
12/9/1958	Mr. Wolheim	H1 W864	
1/31/1959	William L. Hamling	H1 H223	
1/31/1959	Mr. Wolheim	H1 W864	
1/11/1967	Carl-Olof Jonsson	H1 J54	
7/18/1967	Carl-Olof Jonsson	H1 J54	
5/9/1967	Mr. Hedman	H1 H455	
5/9/1967	Carl-Olof Jonsson	H1 J54	
5/5/1968	L. Cruikshank	H1 C955	
10/29/1968	Carl-Olof Jonsson	H1 J54	
11/30/1968	Carl-Olof Jonsson	H1 J54	
5/27/1969	Carl-Olof Jonsson	H1 J54	
6/15/1969	Carl-Olof Jonsson	H1 J54	
8/12/1969	Carl-Olof Jonsson	H1 J54	
3/21/1972	Carl-Olof Jonsson	H1 J54	
4/7/1972	Carl-Olof Jonsson	H1 J54	
11/6/1974	E. Hoffman Price	H1 P946	
1/14/1975	E. Hoffman Price	H1 P946	
5/30/1975	E. Hoffman Price	H1 P946	
2/2/1976	E. Hoffman Price	H1 P946	
2/21/1976	E. Hoffman Price	H1 P946	
7/20/1976	E. Hoffman Price	H1 P946	

Other letters in the Edmond Hamilton collection - By Date

Date	To	From	Ref. No.
11/8/1948	Leigh Brackett	Frederik Pohl	H1 P748
9/20/1950	Oscar J. Friend	Helen M. Herman	H1 F865
1/4/1951	Oscar J. Friend	Gerald J. Pollinger	H1 F865
2/21/1951	Roger F. Foley	E. Hoffman Price	H1 P946
2/21/1951	Esther	E. Hoffman Price	H1 P946
3/5/1953	Mr. Day	L. Sprague DeCamp	H1 D291
1/16/1954	Brad(ford M. Day)	L. Sprague DeCamp	H1 D291
6/19/1954	Oscar J. Friend	JD Ewing	H1 F865
12/5/1954	Brad(ford M. Day)	L. Sprague DeCamp	H1 D291
6/3/1959	Davis Dresser	Clark Kinnaird	H1 M331
Hand written Note to Ed.			
11/28/1962	Isabelle Taylor	Edward E. Smith	H1 S646
3/14/1963	Mr. Wollheim	Andre Norton	H1 W864
3/18/1963	Leigh	Donald A. Wollheim	H1 W864
6/30/1967	Bengt-Olaf Ringberg	Bengt-Olaf Ringberg	H1 R581
8/11/1967	Carl-Olof Jonsson	Carol L. Klapper	H1 J54
8/29/1967	Bengt-Olaf Ringberg	Bengt-Olaf Ringberg	H1 R581
2/5/1968	Carl-Olof Jonsson	Erich Pabel Verlag	H1 J54
12/22/1971	Bengt-Olaf Ringberg	Bengt-Olaf Ringberg	H1 R581
4/9/1972	Bengt-Olaf Ringberg	Bengt-Olaf Ringberg	H1 R581
5/18/1973	Bengt-Olaf Ringberg	Bengt-Olaf Ringberg	H1 R581

Letters By Golden Library Catalog Reference Number

H1 A182 **Forrest J. Ackerman**

Date	To	From
8-Jun-56	E. Hamilton	F.J. Ackemann
20-Jun-56	E. Hamilton	F.J. Ackemann
28-Jun-56	E. Hamilton	F.J. Ackemann
4-Aug-56	E. Hamilton	F.J. Ackemann
2-Dec-60	E. Hamilton	F.J. Ackemann
29-Oct-56	E. Hamilton	F.J. Ackemann
21-Dec-56	E. Hamilton	F.J. Ackemann
12-Jan-57	E. Hamilton	F.J. Ackemann
23-Jan-57	E. Hamilton	F.J. Ackemann
29-Jun-50	E. Hamilton	F.J. Ackemann
28-Jul-50	E. Hamilton	F.J. Ackemann
13-Ma-57	E. Hamilton	F.J. Ackemann
17-Feb-56	F.J. Ackemann	E. Hamilton
17-Feb-56	F.J. Ackemann	E. Hamilton
23-Jun-56	F.J. Ackemann	E. Hamilton
30-Jun-56	F.J. Ackemann	E. Hamilton
30-Jun-56	W. J. Delaney	E. Hamilton
30-Jun-56	Selwyn & Blount, Ltd	E. Hamilton
11-Oct-56	William K. Friedman	E. Hamilton
25-Oct-56	F.J. Ackemann	E. Hamilton
25-Oct-56	William K. Friedman	E. Hamilton
15-Mar-57	F.J. Ackemann	E. Hamilton
15-Mar-57	F.J. Ackemann	E. Hamilton
10-Mar-59	F.J. Ackemann	E. Hamilton

H1 A489 **Amazing Stories**

Date	To	From
20-Oct-32	E. Hamilton	Florence C. Bothmer
15-Feb-34	E. Hamilton	Florence C. Bothmer
29-Aug-27	E. Hamilton	Miriam Bourne
28-Sep-27	E. Hamilton	Miriam Bourne
2-Mar-29	E. Hamilton	Miriam Bourne
6-Mar-29	E. Hamilton	Miriam Bourne
10-May-29	E. Hamilton	Miriam Bourne
12-Nov-29	E. Hamilton	Miriam Bourne
14-Jan-30	E. Hamilton	Miriam Bourne
15-Aug-30	E. Hamilton	Miriam Bourne
26-Nov-30	E. Hamilton	Miriam Bourne

Date	To	From
26-Jan-38	E. Hamilton	BG Davis
	E. Hamilton	BG Davis
15-Mar-56	E. Hamilton	Paul W. Fairman
3-Sep-27	E. Hamilton	H. Gernsback
26-Oct-28	E. Hamilton	H. Gernsback
28-Nov-28	E. Hamilton	H. Gernsback
14-Nov-60	E. Hamilton	Cele Goldsmith
6-Sep-62	Leigh & Ed	Cele Goldsmith
1-Nov-62	E. Hamilton	Cele Goldsmith
1-Nov-62	E. Hamilton	Cele Goldsmith
27-Mar-62	E. Hamilton	Cele Goldsmith
2-Oct-64	E. Hamilton	Cele G. Lalli
29-Mar-65	E. Hamilton	Cele G. Lalli
8-May-62	E. Hamilton	Cele Goldsmith
11-Jun-42	Raymond Palmer	E. Hamilton
19-May-44	Raymond A. Palmer	E. Hamilton
28-Mar-45	Raymond A. Palmer	E. Hamilton
14-Jun-54	Ray Palmer	E. Hamilton
2-Aug-54	Ray Palmer	E. Hamilton
10-Oct-38	E. Hamilton	Raymond A Palmer
11-Mar-38	E. Hamilton	Raymond A palmer
	E. Hamilton	Raymond A Palmer
	E. Hamilton	Raymond A Palmer
8-Oct-45	E. Hamilton	Raymond A. Palmer
20-Mar-46	E. Hamilton	Raymond A Palmer
3-Dec-53	E. Hamilton	Bea Mahaffey
19-Dec-33	E. Hamilton	T. O'Conor Sloane PhD.
30-Aug-35	E. Hamilton	T. O'Conor Sloane PhD.
12-Apr-40	E. Hamilton	David Vern
22-May-40	E. Hamilton	David Vern
	E. Hamilton	David Vern
25-Jun-40	E. Hamilton	David Vern

H1 B329 **Harry Bates**

Date	To	From
18-Jan-30	E. Hamilton	Harry Bates
28-Apr-32	E. Hamilton	Harry Bates
28-Oct-32	E. Hamilton	Harry Bates

H1 B378 **Charles Beaumont**

Date	To	From
17-Oct-60	E. Hamilton	Charles Beaumont
30-Oct-60	E. Hamilton	Charles Beaumont

Date	To	From
5-Mar-62	E. Hamilton	Charles Beaumont

H1 B613 **Otto Binder**

Date	To	From
14-Sep-56	E. Hamilton	Otto Binder
29-Sep-56	E. Hamilton	Otto Binder

H1 B645 **Albert P. Blaustein**

Date	To	From
	E. Hamilton	Albert P. Blaustein
	E. Hamilton	Albert P. Blaustein

H1 B753 **Anthony Boucher**

Date	To	From
28-Sep-53	E. Hamilton	Anthony Boucher
23-Jan-54	E. Hamilton	Mick McCowas
28-Mar-54	E. Hamilton	A. Boucher
	E. Hamilton	Avram Davidson

H1 B798 **Ray Bradbury**

Date	To	From
7-Oct-43	E. Hamilton	Ray Bradbury
	E. Hamilton	Ray Bradbury
8-Jun-49	Ed & Leigh	Ray Bradbury
2-Jul-49	Ed & Leigh	Ray Bradbury
3-Aug-49	Ed & Leigh	Ray Bradbury
12-Sep-49	Ed & Leigh	Ray Bradbury
7-Nov-49	Ed & Leigh	Ray Bradbury
30-Nov-49	Ed & Leigh	Ray Bradbury
13-Jan-50	Ed & Leigh	Ray Bradbury
20-Jan-50	Ed & Leigh	Ray Bradbury
7-Apr-50	Ed & Leigh	Ray Bradbury
7-Mar-50	Ed & Leigh	Ray Bradbury
8-Jun-50	Ed & Leigh	Ray Bradbury
8-Aug-50	Ed & Leigh	Ray Bradbury
8-Oct-50	Ed & Leigh	Ray Bradbury
28-Dec-50	Ed & Leigh	Ray Bradbury
22-Mar-51	Ed & Leigh	Ray Bradbury
30-Mar-51	Ed & Leigh	Ray Bradbury
25-Jun-51	Ed & Leigh	Ray Bradbury
Nov-51	Ed & Leigh	Ray Bradbury
23-Aug-53	Ed & Leigh	Ray Bradbury

Date	To	From
14-Oct-53	Ed & Leigh	Ray Bradbury
17-Sep-53	Ed & Leigh	Ray Bradbury
30-Mar-58	Ed & Leigh	Ray Bradbury
24-Aug-44	Ed	Ray Bradbury
26-Oct-49	Ed	Ray Bradbury
7-Nov-49	Ed	Ray Bradbury
29-Aug-50	Ed & Leigh	Ray Bradbury
19-Sep-50	Ed & Leigh	Ray Bradbury

H1 B842 **Bernard Breslaner**

Date	To	From
30-Oct-45	E. Hamilton	Bernard Breslaner

H1 B897 **John Brunner**

Date	To	From
4-Mar-63	E. Hamilton	John Brunner

H1 B919 **Lamont Buchanan [Weird Tales]**

Date	To	From
8-Sep-44	E. Hamilton	Lamont Buchanan
10-Nov-44	E. Hamilton	Lamont Buchanan
23-May-44	E. Hamilton	Lamont Buchanan
2-Jan-45	E. Hamilton	Lamont Buchanan
15-Mar-45	E. Hamilton	Lamont Buchanan
27-Mar-45	E. Hamilton	Lamont Buchanan
1-Jun-45	E. Hamilton	Lamont Buchanan
2-Jul-45	E. Hamilton	Lamont Buchanan
7-Feb-46	E. Hamilton	Lamont Buchanan
1-Mar-46	E. Hamilton	Lamont Buchanan
5-Mar-46	E. Hamilton	Lamont Buchanan
1-Jul-46	E. Hamilton	Lamont Buchanan
20-Mar-47	E. Hamilton	Lamont Buchanan
18-Jul-47	E. Hamilton	Lamont Buchanan
2-Sep-47	E. Hamilton	Lamont Buchanan
30-Apr-48	E. Hamilton	Lamont Buchanan
21-Jul-49	E. Hamilton	Dorthy McIlwraith

H1 C188 **John W. Campbell Jr.**

Date	To	From
6-Jun-38	E. Hamilton	John W. Campbell Jr.
27-Oct-38	E. Hamilton	John W. Campbell Jr.

H1 C323 **Lin Carter**

Date	To	From
28-Nov-61	E. Hamilton	Lin Carter

H1 C455 **A. Bertram Chandler**

Date	To	From
14-Mar-68	Leigh & Ed	A. Bertram Chandler

H1 C955 **Lawrence Cruikshank**

Date	To	From
2-May-68	E. Hamilton	Lawrence Cruikshank
5-May-68	L. Cruikshank	E. Hamilton

H1 D251 **David**

Date	To	From
6-Jan-75	E. Hamilton	David ?

H1 D291 **Lyon Sprague DeCamp**

Date	To	From
16-Jan-54	Brad(ford M. Day)	L. Sprague DeCamp
5-Dec-54	Brad(ford M. Day)	L. Sprague DeCamp
5-Mar-53	Mr. Day	L. Sprague DeCamp
27-May-61	Hamiltons	L. Sprague DeCamp
5-May-60	Hamiltons	L. Sprague DeCamp
28-Dec-59	Ed & Leigh	L. Sprague DeCamp
24-May-58	Hamiltons	L. Sprague DeCamp
21-Aug-56	Hamiltons	L. Sprague DeCamp
3-Nov-54	Hamiltons	L. Sprague DeCamp
9-Oct-53	Hamiltons	L. Sprague DeCamp
4-Sep-53	Hamiltons	L. Sprague DeCamp
6-Feb-53	Hamiltons	L. Sprague DeCamp
14-Nov-52	Hamiltons	L. Sprague DeCamp
13-Nov-52	Hamiltons	L. Sprague DeCamp
19-Aug-52	Hamiltons	L. Sprague DeCamp
9-Aug-52	Hamiltons	L. Sprague DeCamp
3-Dec-51	Hamiltons	L. Sprague DeCamp
16-Mar-50	Hamiltons	L. Sprague DeCamp
26-Sep-49	Hamiltons	L. Sprague DeCamp
10-Sep-52	Hamiltons	L. Sprague DeCamp
17-Oct-52	Hamiltons	L. Sprague DeCamp
17-Sep-53	Hamiltons	L. Sprague DeCamp

H1 D389 **Michel Demuth**

Date	To	From
8-Oct-69	E. Hamilton	Michel Demuth

H1 D431 **August Derleth**

Date	To	From
26-Jul-49	E. Hamilton	August Derleth
1-Aug-49	E. Hamilton	August Derleth
17-Sep-49	E. Hamilton	August Derleth
24-Sep-49	E. Hamilton	August Derleth

Date	To	From
29-Jan-52	E. Hamilton	August Derleth
2-Apr-55	E. Hamilton	August Derleth
10-Oct-58	E. Hamilton	August Derleth

H1 D576 **T. E. Dikty**

Date	To	From
27-May-54	E. Hamilton	T. E. Dikty
28-Jun-54	E. Hamilton	T. E. Dikty
	E. Hamilton	T. E. Dikty

H1 E58 **V. R. Emanuel**

Date	To	From
16-Aug-58	E. Hamilton	V. R. Emanuel
3-Sep-58	E. Hamilton	V. R. Emanuel
12-Sep-58	E. Hamilton	V. R. Emanuel

H1 F317 **Frederick Fell**

Date	To	From
6-Jan-50	E. Hamilton	Ruth Amslow
15-Jan-51	E. Hamilton	Sidney Soloman
18-Oct-51	E. Hamilton	F. Fell
26-Nov-51	E. Hamilton	Wayne DaMetz
	E. Hamilton	Sidney Soloman
23-Jul-54	E. Hamilton	F. Fell
1-Oct-56	E. Hamilton	F. Fell
23-Oct-57	E. Hamilton	F. Fell
18-Feb-58	E. Hamilton	F. V. Fell
23-May-58	E. Hamilton	F. V. Fell
23-Jun-58	E. Hamilton	F. V. Fell
28-Mar-58	E. Hamilton	Winifred Glass
23-Nov-51	E. Hamilton	F. Fell Inc. w/O. Kiln
23-Nov-51	E. Hamilton	F. Fell Inc. w/O. Kiln
23-May-52	E. Hamilton	F. Fell Inc. w/O. Kiln
24-Nov-52	E. Hamilton	F. Fell Inc. w/O. Kiln

Date	To	From
24-Nov-52	E. Hamilton	F. Fell Inc. w/O. Kiln
10-Dec-53	E. Hamilton	F. Fell Inc. w/O. Kiln
24-Nov-52	E. Hamilton	F. Fell Inc. w/O. Kiln
10-Dec-53	E. Hamilton	F. Fell Inc. w/O. Kiln
2-Aug-54	E. Hamilton	F. Fell Inc. w/O. Kiln
30-Sep-57	E. Hamilton	F. Fell Inc. w/O. Kiln
31-May-58	E. Hamilton	F. Fell Inc. w/O. Kiln
24-Sep-56	Frederick V. Fel	E. Hamilton
16-Oct-57	Frederick V. Fel	E. Hamilton
5-Nov-57	Frederick V. Fel	E. Hamilton
6-Feb-58	Frederick V. Fel	E. Hamilton
19-May-58	Frederick V. Fel	E. Hamilton

H1 F736 **Charles Fort**

Date	To	From
29-Mar-26	E. Hamilton	Charles Fort
27-May-26	E. Hamilton	Charles Fort
25-Oct-26	E. Hamilton	Charles Fort
27-Feb	E. Hamilton	Charles Fort
17-Feb-31	E. Hamilton	Charles Fort
13-Feb-37	E. Hamilton	Charles Fort

H1 F865 **Oscar J. Friend**

Date	To	From
27-Feb-42	E. Hamilton	Oscar J. Friend
7-May-42	E. Hamilton	Oscar J. Friend
9-Jun-42	E. Hamilton	Oscar J. Friend
9-Dec-42	E. Hamilton	Oscar J. Friend
22-Mar-43	E. Hamilton	Oscar J. Friend
3-Jun-43	E. Hamilton	Oscar J. Friend
1-Oct-43	E. Hamilton	Oscar J. Friend
19-Jan-44	E. Hamilton	Oscar J. Friend
24-Jan-44	E. Hamilton	Oscar J. Friend
26-Jan-44	E. Hamilton	Oscar J. Friend
31-Jan-44	E. Hamilton	Oscar J. Friend
9-Feb-44	E. Hamilton	Oscar J. Friend
1-Dec-48	E. Hamilton	Oscar J. Friend
22-Jul-49	E. Hamilton	Oscar J. Friend
28-Jan-49	E. Hamilton	Oscar J. Friend
28-Feb-49	E. Hamilton	Oscar J. Friend
2-Mar-49	E. Hamilton	Oscar J. Friend
28-Jul-49	E. Hamilton	Oscar J. Friend

Date	To	From
4-Oct-49	E. Hamilton	Oscar J. Friend
8-Oct-49	E. Hamilton	Oscar J. Friend
11-Nov-48	E. Hamilton	Oscar J. Friend
18-Nov-49	E. Hamilton	Oscar J. Friend
1-Dec-49	E. Hamilton	Oscar J. Friend
17-Dec-49	E. Hamilton	Oscar J. Friend
15-Feb-50	E. Hamilton	Oscar J. Friend
8-Mar-50	E. Hamilton	Oscar J. Friend
1-Apr-50	E. Hamilton	Oscar J. Friend
11-Apr-50	E. Hamilton	Oscar J. Friend
12-Jul-50	E. Hamilton	Oscar J. Friend
19-Apr-50	E. Hamilton	Oscar J. Friend
24-Apr-50	E. Hamilton	Oscar J. Friend
23-May-50	E. Hamilton	Oscar J. Friend
12-Jul-50	E. Hamilton	Oscar J. Friend
18-Jul-50	E. Hamilton	Oscar J. Friend
17-Aug-50	E. Hamilton	Oscar J. Friend
24-Aug-50	E. Hamilton	Oscar J. Friend
23-Sep-50	E. Hamilton	Oscar J. Friend
25-Oct-50	E. Hamilton	Oscar J. Friend
30-Oct-50	E. Hamilton	Oscar J. Friend
1-Nov-50	E. Hamilton	Oscar J. Friend
6-Dec-50	E. Hamilton	Oscar J. Friend
13-Dec-50	E. Hamilton	Oscar J. Friend
9-Apr	E. Hamilton	Oscar J. Friend
17-May	E. Hamilton	Oscar J. Friend
23-Nov	E. Hamilton	Oscar J. Friend
5-May	E. Hamilton	Oscar J. Friend
6-Aug	E. Hamilton	Oscar J. Friend
10-Jan-51	E. Hamilton	Oscar J. Friend
3-Mar-51	E. Hamilton	Oscar J. Friend
18-Apr-51	E. Hamilton	Oscar J. Friend
26-Apr-51	E. Hamilton	Oscar J. Friend
21-Aug-51	E. Hamilton	Oscar J. Friend
28-Nov-51	E. Hamilton	Oscar J. Friend
5-Dec-51	E. Hamilton	Oscar J. Friend
5-Jan-52	E. Hamilton	Oscar J. Friend
5-Mar-52	E. Hamilton	Oscar J. Friend
3-Apr-52	E. Hamilton	Oscar J. Friend
10-Jun-52	E. Hamilton	Oscar J. Friend
21-Jul-52	E. Hamilton	Oscar J. Friend
5-Sep-52	E. Hamilton	Oscar J. Friend
22-Sep-52	E. Hamilton	Oscar J. Friend

Date	To	From
17-Dec-52	E. Hamilton	Oscar J. Friend
17-Mar-58	E. Hamilton	Oscar J. Friend
5-Jul-52	E. Hamilton	Oscar J. Friend
30-Nov-50	E. Hamilton	Oscar J. Friend
	E. Hamilton	Oscar J. Friend
	E. Hamilton	Oscar J. Friend
7-May-53	E. Hamilton	Oscar J. Friend
8-Oct-53	E. Hamilton	Oscar J. Friend
26-Feb-54	E. Hamilton	Oscar J. Friend
19-Jun-54	E. Hamilton	Oscar J. Friend
26-Aug-54	E. Hamilton	Oscar J. Friend
29-Sep-54	E. Hamilton	Oscar J. Friend
11-Apr-56	E. Hamilton	Oscar J. Friend
22-Oct-56	E. Hamilton	Oscar J. Friend
23-Aug-56	E. Hamilton	Oscar J. Friend
19-Sep-57	E. Hamilton	Oscar J. Friend
20-Dec-57	E. Hamilton	Oscar J. Friend
29-May-58	E. Hamilton	Oscar J. Friend
19-Apr-59	E. Hamilton	Oscar J. Friend
9-Jul-56	E. Hamilton	Oscar J. Friend
3-Dec-49	Oscar J. Friend	E. Hamilton
15-Jul-50	Oscar J. Friend	E. Hamilton
26-Feb-57	Oscar J. Friend	E. Hamilton
10-Aug-57	Oscar J. Friend	E. Hamilton
4-Jan-51	Oscar J. Friend	Gerald J. Pollinger
20-Sep-55	E. Hamilton	Gerald J. Pollinger
19-Jun-54	Oscar J. Friend	J.D. Ewing
25-Oct-51	E. Hamilton	Avgust Petrisic
20-Sep-50	Oscar J. Friend	Helen M. Herman

H1 G376 **Hugo Gernsback**

Date	To	From
5-Mar-29	E. Hamilton	H. Gernsback
11-Mar-29	E. Hamilton	H. Gernsback
5-Apr-29	E. Hamilton	H. Gernsback
12-Aug-29	E. Hamilton	H. Gernsback
13-Nov-29	E. Hamilton	H. Gernsback
12-Dec-29	E. Hamilton	H. Gernsback
7-Jan-30	E. Hamilton	H. Gernsback
25-Feb-30	E. Hamilton	H. Gernsback
24-Feb-32	E. Hamilton	H. Gernsback
5-Feb-34	E. Hamilton	H. Gernsback

H1 G481 **Walter H. Gillinger**

Date	To	From
28-Nov-38	E. Hamilton	Walter H. Gillinger
7-May-40	E. Hamilton	Walter H. Gillinger
15-Jul-40	E. Hamilton	Walter H. Gillinger
9-Sep-41	E. Hamilton	Walter H. Gillinger
25-Jan-44	E. Hamilton	Walter H. Gillinger
21-Jun-45	E. Hamilton	Walter H. Gillinger
3-Oct-45	E. Hamilton	Walter H. Gillinger
29-Nov-45	E. Hamilton	Walter H. Gillinger
28-Jan-46	E. Hamilton	Walter H. Gillinger
16-Mar-46	E. Hamilton	Walter H. Gillinger
6-May-46	E. Hamilton	Walter H. Gillinger
9-Nov-46	E. Hamilton	Walter H. Gillinger

H1 G976 **James E. Gunn**

Date	To	From
18-Mar-57	Ed & Leigh	James E. Gunn

H1 H223 **William L. Hamling**

Date	To	From
16-Aug-48	E. Hamilton	William L. Hamling
25-Feb-53	E. Hamilton	William L. Hamling
5-May-53	E. Hamilton	William L. Hamling
12-Oct-55	E. Hamilton	William L. Hamling
27-Oct-55	E. Hamilton	William L. Hamling
5-Nov-55	E. Hamilton	William L. Hamling
30-Nov-55	E. Hamilton	William L. Hamling
10-Dec-55	E. Hamilton	William L. Hamling
3-Feb-56	E. Hamilton	William L. Hamling
5-Mar-56	E. Hamilton	William L. Hamling
4-Apr-56	E. Hamilton	William L. Hamling
29-May-56	E. Hamilton	William L. Hamling
7-Jul-56	E. Hamilton	William L. Hamling
20-Aug-56	E. Hamilton	William L. Hamling
16-Oct-56	E. Hamilton	William L. Hamling
30-Oct-56	E. Hamilton	William L. Hamling
27-Nov-56	E. Hamilton	William L. Hamling
27-Dec-56	E. Hamilton	William L. Hamling
26-Feb-56	E. Hamilton	William L. Hamling
4-Mar-57	E. Hamilton	William L. Hamling
9-Mar-57	E. Hamilton	William L. Hamling

Date	To	From
29-Apr-57	E. Hamilton	William L. Hamling
22-May-57	E. Hamilton	William L. Hamling
2-Jul-57	E. Hamilton	William L. Hamling
2-Jul-57	E. Hamilton	William L. Hamling
27-Sep-57	E. Hamilton	William L. Hamling
20-Dec-57	E. Hamilton	William L. Hamling
31-Dec-57	E. Hamilton	William L. Hamling
4-Feb-58	E. Hamilton	William L. Hamling
28-Feb-58	E. Hamilton	William L. Hamling
26-Mar-58	E. Hamilton	William L. Hamling
7-May-58	E. Hamilton	William L. Hamling
7-Feb-59	E. Hamilton	William L. Hamling
18-Jun-60	E. Hamilton	William L. Hamling
31-Jan-59	William L. Hamling	E. Hamilton

H1 H296 **T. Everett Harre**

Date	To	From
30-Oct-28	E. Hamilton	T. Everett Harre
8-Dec-28	E. Hamilton	T. Everett Harre
7-Aug-29	E. Hamilton	T. Everett Harre
14-Aug-29	E. Hamilton	T. Everett Harre
29-Aug-29	E. Hamilton	T. Everett Harre

H1 H318 **Harry Harrison**

Date	To	From
19-Feb-64	E. Hamilton	Harry Harrison

H1 H455 **Hedman**

Date	To	From
9-May-67	Mr. Hedman	E. Hamilton

H1 H688 **Russ Hodgkins**

Date	To	From
2-Jun-47	E. Hamilton	Russ Hodgkins
1-Jul-47	E. Hamilton	Russ Hodgkins
20-Aug-47	E. Hamilton	Russ Hodgkins
7-Jul-47	Russ Hodgkins	E. Hamilton

H1 H815 **Charles D. Hornig [Wonder Stories]**

Date	To	From
18-Dec-33	E. Hamilton	Charles D. Hornig
4-Jan-34	E. Hamilton	Charles D. Hornig

Date	To	From
8-Feb-35	E. Hamilton	Charles D. Hornig
7-Feb-36	E. Hamilton	Charles D. Hornig

H1 J54 **Robert Jennings**

Date	To	From
16-Feb-62	E. Hamilton	Robert Jennings
12-May-62	E. Hamilton	Robert Jennings

H1 J81 **Carl-Olof Jonson**

Date	To	From
18-Jan	E. Hamilton	Carl-Olof Jonsson
14-Apr	E. Hamilton	Carl-Olof Jonsson
18-Apr	E. Hamilton	Carl-Olof Jonsson
31-May	E. Hamilton	Carl-Olof Jonsson
18-Jun	E. Hamilton	Carl-Olof Jonsson
11-Nov	E. Hamilton	Carl-Olof Jonsson
23-Nov	E. Hamilton	Carl-Olof Jonsson
11-Aug-67	Carl-Olof Jonsson	Carol L. Klapper
6-Dec	E. Hamilton	Carl-Olof Jonsson
5-Feb-68	Carl-Olof Jonsson	Erich Pabel Verlag
5-Sep	E. Hamilton	Carl-Olof Jonsson
9-May-67	Carl-Olof Jonsson	E. Hamilton
18-Jul-67	Carl-Olof Jonsson	E. Hamilton
30-Nov-68	Carl-Olof Jonsson	E. Hamilton
27-May-69	Carl-Olof Jonsson	E. Hamilton
15-Jun-69	Carl-Olof Jonsson	E. Hamilton
11-Jan-68	Carl-Olof Jonsson	E. Hamilton
29-Oct-68	Carl-Olof Jonsson	E. Hamilton
12-Aug-69	Carl-Olof Jonsson	E. Hamilton
21-Mar-72	Carl-Olof Jonsson	E. Hamilton
7-Apr-72	Carl-Olof Jonsson	E. Hamilton

H1 K71 **Damon Knight**

Date	To	From
18-Mar-60	Ed & Leigh	Damon Knight
5-Oct-61	E Hamilton	Damon Knight

H1 K97 **Henry Kuttner**

Date	To	From
14-Jun-49	Leigh & Ed	Henry Kuttner
16-Jun-49	Leigh & Ed	Henry Kuttner
6-Jul-49	Leigh & Ed	Henry Kuttner
20-Jun	Leigh & Ed	Henry Kuttner

Date	To	From
17-Nov-49	Leigh & Ed	Henry Kuttner
12-Apr-50	Leigh & Ed	Henry Kuttner
3-Sep-51	Leigh & Ed	Henry Kuttner
14-Sep-52	Leigh & Ed	Henry Kuttner

H1 L347 **David Lasser**

Date	To	From
16-Nov-29	E. Hamilton	David Lasser
11-Mar-30	E. Hamilton	David Lasser
17-Mar-30	E. Hamilton	David Lasser
4-Jun-30	E. Hamilton	David Lasser
3-Jul-30	E. Hamilton	David Lasser
19-Nov-31	E. Hamilton	David Lasser
4-Dec-31	E. Hamilton	David Lasser
5-Jul-30	David Lasser	E. Hamilton

H1 M331 **Leo Margulies [Standard Magazine, Inc.]**

Date	To	From
21-Feb-36	E. Hamilton	Leo Margulies
10-Oct-41	E. Hamilton	Leo Margulies
14-Apr-42	E. Hamilton	Leo Margulies
21-Apr-42	E. Hamilton	Leo Margulies
22-May-42	E. Hamilton	Leo Margulies
28-Aug-42	E. Hamilton	Leo Margulies
7-May-43	E. Hamilton	Leo Margulies
20-Aug-43	E. Hamilton	Leo Margulies
21-Jan-44	E. Hamilton	Leo Margulies
9-May-44	E. Hamilton	Leo Margulies
17-May-44	E. Hamilton	Leo Margulies
16-Jun-44	E. Hamilton	Leo Margulies
21-Jul-44	E. Hamilton	Leo Margulies
25-Sep-44	E. Hamilton	Leo Margulies
15-Dec-44	E. Hamilton	Leo Margulies
20-Dec-44	E. Hamilton	Leo Margulies
5-Jan-45	E. Hamilton	Leo Margulies
23-Feb-45	E. Hamilton	Leo Margulies
21-Mar-45	E. Hamilton	Leo Margulies
18-Jan-46	E. Hamilton	Leo Margulies
21-Feb-46	E. Hamilton	Leo Margulies
1-Mar-46	E. Hamilton	Leo Margulies
15-Mar-46	E. Hamilton	Leo Margulies
22-Mar-46	E. Hamilton	Leo Margulies

Date	To	From
26-Apr-46	E. Hamilton	Leo Margulies
1-Nov-46	E. Hamilton	Leo Margulies
24-Oct-47	E. Hamilton	Leo Margulies
3-Mar-50	E. Hamilton	Leo Margulies
14-May-58	E. Hamilton	Leo Margulies
20-May-58	E. Hamilton	Leo Margulies
29-May-58	E. Hamilton	Leo Margulies
24-Jun-58	E. Hamilton	Leo Margulies
27-Jun-58	E. Hamilton	Leo Margulies
8-Jul-58	E. Hamilton	Leo Margulies
21-Jul-58	E. Hamilton	Leo Margulies
6-Aug-58	E. Hamilton	Leo Margulies
13-Aug-58	E. Hamilton	Leo Margulies
25-Aug-58	E. Hamilton	Leo Margulies
9-Sep-58	E. Hamilton	Leo Margulies
3-Oct-58	E. Hamilton	Leo Margulies
10-Oct-58	E. Hamilton	Leo Margulies
16-Dec-58	E. Hamilton	Leo Margulies
7-Jan-59	E. Hamilton	Leo Margulies
19-Jan-59	E. Hamilton	Leo Margulies
12-Feb-59	E. Hamilton	Leo Margulies
21-Mar-59	E. Hamilton	Leo Margulies
23-Mar-54	E. Hamilton	Cylvia Klieinman
14-May-59	E. Hamilton	Cylvia K. Margulies
3-Jun-59	Davis Dresser	Clark Kinnaird
26-Jun-59	E. Hamilton	Leo Margulies
15-Jul-59	E. Hamilton	Leo Margulies
21-Jul-59	E. Hamilton	Cylvia K. Margulies
29-Jul-59	E. Hamilton	Cylvia K. Margulies
19-Aug-59	E. Hamilton	Cylvia K. Margulies
15-Oct-59	E. Hamilton	Leo Margulies
4-Nov-59	E. Hamilton	Leo Margulies
18-May-1960	E. Hamilton	Ann Stern
14-Jun-60	E. Hamilton	Leo Margulies
19-Sep-60	E. Hamilton	Ann Stern
1-Nov-60	E. Hamilton	Torquil & Co, Inc.
20-Feb-61	E. Hamilton	Cylvia K. Margulies
27-Feb-61	E. Hamilton	Cylvia K. Margulies
8-May-61	E. Hamilton	Leo Margulies
27-Jun-61	E. Hamilton	Mrs. Saima Heckmeyer
6-Nov-62	E. Hamilton	Torquil & Co, Inc.
22-Aug-62	E. Hamilton	Cylvia K. Margulies
17-Dec-62	E. Hamilton	Leo Margulies

Date	To	From
1-May-63	E. Hamilton	Torquil & Co, Inc.
6-Nov-63	E. Hamilton	Torquil & Co, Inc.
21-Dec-61	E. Hamilton	Leo Margulies
13-Mar-62	E. Hamilton	Cylvia K. Margulies
19-May-61	E. Hamilton	Helen McCloy Dresser
	E. Hamilton	Helen McCloy Dresser
31-Aug-61	E. Hamilton	Helen McCloy Dresser
25-Sep-61	E. Hamilton	Helen McCloy Dresser
24-Dec-61	E. Hamilton	Helen McCloy Dresser
6-Jan-62	E. Hamilton	Brett Halliday
17-Feb-63	E. Hamilton	Brett Halliday
1-May-62	E. Hamilton	Torquil & Co, Inc.
19-May-58	Leo Margulies	E. Hamilton
24-May-58	Leo Margulies	E. Hamilton
27-May-58	Leo Margulies	E. Hamilton
26-Jun-58	Leo Margulies	E. Hamilton
9-Aug-58	Leo Margulies	E. Hamilton

H1 M572 **Abraham Merritt**

Date	To	From
7-Sep-31	E. Hamilton	Abraham Merritt
25-Mar-32	E. Hamilton	Abraham Merritt

H1 M576 **Sam Merwin Jr.**

Date	To	From
22-Jun-45	E. Hamilton	Sam Merwin Jr.
2-Jul-45	E. Hamilton	Sam Merwin Jr.
3-Aug-45	E. Hamilton	Sam Merwin Jr.
23-Nov-45	E. Hamilton	Sam Merwin Jr.
30-Dec-46	E. Hamilton	Sam Merwin Jr.
22-Apr-47	E. Hamilton	Sam Merwin Jr.
8-Aug-47	E. Hamilton	Sam Merwin Jr.
12-Dec-47	E. Hamilton	Sam Merwin Jr.
9-Apr-48	E. Hamilton	Sam Merwin Jr.
23-Mar-49	E. Hamilton	Sam Merwin Jr.
10-Jun-49	E. Hamilton	Sam Merwin Jr.
19-Aug-49	E. Hamilton	Sam Merwin Jr.
22-Sep-49	E. Hamilton	Sam Merwin Jr.
16-Dec-49	E. Hamilton	Sam Merwin Jr.
30-Dec-49	E. Hamilton	Sam Merwin Jr.
12-May-50	E. Hamilton	Sam Merwin Jr.
10-Jul-50	E. Hamilton	Sam Merwin Jr.

Date	To	From
28-Jun-50	E. Hamilton	Sam Merwin Jr.
28-Jul-50	E. Hamilton	Sam Merwin Jr.
6-Oct-50	E. Hamilton	Sam Merwin Jr.
23-Feb-51	E. Hamilton	Sam Merwin Jr.
6-Mar-51	E. Hamilton	Sam Merwin Jr.
10-Oct-45	E. Hamilton	Samuel Mines
29-Mar-49	E. Hamilton	Samuel Mines
3-Aug-51	E. Hamilton	Samuel Mines
27-Nov-51	E. Hamilton	Samuel Mines
27-Mar-52	E. Hamilton	Samuel Mines
6-Jun-52	E. Hamilton	Samuel Mines
25-Jun-52	E. Hamilton	Samuel Mines
28-Nov-52	E. Hamilton	Samuel Mines
6-Mar-53	E. Hamilton	Samuel Mines
10-Mar-53	E. Hamilton	Samuel Mines
10-Jun-54	E. Hamilton	Samuel Mines
	E. Hamilton	Samuel Mines
9-Jul-54	E. Hamilton	Samuel Mines
10-Aug-45	E. Hamilton	Charles S. Strong
	E. Hamilton	Charles S. Strong
9-Apr-53	E. Hamilton	Fanny Ellsworth
29-Apr-53	E. Hamilton	Fanny Ellsworth
23-Sep-47	E. Hamilton	Joseph Green
8-Feb-57	E. Hamilton	Jim Hendryx, Jr
11-Apr-57	E. Hamilton	Jim Hendryx, Jr.
31-Jul-58	E. Hamilton	Jim Hendryx, Jr.
16-Apr-51	Mr. N. L. Pines	E. Hamilton

H1 M651 **Schuyler Miller**

Date	To	From
27-Oct-59	E. Hamilton	Schuyler Miller
	E. Hamilton	Schuyler Miller

H1 M657 **Robert P. Mills**

Date	To	From
1-Apr-54	E. Hamilton	Robert P. Mills
10-Jan-58	E. Hamilton	Sondra Mandell
3-Jan	E. Hamilton	Robert P. Mills
10-Jan	E. Hamilton	Robert P. Mills
25-Feb	E. Hamilton	Robert P. Mills
8-Jul	E. Hamilton	Robert P. Mills
25-Nov	E. Hamilton	Robert P. Mills
June	E. Hamilton	Robert P. Mills

Date	To	From
8-Jul-57	E. Hamilton	

H1 M678a **Miscellaneous [Agents, Editors]**

Date	To	From
25-Nov-53	E. Hamilton	Bea Mahaffey
7-May-54	E. Hamilton	Ray
20-Dec-59	E. Hamilton	Ted Carnell
1-Nov-33	E. Hamilton	William Crawford
16-Oct-35	E. Hamilton	Doone Burks
5-Aug-48	E. Hamilton	Drayton S. Haff
21-Jul-60	E. Hamilton	Harry Jacobson
	E. Hamilton	
12-Sep-67	E. Hamilton	Jacques Sadoul
31-Jan-68	E. Hamilton	Jacques Sadoul
12-Oct-53	E. Hamilton	Ruth Stark
8-Aug-1960	E. Hamilton	Pierre Versins
2-May-61	E. Hamilton	Pierre Versins
14-Oct-68	E & L Hamilton	Sebastian Martinez
20-Oct-58	E. Hamilton	Marty Greenberg
17-May-50	E. Hamilton	Ned Brown
21-Nov-61	E. Hamilton	Lin Carter
20-Jun-57	E. Hamilton	Isabelle Taylor
	E. Hamilton	The Pub. Fiscal Corp
	E. Hamilton	Penguin Press
	E. Hamilton	Scwartz & Weisinger
6-May-31	E. Hamilton	S.J.
3-Mar-31	E. Hamilton	Astounding
14-Mar-30	E. Hamilton	Astounding
10-Jan-30	E. Hamilton	Astounding

H1 M678b **Miscellaneous [Fans]**

Date	To	From
7-Jan-59	E. Hamilton	Manfred Alex
1-Nov-63	E. Hamilton	Bill Allen
23-Jun-52	E. Hamilton	Arthur Brandwein
2-Jun-69	E. Hamilton	Joanne Burger
	E. Hamilton	K.G. Dunn
5-May-69	E. Hamilton	Dan Followell
14-Jun-69	E. Hamilton	Dan Followell
26-Aug-61	E. Hamilton	Ingrid Fritzsch
11-Jan-65	E. Hamilton	E. J. Frost
8-Oct-64	E. Hamilton	Owen C Girley

Date	To	From
	E. Hamilton	David Jones
22-Apr-54	E. Hamilton	John Keipp
10-May-54	E. Hamilton	Jahn Keipp
10-Jan-56	E. Hamilton	Alberta Leek
18-Mar-45	E. Hamilton	S. A. McElfresh
30-Mar-45	E. Hamilton	S. A. McElfresh
4-May-45	E. Hamilton	Thos. O. Mabott
21-Apr-55	E. Hamilton	Art Nyman
26-Nov-52	E. Hamilton	Robert W. Pratt
21-Jul-69	E. Hamilton	Theodore Quock
1-Dec-69	E. Hamilton	Jeffrey Rothenberg
7-Mar-55	E. Hamilton	Robert H. Searcy
7-Apr-55	E. Hamilton	Robert H. Searcy
28-Apr-55	E. Hamilton	Robert H. Searcy
29-Oct-62	E. Hamilton	Robert G. Shively
3-Feb-68	E. Hamilton	Blane Smith
28-Dec-51	E. Hamilton	Amaryllis Sponagle
28-Feb-51	E. Hamilton	Ernest O. Stout
15-Jan-52	E. Hamilton	Thos. Taylor
24-May-52	E. Hamilton	Thos. Taylor
12-Oct-56	E. Hamilton	Oswald Train
27-Jun-68	E. Hamilton	Jas. P. Young
31-Mar-56	Edmond & Leigh	Miss R. Wild

H1 M678c **Miscellaneous [Fanzines]**

Date	To	From
4-Oct-47	E. Hamilton	Donald B. Day
30-Nov-50	E. Hamilton	James J. Klinikowski
24-Oct-50	E. Hamilton	Miss Betty Steward
7-Oct-50	E. Hamilton	Mr. Gene Garretson
6-Nov-55	E. Hamilton	Larry Farsace
6-Apr-57	E. Hamilton	Allan Howard
16-Apr	E. Hamilton	Howard DeVore
Mar-58	E. Hamilton	MI SF Society
1-Apr-64	E. Hamilton	A. H. Mercer (BSFA)
22-Dec-64	E. Hamilton	Steve Perrin
27-Apr-65	E. Hamilton	Roger G. Peyton
24-Sep-68	E. Hamilton	John H Guidry
	E. Hamilton	John H Guidry (NOSFA
11-Apr-69	E. Hamilton	Iwan Hedman
27-Jan-57	E. Hamilton	Robert Wild
	E. Hamilton	Henry Moskowitz
	E. Hamilton	First Fandom

Date	To	From
	E. Hamilton	The Science Fiction

H1 M678d **Miscellaneous - Cover Art [Publishers]**

Date	To	From
2-Jan-46	E. Hamilton	Lamont Buchanan
30-Nov-45	E. Hamilton	Lamont Buchanan
6-Feb-48	E. Hamilton	Lamont Buchanan
28-Jun-61	E. Hamilton	Cele Goldsmith
20-Jan-64	E. Hamilton	Cele Goldsmith
14-Jan-64	E. Hamilton	Cele Goldsmith
24-Jan-46	E. Hamilton	R. G. (Bob) Jones
9-Apr-42	E. Hamilton	Ray Palmer
14-Apr-53	E. Hamilton	Ray Palmer

H1 M678e **Miscellaneous [Writers]**

Date	To	From
27-Sep-64	E. Hamilton	Alva Rogers
14-Dec-46	E. Hamilton	Robert E. Briney
2-Aug-52	E. Hamilton	Merle I. Franklin
21-Dec-64	E. Hamilton	E. J. Frost
24-Feb-32	E. Hamilton	J. Harvey Haggard
	E. Hamilton	John Jakes
23-Mar-65	E. Hamilton	Terry Lowry
12-May-62	E. Hamilton	Douglas Mackey
	E. Hamilton	Evelyn Paige
1969	E. Hamilton	John J. Piera
20-Aug-62	E. Hamilton	Douglas Taylor
19-Sep-62	E. Hamilton	Douglas Taylor
13-Aug-40	E. Hamilton	Monte
	E. Hamilton	Danny Rowe

H1 M819 **Mike Moorcock**

Date	To	From
27-May-64	E. Hamilton	Mike Moorcock

H1 M912 **Sam Moskowitz**

Date	To	From
17-Jun-62	E. Hamilton	Sam Moskowitz
29-Jan-65	E. Hamilton	Sam Moskowitz

H1 N535 **Eleanor Newburger**

Date	To	From
7-Aug-59	E. Hamilton	Eleanor Newburger
8-Aug-59	E. Hamilton	Eleanor Newburger
31-Dec-59	E. Hamilton	Eleanor Newburger
15-Sep-59	E. Hamilton	Indian S.L.B.T report
	E. Hamilton	Indian S.L.B.T report

H1 N882 **Andre Norton**

Date	To	From
6-Jun-54	Mr & Mrs. Hamilton	Andre Norton

H1 P748 **Frederik Pohl**

Date	To	From
8-Nov-48	Leigh Brackett	Frederik Pohl
24-Nov-48	E. Hamilton	Frederik Pohl
14-Feb-49	E. Hamilton	Frederik Pohl

H1 P946 **E. Hoffman Price**

Date	To	From
3-Jun-44	E. Hamilton	E. Hoffman Price
29-Jan-50	E. Hamilton	E. Hoffman Price
12-Jan-51	E. Hamilton	E. Hoffman Price
21-Feb-51	Roger F. Foley	E. Hoffman Price
21-Feb-51	Esther	E. Hoffman Price
6-Mar-52	E. Hamilton	E. Hoffman Price
20-May-52	E. Hamilton	E. Hoffman Price
22-Jan-55	E. Hamilton	E. Hoffman Price
11-Jun-56	E. Hamilton	E. Hoffman Price
24-Jun-56	E. Hamilton	E. Hoffman Price
15-May-57	E. Hamilton	E. Hoffman Price
27-May-56	E. Hamilton	E. Hoffman Price
6-Jul-59	E. Hamilton	E. Hoffman Price
10-Oct-59	E. Hamilton	E. Hoffman Price
25-Nov-61	E. Hamilton	E. Hoffman Price
26-Jun-62	E. Hamilton	E. Hoffman Price
	E. Hamilton	E. Hoffman Price
3-Jun-62	E. Hamilton	E. Hoffman Price
7-Dec-63	E. Hamilton	E. Hoffman Price
18-Mar-64	E. Hamilton	E. Hoffman Price
10-Apr-68	E. Hamilton	E. Hoffman Price
19-Jun-68	E. Hamilton	E. Hoffman Price
23-Aug-68	E. Hamilton	E. Hoffman Price
13-Feb-47	E. Hoffman Price	E. Hamilton
5-Jan-47	E. Hoffman Price	E. Hamilton

Date	To	From
6-Nov-74	E. Hoffman Price	E. Hamilton
14-Jan-75	E. Hoffman Price	E. Hamilton
30-May-75	E. Hoffman Price	E. Hamilton
2-Feb-76	E. Hoffman Price	E. Hamilton
21-Feb-76	E. Hoffman Price	E. Hamilton
20-Jul-76	E. Hoffman Price	E. Hamilton

H1 R581 **Bengt-Olaf Ringberg**

Date	To	From
8-Jul-67	E. Hamilton	Bengt-Olaf Ringberg
10-Dec-67	E. Hamilton	Bengt-Olaf Ringberg
10-Sep-68	E. Hamilton	Bengt-Olaf Ringberg
1-Dec-68	E. Hamilton	Bengt-Olaf Ringberg
4-Feb-69	E. Hamilton	Bengt-Olaf Ringberg
29-Aug-67	Bengt-Olaf Ringberg	Bengt-Olaf Ringberg
22-Dec-71	Bengt-Olaf Ringberg	Bengt-Olaf Ringberg
9-Apr-72	Bengt-Olaf Ringberg	Bengt-Olaf Ringberg
18-May-73	Bengt-Olaf Ringberg	Bengt-Olaf Ringberg
30-Jun-67	Bengt-Olaf Ringberg	Bengt-Olaf Ringberg

H1 R747 **Robert N. Rolfe**

Date	To	From
15-Dec-53	E. Hamilton	Robert N. Rolfe

H1 R961 **Eric Frank Russell**

Date	To	From
24-Apr-64	E. Hamilton	Eric Frank Russell
12-Oct-64	E. Hamilton	Eric Frank Russell

H1 S387 **Stephen F. Schultheis**

Date	To	From
31-Dec-56	E. Hamilton	Stephen F. Schultheis
24-Jun-62	E. Hamilton	Stephen F. Schultheis

H1 S411 **Julius Schwartz**

Date	To	From
25-May-34	E. Hamilton	Julius Schwartz
25-May-35	E. Hamilton	Julius Schwartz
10-Aug-43	E. Hamilton	Julius Schwartz
17-Nov-43	E. Hamilton	Julius Schwartz
10-Dec-43	E. Hamilton	Julius Schwartz
31-Jan-44	E. Hamilton	Julius Schwartz

Date	To	From
7-Feb-44	E. Hamilton	Julius Schwartz
4-Mar-44	E. Hamilton	Julius Schwartz
17-May-44	E. Hamilton	Julius Schwartz
10-Jun-44	E. Hamilton	Julius Schwartz
4-Jul-44	E. Hamilton	Julius Schwartz
2-Sep-44	E. Hamilton	Julius Schwartz
9-Jun-45	E. Hamilton	Julius Schwartz
28-Apr-58	E. Hamilton	Julius Schwartz
28-Nov-60	E. Hamilton	Julius Schwartz
1-Mar-56	E. Hamilton	Julius Schwartz
30-Apr-56	E. Hamilton	Julius Schwartz
22-May-56	E. Hamilton	Julius Schwartz
3-Feb-44	Julius Schwartz	E. Hamilton
21-Aug-45	Mort (Weisinger)	E. Hamilton

H1 S535 **Larry Shaw**

Date	To	From
9-Jul-56	E. Hamilton	Larry Shaw
13-Jul-56	E. Hamilton	Larry Shaw
31-Jul-56	E. Hamilton	Larry Shaw
23-Aug-56	E. Hamilton	Larry Shaw
26-Aug-56	E. Hamilton	Larry Shaw
26-Dec-56	E. Hamilton	Larry Shaw
2-Oct-57	E. Hamilton	Larry Shaw

H1 S571 **James R. Sieger**

Date	To	From
8-Feb-61	E. Hamilton	James R. Sieger

H1 S587 **Robert Silverberg**

Date	To	From
29-Apr-61	E. Hamilton	Bob Silverberg

H1 S646 **Edward E. Smith**

Date	To	From
26-Jul-54	E. Hamilton	Edward E. Smith
6-Aug-54	E. Hamilton	Edward E. Smith
30-Sep-55	E. Hamilton	Edward E. Smith
22-Jun-57	E. Hamilton	Edward E. Smith
28-Nov-62	E. Hamilton	Edward E. Smith
18-Nov-64	E. Hamilton	Edward E. Smith
28-Nov-62	Isabelle Taylor	Edward E. Smith
14-Mar-57	E. Hamilton	C. L. Barrett, M.D.

Date	To	From
1-Sep-65	E. Hamilton	C. L. Barrett, M.D.

H1 S768 **William R. Sprenger**

Date	To	From
31-Aug-26	E. Hamilton	William R. Sprenger
29-Nov-26	E. Hamilton	William R. Sprenger
16-Dec-26	E. Hamilton	William R. Sprenger
24-Jun-31	E. Hamilton	William R. Sprenger
24-Nov-33	E. Hamilton	William R. Sprenger
27-Dec-33	E. Hamilton	William R. Sprenger
30-Jan-34	E. Hamilton	William R. Sprenger
13-Aug-34	E. Hamilton	William R. Sprenger
31-Jan-35	E. Hamilton	William R. Sprenger
22-Dec-37	E. Hamilton	William R. Sprenger

H1 S885 **Jannick Storm**

Date	To	From
4-May-68	E. Hamilton	Jannick Storm
16-Apr-68	E. Hamilton	Jannick Storm

H1 S976 **Tom Swicegood**

Date	To	From
	E. Hamilton	Tom Swicegood
	E. Hamilton	Tom Swicegood
	E. Hamilton	Tom Swicegood

H1 W428 **Mort Weisinger**

Date	To	From
V-J-Day	E. Hamilton	Mort Weisinger
9-Jul-45	E. Hamilton	Mort Weisinger
23-Aug-45	E. Hamilton	Mort Weisinger
1-Oct-45	E. Hamilton	Mort Weisinger
16-Oct-45	E. Hamilton	Mort Weisinger
12-Jul-46	E. Hamilton	Mort Weisinger
2-Jan-50	E. Hamilton	Mort Weisinger
7-Dec-56	E. Hamilton	Mort Weisinger
	E. Hamilton	Mort Weisinger
	E. Hamilton	Mort Weisinger
24-Oct-34	E. Hamilton	Mort Weisinger
3-Nov-34	E. Hamilton	Mort Weisinger
31-May-34	E. Hamilton	Mort Weisinger
13-Jun-39	E. Hamilton	Mort Weisinger

Date	To	From
23-Jul-58	E. Hamilton	Mort Weisinger

H1 W452 **Manly Wade Wellman**

Date	To	From
Tues-Morn	E. Hamilton	Manly Wade Wellman

H1 W453 **Basil Wells**

Date	To	From
4-Jun-54	E. Hamilton	Basil Wells
10-Jun-54	E. Hamilton	Basil Wells
20-Jan-56	E. Hamilton	Basil Wells
12-Jul-56	E. Hamilton	Basil Wells
3-Jan-57	E. Hamilton	Basil Wells
11-Mar-60	E. Hamilton	Basil Wells

H1 W731 **Jack Williamson**

Date	To	From
17-Dec-43	E. Hamilton	Jack Williamson
18-Feb-44	E. Hamilton	Jack Williamson
4-May-44	E. Hamilton	Jack Williamson
10-Jul-44	E. Hamilton	Jack Williamson
23-Oct-44	E. Hamilton	Jack Williamson
2-Nov-44	E. Hamilton	Jack Williamson
Wed-Noon-44?	E. Hamilton	Jack Williamson
18-Dec-44	E. Hamilton	Jack Williamson
11-Apr-45	E. Hamilton	Jack Williamson
20-May-45	E. Hamilton	Jack Williamson
2-Jul-45	E. Hamilton	Jack Williamson
27-Sep-45	E. Hamilton	Jack Williamson
10-Feb-46	E. Hamilton	Jack Williamson
8-Jun-49	E. Hamilton	Jack Williamson
12-Jul-54	E. Hamilton	Jack Williamson
29-Oct-59	E. Hamilton	Jack Williamson
16-Mar-60	E. Hamilton	Jack Williamson

H1 W864 **Donald A. Wollheim**

Date	To	From
22-Apr-47	E. Hamilton	Donald A. Wollheim
18-Mar-60	E. Hamilton	Donald A. Wollheim
5-Dec-58	E. Hamilton	Donald A. Wollheim
11-Dec-58	E. Hamilton	Donald A. Wollheim
12-Mar-59	E. Hamilton	Donald A. Wollheim
17-Apr-61	E. Hamilton	Donald A. Wollheim

Date	To	From
9-May-61	E. Hamilton	Donald A. Wollheim
21-Feb-63	E. Hamilton	Donald A. Wollheim
18-Mar-63	Leigh	Donald A. Wollheim
14-Mar-63	Mr. Wollheim	Andre Norton
9-Dec-58	Mr. Wollheim	E. Hamilton
31-Jan-59	Mr. Wollheim	E. Hamilton

H1 W949 **Farnsworth Wright**

Date	To	From
1-Feb-26	E. Hamilton	Farnsworth Wright
9-Feb-26	E. Hamilton	Farnsworth Wright
22-Mar-26	E. Hamilton	Farnsworth Wright
22-Mar-26	E. Hamilton	Farnsworth Wright
25-Feb-25	E. Hamilton	Farnsworth Wright
26-Mar-26	E. Hamilton	Farnsworth Wright
8-Jan-27	E. Hamilton	Farnsworth Wright
14-May-26	E. Hamilton	Farnsworth Wright
18-May-26	E. Hamilton	Farnsworth Wright
12-Jul-26	E. Hamilton	Farnsworth Wright
15-Jul-26	E. Hamilton	Farnsworth Wright
11-Sep-26	E. Hamilton	Farnsworth Wright
23-Feb-27	E. Hamilton	Farnsworth Wright
13-Jun-27	E. Hamilton	Farnsworth Wright
21-Jan-28	E. Hamilton	Farnsworth Wright
17-Mar-28	E. Hamilton	Farnsworth Wright
19-Jan-29	E. Hamilton	Farnsworth Wright
30-Apr-30	E. Hamilton	Farnsworth Wright
8-Jun-31	E. Hamilton	Farnsworth Wright
9-Dec-31	E. Hamilton	Farnsworth Wright
24-Oct-32	E. Hamilton	Farnsworth Wright
14-Feb-33	E. Hamilton	Farnsworth Wright
7-Mar-33	E. Hamilton	Farnsworth Wright
15-Jun-33	E. Hamilton	Farnsworth Wright
28-Aug-33	E. Hamilton	Farnsworth Wright
28-Sep-33	E. Hamilton	Farnsworth Wright
31-Mar-34	E. Hamilton	Farnsworth Wright
16-May-34	E. Hamilton	Farnsworth Wright
13-Feb-35	E. Hamilton	Farnsworth Wright
16-Feb-35	E. Hamilton	Farnsworth Wright
2-May-35	E. Hamilton	Farnsworth Wright
7-Jul-36	E. Hamilton	Farnsworth Wright
25-Jan-37	E. Hamilton	Farnsworth Wright

Date	To	From
16-Apr-37	E. Hamilton	Farnsworth Wright
26-OCt-37	E. Hamilton	Farnsworth Wright
16-Feb-38	E. Hamilton	Farnsworth Wright
21-Jul-38	E. Hamilton	Farnsworth Wright
17-Feb-39	E. Hamilton	Farnsworth Wright
20-Oct-39	E. Hamilton	Farnsworth Wright
11-Dec-39	E. Hamilton	Farnsworth Wright
29-Jan-40	E. Hamilton	Farnsworth Wright
	E. Hamilton	Farnsworth Wright

D
Non-Fiction

D1 "The Excitements of Science." Tales of Wonder, #5 (Winter, 1938) Pg. 126.

D2 "Why I Selected The Inn Outside the World" in **My Best Science Fiction Story** [12 of 25]. Edited by Leo Margulies and Oscar J.Friend. _: Merlin Press, 1949, p.

aa in **My Best Science Fiction Story** [12 of 25]. Edited by Leo Margulies and Oscar J.Friend. _: Pocket, 1954, p.

D3 "Writing the Pseudo-Scientific Story."[cxx]

D4 "The Story Behind the Story for FORGOTTEN WORLD."[cxxi]

D5 "Terror In Installments."[cxxii]

D6 "Time-Travelling in Ohio."[cxxiii]

D7 "Untitled."[cxxiv]

D8 "Introducing the Author: Edmond Hamilton" in Imagination Science Fiction. (April, 1956) Pg. 2. Photo.

D9 "Author's Lot, No. 4" in Vector 28. (September 1964): pp. 14-15.

D10 "Tribute to 'Doc' Smith" in <u>Vector</u> 36 (November 1965): pp. 9-10.

D11 "He That Hath Words" in **Deeper than you Think**. (July, 1968): Pg.

b in <u>WT 50: A Tribute to Weird Tales</u>. () Pg. 88.

c in **Weird Tales Story**. Edited by Robert Weinberg. _: FAX Collector's Editions, 1977, p.

D12 "Look Forward, Look Back" in <u>Return to Wonder</u>, #9. (1970?): pp. 6-7.

D13 "An Inside Look at Captain Future" in <u>Pulp</u> 1:3 (Summer, 1971) Pg. 3.

D14 "John W. Campbell" in <u>Locus</u> No. 91. (July 22, 1971) Pg. 8.

D15 The Story of Monroe: Its Past and Its Progress Toward the Present. Monroe Public Schools, Print Shop. 1976, p.

D16 "Afterward." **The Best of Edmond Hamilton**. Edited by Leigh Brackett. Garden City, NY.: Nelson Doubleday, 1977, p.cloth.

aa in **The Best of Edmond Hamilton**. Edited by Leigh Brackett.: Ballentine, 1977, p. paper.

b in **The Vampire Master and Other Tales of Terror**, Royal Oak, MI: Haffner Press. 2000, p. cloth.

D17 "Story Teller of Many Worlds." **The Best of Leigh Bracket**. 1977, p.

aa in **The Best of Leigh Bracket**. 1977.

D18 "Fifty Years of Heroes: The Edmond Hamilton Papers" in **Weird Heroes**, edited by Byron Preiss. Vol. 6 (April, 1977): 111. _: Pyramid, 1977, p.

E
Teleplays

E1 "The Children of the Moon," for **Crater Base One.**[cxxv] (EDH#1)

E2 "The Man Who Watched the Earth," for **Crater Base One**. (EDH#2)

E3 "Forgotten Earth," for **Crater Base One**. (EDH#3)

E4 "The Moon-Born," for **Crater Base One**. (EDH#4)

F
Comic Books

F1 *Black Terror*. Edmond Hamilton was the principle author from 1941-1945.[cxxvi]

F2 "Isle of Yesterday."[cxxvii] in Superman.(12 July 1946) Pg.

F3 <unknown>.[cxxviii] in Detective Comics #144 (February 1949) Pg.

F4 "The Adventures of Chris KL-99 - The World of Giant Robots" in Strange Adventures #2, (October – November, 1950) Pg.

F5 "The Adventures of Chris KL-99 - The Metal World" in Strange Adventures #3, (December, 1950) : Pg.

F6 "The Crime Chase Through Time" in Strange Adventures #4, (January, 1951) Pg.

F7 "The Adventures of Chris KL-99 - The World Inside the Atom" in Strange Adventures #5, (February, 1951) Pg.

F8 "The Adventures of Chris KL-99 - The Lost Earthman" in Strange Adventures #7, (April, 1951) Pg.

F9 "The Adventures of Chris KL-99 - The Missing Moon" in Strange Adventures #11, (August, 1951) Pg.

F10 "Artist of Other Worlds" in Strange Adventures #13, (October, 1951) Pg.

F11 "Superman vs. It" in Action Comics #162, (November, 1951) Pg.

F12 "The Micromen" in Mystery in Space,[cxxix] (1951) Pg.

F13 "The Danger Club" in Batman #76 (April-May, 1953) Pg.

F14 "The Pengiun's Fabulous Fowls" in Batman #76 (April-May, 1953) Pg. Art: Lew Sayre Schwartz and Charles Paris.

REPRINTS:

b in **The Greatest Batman Stories Ever Told Volume 2**. Edited by Paul Kupperberg and Robert Greenberger. New York, NY: Warner Books, Inc. 1992, pp 53-62.

F15 "Crimes of the Catwoman" in Detective Comics, #203 (January 1954) Pg. Art: Lew Sayre Schwartz and Charles Paris. Lettering: Pat Gordon.

REPRINTS:

b in **The Greatest Batman Stories Ever Told Volume 2**. Edited by Paul Kupperberg and Robert Greenberger. New York, NY: Warner Books, Inc. 1992, pp 53-62.

F16 "The Man with Four Minds." in Strange Adventures,[cxxx] (1954) Pg.

F187 "The Batman of Tomorrow!" in Detective Comics #216

(February 1955) Pg. Pencils: Dick Sprang; Inks: Charles Paris.

REPRINTS:

b in **Batman in the Fifties**. Edited by D. C. Comics. New York, NY: D. C. Comics, 2002, p. pp. 148-159.

F18 "The Map of Mystery" in Batman #91 (April, 1955) Pg.

F19 "The Living Batplane" in Batman #91 (April, 1955) Pg.

F20 "The Caveman Batman" in Batman #93 (August, 1955) Pg.

F21 "Batman - Baby Sitter" in Batman #93 (August, 1955) Pg.

F22 "The Synthetic Hero." (1 March 1956) Pg.

F23 "The True History of Superman and Batman" in World's Finest Comics #81 (March/April 1956) Pg. Pencils Sheldon Moldoff; Inks: Charles Paris.

REPRINTS:

b in **Batman in the Fifties**. Edited by D. C. Comics. New York, NY: D. C. Comics. 2002, p 36-47.

F24 "The Batwoman" in Detective Comics #233 (July, 1956) Pg. Splash Page: Sheldon Moldoff.

REPRINTS:

b in **Batman in the Fifties**. Edited by D. C. Comics. New York, NY: D. C. Comics. 2002, p 70-81.

F25 "The 1,001 Inventions of Batman" in Batman #109, (August, 1957) Pg.

F26 <unknown> in Giant Superman Annual #6 (1962) Pg.

F27 <unknown> in Action Comics #290 (July, 1962) Pg.

F28 "Superman Under The Green Sun" in Superman #155, (August, 1962) Pg.

F29 "The Last Days of Superman" in Superman #156, (October, 1962) Pg. Pencils: Curt Swan; Inks: George Klien.

REPRINTS:

b in **Superman in the Sixties**. Edited by Dale Crane. New York, NY:DC Comics. 19999, p 89-104.

c in **Superman: The Greatest Stories Ever Told, Volume 1**. Edited by ?. New York, NY: DC Comics. 2004, 192 pp. (10.1 x 6.6 x 0.4 inches) ISBN-10: 1401203396; ISBN-13: 978-1401203399.

F30 <unknown> in Action Comics #291 (August, 1962) Pg.

F31 <unknown> in Adventure #300 (September, 1962) Pg.

F32 <unknown> in Adventure #304 (January, 1963) Pg.

F33 "The Legion of Substitute Heroes" in Adventure #306, (March, 1963) Pg.

F34 "The Secret Power of the Mystery Super-Hero" in

Adventure #307, (April, 1963) Pg.

F35 "Superman Under the Red Sun!" in Action Comics #300 (May, 1962) Pg.

F36 "The Return of Lightning Lad" in Adventure #308, (May, 1963) Pg.

F37 "The Legion of Super Monsters" in Adventure #309, (June, 1963) Pg.

F38 "The Legion's Super-Showdown" in Adventure #309, (June, 1963) Pg.
Note: This is part two of the story begun in "The Legion of Super Monsters".

F39 "The Doom of the Super-Heroes" in Adventure #310, (July, 1963) Pg.

F40 "The Last Stand of the Legion" in Adventure #310, (July, 1963) Pg.
Note: This is part two of the story begun in "The Doom of the Super-Heroes".

F41 "The War Between the Substitute Heroes and the Legionaires" in Adventure #311, (August, 1963) Pg.

F42 "The Duel of the Legions" in Adventure #311, (August, 1963): Pg.
Note: This is part two of the story begun in "The War Between the Substitute Heroes and the Legionaires".

F43 "Menace of the Future Man" in World's Finest #135 (August, 1963) Pg.

F44 "The Super-Sacrifice of the Legionaires" in Adventure #312, (September, 1963) Pg.

F45 "The Bravest Legionaire" in Adventure #312, (September, 1963): Pg.
Note: This is part two of the story begun in "The Super-Sacrifice of the Legionaires".

F46 "The Condemned Legionaires" in Adventure #313, (October, 1963) Pg.

F47 "The Secret of Satan Girl" in Adventure #313, (October, 1963): Pg.
Note: This is part two of the story begun in "The Condemned Legionaires".

F48 "The Showdown Between Luthor and Superman[cxxxi]" in

Superman #164 (October 1963) Pg. Pencils: Curt Swan; Inks: George Klein. Cover: Curt Swan & George Klein.

REPRINTS:

b in **Superman in the Sixties**. Edited by Dale Crane. New York, NY: DC Comics. 1999, p 150-166.

c in **Superman: The Greatest Stories Ever Told, Volume 1**. Edited by ?. New York, NY: DC Comics. 2004, 192 pp. (10.1 x 6.6 x 0.4 inches) ISBN-10: 1401203396; ISBN-13: 978-1401203399.

CHAPTERS:

Part I: The Showdown Between Luthor and Superman
Part II: The Super Duel

F49 "The Super-Villians of All Ages" in Adventure #314, (November, 1963) Pg.

F50 "The Civil War of the Legion" in Adventure #314, (November, 1963) Pg.
Note: This is part two of the story begun in "The Super-Villians of All Ages".

F51 "The Legionnaires Super-Contest" in Adventure #315, (December, 1963) Pg.

F52 "The Winner of the Super-Tests" in Adventure #315, (December, 1963) Pg.
Note: This is part two of the story begun in "The Legionnaires Super-Contest".

F53 "The Renegade Super-Hero" in Adventure #316, (January, 1964) Pg.

F54 "The Zodiac Master" in Detective Comics #323 (January, 1964): Pg.

F55 "The End of a Super-Traitor" in Adventure #316, (January, 1964) Pg.
Note: This is part two of the story begun in "The Renegade Super-Hero".

F56 "The Menace of Dream Girl" in Adventure #317, (February, 1964) Pg.

F57 "The Doom of the Legion" in Adventure #317, (February, 1964): Pg.

Note: This is part two of the story begun in "The Menace of Dream Girl".

F58 "The Mutiny of the Legionnaires" in Adventure #318, (March, 1964) Pg.

F59 "The Castaway Legionnaires" in Adventure #318, (March, 1964) Pg.

Note: This is part two of the story begun in "The Mutiny of the Legionnaires".

F60 "Robin's New Secret Identity" in Batman #162 (March, 1964): Pg.

F61 "The Batman Creature" in Batman #162 (March, 1964) Pg.

F62 "The Legion's Suicide Squad" in Adventure #319, (April, 1964): Pg.

F63 "The Charge of the Substitute Heroes" in Adventure #319, (April, 1964) Pg.

Note: This is part two of the story begun in "The Legion's Suicide Squad".

F64 "The Code of the Legion" in Adventure #321, (June 1964) Pg.

F65 "The Weakest Legionnaire" in Adventure #321, (June 1964) Pg.

Note: This is part two of the story begun in "The Code of the Legion".

F66 "The Super-Tests of the Super-Pets" in Adventure #322, (July, 1964) Pg.

F67 "The Pet of a Thousand Faces" in Adventure #322, (July, 1964) Pg.
Note: This is part two of the story begun in "The Super-Tests of the Super-Pets".

F68 "The Legion of Super-Outlaws" in Adventure #324, (September, 1964) Pg.

F69 "The Battle of the Super-Teams" in Adventure #324, (September, 1964) Pg.
Note: This is part two of the story begun in "The Legion of Super-Outlaws".

F70 "Lex Luthor Meets the Legion of Super-Heroes" in Adventure #325, (October, 1964) Pg.

F71 "The Super-Vengence of Lex Luthor" in Adventure #325, (October, 1964) Pg.
Note: This is part two of the story begun in "Lex Luthor Meets the Legion of Super-Heroes".

F72 "The Lone Wolf Legionnaire" in Adventure #327, (December, 1964) Pg.

F73 "The Youth Who Wasn't Human" in Adventure #327, (December, 1964) Pg.
Note: This is part two of the story begun in "The Lone Wolf Legionnaire".

F74 "The Super-Moby Dick of Space" in Adventure #332, (May, 1965) Pg.

F75 "The Cosmic Quest of Lightning Lad" in Adventure #332, (May, 1965) Pg.
Note: This is part two of the story begun in "The Super-Moby Dick of Space".

F76 "The Unknown Legionnaire" in Adventure #334, (July, 1965): Pg.

F77 "The Secret of Unknown Boy" in Adventure #334, (July, 1965) Pg.
Note: This is part two of the story begun in "The Unknown Legionnaire".

F78 "Starfinger" in Adventure #335, (August, 1965) Pg.

F79 "Starfinger Against The Legion" in Adventure #335, (August, 1965) Pg.
Note: This is part two of the story begun in "Starfinger".

F80 "The True Identity of Starfinger" in Adventure #336, (September, 1965) Pg.

F81 "The Secret of Starfinger" in Adventure #336, (September, 1965) Pg.
Note: This is part two of the story begun in "The True Identity of Starfinger".

F82 "The Weddings That Wrecked the Legion" in Adventure #337, (October, 1965) Pg.

F83 "The Legionnaire Drop-outs" in Adventure #337, (October, 1965) Pg.
Note: This is part two of the story begun in "The Weddings That Wrecked the Legion".

F84 "Hunters of the Super-Beasts" in Adventure #339, (December, 1965) Pg.

F85 "The Menace of Beast Boy" in Adventure #339, (December, 1965) Pg.
Note: This is part two of the story begun in "Hunters of the Super-Beasts".

F86 "Colossal Boy's One-Man War" in Adventure #341, (February, 1966) Pg.

F87 "The Weirdo Legionnaire" in Adventure #341, (February, 1966): Pg.
Note: This is part two of the story begun in "Colossal Boy's One-Man War".

F88 "The Strategy of Brainiac 5" in Adventure #341, (February, 1966) Pg.
Note: This is part three of the story begun in "Colossal Boy's One-Man War".

F89 "The Legionnaire Who Killed" in Adventure #342, (March, 1966) Pg.

F90 "The Verdict of the Legion" in Adventure #342, (March, 1966): Pg.

Note: This is part two of the story begun in "The Legionnaire Who Killed".

F91 "The Evil Hand of the Luck Lords" in Adventure #343, (April, 1966) Pg.

F92 "The Secret of the Luck Lords" in Adventure #343, (April, 1966) Pg.
Note: This is part two of the story begun in "The Evil Hand of the Luck Lords".

F93 "The Super-Stalag of Space" in Adventure #344, (May, 1966): Pg.

F94 "The Testing of Brainiac 5" in Adventure #344, (May, 1966): Pg.
Note: This is part two of the story begun in "The Super-Stalag of Space".

F95 "The Execution of Matter-Eater Lad" in Adventure #345, (June, 1966) Pg.

F96 "Duo Damsel's Double-Play" Adventure #345, (June, 1966): Pg.
Note: This is part two of the story begun in "The Execution of Matter-Eater Lad".

The following stories or scripts were found in the Edmond Hamilton papers housed in the Jack Williamson Collection at Golden Library at Eastern New Mexico University. All of the stories have no byline, however there is a letter from Mort Weisinger stating "Here's a check for the Tommy Tomorrow yarn" dated 2 January 1950. Some of the scripts have a date sent typed on them. However, they do not state which issue, or series the story was published in.

F97 "Bandits in Toyland"[cxxxii] in Batman.

Bruce Wayne is called to Jury Duty in the case of an employee accused of robbing the Luxury store where he was employed. During the trial Bruce discovers that Willard, the employee, was framed.

Bruce sneaks out of the hotel where the jury is being put up for the night. He and Robin trace a mysterious rash of toy robberies to the gangster Muscles Malone.

F98 "The Connoisseur of Crime"[cxxxiii] in Green Lantern.

Alan Scott (Green Lantern) and Doiby Dickles are walking homeward when they encounter a group of boys in Green Lantern costumes. Scott decides to investigate because they are unauthorized products.

F99 "The Dynamic Duo of Kandor!"[cxxxiv] in Jimmy Olsen #69. Pencils by Curt Swan and inked by George Klien.

F100 "The Dynamic Duo of Kandor!, Part II" in Jimmy Olsen #69. Pencils by Curt Swan and inked by George Klien.

F101 "Robotman - Around the World in 24 Hours" in Detective Comics.

F102 "Robotman - The Human Armored Car" in Detective Comics.

F103 "Robotman - Robbie Shows his Teeth" in Star Spangled Comics.

F104 "Robotman - The Ghost Dog" in Star Spangled Comics.

F105 "Robotman - Lightning Strikes Twice" in Star Spangled Comics.

F106 "Robotman - Emergency Kit for Crime" in Star Spangled Comics.

F107 "The Substitute Superman!"[cxxxv] in ?

This is chapter two [see L61] of the story that began in "The World that was Krypton's Twin." Kell Orr is impersonating Superman on Earth while Superman is on Xenon. Lois Lane begins to suspect that Clark Kent is Superman because he's made several 'super' mistakes since he's not used to having super-powers or is he accoustomed to Earth life. He also avoids the schemes of Sparkler Staines who trying to kill Superman with Kryptonite bullets.There may be a third chapter for this story because it ends without returning Superman to Earth and Kell Orr to Xenon.

F108 "Superboy - The Miracle Plane" in ?

F109 "Superboy - Superboy meets Girl" in ?

F110 "Superboy - Superboy, Toy-Tester" in ?

F111 "Superboy - The Adventure of Jaguar Boy" in ?

F112 "Superboy - The Hobby Robber" in ?

F113 "Superboy - Doll of Danger" in ?

F114 "Superman - The City That Forgot Superman" in ?

F115 "Superman - Mr. Mxyxtplk, Hero!" in ?

F116 "Tommy Tomorrow - The Largest Man in the World" in Action Comics.

F117 "Tommy Tomorrow - The Seven Wonders of Space" in Action Comics.

F118 "The World that was Krypton's Twin!"[cxxxvi] in ?

Scientists discover a planet far out in space. This world is almost an exact twin of Krypton. Superman decides to go investigate. There he saves an animal preserve from an erupting volcano. He befriends a local scientist Zell Orr and meets his son Kell Orr. He craves adventure, so Superman and Kell decide to switch places. He flies Kell to earth and gives him a crash course in being \ Superman and Clark Kent. Superman then returns to Xenon, where he performs several more super feats. And much like Superman's first appearance on Earth, he is pestered by a woman reporter named Vana Vair. While dealing with an ever growing number of catastrophies, Superman makes a terrible discovery.

F119 "The Super-Partners" in World's Finest.

Superman rescues a young boy from a wrecked space ship. It turns out that he has super-powers like Superman. He has amnesia and does not remember who he his or where he's from. Batman, Robin and Superman give him the name Skyboy and he becomes Superman's partner. With Skyboy's help they perform several superfeats to keep Metropolis from harm. They solve the mystery of who's stealing all of the copper.

The following items are also included in the Edmond Hamilton papers in the Jack Williamson Collection at Golden Library, Eastern New Mexico University. It is not known whether Mr. Hamilton wrote the stories associated with these. They may have been sent to him to suggest plots for a story; these are listed by call number.

F120 H5 M678a

Copy of cover to Action Comics #314 (July) Pg.
Featuring "The Day Superman became the Flash."

Copy of World's Finest #141 (May) Pg.
Featuring "The Olsen-Robin Team versus The Superman-Batman Team!"
Note: There is a hand-written on it: "Ed. here's the cover scene – please incorporate in the story as
..."

F121 H8 C733

Action Comics #290, (July, 1962)
Action Comics #291, (August, 1962)
Action Comics #300, (May, 1963)
Adventure Comics #300, (September, 1962)
Adventure Comics #310, (October, 1962)
Adventure Comics #304, (January, 1963)
Giant Superman Annual #6, (1962-63)
World's Finest #151, (August, 1965)
World's Finest #157, (May, 1966)

Notes

An item of note to comic book fans. In a letter from Mort Weisinger, dated 7 December 1956, the name Lightning Man was okayed.

In researching Mr. Hamilton's involvement I have run across speculation that he may have been involved with a story (or stories) in the following comic books.

Action Comics

118	
119	
121	
135	
137	
138	
147	
148	
151	
158	
186	
189	
191	
223	
229	
234	
239	
293	
301	
303	
309	
314	The Day Superman became the Flash
318	
319	
321	
327	
329	
330	
338	
339	

Adventure

144
145
146
156
161
167

172			
208			
240			
268			
301		(Superboy)	
321			
333			

Batman

38		Peril in Greece	
77		The Crime Predictor	
78		The Manhunter from Mars	
83		The Testing of Batman	
85		The Guardian of the Bat-Signal	
86	1954	The Voyage of the First Batmarine	
88	1954	The Mystery of the Four Batmen	
90	1955		
94	1955		
95		Mystery of the Sky Museum	
		The Ballad of Batman	
98		The Desert Island Batman	
99		Batman -- Frontier Marshall	
		The Phantom of the Bat-Cave	
101		The Vanished Batman	
		The Six Strangest Sleuths	
104		The Man Who Knew Batman's Secret	
110		The Phantom Batman	
111		The Armored Batman	
112	1957	Batman's Roman Holiday	

Detective Comics

124			
127			
133			
135			
158			
165	1950		
198	1953	The Lord of Batmanor	co-written by Leigh Brackett
211	1954	The Jungle Cat-Queen	
217	1955		
225	1955		
226	1955	When Batman Was Robin	
235	1956		

245	1957	

From Beyond the Unknown

5	Jun-Jul 1970	The Gorilla Who Challenged the World
		The Jungle Emperor
8	Dec-Jan 1970-71	The Incredible Eyes of Arthur Gail!

Strange Adventures

67		Search for a Lost World (reprinted in #230)

Superboy

22		The Noah's Ark from Space
23		Clark Kent, Miser
27		The Movie Star of Tomorrow
99		The Doom That Destroyed Clark Kent
101		The Valhalla of Super-Companian (reprinted in Adventure 371)
103		The Three Ages of Superboy
119		Superbaby's First time-Adventure
120		The Invulnerable Imp

Superman

52		Superman in Valhalla
64		The Isle of Giant Insects
68		Six Elements of Crime
70		The Life of Superman
		The Pied Piper Pransker
71		The Anti-Superman Club
		The Man Who Stole the Oceans
72		The Private Life of Perry White
74		The Lost Secrets of Krypton
		The Secret of Superman's House
75		The Prankster's Star Pupil
		Superman--Thrill Salesman
76		The Mightiest Team in the World
78	9/10-1952	The Girls in Superman's Life
79		Citadel of Doom
80		Superman's Big Brother
		Men of Fire
81		Superman's Secret Workshop
90		Superman's Secret Past
102		Superman's 3 Mistakes
106	1956	Superman's First Exploits

119		The Second Superman
154		The Underwater Pranks of Mr. Mzyzptlk
158		Superman in Kandor
161		Superman Goes to War
163		Wonder-Man, The New Hero of Metropolis
166		The Fantastic Story of Superman's Sons
167		The Team of Luthor and Brainiac
168		Luthor-Super-Hero
171		The Nightmare Ordeal of Superman
174		Clark Kent;s Incredible Delusion
175		Clark Kent's Brother
181		The Superman of 2965

Superman's Girlfriend Lois Lane

54	1967	The Monster Who Loved Lois
57	1967	The Return of Lois' Monster Sweetheart

Superman's Pal Jimmy Olsen

64		Jimmy Olsen's Fiery Friends
66	1963	The Burglar Kit from the Future
67		The Dummy That Haunted Jimmy Olsen
71		(all 3 stories)
85		King Olsen's Private Island

World's Finest

35		
39		
62		
73		
76		
77		The Super Bat-Man
79		
80		
81		
82		
84		
85		
86		
88	1957	Supreman's & Batman's Greatest Foes (reprinted in the Greatest Joker Stories Ever Told)
89		
90		

91		
92		
93		
94	1958	Origin of the Superman-Batman (reprinter in the Greatest Joker Stories Ever Told)
96		
141		The Superman-Batman Team!
142		
143		
144		
145		
146		
147		
148		
149		
150		
151		
152		
153		
154		
155		
156		
157		
158		
159		

G
Interviews

G1 Interview conducted by person(s) unknown.
Interview of Edmond Hamilton, Leigh Brackett, Bertil Falk, Kathleen J. Prestwidge and Ulf R. Johnson. Conducted in the office of Hans Stefen Santesson, February 23, 1974, p.
[Film Reel]

G2 "Interview with Edmond Hamilton," conducted by Patrick Hayden, in Twibbet 7, [n.d. c1975] pp. 4-8. [fanzine]

REPRINTS:

b in Alien Contact: Das Magazin für Science Fiction und Fantasy, August 19, 2003, p. (#55),

G3 "An Interview with Leigh Brackett & Edmond Hamilton," conducted by David Truesdale with Paul MaGuire, in Tangent, September 1976, p. [fanzine]

REPRINTS:

b Science Fiction Review, (V6#2 [#21]) May 1977, pp. 6-15.

G4 "The Amazing Interview: Edmond Hamilton & Leigh Brackett," conducted by Darrell Schweitzer, in Amazing Science Fiction, (51:2) January 1978, p. Pg. 116.

REPRINTS:

b in **Science Fiction Voices #5**. San Bernardino, CA: Borgo Press. 1979, p. paper, pp. 35-41.

G5 "Edmond Hamilton: Interview," conducted by Paul Walker, in **Speaking of Science Fiction: The Paul Walker Interviews**. _: Luna Publications, September 1978, 425 p.

ISBN: 0-930346-01-7. Illustrator: David Ludwig.

H
Citings

The following is a list of books that mention Mr. Hamilton, or one of his works, in passing. No real detail is given about the author, but in some instances these passages place Mr. Hamilton at a certain event or credit him with some accomplishment.

H1 Ash, Brian. **The Visual Encyclopedia of Science Fiction**. New York: Harmony Books, 1977.

Pgs. 70, 75, 76, 81, 82, 87, 93, 97, 98, 103, 105, 108, 110, 112, 133, 134, 139, 142, 150, 157, 173, 180, 185, 191, 193, 307, 334.

H2 Ashley, Mike. **The History of Science Fiction Magazines: 1926 -1935**. Chicago: Henry Regnery Company, 1974.

Pg. 153.

H3 Ashley, Mike. **The Supernatural Index: 1926 -1935**. Chicago: Henry Regnery Company, 1974.

Pg. 153.

H4 Bainbridge, William Sims. **Dimensions of Science Fiction**. Cambridge, MA: Harvard University Press, 1986.

Pgs. 28, 79, 124, 126-127.

H5 Barmeyer, Eike. **Science Fiction: Theorie und Geschichte**. Munchen 40, Germany: Wilhelm Fink Verlag, 1970.

Pg. 120.

H6 Barron, Neil. **Anatomy of Wonder: A Critical Guide to Science Fiction 2nd Ed**. New York: R.R. Bowker Co. 1981.

Pgs.	2-2	(The Accursed Galaxy)
	2-38	(Crashing Suns)
		(The Horror on the Asteroid)
		(Outside the Universe)
	3-365	(The Best of Edmond Hamilton)
	3-366	(The Star of Life)

H7 Beaumont, Charles "The Bloody Pulps" in Playboy (September, 1962).

Pg 9.

H8 Benton, Mike. **The Illustrated History Science Fiction Comics**. Dallas, TX.: Taylor Publishing Co. 1992.

Pgs: 4, 22, 59, 60, 63.

H9 Benton, Mike. **Superheroes Comics of the Golden Age**. Dallas, TX: Taylor Publishing Co.

Pg. 78.

H10 Berger, Albert L. "The Triumph of Prophecy: Science Fiction and Nuclear Power in the Post-Hiroshima Period" in <u>Science Fiction Studies</u>, Number 9, Volume 3, Part 2 (July 1976).

H11 Bleiler, E. F. **The Checklist of Science-Fiction & Supernatural Fiction**. Glen Rock, NJ: Fireball Books, 1979.

Pg. 92 "The Horror on the Asteroid, & Other Tales of Planetary Horror," 1936. 256 p.
Pg. 92 "The Metal Giants," nd. 34

H12 Bleiler, Everett, F. **Science Fiction: The Early Years**. Kent, Ohio: Kent State University Press, 1990.

Pg. 331

H13 Bretnor, Reginald. Ed. **Modern Science Fiction**. Chicago, IL: Advent Publishers, Inc. 1979.

Pgs. 169, 304.
Pg. 77. **The Star Kings**

H14 Bretnor, Reginald. Ed. **Science Fiction Today and Tomorrow**. NY: Harper & Row Publishers, 1974.

Pgs. 189, 190, 290, 309.

H15 Budrys, Algis. **Benchmarks: Galaxy Bookshelf of Algis Budrys**. Carbondale & Edwardsville, IL.: Southern Illinois Unversity Press, 1985.

Pg. 86 ("Requiem," Modern Masterpieces of Science Fiction)
Pg. 132 ("Sunfire")
Pg. 213 ("What's It Like Out There?," Science Fiction For People Who Hate Science Fiction).

H16 Clareson, Thomas D. **Contemporary American Science Fiction**. Columbia, SC: University of Southern Carolina Press, 1990.

Pgs. 14, 19, 22.

H17 Daniels, Les. **Batman: The Complete History**. San Francisco, CA: Chronicle Books, 1998.

H18 Daniels, Les. **DC Comics: Sixty Years of the World's Favorite Comic Book Heroes**. New York, NY: Bulfinch Press Book; Little, Brown and Company, 1995.

Pgs. 28, 102, 122

H19 Daniels, Les. **Superman: The Complete History**. San Francisco, CA: Chronicle Books, 1998.

Pgs. 105, 109

H20 Davenport, Basil, Robert A. Heinlein, C. M. Kornbluth, Alfred Bester, Robert Bloch. **The Science Fiction Novel: Imagination & Social Criticism**. Chicago: Advent Publishing Co. 1969.

Pg. 30-1.

H21 Haining, Peter. **Weird Tales**. NY: Carroll & Graf Publishers, Inc. 1976, 1990.

Pg. 15.

H22 Hartwell, David. **Age of Wonders: Exploring the Worlds of Science Fiction**. New York, NY.: Walker & Co. 1984.

Pg. 45.

H23 Hudgeons, Thomas E. III. **The Official 1981 Price Guide to Comic & Science Fiction Books**. Orlando, FL: The House of Collectibles, 1981.

Pgs. 403, 416, 430.

H24 James, Edward. **Science Fiction in the 20th Century**. Oxford: Oxford University Press, 1994.

Pgs. 73, 75.

H25 Kaye, Marvin & Saralee Kaye. **The Magazine that Never Dies: Weird Tales**. Garden City, NY: Doubleday Book & Music Clubs, Inc. 1988.

Pgs, xvii
582
579 "The Man Who Returned"
580 "He That Hath Wings"
"The Man Who Returned"
581 "Evolution Island"

H26 Latham, Rob. "Recent Works of Reference on SF, Fantasy, and Horror" in Science Fiction Studies #85 Volume 28, Part 3 (November 2001).

H27 Magic Dragon Multimedia. **SF Timeline 1920-1930**. http://www.magicdragon.com/UltimateSF/timeline1930.html.

H28 Magic Dragon Multimedia. **SF Timeline 1930-1940**. http://www.magicdragon.com/UltimateSF/timeline1940.html.

H29 Magic Dragon Multimedia. **SF Timeline 1940-1950**. http://www.magicdragon.com/UltimateSF/timeline1950.html.

H30 Magic Dragon Multimedia. **SF Timeline 1950-1960**. http://www.magicdragon.com/UltimateSF/timeline1960.html.

H31 Magic Dragon Multimedia. **SF Timeline 1960-1970**. http://www.magicdragon.com/UltimateSF/timeline1970.html.

H32 Madle, Robert A. "My Pal Johnny." Mimosa 23 (January 1999). Pg. 34.

H33 Merril, Judith. **9th Annual Edition of the Years's Best Science Fiction**. New York, NY: Dell Publishing Company, Inc. 1963.

Pg. 380.

H34 - - - **10th Annual Edition of the Years's Best Science Fiction**. New York, NY: Dell Publishing Company, Inc. 1963.

Pg. 381.

H35 Moskowitz, Sam. **Explorers of the Infinite: Shapes of Science Fiction**. Westport, CT: Hyperion Press, Inc. 1974.

Pgs. 194, 205, 297.

H36 Moskowitz, Sam. **The Immortal Storm**. Westport, CT: Hyperion Press, Inc. 1974.

Pgs. 16, 75, 83, 213.

H37 Moskowitz, Sam. **Seekers of Tomorrow**. Westport, CT: Hyperion Press, Inc. 1974.

Pgs. 3, 10, 19, 90, 107, 108, 117, 134-35, 144, 238, 309, 329, 359, 364.

H38 Moskowitz, Sam. **Strange Horizons: The Spectrum of Science Fiction**. NY: Charles Scribner's Sons, 1976.

Pgs. 82-83, 88, 148, 220, 242-243, 251.

H39 Nichols, Peter. **The Science Fiction Encyclopedia**. Garden City, NY: Dolphin Books, Doubleday & Co. Inc. 1979.

Pg. 270.

H40 Pringle, David. **Science Fiction The 100 Best Novels**. New York, NY: Carroll & Graf Publishers, Inc. 1985.

Pg. 56.

H41 Rodgers, Alva. **A Requiem For Astounding**. Chicago, IL: Advent Publishers, Inc. 1964.

Pgs. 2, 6, 46, 47, 65, 110, 212.

H42 Rottensteiner, Frank. **The Science Fiction Book: An Illustrated History**. New York, NY: The Seabury Press, 1975.

Pg.55 "The Star-Stealers" cover Weird Tales February 1929.

H43 Sadoul, J. **Historie de La Science Fiction Moderne**. Paris: Albin Michel. 1973.

Pgs. 75, 92, 93, 124, 128, 131, 159, 160, 161, 162, 164, 170, 199, 236, 259, 297, 389.

H44 Sampson, Robert. **Yesterday's Faces: A Study of Series Characters in the Early Pulp Magazines: Vol. 2 Strange Days**. Bowling Green, OH: Bowling Green University Popular Press, 1984.

Pgs. 214, 216, 218, 247, 255.

H45 Schultz, Hans-Joachim. **Science Fiction**. Stuttgart: J.B. Metzlerghe Vertagsbuchhandlung, 1986.

Pgs. 136, 137.

H46 Schwartz, Julius & Brian M. Thomsen. **Man of Two Worlds**. New York,

NY: Harper Collins Publishing Inc, 2000.

Pgs, frontpiece, 25, 34-35, 48, 56-58, 61-63, 83, 114, 158.

H47 Tymn, Marshall B. **Horror Literature: A Core Collection and Reference Guide**. New York, NY: R.R. Bowker Co. 1981. 520p.

Pgs. 348 (4-243): 356 (4-273), 357 (4-275), 361 (4-285 and 4-286), 367 (4-305), 393 Thrilling Mystery.

H48 Warner, Harry Jr. **All Our Yesterdays**. Chicago, IL: Advent Publishers, Inc. 1969.

Pgs. 28, 52, 225.

H49 Wolheim, Donald A. **Universe Makers**. <publisher unknown> 1971.

pp. 30-32.

H50 Wuckel, Dicter & Bruce Cassidy. **The Illustrated History of Science Fiction**. New York, NY: Ungar, 1986.

H51 Zgorzelski, Andrzes. **Fantastyka Utopia: Science Fiction: Ze studiow nad rozwojen gatunkow**. Warszawa: Pantswone Wydawnictwo Nawkowe, 1980.

Pgs. 127-137, 138, 141, 145, 146, 153, 154, 168, 169.

I
About the Author

I1 Akerman, Forrest J. “Edmond Hamilton: The World Saver” in **Weird Heroes. Vol. 6**. April, 1977, p. Pg. 142.

I2 --- “Eulogy” in Xenofile, #30. Pg. 13.

I3 Barron, Neil. **Anatomy of Wonder**. New York, NY: R. R. Bowker Co. 1981, p.

I4 Benson, Gordon and Phil Stephensen-Payne. **Leigh Douglas Bracket & Edmond Hamilton: A Working Bibliograhy**. San Bernardino, CA: The Borgo Press, Galatic Central Bibliographies (Galactic Central Bibliographies for the Avid Reader; Volume 20). 1992, 25 p.

I5 Bloch, Robert & Julius Schwartz. “Afterwards” in **Weird Heroes. Vol. 6**. April, 1977, Pg. 145.

I6 Brackett, Leigh. <Untitled> in Return to Wonder. #9. Pg. 8.

I7 Bradbury, Ray & Leigh Bracket. “Preface.” **Ocean de Venus**. _: Tems Futurs, 1982, p. Translated by Mary Rosenthal & Brian Hester.

I8 Bull, Terry. <unknown>“[1] in Vector. 1965, p.

I9 Clute, John. “Edmond Hamilton.” **The Encyclopedia of Science Fiction**. New York, NY: Doubleday, 1979, pp. 270-1.

I10 Clute, John and Peter Nicholes. **The Encyclopedia of Science Fiction**. New York, NY: St. Martin's Griffin, 1993, pp. 538-9.

I11 DeCamp, L. Sprague **Science Fiction Handbook**. Hermatige House, 1952, p.

I12 De La Ree, Gerry. "Introduction." **The Horror on the Asteroid and Other Tales of Planetary Horror**. Gregg Press, 1976, p.

I13 De Vore, Howard. "Edmond Hamilton, A Recollection." <u>Lan's Lantern Six</u>. (Autumn 1977) Pg. 3.

I14 Gammell, Leon L. **The Annotated Guide to Startling Stories**. Mercer Island, WA: Starmont House. 1986, p.

4	The Prisoner of Mars
6	The Three Planeteers
9	A Yank at Valhalla
19	Outlaw World
21	The Star of Life
24	The Valley of Creation
28	The City at World's End
44	The Fear Neutralizer
45	The Space Visitors
47	The Man who Evolved
54	The Island of Unreason
55	Trouble on Triton
57	The Man with X-Ray Eyes
58	Proxy Planeteers
59	The Conquest of Two Worlds
65	The Return of Captain Future
66	Children of the Sun
68	The Harpers of Titan
68	Pardon my Iron Nerves
70	Moon of the Unforgotten

70 Earthmen No More
71 Birthplace of Creation
82 The Unforgiven

I15 Garman, Gerald M. "Edmond Hamilton." **Twentieth-Century American Science-Fiction Writers, Vol. 1**. New York, NY: Gale, 1981, pp. 201-4.

I16 Gunn, James E. "The World - Wrecker on Mars" in **The Road to Science Fiction #2: From Wells to Heinlein**. _: Rowman & Littlefield Pub Inc. October 2002, 325 p. ISBN: 0810844397. paper.

I17 Hamilton, Esther. "Around Town" in The Youngstown Vindicator, (27 February 1977) Pg. B1.

I18 --- "Around Town" in The Youngstown Vindicator. () Pg.

I19 Horn, Maurice. **The World Encyclopedia of Comics Vol. 1 & Vol. 2**. New York, NY: Chelsea House Publishers, 1976, Pg. 117 & 642.

I20 Jones, Robert Kenneth. **The Shudder Pulps**. New York, NY: Plume. 1975, p.

Edmond Hamilton writing as Robert Wentworth. Pg. 189.

I21 Kankowski, Joseph. "Fiction by Edmond Hamilton" in Xenofile #30. (1977) Pp. 14-15.

I22 Kettlitz, Hardy. **Edmond Hamilton. Weltenzerstörer und Autor von Captain Future**. (SF Personality 13). <year>, 151 p. [paperback] ISBN 3-926126-25-6.

I123 Korber, Joachim. **Bibliograhisches Lexikon: der Utopisch Phantatischen Literatur**. _: Corian. Band 4 Gr-Ki, <year>, p.

Hamilton, Edmond (Hans-Ulrich Bolttcher).

I124 Litowitz, Pat. "New Castle High grads make mark in World" in New Castle News (May 5, 2006) pp.

I125 Lovisi, Gary. "Comet Kings: From Pulps to Paperbacks" in Paperback Parade #1 (October 1986) Pp. 16-18.

I126 Meyers, W. E. "One Hundred Most Important People in Science Fiction/Fantasy: Edmond Hamilton" in Starlog #100 (November 1985) Pg. 62.

I127 Moskowitz, Sam. "Edmond Hamilton" in **Explorers of the Infinite: Shapes of SF**. _: <publisher unknown> <year> p. Pgs. 194, 205, 297.

I128 --- "Edmond Hamilton" in **Seekers of Tomorrow**. Westport, CT. Hyperion Press, Inc. 1966, pp. 66-83.

I129 --- **The Immortal Storm**. Westport, CT. Hyperion Press, Inc. 1954, p.

Pgs. 16, 75, 83, 213.

I130 --- "Introduction to 'The Man Who Saw the Future" in Amazing Stories. (February, 1961) Pg.

I131 --- "SF Profile: Edmond Hamilton" in Amazing Stories. (__, 1963): Pg.

I32 --- "Why 'The Man Who Evolved' is my Favorite Story." Startling Stories, (November, 1940) Pg. 113.

I33 Palm, Anders. "Edmond Hamilton ar dod - men Kapten Frank Lever" in Dagens Nyheter. Wednesday, 23 February 1977, p.

I34 Preiss, Byron. "Eulogy" in **Weird Heroes. Vol. 6**. (April, 1977) Pg. 145.

I35 Ringberg, Bengt-Olaf. "Edmond Hamilton Bibliografi" in Future Fan. #15. () Pp. 11-17.

I36 Robins, Leonard A. **The Pulp Magazine Index: First Series**. Mercer Island, WA: Starmont House, 1989, p. Pg 648.

I37 Sampson, Robert. **Yesterday's Faces Vol. 2: Strange Days**. Bowling Green, OH. Bowling Green University Popular Press, 1984, p.

Pgs. 214, 216, 218, 247, 255n.

I38 Smith, David C. "A Remembrance of Edmond Hamilton" in Outre 2:1 #5. (May, 1977) Pg. 2.

I39 Stableford, Brian M. "Edmond Hamilton and Leigh Bracket: An Appreciation" in **Masters of Science Fiction #1**. San Bernardino, CA: Borgo Press, 1981, p. Pgs. 6, 14.

a in **Masters of Science Fiction #1**. San Bernardino, CA: Borgo Press. 1981, pp. 6-14.

ab in **Outside the Human Aquarium: Masters of Science Fiction**. San Bernardino, CA: Borgo Press, 1995, pp. 7- 17.

I40 Terry, P. A. M. "Kings cross in orbit: Edmond Hamilton and eigh Bracket in Sydney” in Australian Science Fiction Review #14 (February 1968) Pp 25-31.

I141 Thompson, Don & Maggie. **The Official Price Guide to Science Fiction & Fantasy Collectibles 3rd. Edition**. _: <publisher unknown> <year> p. Pgs. 156, 294.

I142 Unknown. “The Authors” in **Amazing SF Anthology: The Wonder Years 1926-1935**. Edited by Martin H. Greenberg. _: <publisher unknown> <year>, p. 318.

I143 --- “The Authors.” **Amazing SF Anthology: The War Years 1936-1945**. Edited by Martin H. Greenberg. _: <publisher unknown> <year>, p. 333.

I144 --- Author’s Works Listings Series III by Donald H. Tuck. _: <publisher unknown> (February, 1962): 8 p.

I145 --- “Biography Sketch” in Amazing Science Fiction. (November, 1938) Pg. 143.

I146 --- “Biography Sketch” in Thrilling Wonder. (June, 1939) Pg. 88. With Photo.

I147 --- “Edmond Hamilton & the ____”[cxxxvii] in Future Fan, #7. () Pp. 12-15.

I148 --- “Edmond Hamilton in Weird Tales, Checklist” in Weird Tales Collector. #1. () Pg. 9.

I149 --- “Hamilton, cont.” in Book West. () Pg. 22.

I50 --- "Inside Hamilton"in Thrilling Wonder Stories. (December, 1952): Pg. 69.

I51 --- "Introduction." **Weird Heroes. Vol. 6**. (April, 1977) Pg. 145.

I52 --- "Meet the Author - Edmond Hamilton" in Startling Stories, 13:1 (Winter, 1946) Pg. 95. (Photo).

I53 --- "Meet the Author - Edmond Hamilton" in Startling Stories, 14:1 (January, 1947) Pg. 108.

I54 --- "Spalten" in Aftonbladet. (Saturday, 26 February 1977) Pg.. 5.

I55 --- "The Story Behind the Story" in Thrilling Wonder Stories, (June, 1938) Pg. 6.
Note: Includes "Murder in the Void" with excerpt from a letter by Mr. Hamilton.

I56 --- "The Story Behind the Story" in Thrilling Wonder Stories, (Winter, 1946) Pg. 110.
Note: Includes a photo with excerpt from a letter by Mr. Hamilton.

I57 --- "Writers Complete River Trip to New Orleans on Steamboat" in ?

I58 --- "Youngstown's Jules Verne" in Youngstown Vindicator, (February, 1977) Pg.

I59 --- <unknown>[cxxxviii] in East Fanglian Times, 2:4 (March, 1964) Pg. 9.

I60 --- LibraryThing. http://www.librarything.com/author/hamiltonedmond

I61 --- http://www.btinternet.com/~mycity/db/staff/hamilton.htm

I63 --- Wikipedia - http://en.wikipedia.org/wiki/Edmond_Hamilton

I64 --- Noted New Castle High School Graduates – http://blogs.myspace.com/index.cfm?fuseaction=blog.view&friendId=75754029&blogId=164399677

I65 Walker, Paul. "Edmond Hamilton" in Luna Monthly #60. (1975) Pg 1-4, 12.

a in **Speaking of Science Fiction** by Paul Walker. Luna Publications: Oradell, NJ. 1978, pp. 3612-369.

I66 Weinberg, Robert. "A Checklist of Edmond Hamilton's Stories" in Return to Wonder. #9. () Pg. 14.

I67 --- "Edmond Hamilton" in Weird Tales Collector, #1. () Pp. 7-8.

I68 --- "Some Lost Stories of Edmond Hamilton" in Return to Wonder. #9. () Pg. 11.

I69 --- "Introduction." in **The Metal Giants and Others, The Collected Edmond Hamilton, Volume One** . Edited by Stephen Haffner. Royal Oak, Michigan: Haffner Press. 1 July 2009, 648 p. Hardback. Illustrated by Hugh Rankin. ISBN-10: 1893887316; ISBN-13: 978-1893887312

I70 Weinstock, Matt. "Around Town"[cxxxix] in ?

I71 Weisinger, Mort. "A Eulogy, of a Sort" in Astounding Stories, "The Readers' Corner." () Pg. 283.

I72 Williams, Wlater Jon. "Introduction." **In The Star-Stealers: The Complete Adventures of The Interstellar Patrol, The Collected Edmond Hamilton, Volume Two** . Edited by Stephen Haffner. Royal Oak, Michigan: Haffner Press. 1 July 2009, 648 p. Hardback.Illustrated by C. Barker Petrie, Jr. ISBN-10 1893887316; ISBN-13 9781893887131 2.

I73 Williamson, Jack. An interview with Elliot, Jeffery M. "In at the Creation" in **Pulp Voices: or Science Fiction Voices #6**. San Bernardino, CA.: Borgo Press, 1983, p. Pg. 15.

I74 Williamson, Jack. in MWestercon Program Book. (July 1970) Pg.

I75 Williamson, Jack. "Introducing the Guests of Honor: Edmond Hamilton, Leigh Brackett, Makers of Myths" in Minicon Program Book. 16-18 April 1976, p. pp. 10-13.

I76 Williamson, Jack. "Edmond Hamilton: an Appreciation" in Locus 10 (January 30, 1977) Pg.. 2.

I77 Williamson, Jack. "Edmond Hamilton: As I Knew Him" in New York Review of Science Fiction #137 (January 2000) Pp. 1, 4-5.

I78 Wollheim, Donald A. "Headquarters: Canopus" **in The Universe Makers**. New York, NY: Harper & Row, 1971,. pp. 30-2.

J
Computer Archives

J1 Edmond Hamilton

a http://www.mygale.org/02/perry/sf/hamilton/hedm.html
b http://sport-books-
online.net/search_Edmond_Hamilton/searchBy_Author.html

J2 E. Hamilton - Bibliography Summary

a http://www.sfsite.com/isfdb_bin/extract_author.cgi?Edmond_Hamilton

J3 MIT Science Fiction Archives

a http://www.mit.edu:8001/pinkdex
Search: Hamilton

J4 Haffner Press

a http://www.haffnerpress.com/authors.html

J4 Science Fiction Lovers Archives

a ftp://sflovers.rutgers.edu/pub/sf-lovers/bibliographies/authorlists/
Hamilton.Edmond[cxl]

J5 Science Fiction Resource Guide

a http://sf.www.lysator.liu.se/sf_archive/sf-texts/authors/H/Hamilton,
Edmond.mbox
b http://sf.www.lystor.liu.se/sf_archive/sf-texts/authors/H/Hamilton,EdmL

J6 Author Lists

a http://julmara.ce.chalmers.se/SF_archive/Authorlists/Hamilton.Edmond

Abstract:

Subject: Author Lists: Edmond Hamilton

Edmond Hamilton was one of the original space opera hacks, known as "World Destroyer/Saver" Hamilton. (Hack being used in the purely good sense). If you have a taste for this sort of thing, it's all in good fun, even if his work hasn't aged as well as E. E. "Doc" Smith. Towards the end of his career he did write several much more "literary" short stories, many of which are collected in "The Best of Edmond Hamilton."

J7 Newspage

a http://cigww2.ecom.dec.com/NEWSPAGE/info/d18/d2/d2/public/B.r1222132.900.rtr77100.htm

Abstract: Edmond Hamilton

J8 Bertil Falk's Homepage

a http://www.sbbs.se/bfalk/ed.htm

A nice page about Mr. Hamilton by Mr. Falk the translator of most of Mr. Hamilton's stories to Swedish.

J9 Past Minicons: Our Family Album

a http://www.spedro.com/Minn-StF/minicon/history

J10 Science Fiction published in 1945 magazines.

This is a listing of all Science Fiction published in 1945 that are eligible for the 1996 Retro Hugo Awards, prizes that are

awarded for stories published before the inception of the Hugo award.
Listed below are the pages that Mr. Hamilton appears on, either as himself or under a pseudonym.

a Novelettes http://lacon3.worldcan.org/retro.nt
b Short Stories http://lacon3.worldcan.org/retro.ss
c Magazines http://lacon3.worldcan.org/retro.mags

J11 Weird Tales

a http://members.aol.com/weirdtales/

The following computer archives primarily deal with comic books. The information, while not devoted to Mr. Hamilton, is of interest in placing the period and events before, during and after Mr. Hamilton's authorship.

J12 Batman

a http://www.acmecity.com/batman/
b Golden Age Batman
http://ocsnet.acsonline.com/~bjordian/
c Batman: Forever Knights
http://batman.techv.net

J13 The Catwoman Center

a http://www.infinet.com/~jsulliva/catwoman/

J14 Green Lantern

a http://www.geocities.com/Area51/3676
b http://www3.cybercity.hko.net/boston/sinofsky/characters/gl/index.html
c http://www.unlv.edu/~lauv/gl/
d Green Lantern Corps Web Page http://www.glcorps.org/

J15 Legion of Superheroes

a http://ourworld.compuserve.com/homepages/MeerkatMeade/lshdnta.htm
b http://www.cs.cmu.edu/afs/cs/user/vernon/www/lsh.html
c http://www.geocities.com/SunsetStrip/6432/legin.htm
d http://www/peak.org/~djuilli/lsh.html
e http://www.geocities.com/Hollywood/Hills/2223/lsh.htm
f http://home.earthlink.net/~lerkowman/lsh/lsh.htm
g Legion of Super Resources
http://www.idyllmtn.com/rac/dc/lsh/lsh_res.htm

J16 Superboy

a The Unofficial Superboy Website http://fly.to/superboy

J17 Superman

a http://www.acmecity.com/superman/
b Superman - Kryptonian Cybernet
http://www.ms.uky.edu/~sykes/kc/indec.html

J18 Various - Strange Days

a http://www.geocities.com/Area51/Corridor/3543

J19 Comics

a http://members.tripod.com/~GILLENTOONS/index-7.html
b http://www.geocities.com/soho/cafe/6707
c Comic Books http://sigma.net/marvel
d Comic Book Awards Almanac
http://www.enteract.com/~aardy/comics/awards/
e Comic Book Resources
http://www.comicbookresources.com/
f Your Guide to the History of Comics
http://www.dereksantos.com/comicpage/
g History of Superhero Comic Books
http://www.geocities.com/Athens/8580

h The Incomplete Comicbook Artists checklist
http://www.caseman.net/~pafranklin

J20 DC Comics

a The Unofficial Guide to the DC Universe
http://welcome.to/the.DC.Guide/

b The Unofficial DC Comics Big Events Homepage

http://www.geocities.com/Area51/Labryrinth/6190/events.html

J21 Captain Future

a Captain Future in Europe
http://www.geocities.com/Area51/Corridor

K
Obituaries

K1 "A Eulogy to Mr. Hamilton" in The Book Review. ()" Pg.

K2 "Edmond Hamilton, Writer, Dies in West" in Youngstown Vindicator, (2 February 1977) Pg. 1.

K3 "Science Fiction Writer Edmond Hamilton Dies" in Antelope Valley Press, (3 February 1977) Pg.

K4 "E. Hamilton dies, dean of science fiction writers" in Tribune Chronicle, # (February 1977) Pg. 5.

K5 Ackerman, Forrest J. "Obituary Note" in Publishers Weekly, #14 (March, 1977) Pg. 46.

K6 Bloch, Robert. "Memoir on Edmond Hamilton" in **Weird Heroes #6**, (1977) Pg.

K7 Price, E. Hoffman. "Edmond Hamilton: In Memoriam," in ?

K8 Unknown. "S-F Writer Edmond Hamilton Dies" in Antelope Valley Press. Thursday (3 February 1977) Pg.

K9 --. "Death of Edmond Hamilton" in The Comics Journal #3 (April 1977): Pg. 4.

L
Miscellanea

L1 Library Collections

A. The Golden Library Eastern New Mexico University is the acknowledged repository for the majority of Mr. Hamilton's papers.

a Correspondence: Rejection slips, business letters, personal correspondence, letters from fans. See chapter C for a complete listing. 914 items.

b Manuscripts: *Ammageddon; Author, Author; Batman; Captain Future Novels; Castaway; City At World's End; Colonists of Mars; Comic Scripts; Carter Base One; Doomstar; Fifty Years of Heroes; Forgotten World; Fugitive of the Stars; Galleys; Green Lantern; The Haunted Stars; He That Hath Wings; The Planet that was Alive; Princess of the Labyrinth; Requiem For A Planet; Science Fiction; Star of Life; Star Kings; Starwolf [Series];Superman; Terror in Installments; Time-Travelling in Ohio; Twilight of the Gods; What's It Like Out There?; World of the Starwolves; Writing the Pseudo-Scientific Story*. 135 items.

c Biographical material: 40 items.

d Clippings, Artwork, Bookjackets, etc.: Artwork, 1 item; Cover Photostat of Beyond Fantasy Fiction, 1 item; Bookcover by Jospeh Doolin, 1 item; Framed Bookjacket, **The Comet-Drivers**, 1 item; Framed Bookjacket, **The Metal Giants**, 1 item; Miscellaneous - Clippings, 7 items.

e Tearsheets/Photocopies of printed materials: "Castaway," 1 item; "Look Forward, Look Back," 1 item.

f Periodicals: *The Amazing World of DC Comics; Action Comics; Adventure Comics; Giant Superman Annual; World's First Comics; Fantastic Adventers; Future Fan; HAPNA!; Len's Lantern; Lost Fantasies; Outre; Pulp; Retrun to Wonder;*

Science Fiction Classics Annual; The Science Fiction Review Monthly; Science Fantasy Correspondent; Screen Stories;Twibbet; WT50: A tribute to Weird Tales. 35 items.

g Other Writers: 13 items.

h General Miscellaneous: 5 items.

i Novels: *Arma do Alem; Battle For the Stars; Beyond the Moon; Calling Captain Future; Captain Future's Challenge; City at World's End; The Closed World: Starwolf No. 2; The Comet Kings; Crashing Suns; Danger Planet; Doomstar; Fugitive of the Stars; Galaxy Mission; Gli Incappucciati d'Ombre; The Haunted Stars; DieHeimat der Astronauten; Horror on the Asteroid and Othe Tales of Planetary Horror; Il Lupo deiCieli; Luta Intergalactica; The Monsters of Juntonheim: a Complete Book-length Novel of Amazing Adventure; Outlaws of the Moon; Patrulha Interstlar; Quest Beyond the Stars; Return to the Stars; Les Rois des Etoiles; Les Rois des Etoiles et Retour Aux Etoiles; La Spedizione della V Flotta; The Star Kings; The Star of Life; The Sun Smasher; Tharkol, Lord of the Unknown: a Novel; The Valley of Creation; The Weapon From Beyond: Starwolf No. 1; The World of the Starwolves: Starwolf No. 3*. 45 items.

j Anthologies: *Avite Aarum Seschilla; Bala Methavi; Alien Worlds; Alien Earth and Other Stories; Beware After Dark! The World's Most Stupendous Tales of Mystery, Hooro, Thrills, and Terror; A Century of Science Fiction; The Ghoul Keepers: Nine Fantastic Stories; The Giant Anthology of Science Fiction; My Best Science Fiction Stories, as Selected by 12 Outstanding Authors; Weird Tales: Stories of Fantasy; The Best From Startling Stories; Exploring Other Worlds; The Man Who Called Himself Poe; Modern Masterpieces of Science Fiction; Seekers of Tomorrow: Masters of Modern Science Fiction; The Vortex Blasters and Other Stories from Modern Masterpieces of Science Fiction; Science Fiction Adventure Classics; Great Science Fiction Adventures; Science Fiction Yearbook, No. 2; Science Fiction Yearbook, No. 3; The End of the World; Every Boy's Book of Science-Fiction; Swordsmen in the Sky*. 23 items.

B. The University Library, University of Winnipeg.

L2 Agent: Scott Meredith[cxli], 580 Fith Avenue, New York, NY 10036

L3 Memberships: Authors Guild of America.

L4 Pseudonyms[cxlii]**:** Alexander Blade, Robert Castle, Hugh Davidson, Will Garth, Brett Sterling, S.M. Tenneshaw.

L5 Cataloging:

Alphabetical List of Stories

Titles in intalics indicate that these were orginally published under one of Mr. Hamilton's pseudonyms. In the last list in this section the initials of the pseudonym are listed.

A Brother To Him
A Conquest of Two Worlds
A Million Years Ahead
A Yank at Valhalla
Abysmal Invaders, The
Accursed Galaxy, The
Across Space
After a Judgement Day
Alien Earth
Armies of the Past
Atomic Conqueors, The
Avenger from Atlantis, The

Babylon in the Sky
Ball Baring Death
Battle For the Stars
Beasts that Once were Men
Best of Leigh Brackett, The
Beyond the Moon
Birthplace of Creation
Bride of The Lightning
Broken Stars, The

Calling Captain Future
Captain Future & the 7 Space Stones
Captain Future & the Space Emperor
Captain Future's Challenge
Castaway
Child of Atlantis
Child of the Wind
Children of Terror
Children of The Sun
Citadel of the Star Lords
Cities in the Air
City at the World's End
City From the Sea, The
Closed Worlds, The
Come Home From Earth
Comet Doom, The
Comet Drivers, The
Comet Kings, The
Comrades of Time
Conqueror's Voice, The
Copper Proof
Corpse Died Twice, The
Corridor of the Suns
Corsairs of the Cosmos
Cosmic Cloud, The
Cosmic Hiss, The
Cosmic Kings, The
Cosmic Looters, The
Cosmic Pantograph, The
Cosmic Quest
Cosmos End
Crashing Suns
Crater Base One: The Children of the Moon
Crater Base One: Forgotten Earth
Crater Base One: The Man Who Watched the Earth
Crater Base One: The Moon-Born
Creatures of the Comet
Crime Crusader, The
Crimson Gold
Crooked Cop

Danger Planet
Dark Backward, The
Daughter of Thor, The
Day of Judgement
Day of the Micro-Men
Days of Creation
Dead Legs
Dead Planet, The

Death Comes in Glass
Death Doll
Death Lord, The
Debtor at Eight
Deconventionalizers, The
Devolution
Dictators of Creation, The
Dimension Terror, The
Dogs of Dr. Dwann, The
Doom over Venus
Doomstar
Door Into Infinity, The
Dreamer's Worlds
Dweller in the Darkness

Earth Brain, The
Earth Dwellers, The
Earth-Owners, The
Earthmen No More
Easy Money
Emphemerae, The
Eternal Cycle, The
Evans of the Earth Guard
Evolution Island
Exile

Face of The Deep
Face to Face
Fear Neutralizer, The
Fessenden's Worlds
Fire Creatures, The
Fire Princess, The
Forgotten World
Free-Lance of Space, The
Fugitive of the Stars

Gift from the Stars
Godmen, The
Great Brain of Kaldar, The
Great Illusion, The

Harpers of Titan
Haunted Stars, The
He That Hath Wings
Hell Train
Hidden World
His Sworn Duty
Holmes' Folly
Horror City, The
Horror From the Magellanic
Horror in the Telescope
Horror on the Asteroid
Horror out of Carthage
Horse that Talked, The
House of Living Music, The
House of the Evil Eye, The

In the World's Dusk
Indestructible Man, The
Inn Outside the World, The
Intelligence Undying
Interplanetary Graveyard
Invaders from the Monster World
Invisible Master, The
Iron One
Island of Unreason, The
Isle of Changing Life, The
Isle of The Sleeper, The

Kaldar, World of Antares
Kid Stuff
King of Shadows, The
Kingdom of the Stars
Knowledge Machine, The

Lake of Life, The
Last Bequest
Last Call for Doomsday
Leopard's Paw
Legion of Lazarus, The
Life Masters, The
Lilene, the Moon Girl
Locked Worlds
Look Forward, Look Back
Lords of the Morning
Lost City of Burma

Lost Elysium
Lost Treasure of Mars
Lost World of Time, The

Magic Moon, The
Magician of Mars, The
Man Who Conquered Age, The
Man Who Evolved, The
Man Who Lived Twice, The
Man Who Returned, The
Man Who Saved the Earth, The
Man Who Saw the Future, The
Man Who Solved Death, The
Man With X-Ray Eyes, The
Master of Genes
Men of the Morning Star
Metal Giants, The
Might-Have-Been, The
Mind-Master, The
Monster-God of Mamurth, The
Monsters of Mars
Moon Menace, The
Moon of The Unforgotten
Murder Asteroid
Murder at Weed Key
Murder in the Clinic, The
Murder in the Grave
Murder in the King Family
Murder in the Void
Murder Mountain
Murder Press
Mutiny on Europa
Mystery Moon, The

Never the Twain Shall Meet
Night the World Ended, The
No Earthman I
No-Man's-Land of Time

Other Side of the Moon, The
Outlaw World
Outlaws of The Moon
Outside the Universe

Pardon My Iron Nerves
Pigmy Island
Plant Revolt, The
Planet of Exile
Planets In Peril
Polar Doom, The
Priestess of The Labyrinth
Prisoner of Mars, The
(Prize Title Contest Story)
Pro, The
Proxy Planeteers

Quest Beyond The Stars, The
Quest in Time, The

Ramrod Key Killings, The
Red Sun of Danger
Reign of the Robots, The
Requiem
Return of Captain Future
Return to the Stars
Revolt on the Tenth World, The

Sacrifice Hit
Sargasso of Space, The
Sea Born, The
Sea Horror, The
Sea Murder
Sea Terror, The
Second Satellite, The
Seeds from Outside, The
Serpent Princess
Shadow Folk, The
Shining Land, The
Ship From Infinity, The
Shores of Infinity, The
Short-Wave Madness
Shot from Saturn, The
Sinister Invasion, The
Six Sleepers, The
Snake-Man
Snake-Men of Kaldar
Snow Clue, The
Son of Two Worlds

Space Beings, The
Space Mirror
Space Rocket Murders, The
Space Visitors, The
Star Hunter, The
Star Kings, The
Star of Dread
Star of Life, The
Star-Roamers, The
Star Trail To Glory, The
Star-Stealers, The
Star Wars of the Galaxy
Starcombers, The
Stark & the Star Kings
Starman Come Home
Stars, My Brothers, The
Starwolf: The Classic Space
Adventure Trilogy
Story of Monore, The
Sun People, The
Sunfire!

Tattooed Man, The
Ten Million Years Ahead
Terror Planet, The
Tharkol, Lord of the Unknown
Three from the Tomb, The
Three Planeteers, The
Through Invisible Barriers
Thunder World
Thundering Worlds
Tiger Girl
Time Raider, The
Transuranic
Treasure on Thunder Moon
Triumph of Captain Future, The
Trouble on Titan
Truth Gas, The
Twilight of the Gods

Under the White Star
Unforgiven, The
Universe Wreckers, The

Valley of Creation, The
Valley of Invisible Men, The
Valley Of The Assassins, The
Valley of The Gods, The
Vampire Master, The
Vampire Village, The

Wacky World
War of the Sexes, The
Watcher of Ages, The
Weapon from Beyond, The
What's It Like Out There?
When Space Burst
When The World Slept
Within The Nebula
Woman From the Ice
World Atavism
World of Never-Men
World Of The Dark Dwellers
World of the Starwolves
World with a Thousand Moons, The
World Without Sex
Worlds to Come

Chronological List of Stories

Abbreviations

Adv	Adventure(s)
Ann	Annual
Cdn	Canadian
Class	Classic(s)
con	conclusion
Fant	Fantastic (Fantasy)
M	Magazine
M-T	Most Thrilling
Myst	Mysteries
p2	part two
p3	part three
Q	Quarterly
rep	reprint
SF	Science Fiction
St	Stories (Story)
T	Told
UK	British

Brackets ([]) around a title indicate that the title was translated into the native language. Please see sections A and B for the title as it appeared in the native language.

1926

Date	Title	Magazine
Aug	The Monster-God of Mamurth	Weird Tales
Sep	Across Space	Weird Tales
Oct	Across Space (P2)	Weird Tales
Nov	Across Space (Con)	Weird Tales
Dec	The Metal Giant	Weird Tales

1927

Date	Title	Magazine
Feb	The Atomic Conquerors	Weird Tales
Mar	Evolution Island	Weird Tales
Sep	The Moon Menace	Weird Tales
Oct	The Time Raider	Weird Tales
Nov	The Time Raider (p2)	Weird Tales

Date	Title	Magazine
Dec	The Time Raider (p3)	Weird Tales

1928

Date	Title	Magazine
Jan	The Comet Doom	Amazing Stories
Jan	The Time Raider (con)	Weird Tales
Jun	The Dimension Terror	Weird Tales
Aug	Crashing Suns	Weird Tales
Sep	Crashing Suns (p2)	Weird Tales
Sep	The Polar Doom	Weird Tales

1929

Date	Title	Magazine
Feb	The Star-Stealers	Weird Tales
Spr	Locked Worlds	Amazing Stories Quarterly
Mar	The Sea Horror	Weird Tales
May	Within The Nebula	Weird Tales
Jun	The Abysmal Invaders	Weird Tales
Jul	Outside the Universe	Weird Tales
Aug	Outside the Universe (p2)	Weird Tales
Sep	Outside the Universe (p3)	Weird Tales
Oct	Outside the Universe (con)	Weird Tales
Fal	The Other Side Of the Moon	Amazing Stories Quarterly
Fal	Hidden World	ScienceWonder Quarterly
Nov	Cities in the Air	Air Wonder Stories

1930

Date	Title	Magazine
Win	Cities in the Air (con)	Air Wonder Stories
Jan	The Life Masters	Weird Tales
Feb	The Comet Drivers	Weird Tales
Mar	The Space Visitors	Air Wonder Storeis
Apr	Evans of the Earth Guard	Air Wonder Stories
Apr	The Invisible Master	Scientific DM
Apr	The Plant Revolt	Weird Tales
May	The Murder In the Clinic	Scientific DM
May	The Sun People	Weird Tales
May	The Universe Wreckers	Amazing Stories
Jun	The Universe Wreckers (p2)	Amazing Stories
Jul	The Universe Wreckers (con)	Amazing Stories

Date	Title	Magazine
Jul	The Death Lord	Weird Tales
Aug	World Atavism	Amazing Stories
Aug	The Second Sattelite	Astounding
Aug	Comet Doom (rep)	Tales of Wonder (Brit)
Aug	Pigmy Island	Weird Tales
Oct	The Man Who Saw the Future	Amazing Stories
Oct	The Mind-Master	Weird Tales
Nov	The Cosmic Cloud	Weird Tales

1931

Date	Title	Magazine
F-M	The Horror City	Weird Tales
Apr	Monsters of Mars	Astounding
Apr	The Man Who Evolved	Wonder Stories
A-M	Ten Million Years Ahead	Weird Tales
Aug	The Sargasso of Space	Astounding Stories
Oct	The Shot from Saturn	Weird Tales
Dec	Creatures of the Comet	Weird Tales
Dec	The Reign of the Robots	Wonder Stories

1932

Date	Title	Magazine
Jan	Dead Legs	Strange Tales
Feb	A Conquest of Two Worlds	Wonder Stories
Feb	The Three from the Tomb	Weird Tales
Apr	The Earth Brain	Weird Tales
May	The Terror Planet	Weird Tales
Oct	The Space Rocket Murders	Amazing Stories
Oct	The Dogs of Dr. Dwann	Weird Tales
Nov	*Vampire Village*	Weird Tales
Dec	The Man Who Conquered Age	Weird Tales

1933

Date	Title	Magazine
Jan	*Snake-Man*	Weird Tales
Apr	Kaldar, World of Antares	Magic Carpet
Apr	The Star-Roamers	Weird Tales
May	The Island of Unreason	Wonder Stories
Jul	The Fire Creatures	Weird Tales
Sep	Horror on the Asteroid	Weird Tales
Oct	Snake-Men of Kaldar	Magic Carpet

Date	Title	Magazine
Oct	*The Vampire Master*	Weird Tales
Nov	The War of the Sexes	Weird Tales
Nov	The Man with X-Ray Eyes	Wonder Stories
Nov	*The Vampire Master (p2)*	Weird Tales
Dec	*The Vampire Master (p3)*	Weird Tales

1934

Date	Title	Magazine
Jan	*The Vampire Master* (con)	Weird Tales
Feb	The Man who Returned	Weird Tales
Mar	Thundering Worlds	Weird Tales
Apr	Corsairs of the Cosmos	Weird Tales
Dec	Cosmos End	Fantasy Magazine

1935

Date	Title	Magazine
Jan	Master of Genes	Wonder Stories
Feb	Murder in the Grave	Weird Tales
Feb	The Truth Gas	Wonder Stories
Mar	The Eternal Cycle (rep)	Wonder Stories
May	Murder and Weed Key	Thrilling Detective
Jul	The Accursed Galaxy	Astouding Stories
Jul	The Avenger from Atlantis	Weird Tales
Jul		Weird Tales (Canadian)
Sep	The Monster-God Of Mamurth (rep)	Weird Tales
Oct	The Cosmic Pantograph	Wonder Stories
Oct	The Six Sleepers	Weird Tales
Dec	The Great Brain of Kaldar	Weird Tales

1936

Date	Title	Magazine
Feb	The Ramrod Key Killings	Popular. Detective
Mar	Leopard's Paw	Popular. Detective
Mar	In the Worlds Dusk	Weird Tales
Apr	Intelligence Undying	Amazing Stories
Apr	Murder Mountain	Popular Detective
Apr	The Earth Dweller	Thrilling Mystery
May	Carter Makes a Squeal	Popular Detective
May	Crimson Gold	Popular Detective
May	Copper Proof	Thrilling Detective

Date	Title	Magazine
Apr	Murder in the King Family	Thrilling Detective
May	Beasts that Once were Men	Thrilling Mystery
May	Child of the Winds	Weird Tales
Jun	Hell Train	G-Men
Jun	*The House of the Evil Eye*	Weird Tales
Jul	When the World Slept	Weird Tales
Aug	Crooked Cop	Popular Detective
Aug	The Crime Crusader	Thrilling Detective
A-S	The Door Into Infinity	Weird Tales
Sep	Snow Clue	Popular Detective
Sep	Children of Terror	Thrilling Mystery
Oct	Last Bequest	Popular Detective
Oct	Cosmic Quest	Thrilling Wonder
Dec	Devolution	Amazing Stories
Dec	Face to Face	Popular Detective
Dec	Sea Murder	Thrilling Detective
Dec	Mutiny on Europa	Thrilling Wonder

1937

Date	Title	Magazine
Jan	Murder Press	Popular. Detective
Feb	Ball Bearing Death	Popular Detective
Mar	Kid Stuff	Phantom Detective
Mar	The Seeds from Outside	Weird Tales
Apr	The Corpse Died Twice	Popular Detective
Apr	A Million Years Ahead	Thrilling Wonder
Apr	Fessenden's Worlds	Weird Tales
May	Death Dolls	Thrilling Detective
Jun		Thrilling Wonder
Jul	His Sworn Duty	Phantom Detective
Aug	Space Mirror	Thrilling Wonder
Aug	World Of The Dark Dwellers	Weird Tales
Sep	Death Comes in Glass	Thrilling Detective
Sep	The Lake of Life	Weird Tales
Oct	(Prize Title Contest Story)	Phantom Detective
Oct	Holmes' Folly	Thrilling Wonder Stories
Oct	The Lake of Life (p2)	Weird Tales
Nov	The Lake of Life (con)	Weird Tales
Dec	When Space Burst	Thrilling Wonder
Dec	Child Of Atlantis	Weird Tales

1938

Date	Title	Magazine
Win	The Space Beings	Tales of Wonder (British)
Jan	The House of Living Music	Weird Tales
Feb	Power Pit 13	Thrilling Adventure
Mar	*The Conqueror's Voice*	Science Fiction Stories
Apr	Easy Money	Thrilling Wonder Stories
May	The Isle of The Sleeper	Weird Tales
Jun	*The Great Illusion*	Thrilling Wonder Annual
Jun	Murder in The Void	Thrilling Wonder Stories
Sum	Horror in the Telescope	Tales of Wonder
Jul	He That Hath Wings	Weird Tales
Aug	The Sea Terror	Tales of Wonder
Aug	The Fire Princess	Weird Tales
Sep	Woman from the Ice	Thrilling Mystery
Sep	The Fire Princess (p2)	Weird Tales
Oct	The Fire Princess (con)	Weird Tales
Nov	The Man Who Lived Twice	Amazing Stories
Dec	The Emphemerae	Astounding Science Fiction
Dec	The Cosmic Hiss	Thrilling Wonder

1939

Date	Title	Magazine
Jan	Bride of The Lightning	Weird Tale
Mar	Valley of Invisible Men	Amazing Stories
Mar	Under the White Star	Science Fiction
Mar	The Fear Neutralizer	Startling Stories
Mar	Comrades of Time	Weird Tales
Apr	Armies of the Past	Weird Tales
May	The Prisoner of Mars	Startling Stories
Jun	*Short-Wave Madness*	Science Fiction Stories
Aug	The Man who Solved Death	Science Fiction
Sep	Debtor at Eight	Detective Short Stories
Sep	Horror Out of Carthage	Fantastic Adventure
Sep	The Space Visitors	Startling Stories
Oct	Dweller in Darkness	Science Fiction

1940

Date	Title	Magazine
Win	Capt. Future & the Space Emperor	Captian Future
Jan	The Three Planeteers	Startling Stories
Feb	Doom Over Venus	Thrilling Wonder Storeis
Feb	Dweller in the Darkness	Thrilling Wonder Stories

Date	Title	Magazine
Mar	Interplanetary Graveyard	Future Fiction
May	Lilene, the Moon Girl	Amazing Stories
May	Dictators of Creation	Thrilling Wonder Stories
May	Doom over Venus	Thrilling Wonder Stories
May	The City From The Sea	Weird Tales
May	*World Without Sex*	Marvel Science Stories
Spr	Calling Captain Future	Capt Future
Jun	The Isle of Changing Life	Thrilling Wonder
Sum	Captain Future's Challenge	Capt Future
Sum	The Man Who Saw the Future (rep)	Tales of Wond
Aug	Lost Treasure of Mars	Amazing Stories
Sep	The Night the World Ended	Thrilling Wonder Stories
Sep	Sea Born	Weird Tales
Fal	Triumph of Captain Future	Capt Future
Oct	Murder Asteroid	Thrilling Wonder Stories
Nov	Revolt on the Tenth World	Amazing Stories
Nov	The Man Who Evolved (rep)	Startling Stories
Dec	A Brother to Him	Thrilling Detective
Dec	Gift From the Stars	Thrilling Wonder Stories
6	[The Night the World Ended] (rep)	Jules Verne

1941

Date	Title	Magazine
Win	Captian Future & the Seven Space Stones	Capt Future
Jan	Mystery Moon	Amazing St ories
Jan	The Horse that Talked	Fantastic Adventure
Jan	A Yank at Valhalla	Startling Stories
Spr	Star Trail To Glory	Capt Future
Sum	The Magician of Mars	Capt Future
Aug	Son of Two Worlds	Thrilling Wonder Stories
Sep	Day of the Micro-Men	Science Fiction
Fal	The Lost World of Time	Capt Future
Nov	Dreamers Worlds	Weird Tales
18-19	[The valley of Invisible Men] (rep)	Jules Verne
26-27	[Gift From the Stars] (rep)	Jules Verne
32-43	[Triumph of Captain Future] (rep)	Jules Verne
38-39	[The Horse that Talked] (rep)	Jules Verne
46/41-6/42	[The Magician of Mars] (rep)	Jules Verne

1942

Date	Title	Magazine
Win	The Quest Beyond The Stars	Capt Future

Date	Title	Magazine
Mar	Wacky World	Amazing Stories
Apr	Treasure on Thunder Moon	Amazing Stories
Spr	Outlaws of The Moon	Capt Future
Jun	The Quest in Time	Fant Adventure
Sum	The Comet Kings	Capt Future
Aug	The Daughter of Thor	Fantastic Adventure
Fal	Planets In Peril	Capt Future
Oct	Through Invisible Barriers	Thrilling Wonder Stories
Dec	The World with a Thousand Moons	Amazing Stories
Dec	Lost City of Burma	Fantastic Adventure
10-25	[Capt Future & the 7 Space Stones](rep)	Jules Verne
18	[Murder Asteroid] (rep)	Jules Verne
26-41	[Star Trail to Glory] (rep)	Jules Verne
1/42-2/43	[Outlaws of the Moon] (rep)	Jules Verne

1943

Date	Title	Magazine
Win	Face of the Deep	Capt Future
Apr	No-Man's-Land of Time	Science Fiction
May	Exile	Super Science Stories
Sum	*Star of Dread*	Capt Future
Nov	The Valley of the Assassins	Weird Tales
5-18	[The Lost World of Time]	Jules Verne
13-16	[Face of the Deep]	Jules Verne
19-33	[A Yank at Valhalla]	Jules Verne
28-40	[Quest Beyond the Stars]	Jules Verne
37-43	[Through Invisible Barriers] (rep)	Jules Verne

1944

Date	Title	Magazine
Win	*Magic Moon*	Capt Future
Apr	Exile	Super Science Stories (CDN)
May	The Free-Lance of Space	Amazing Stories
Sep	The Shadow Folk	Weird Tales
13-17	[The World with a Thousand Moons] (rep)	Jules Verne
39/44 - 32/45	[Planets in Peril] (rep)	Jules Verne

1945

Date	Title	Magazine
Jan	Priestess of the Labyrinth	Weird Tales

Date	Title	Magazine
May	The Shining Land	Weird Tales
Spr	The Island of Unreason (rep)	Startling Stories
Spr	*Red Sun of Danger*	*Startling Stories*
Jun	Invader from the Monster World	Amazing Stories
Sum	The Deconventionalizers	Thrilling Wonder Stories
Jul	The Inn Outside the World	Weird Tales
Nov	Lost Elysium	Weird Tales
Fal	Trouble on Titan	Startling Stories
33	[Magic Moon] (rep)	Jules Verne

1946

Date	Title	Magazine
	The Man Who Saved the Earth	Best Of SF
	Master of Genes	Thrilling Stories (UK)
Win	Outlaw World	Startling Stories
Win	Forgotten World	Thrilling Wonder
May	The Valley of the Gods	Weird Tales
Spr	The Dead Planet	Startling Stories
Spr	The Indestructible Man	Thrilling Wonder
Sum	The Man with X-ray Eyes (rep)	Startling Stories
Jul		Weird Tales(Cdn)
Sep	Day of Judgement	Weird Tales
Fal	*Never the Twain Shall Meet*	*Thrilling Wonder*
Nov		Weird Tales(Cdn)
13	[The Free-Lance of Space] (rep)	Jules Verne
42	[The Revolt of the Tenth World] (rep)	Jules Verne

1947

Date	Title	Magazine
Jan	The Star of Life	Startling Stories
Jan	The King of Shadows	Weird Tales
Feb	Come Home From Earth	Thrilling Wonder
Jul	Proxy Planeteer	Startling Stories
Sep	The Star Kings	Amazing Stories
6-8	[Son of Two Worlds] (rep)	Jules Verne

1948

Date	Title	Magazine
	The Star Stealers	Avon Fantasy Reader #6
Jan	A Conquest of Two Worlds (rep)	Startling Stories
Jan	Serpent Princess	Weird Tales

Date	Title	Magazine
Feb	Transuranic	Thrilling Wonder
Mar	The Might-Have-Been	Weird Tales
Jun	The Knowledge Machine	Thrilling Wonder
Jul	The Valley of Creation	Startling Stories
Jul	Twilight of the Gods	Weird Tales
Sep	The Watcher of Ages	Weird Tales
Sep		Weird Tales

1949

Date	Title	Magazine
Apr	Alien Earth	Thrilling Wonder

1950

Date	Title	Magazine
Jan	Return of Captain Future	Startling Stories
May	Children of The Sun	Startling Stories
Spr	Hidden World (rep)	Fant Story Quarterly
Jul	City at World's End	Startling Stories
Sep	Harpers of Titan	Startling Stories
Nov	Pardon My Iron Nerves	Startling Stories

1951

Date	Title	Magazine
Jan	Moon of the Unforgotten	Startling Stories
Mar	Earthmen No More	Startling Stories
May	Birthplace of Creation	Startling Stories
May	Isle of the Sleeper (rep)	Weird Tales
Spr	The Star Kings (Rep)	Two Comp SF-Adventures
Fal	The Cosmic Pantograph (rep)	Fantasy Story

1952

Date	Title	Magazine
Mar	City at the World's End (Rep)	Galaxy SF Novel
Aug	Lords of the Morning	Thrilling Wonder
Dec	What's It Like Out There?	Thrilling Wonder

1953

Date	Title	Magazine

Date	Title	Magazine
Oct	The Unforgiven	Startling Stories

1954

Date	Title	Magazine
July 8 - Sept 15	[The Star Kings]	Jules Verne
Sep	Starman Come Home	Universe
Fal	Forgotten World (rep)	Fantasy Story
Nov	Sacrifice Hit	Fantasy & SF

1956

Date	Title	Magazine
Apr	Wacky World (rep)	Amazing Stories
Apr	The Legion of Lazarus	Imagination
Jun	*Battle for the Stars*	Imagination
Jul	Thunder World	Imaginative Tales
Oct	Citadel of the Star Lords	Imagination
Nov	*The Cosmic Kings*	Imiginative Tales
Dec	*Last Call For Doomsday*	Imagination SF
Dec	The Starcombers	SF Adventure

1957

Date	Title	Magazine
Mar	*The Tattooed Man*	Imaginative Tales
Jun	*The Sinister Invasion*	Imagination SF
Jul	World of Never-Men	Imaginative Tales
Nov	The Ship From Infinity	Imaginative Tales
Nov	No Earthman I	Venture SF
Dec	Fuguitive of the Stars	Imagination

1958

Date	Title	Magazine
Jan	A Yank at Valhalla (rep)	Fantastic Story Magazine
Feb	*The Cosmic Looters*	Imagination SF
Mar	Men of the Morning Star	Imaginative Tales
Apr	Corridor of the Sun	Imagination
May	The Dark Backward	Venture SF
Jul	Planet of Exile	Space Travel
Sep	The Star Hunter	Space Travel
Nov	The God Men	Space Travel

1959

Date	**Title**	**Magazine**
Aug 15	The Man Who Missed the Moon	Toronto Star Weekly

1961

Date	**Title**	**Magazine**
Feb	The Man Who Saw the Future (rep)	Amazing Stories
Apr	Devolution (rep)	Amazing Stories

1962

Date	**Title**	**Magazine**
Apr	Requiem	Amazing Stories
May	The Stars My Brothers	Amazing Stories
Sep	Sunfire!	Amazing Stories

1963

Date	**Title**	**Magazine**
Mar	Babylon in the Sky	Amazing Stories
Jul	He that Hath Wings	Fantastic St M
Dec	After a Judgement Day	Fantastic St M

1964

Date	**Title**	**Magazine**
Sep	Kingdom of the Stars	Amazing Stories
Oct	The Pro	Fant & SF

1965

Date	**Title**	**Magazine**
	What's It Like Out There?	Treasury of Great SF
Apr	The Shores	
of Infinity	Amazing Stories	
Dec	The Comet Doom (rep)	Amazing Stories

1966

Date	**Title**	**Magazine**
Apr	Intelligence Undying (rep)	Amazing Stories
Dec	The Broken Stars	Fantastic

1967

Date	Title	Magazine
	World Atavism (rep)	
Win	The Monster-God of Mamurth (rep)	Mag of Horror
Win	Requiem (rep)	Most Thrilling SF Ever T
Win	Quest in Time	SF Yearbook
Spr	The Moon Menace (rep)	Famous SF
Oct	Pigmy Island	Man From U.N.C.L.E.

1968

Date	Title	Magazine
	Castaway	Man Called Poe
	Serpent Princess (rep)	Man Called Poe
Spr	The Stars, My Brothers (rep)	MT-SF-et
Spr	The Three from the Tomb (rep)	Start Myst
Jul	Locked Worlds (rep)	Amazing Stories
Aug	Horror out of Carthage (rep)	Fantastic Stories
Fal	Space-Rocket Murders (rep)	SF Adv Class
Dec	The Broken Stars	Fantastic Stories

1969

Date	Title	Magazine
	The Unforgiven	SF Yearbook #3
Win	The Dogs of Dr. Dwan (rep)	Start Mystery Stories
Win	The Other Side of the Moon (rep)	SF Adventure Classics
Win	The Man Who Lived Twice (rep)	SF Adventure Classics
Win	The Revolt on the Tenth World (rep)	SF Adventure Classics
May	Horror From the Magellanic	Amazing Stories
Sep	Lost Treasure of Mars (rep)	Amazing Stories
Fal	Wacky World (rep)	SF Classics

1970

Date	Title	Magazine
	Look Forward, Look Back	Return to Wonder #9
	Devolution (rep)	SF Classics Annual
#4	[The Return of Captain Future] (rep)	Jules Verne
Fal	Kingdom of the Stars	SF Greats
Win	Dead Legs (rep)	Weird Terror Tales

1971

Date	Title	Magazine
Spr	Liline, the Moon Girl (rep)	SF Adventure Classics

1972

Date	Title	Magazine
	Iron One	Signs & Wonder
Oct	After A Judgement Day (rep)	Most Thrilling SF Ever Told
Nov	Valley of Invisible Men (rep)	SF Adv Class

1973

Date	Title	Magazine
Feb	Sunfire! (rep)	Most Thrilling SF Ever Told
Aug		Thrilling Science Stories
Aug	The Shores of Infinity (rep)	Most Thrilling SF Ever Tpld

1976

Date	Title	Magazine
Fal	Birthplace of Creation (rep)	Starwind

1977

Date	Title	Magazine
	Comrades of Time (rep)	Lost Fantasies #5

1979

Date	Title	Magazine
Apr	Intelligence Undying (rep)	Fantastic
May	Devolution (rep)	Amazing Stories
Jul	The Man Who Evolved (part 1 - rep)	Enigmas
Aug	The Man Who Evolved (part 2 - rep)	Enigmas
Aug	Sunfire! (rep)	Amazing Stories

1980

Date	Title	Magazine
	[Capt Future & the Space Emperor] (rep)	Kapten Franks

1984

Date	Title	Magazine
	What's It Like Out There	Nova SF

Magazine List

Air Wonder Stories

Volume	Is/Date	Page	Title
?	Nov 1929	Pg. 390	Cities in the Air
?	Win 1930	?	Cities in the Air [con]
?	Mar 1930	Pg. 804	The Space Visitors
?	Apr 1930	Pg. 902	Evans of the Earth Guard

Amazing Stories

Volume	Is/Date	Page	Title
?	Jan 1928	Pg. 926	The Comet Doom
?	May 1930	Pg. 102	The Universe Wreckers
?	Jun 1930	Pg. 254	The Universe Wreckers [p2]
?	Jul 1930	Pg. 346	The Universe Wreckers [con]
?	Aug 1930	Pg. 428	World Atavism
?	Oct 1930	Pg. 600	The Man Who Saw the Future
?	Oct 1932	Pg. 582	The Space Rocket Murders
?	Apr 1936	Pg. 13	Intelligence Undying
?	Dec 1936	Pg. 90	Devolution
	Nov 1938	Pg. 76	The Man Who Lived Twice
	Mar 1939	Pg. 22	Valley of Invisible Men
	May 1940	Pg. 66	Lilene, the Moon Girl
14:8	Aug 1940	Pg. 68	Lost Treasure of Mars
	Nov 1940	Pg. 60	The Revolt on the Tenth World
15:1	Jan 1941	Pg. 72	Mystery Moon
	Mar 1942	Pg. 198	Wacky World
	Apr 1942	Pg. 198	Treasure on Thunder Moon
	Dec 1942	Pg. 64	The World With a Thousand Moons
18:3	May 1944	Pg. 122	The Free-Lance of Space
	Jun 1945	Pg. 68	Invader from the Monster World
	Sep 1947	Pg. 8	The Star Kings
	Apr 1956	Pg. 60	Wacky World
	Feb 1961	Pg. 85	The Man Who Saw the Future
	Apr 1961	Pg. 25	Devolution
	Apr 1962	Pg. 48	Requiem
	May 1962	Pg. 6	The Stars, My Brothers
	Sep 1962	Pg. 6	Sunfire!
	Mar 1963	Pg. 6	Babylon in the Sky
39:4	Sep 1964	Pg. 6	Kingdom of the Stars
	Apr 1965	Pg. 7	The Shores of Infinity
40:3	Dec 1965	Pg. 64	The Comet Doom

Volume	Is/Date	Page	Title
	Apr 1966	Pg. 45	Intelligence Undying
	Jul 1968	Pg. 39	Locked Worlds
	May 1969	Pg. 6	The Horror from the Magellanic
43:3	Sep 1969	Pg. 84	Lost Treasure of Mars
52:3	May 1979	Pg. 32-48	Devolution
	Aug 1979	Pg.	Sunfire!

Amazing Stories Quarterly

Volume	Is/Date	Page	Title
	Spr 1929	Pg. 222	Locked Worlds
	Fal 1929	Pg. 516	The Other Side of the Moon
	Sum 1941	Pg.	

Astounding Science Fiction

Volume	Is/Date	Page	Title
3:2	#8 Aug 1930	Pg. 175	The Second Sattelite
6:1	#16 Apr 1931	Pg. 4	Monsters of Mars
7:3	#21 Sep 1931	Pg. 390	The Sargasso of Space
15:5	#56 Jul 1935	Pg. 64	The Accursed Galaxy
22:4	#97 Dec 1938	Pg. 50	The Ephemerae

Avon Fantasy Reader

Volume	Is/Date	Page	Title
	#6 (1948)	Pg. 65	The Star-Stealers

Avon Science Fiction Reader

Volume	Is/Date	Page	Title
	#1 1951	Pg. 3	The War of the Sexes

Bombay Chonicle

Volume	Is/Date	Page	Title
	#27 Oct 54	Pg. 5	[Beyond The Moon] (Serialized)

Captain Future

Volume	Is/Date	Page	Title
1:1	Win 1940	Pg. 12	Captain Future & the Space Emperor
1:2	Spr 1940	Pg. 12	Calling Captain Future
1:3	Sum 1940	Pg. 14	Captain Future's Challenge
2:1	Fal 1940	Pg. 14	Triumph of Captain Future
2:2	Win 1941	Pg. 14	Captian Future & the Seven Space Stones
2:3	Spr 1941	Pg. 14	Star Trail to Glory
3:1	Sum 1941	Pg. 14	The Magician of Mars

Volume	Is/Date	Page	Title	
3:2	Fal 1941	Pg. 14	The Lost World of Time	
3:3	Win 1942	Pg. 15	The Quest Beyond the Stars	
4:1	Spr 1942	Pg. 14	Outlaws of the Moon	
4:2	Sum 1942	Pg. 11	The Comet Kings	
4:3	Fal 1942	Pg. 13	Planets In Peril	
5:1	Win 1943	Pg. 15	Face of the Deep	
5:3	*Sum 1943*	*Pg. 13*	*The Star of Dread*	Brett Sterling
6:1	*Win 1944*	*Pg. 15*	*Magic Moon*	Brett Sterling

Detective Short Stories

Volume	Is/Date	Page	Title
	Sep 1939		Debtor At Eight

Enigmas of the Universe

Volume	Is/Date	Page	Title
	#26 Jul 1977	Pg. 59-65	[The Man Who Evolved]
	#27 Aug 1977	Pg. 59-65	[The Man Who Evolved]

Famous Science Fiction

Volume	Is/Date	Page	Title
	No. 2		
	#2 Spr 1967		The Moon Menace

Fantastic

Volume	Is/Date	Page	Title
17:6	Aug 1968	Pg. 22-50	Horror Out of Carthage
18:2	Dec 1968	Pg. 6-36	The Broken Stars
	Apr 1979		Intelligence Undying

Fantastic Adventure

Volume	Is/Date	Page	Title
	Sep 1939	pp 6-23	Horror Out of Carthage
	Jan 1941	Pg. 108	The Horse that Talked
4:6	Jun 1942	Pg. 150	The Quest in Time
	Aug 1942	Pg. 10	The Daughter of Thor
	Dec 1942	Pg. 38	Lost City of Burma

Fantastic Story Magazine

Volume	Is/Date	Page	Title
3:1	Fal 1951	Pg. 101	The Cosmic Pantograph
	Sum 1951		Men of Honor
5:1	Jan 1958	Pg. 10	A Yank at Valhalla
7:3	Fal 1954	Pg. 10	Forgotten World

Fantastic Stories of The Imagination

Volume	Is/Date	Page	Title
12:7	Jul 1963	Pg. 22	He that Hath Wings
12:12	Dec 1963	Pg. 6	After a Judgement Day

Fantastic Story Quarterly

Volume	Is/Date	Page	Title
1:1	Spr 1950	Pg. 11	Hidden World
	Fal 1951		

Fantasy Magazine

Volume	Is/Date	Page	Title
	Dec 1934		Cosmos End
	Jan 1953		

Fantasy Story

Volume	Is/Date	Page	Title
	Oct 1953		
	Nov 1953		

Future Fiction

Volume	Is/Date	Page	Title
	Mar 1940	Pg. 56	Interplanetary Graveyard

G-Men

Volume	Is/Date	Page	Title
	Jun 1936		Hell Train

Great Science Fiction

Volume	Is/Date	Page	Title
	#8		Babylon in the Sky

Imagination SCience fiction

Volume	Is/Date	Page	Title	
7:2	#48 Apr 1956	Pg. 6	The Legion of Lazarus	
7:3	*#49 Jun 1956*	*Pg. 6*	*Battle For the Stars*	Alexander Blade
7:5	#51 Oct 1956	Pg. 8	Citadel of the Star Lords	
	#58 Dec 1956		*Last Call for Doomday*	S. M. Tenneshaw
8:3	*#55 Jun 1957*	*Pg. 6*	*The Sinister Invasion*	Alexander Blade
8:6	#58 Dec 1957	Pg. 6	Fugitive Of The Stars	
	Feb 1958		*The Cosmic Looters*	Alexander Blade
9:2	#60 Apr 1958	Pg. 6	Corridor of the Suns	

Imaginative Tales

Volume	Is/Date	Page	Title	
3:4	Jul 1956	Pg. 6	Thunder World	
3:6	*Nov 1956*	*Pg. 8*	*The Cosmic Kings*	Alexander Blade
4:2	*Mar 1957*	*Pg. 6*	*The Tattooed Man*	Alexander Blade
4:4	Jul 1957	Pg. 6	World of Never-Men	
4:6	Nov 1957	Pg. 6	The Ship from Infinity	
5:2	Mar 1958	Pg. 6-59	Men of the Morning Star	

Jules Verne Magazinet

Volume	Is/Date	Page	Title
	#6 1940		[The Night the World Ended]
	#18 1941		[The Valley of Invisible Men - Part 1]
	#19 1941		[The Valley of Invisible Men - Part 2]
	#26 1941		[Gift From the Stars - Part 1]
	#27 1941		[Gift From the Stars - Part 2]
	#32 1941		[Triumph of Captain Future - Part 1]
	#33 1941		[Triumph of Captain Future - Part 2]
	#34 1941		[Triumph of Captain Future - Part 3]
	#35 1941		[Triumph of Captain Future - Part 4]
	#36 1941		[Triumph of Captain Future - Part 5]
	#37 1941		[Triumph of Captain Future - Part 6]
	#38 1941		[The House That Talked - Part 1]
			[Triumph of Captain Future - Part 7]
	#39 1941		[The House That Talked - Part 2]
			[Triumph of Captain Future - Part 8]
	#40 1941		[Triumph of Captain Future - Part 9]
	#41 1941		[Triumph of Captain Future - Part 10]
	#42 1941		[Triumph of Captain Future - Part 11]
	#43 1941		[Triumph of Captain Future - Part 12]
	#46 1941		[The Magician of Mars - Part 1]
	#46 1941		[The Magician of Mars - Part 2]
	#46 1941		[The Magician of Mars - Part 3]
	#46 1941		[The Magician of Mars - Part 4]
	#46 1941		[The Magician of Mars - Part 5]
	#46 1941		[The Magician of Mars - Part 6]
	#46 1941		[The Magician of Mars - Part 7]
	#1 1942		[Outlaws of the Moon - Part 1]
			[The Magician of Mars - Part 8]
	#2 1942		[Outlaws of the Moon - Part 2]
			[The Magician of Mars - Part 9]
	#3 1942		[Outlaws of the Moon - Part 3]
			[The Magician of Mars - Part 10]
	#4 1942		[Outlaws of the Moon - Part 4]

Volume	Is/Date	Page	Title
			[The Magician of Mars - Part 11]
	#5 1942		[Outlaws of the Moon - Part 5]
			[The Magician of Mars - Part 12]
	#6 1942		[Outlaws of the Moon - Part 6]
			[The Magician of Mars - Part 13]
	#7 1942		[Outlaws of the Moon - Part 7]
	#8 1942		[Outlaws of the Moon - Part 8]
	#9 1942		[Outlaws of the Moon - Part 9]
	#10 1942		[Outlaws of the Moon - Part 10]
			[Captain Future and the 7 Space Stones - Part 1]
	#11 1942		[Outlaws of the Moon - Part 11]
			[Captain Future & the 7 Space Stones - Part 2]
	#12 1942		[Outlaws of the Moon - Part 12]
			[Captain Future & the 7 Space Stones - Part 3]
	#13 1942		[Captain Future & the 7 Space Stones - Part 4]
	#14 1942		[Captain Future and the 7 Space Stones - Part 5]
	#15 1942		[Captain Future and the 7 Space Stones - Part 6]
	#16 1942		[Captain Future and the 7 Space Stones - Part 7]
	#17 1942		[Captain Future and the 7 Space Stones - Part 8]
	#18 1942		[Murder Asteroid]
			[Captain Future and the 7 Space Stones - Part 9]
	#19 1942		[Captain Future & the 7 Space Stones - Part 10]
	#20 1942		[Captain Future & the 7 Space Stones - Part 11]
	#21 1942		[Captain Future & the 7 Space Stones - Part 12]
	#22 1942		[Captain Future & the 7 Space Stones - Part 13]
	#23 1942		[Captain Future & the 7 Space Stones - Part 14]
	#24 1942		[Captain Future & the 7 Space Stones - Part 15]
	#25 1942		[Captain Future & the 7 Space Stones - Part 16]
	#26 1942		[Star Trail to Glory - Part 1]
	#27 1942		[Star Trail to Glory - Part 2]
	#28 1942		[Star Trail to Glory - Part 3]
	#29 1942		[Star Trail to Glory - Part 4]
	#30 1942		[Star Trail to Glory - Part 5]
	#31 1942		[Star Trail to Glory - Part 6]
	#32 1942		[Star Trail to Glory - Part 7]
	#33 1942		[Star Trail to Glory - Part 8]
	#34 1942		[Star Trail to Glory - Part 9]
	#35 1942		[Star Trail to Glory - Part 10]
	#36 1942		[Star Trail to Glory - Part 11]
	#37 1942		[Star Trail to Glory - Part 12]
	#38 1942		[Star Trail to Glory - Part 13]
	#39 1942		[Star Trail to Glory - Part 14]

Volume	Is/Date	Page	Title
	#40 1942		[Star Trail to Glory - Part 15]
	#41 1942		[Star Trail to Glory - Part 16]
	#1 1943		[Outlaws of the Moon - Part 13]
	#2 1943		[Outlaws of the Moon - Part 14]
	#5 1943		[The Lost World of Time - Part 1]
	#6 1943		[The Lost World of Time - Part 2]
	#7 1943		[The Lost World of Time - Part 3]
	#8 1943		[The Lost World of Time - Part 4]
	#9 1943		[The Lost World of Time - Part 5]
	#10 1943		[The Lost World of Time - Part 6]
	#11 1943		[The Lost World of Time - Part 7]
	#12 1943		[The Lost World of Time - Part 8]
	#13 1943		[The Lost World of Time - Part 9]
			[Face of the Deep - Part 1]
	#14 1943		[The Lost World of Time - Part 10]
			[Face of the Deep - Part 2]
	#15 1943		[The Lost World of Time - Part 11]
			[Face of the Deep - Part 3]
	#16 1943		[The Lost World of Time - Part 12]
			[Face of the Deep - Part 4]
	#17 1943		[The Lost World of Time - Part 13]
	#18 1943		[The Lost World of Time - Part 14]
	#19 1943		[A Yank at Valhalla - Part 1]
	#20 1943		[A Yank at Valhalla - Part 2]
	#21 1943		[A Yank at Valhalla - Part 3]
	#22 1943		[A Yank at Valhalla - Part 4]
	#23 1943		[A Yank at Valhalla - Part 5]
	#24 1943		[A Yank at Valhalla - Part 6]
	#25 1943		[A Yank at Valhalla - Part 7]
	#26 1943		[A Yank at Valhalla - Part 8]
	#27 1943		[A Yank at Valhalla - Part 9]
	#28 1943		[A Yank at Valhalla - Part 10]
			[Quest Beyond the Stars - Part 1]
	#29 1943		[A Yank at Valhalla - Part 11]
			[Quest Beyond the Stars - Part 2]
	#30 1943		[A Yank at Valhalla - Part 12]
			[Quest Beyond the Stars - Part 3]
	#30 1943		[A Yank at Valhalla - Part 13]
			[Quest Beyond the Stars - Part 4]
	#30 1943		[A Yank at Valhalla - Part 14]
			[Quest Beyond the Stars - Part 5]
	#30 1943		[A Yank at Valhalla - Part 15]
			[Quest Beyond the Stars - Part 6]

Volume	Is/Date	Page	Title
	#30 1943		[Quest Beyond the Stars - Part 7]
	#30 1943		[Quest Beyond the Stars - Part 8]
	#30 1943		[Quest Beyond the Stars - Part 9]
	#30 1943		[Through Invisible Barriers - Part 1]
			[Quest Beyond the Stars - Part 10]
	#30 1943		[Through Invisible Barriers - Part 2]
			[Quest Beyond the Stars - Part 11]
	#30 1943		[Through Invisible Barriers - Part 3]
			[Quest Beyond the Stars - Part 12]
	#40 1943		[Through Invisible Barriers - Part 4]
			[Quest Beyond the Stars - Part 13]
	#41 1943		[Through Invisible Barriers - Part 5]
	#42 1943		[Through Invisible Barriers - Part 6]
	#43 1943		[Through Invisible Barriers - Part 7]
	#51 1943		[The Comet Kings - Part 1]
	#1 1944		[The Comet Kings - Part 2]
	#2 1944		[The Comet Kings - Part 3]
	#3 1944		[The Comet Kings - Part 4]
	#4 1944		[The Comet Kings - Part 5]
	#5 1944		[The Comet Kings - Part 6]
	#6 1944		[The Comet Kings - Part 7]
	#7 1944		[The Comet Kings - Part 8]
	#8 1944		[The Comet Kings - Part 9]
	#9 1944		[The Comet Kings - Part 10]
	#10 1944		[The Comet Kings - Part 11]
	#11 1944		[The Comet Kings - Part 12]
	#12 1944		[The Comet Kings - Part 13]
	#13 1944		[The World with a Thousand Moons - Part 1]
			[The Comet Kings - Part 14]
	#14 1944		[The World with a Thousand Moons - Part 2]
			[The Comet Kings - Part 15]
	#15 1944		[The World with a Thousand Moons - Part 3]
			[The Comet Kings - Part 17]
	#16 1944		[The World with a Thousand Moons - Part 4]
			[The Comet Kings - Part 18]
	#17 1944		[The World with a Thousand Moons - Part 5]
	#39 1944		[Planets in Peril - Part 1]
	#32 1945		[Planets in Peril - Part 16]
	#33 1945		[Magic Moon]
	#13 1946		[The Free-Lance of Space]
	#42 1946		[The Revolt on the Tenth World]
	#6 1947		[Son of Two Worlds - Part 1]

Volume	Is/Date	Page	Title
	#7 1947		[Son of Two Worlds - Part 2]
	#8 1947		[Son of Two Worlds - Part 3]
	8 July 1954		[The Star Kings - Part 1]
	15 Sept 1954		[The Star Kings - Conclusion]
	#4 1970		[The Return of Captain Future]

KAPTEN FRANK RYMDENS HJALTE

Volume	Is/Date	Page	Title
	1980		[Captain Future and the Space Emperor]

Locus

Volume	Is/Date	Page	Title
	211		

Lost Fantasies

Volume	Is/Date	Page	Title
	# 5 (1977)	pp. 5-26	Comrades of Time

The Magazine of Fantasy & Science Fiction

Volume	Is/Date	Page	Title
	Nov 1954	Pg. 100	Sacrifice Hit
27:4	#161 Oct 1964	Pg. 21	The Pro

Magazine of Horror

Volume	Is/Date	Page	Title
	#14 Win 66/67		The Monster-God of Mamurth

Magic Carpet

Volume	Is/Date	Page	Title
	Apr 1933	Pg. 221	Kaldar, World of Antares
	Oct 1933	Pg. 473	Snake-men of Kaldar

Man From U.N.C.L.E. Magazine

Volume	Is/Date	Page	Title
	Oct 1968		Pigmy Island

Marvel Super Stories

Volume	Is/Date	Page	Title	
	May 1940	*Pg. 41*	*The World Without Sex*	Robert Wentworth

The Most Thrilling Science Fiction Ever Told

Volume	Is/Date	Page	Title
	#7 Win 1967	Pg. 28-45	Requiem

Volume	Is/Date	Page	Title
	#8 Spr 1968	Pg. 4-42	The Stars, My Brothers
	Oct 1972		After a Judgement Day
	Feb 1973		Sunfire!
	Aug 1973		The Shores of Infinity

Nova Science Fiction

Volume	Is/Date	Page	Title
4:3	Dec 1984	Pg. 25	Hur ar det dar ute? (What's It Like Out There?)

Planet Stories

Volume	Is/Date	Page	Title
			The Star Kings

The Phantom Detective

Volume	Is/Date	Page	Title
18:2	Mar 1937		Kid Stuff
18:3	Jul 1937		His Sworn Duty
20:3			(Prize Title Contest Story)

Popular Detective

Volume	Is/Date	Page	Title
6:2	Mar 1936		Leopard's Paw
7:1	May 1936		Crimson Gold
	Feb 1936		The Ramrod Key Killings
	Apr 1936		Murder Mountain
	May 1936		Carter Makes a Squeal
	Aug 1936		Crooked Cop
	Sep 1936		Snow Clue
	Oct 1936		Last Bequest
	Dec 1936		Face to Face
	Jan 1937		Murder Press
	Feb 1937		Ball Bearing Death
	Apr 1937		The Corpse Died Twice

Return to Wonder

Volume	Is/Date	Page	Title
	9		Look Forward, Look Back

Science Fiction

Volume	Is/Date	Page	Title
	Mar 1939	Pg. 6	Under the White Star
1:3	Aug 1939	Pg. 32	The Man Who Solved Death

Volume	Is/Date	Page	Title	
	Oct 1939	Pg. 56	Dweller in the Darkness	
	Sep 1941	Pg. 50	Day of the Micro-Men	

Science Fiction Adventure

Volume	Is/Date	Page	Title
	Dec 1956	Pg. 5	The Starcombers
	Nov 1958 (#5)		The Starcombers

Science Fiction Adventure Classics

Volume	Is/Date	Page	Title
	Win 1967	Pg 27	World Atavism
	Fal 1968	Pg 5	The Space Rocket Murders
	Fal 1969 #8	Pg 16	Wacky World
	Win 1969 #7	Pg 88-102	The Man Who Lived Twice
	#7 Win 1969	Pg 4-87	The Other Side of the Moon
	#7 Win 1969	Pg 103-131	The Revolt on the Tenth World
	Spr 1971	Pg 73	Lilene, the Moon Girl
	Nov 1972	Pg 30-70	Valley of Invisible Men

Science Fiction Classic Annual

Volume	Is/Date	Page	Title
	1970	pp 37-52	Devolution

Science Fiction Classics

Volume	Is/Date	Page	Title
	#6		
	#19		
	May 1974		The Free-Lance of Space

Science Fiction Greats

Volume	Is/Date	Page	Title
	Fal 1970		Kingdom of the Stars

Science Fiction Stories

Volume	Is/Date	Page	Title	
	Mar 1939	Pg. 34	The Conqueror's Voice	Robert Castle
	Jun 1939	*Pg. 57*	*Short-Wave Madness*	Robert Castle
	Apr 1943	Pg. 45	No-Man's-Land of Time	

Science Fiction Yearbook

Volume	Is/Date	Page	Title
	1967		The Knowledge Machine
	No. 2	Pg. 4	The Fear Neutralizer

Volume	Is/Date	Page	Title	
	No. 3(1969)		The Unforgiven	
	Win 1971		The Quest in Time	

Science Wonder Quarterly

Volume	Is/Date	Page	Title
	#1 Fal 1929	Pg. 84	The Hidden World

Scientific Detective MONTHLY

Volume	Is/Date	Page	Title
	Apr 1930	Pg. 300	The Invisible Master
	May 1930	Pg. 390	The Murder in the Clinic

Space Travel

Volume	Is/Date	Page	Title
	Jul 1958	Pg. 30	Planet of Exile
5:5	Sep 1958	Pg. 30	The Star Hunter
	Nov 1958	Pg. 6	The Godmen

Startling Mystery Stories

Volume	Is/Date	Page	Title
	#8 Spr 1968		Three From the Tomb
	Win 1969		The Dogs of Dr. Dwann

Startling Stories

Volume	Is/Date	Page	Title	
	Mar 1939	Pg. 108	The Fear Neutralizer	
	May 1939	Pg. 14	The Prisoner of Mars	
	Sep 1939	Pg. 110	The Space Visitors	
	Jan 1940	Pg. 12	The Three Planeteers	
	Nov 1940	Pg. 110	The Man Who Evolved	
	Jan 1941	Pg. 14	A Yank at Valhalla	
12:1	Spr 1945	Pg. 90	The Island of Unreason	
12:1	*Spr 1945*		*Red Sun of Danger*	Brett Sterling
	Fal 1945	Pg. 75	Trouble on Titan	
13:1	Win 1946	Pg. 11	Outlaw World	
	Spr 1946	Pg. 84	The Dead Planet	
14:1	Sum 1946	Pg. 62	The Man with X-Ray Eyes	
14:3	Jan 1947	Pg. 13	The Star of Life	
15:3	Jul 1947	Pg. 88	Proxy Planeteer	
16:3	Jan 1948	Pg. 70	A Conquest of Two Worlds	
	Jul 1948	Pg. 9	The Valley of Creation	
20:3	Jan 1950	Pg. 94	The Return of Captain Future	

Volume	Is/Date	Page	Title
21:2	May 1950	Pg. 98	Children of the Sun
	Jul 1950	Pg. 11	City at World's End
22:1	Sep 1950	Pg. 96	Harpers of Titan
22:2	Nov 1950	Pg. 78	Pardon My Iron Nerves
22:3	Jan 1951	Pg. 118	Moon of The Unforgotten
23:1	Mar 1951	Pg. 76	Earthmen No More
23:2	May 1951	Pg. 120	Birthplace of Creation
31:1	Oct 1953	Pg. 76	The Unforgiven

Starwind

Volume	Is/Date	Page	Title
2:1	Fal 1976	Pg. 46	Birthplace of Creation

Strange Tales of mystery and horror

Volume	Is/Date	Page	Title
	Jan 1932	Pg. 299	Dead Legs

Super Science Stories

Volume	Is/Date	Page	Title
	May 1943	Pg. 88	Exile

Super Science Stories (Canadian?)

Volume	Is/Date	Page	Title
	Apr 1944		Exile

Tales of Wonder

Volume	Is/Date	Page	Title
	Aug 1930	Pg. 4	The Comet Doom
	#3 Sum 1938	Pg. 33	Horror in the Telescope
	#4 Aug 1938	Pg. 72	The Sea Terror
	#5 Win 1938	Pg. 39	The Space Beings
	#11 Sum 1940	Pg. 24	The Man Who Saw the Future

Thirty Thrilling Tales

Volume	Is/Date	Page	Title
			The Cosmic Pantograph

Thrilling Adventure

Volume	Is/Date	Page	Title
	Feb 1938		Power Pit 13

Thrilling Detective

Volume	Is/Date	Page	Title
	May 1935		Murder at Weed Key

Volume	Is/Date	Page	Title
	Apr 1936		Murder in the King Family
	May 1936		Copper Proof
	Aug 1936		The Crime Crusader
	Dec 1936		Sea Murder
	May 1937	Pg. 78	Death Dolls
	Sep 1937	Pg. 54	Death Comes in Glass
	Dec 1940		A Brother to Him

Thrilling Mystery

Volume	Is/Date	Page	Title
2:3	Apr 1936	Pg. 48	The Earth Dwellers
	May 1936		Beasts that Once were Men
4:2	Sep 1936	Pg. 35	Children of Terror
	Sep 1938		Woman From the Ice

Thrilling Science Fiction

Volume	Is/Date	Page	Title
	Aug 1973		

Thrilling Science Stories

Volume	Is/Date	Page	Title
	Fal 1976		

Thrilling Wonder Stories

Volume	Is/Date	Page	Title	
	Oct 1936	Pg. 33	Cosmic Quest	
	Dec 1936	Pg. 64	Mutiny of Europa	
	Apr 1937	Pg. 92	A Million Years Ahead	
	Aug 1937	Pg. 43	Space Mirror	
	Oct 1937	Pg. 59	Holmes Folly	
	Dec 1937	Pg. 90	When Space Burst	
	Apr 1938	Pg. 55	Easy Money	
11:3	Jun 1938	Pg. 14	Murder in the Void	
11:3	*Jun 1938*	*Pg. 97*	*The Great Illusion*	Will Garth
	Dec 1938	Pg. 90	The Cosmic Hiss	
	Feb 1940		Doom Over Venus	
	Feb 1940		Dweller in the Darkness	
	May 1940	Pg. 50	Dictators of Creation	
	Jun 1940	Pg. 33	The Isle of Changing Life	
	Sep 1940	Pg. 82	The Night the World Ended	
	Oct 1940	Pg. 80	Murder Asteroid	
	Dec 1940	Pg. 91	Gift from the Stars	

Volume	Is/Date	Page	Title	
	Aug 1941	Pg. 14	Son of Two Worlds	
	Oct 1942	Pg. 15	Through Invisible Barriers	
	Sum 1945	Pg. 59	The Deconventionalizers	
28:1	Win 1946	Pg. 13	Forgotten World	
	Spr 1946	Pg. 32	The Indestructible Man	
	Fal 1946	*Pg. 60*	*Never the Twain Shall Meet*	Brett Sterling
	Feb 1947	Pg. 91	Come Home From Earth	
	Feb 1948	Pg. 72	Transuranic	
	Jun 1948	Pg. 109	The Knowledge Machine	
34:1	Apr 1949	Pg. 54	Alien Earth	
40:3	Aug 1952	Pg. 12	Lords of the Morning	
	Dec 1952	Pg. 66	What's It Like Out There?	
	Dec 1952	Pg. 69	Inside Hamilton	

Toronto Star Weekly

Volume	Is/Date	Page	Title
	15 Aug 1959		The Man Who Missed the Moon

Treasury of Great Science Fiction

Volume	Is/Date	Page	Title
	#2		What's It Like Out There

Two Complete Science-Adventure Books

Volume	Is/Date	Page	Title
1:2	Spr 1951	Pg. 4	The Star Kings

Universe

Volume	Is/Date	Page	Title
	Sep 1954	Pg. 6	Starman Come Home

Venture Science Fiction

Volume	Is/Date	Page	Title
1:6	#6 Nov 1957	Pg. 85	No Earthman I
	Dec 1957		
2:3	#9 May 1958	Pg. 6	The Dark Backward

VENTURE (British)

Volume	Is/Date	Page	Title
	Jun 1964		No Earthman I

Weird Tales

Volume	Is/Date	Page	Title
	Mar		Evolution Island

Volume	Is/Date	Page	Title	
8:2	Aug 1926	Pg. 207	The Monster-God of Mamurth	
8:3	Sep 1926	Pg. 307	Across Space	
8:4	Oct 1926	Pg. 520	Across Space	
8:5	Nov 1926	Pg. 690	Across Space	
8:6	Dec 1926	Pg. 724	The Metal Giant	
9:2	Feb 1927	Pg. 163	The Atomic Conquerors	
9:3	Mar 1927		Evolution Island	
10:3	Sep 1927	Pg. 311	The Moon Menace	
10:4	Oct 1927	Pg. 459	The Time Raider	
10:5	Nov 1927	Pg. 639	The Time Raider	
10:6	Dec 1927	Pg. 832	The Time Raider	
11:1	Jan 1928	Pg. 105	The Time Raider	
11:6	Jun 1928	Pg. 769	The Dimension Terror	
12:2	Aug 1928	Pg. 193	Crashing Suns	
12:3	Sep 1928	Pg. 375	Crashing Suns	
12:3	Sep 1928		The Polar Doom	
13:2	Feb 1929	Pg. 149	The Star-Stealers	
13:3	Mar 1929	Pg. 351	The Sea Horror	
13:5	May 1929	Pg. 597	Within the Nebula	
13:6	Jun 1929	Pg. 741	The Abysmal Invaders	
14:1	Jul 1929	Pg. 49	Outside the Universe	
14:2	Aug 1929	Pg. 219	Outside the Universe	
41:3	Sep 1929	Pg. 374	Outside the Universe	
14:4	Oct 1929	Pg. 517	Outside the Universe	
15:1	Jan 1930	Pg. 59	The Life Masters	
15:2	Feb 1930	Pg. 172	The Comet Drivers	
15:4	Apr 1930	Pg. 487	The Plant Revolt	
15:5	May 1930	Pg. 606	The Sun People	
16:1	Jul 1930	Pg. 83	The Death Lord	
16:2	Aug 1930	Pg. 175	Pigmy Island	
16:4	Oct 1930	Pg. 489	The Mind-Master	
16:5	Nov 1930	Pg. 631	The Cosmic Cloud	
17:2	Feb-Mar 1931	Pg. 192	The Horror City	
17:3	Apr-May 1931	Pg. 304	Ten Million Years Ahead	
18:1	Aug 1931	Pg. 22	The Earth-Owners	
18:3	Oct 1931	Pg. 343	The Shot from Saturn	
18:5	Dec 1931	Pg. 630	Creatures of the Comet	
19:2	Feb 1932	Pg. 178	The Three from the Tomb	
19:4	Apr 1932	Pg. 466	The Earth Brain	
19:5	May 1932	Pg. 611	The Terror Planet	
20:4	Oct 1932	Pg. 491	The Dogs of Dr. Dwann	
20:5	*Nov 1932*		*Vampire Village*	Hugh Davidson

Volume	Is/Date	Page	Title	
20:6	Dec 1932	Pg. 749	The Man Who Conquered Age	
21:1	*Jan 1933*		*Snake-Men*	Hugh Davidson
21:4	Apr 1933	Pg. 461	The Star-Roamers	
22:1	Jul 1933	Pg. 26	The Fire Creatures	
22:3	Sep 1933	Pg. 298	Horror on the Asteroid	
22:4	*Oct 1933*		*The Vampire Master*	Hugh Davidson
22:5	Nov 1933	Pg. 551	The War of the Sexes	
22:5	*Nov 1933*		*The Vampire Master*	Hugh Davidson
22:6	*Dec 1933*		*The Vampire Master*	Hugh Davidson
23:1	*Jan 1934*		*The Vampire Master*	Hugh Davidson
23:2	Feb 1934	Pg. 219	The Man Who Returned	
23:3	Mar 1934	Pg. 331	Thundering Worlds	
23:4	Apr 1934	Pg. 449	Corsairs of the Cosmos	
25:2	Feb 1935	Pg. 199	Murder in the Grave	
26:1	Jul 1935	Pg. 2	The Avenger From Atlantis	
26:3	Sep 1935	Pg. 381	The Monster-God of Mamurth	
26:4	Oct 1935	Pg. 402	The Six Sleepers	
26:6	Dec 1935	Pg. 707	The Great Brain of Kaldar	
27:3	Mar 1936	Pg. 345	In the World's Dusk	
27:5	May 1936	Pg. 597	Child of the Wind	
27:6	*Jun 1936*		*The House of the Evil Eye*	Hugh Davidson
28:1	Jul 1936	Pg. 36	When the World Slept	
28:2	Aug-Sep 1936	Pg. 130	The Door Into Infinity	
29:3	Mar 1937	Pg. 361	The Seed from Outside	
29:4	Apr 1937	Pg. 413	Fessenden's Worlds	
30:2	Aug 1937	Pg. 179	World of the Dark Dwellers	
30:3	Sep 1937	Pg. 258	The Lake of Life	
30:4	Oct 1937	Pg. 459	The Lake of Life	
30:5	Nov 1937	Pg. 596	The Lake of Life	
30:6	Dec 1937	Pg. 708	Child of Atlantis	
31:1	Jan 1938	Pg. 21	The House of Living Music	
31:5	May 1938	Pg. 588	The Isle of the Sleeper	
32:1	Jul 1938	Pg. 70	He that Hath Wings	
32:2	Aug 1938	Pg. 167	The Fire Princess	
32:3	Sep 1938	Pg. 325	The Fire Princess	
32:4	Oct 1938	Pg. 455	The Fire Princess	
33:1	Jan 1939	Pg. 61	Bride of the Lightning	
33:3	Mar 1939	Pg. 102	Comrades of Time	
33:4	Apr 1939	Pg. 61	Armies of the Past	
34:4	*Oct 1939*		*The Vampire Master*	Hugh Davidson
34:5	*Nov 1939*		*The Vampire Master*	Hugh Davidson
34:6	*Dec 1939*		*The Vampire Master*	Hugh Davidson
35:1	*Jan 1940*		*The Vampire Master*	Hugh Davidson

Volume	Is/Date	Page	Title
35:3	May 1940	Pg. 14	The City From the Sea
35:5	Sep 1940	Pg. 76	Sea Born
36:2	Nov 1941	Pg. 6	Dreamers Worlds
37:2	Nov 1943	Pg. 8	The Valley of the Assassins
38:1	Sep 1944	Pg. 6	The Shadow Folk
38:3	Jan 1945	Pg. 8	Priestess of the Labyrinth
38:5	May 1945	Pg. 30	The Shining Land
38:6	Jul 1945	Pg. 64	The Inn Outside the World
39:2	Nov 1945	Pg. 10	Lost Elysium
39:5	May 1946	Pg. 8	The Valley of the Gods
39:7	Sep 1946	Pg. 20	Day of Judgement
39:9	Jan 1947	Pg. 38	The King of Shadows
40:2	Jan 1948	Pg. 6	Serpent Princess
	Mar 1948		The Might-Have-Been
40:5	Jul 1948	Pg. 4	Twilight of the Gods
40:6	Sep 1948	Pg. 68	The Watcher of Ages
43:4	May 1951	Pg. 42	The Isle of the Sleeper

Weird Tales (Canadian)

Volume	Is/Date	Page	Title
	Sep 1946		
	Jan 1947		
	Sep 1948		

Weird Terror Tales

Volume	Is/Date	Page	Title
	Win 1970(#1)		Dead Legs

Wonder Stories

Volume	Is/Date	Page	Title
	Apr 1931	Pg. 1266	The Man Who Evolved
	Dec 1931	Pg. 848	The Reign of the Robots
	Feb 1932	Pg. 1046	A Conquest of Two Worlds
	May 1933	Pg. 970	Island of Unreason
	Nov 1933	Pg. 386	The Man with X-Ray Eyes
	Jan 1935	Pg. 958	Master of Genes
	Feb 1935	Pg. 1060	The Truth Gas
	Mar 1935	Pg. 1184	Eternal Cycle [Cosmos End]
	Oct 1935	Pg. 554	The Cosmic Pantograph
	May 1938		The Island of Unreason

Wonder Stories Annual

Volume	Is/Date	Page	Title
	1951		Turnabout

Items cited in other reference works, but not found in the cited magazines

---

Where Cited			Where Found
Amazing Stories			
Dec 1938	Pg. 50	The Ephemerae	-> Astounding Stories Dec 38
Jan 1965 Pg. 64	?		
Fantastic Stories Monthly			
Jan 1953		A Yank At Valhalla	-> Fantasy Story Magazine Jan 1958
GALAXY			
Apr 1964		The Haunted Stars	
Saturn: The Magazine of Science Fiction			
Mar 1957		?	
Science Fiction Stories			
1st issue (May/June 1955)		?	
2nd issue		?	
Startling Stories			
Jan 1942	Pg 94	The Return of Captain Future	-> Startling Stories
Jan 1950			
Dec 1952		What's It Like Out There	-> Thrilling Wonder Stories
Dec 1952			
Tales of Wonder			
Aug 1939		The Comet Doom	-> Tales of Wonder Aug 30
Thrilling Wonder Stories			
Apr 1938		Easy Money	-> Wonder Stories Apr 1938
Wierd Tales			
May 1933		The Island of Unreason	-> Wonder Stories May 33
Oct 1933		The Fire Princess	-> Weird Tales A/S/O 1938
Feb 1935		The Man Who Returned	-> Weird Tales Feb 1934
Magazine Unknown			
Dec 1934		Armageddon in Space	
Mar 1948		The Might-Have-Been	

AFTERWORD

What a project this has been. What you have in your hands is the end result of thirty some years of work. This all started back when I was in sixth grade. I bought my first science fiction novel. Up until this time I read mostly mysteries (juvenile) and baseball stories and histories.

One day I was browsing a small paperback rack in a smoke shop (my father smoked a pipe) and I bought *Galaxy Mission.* I read this and I was hooked. I bought all the other Edmond Hamilton books they had over the next couple months. For many year I thought that there were only four Captain Future novels. Then in high school I found out that Edmond Hamilton had written a lot more Captain Future novels and a lot more.

I then started keeping track of what I found out about Edmond Hamilton. My friends and I used to ride the bus downtown so we could visit the used bookstores looking for old pulp magazines.

In the early 1970's I found out that Mr. Hamilton and his wife summered in Kinsman, Ohio. This was only about an hour from where I lived. I wrote Mr. Hamilton and he was gracious enough to allow me to come visit. I convinced my father to drive a couple friends and me out one Saturday. It was fascinating to actually meet an author and I remember thinking that I want a library in my house someday, just like his (floor to ceiling bookcase on almost every wall).

More years passed and Mr. Hamilton passed away. In the 1980's I found out that his papers had been donated to the Jack Williamson collection at Eastern New Mexico University's Golden Library. I wrote to Mrs. Walker (the librarian) asking her about what was donated. She responded that they did not know and did not have a good idea of what Mr. Hamilton had written.

I promptly sent him a copy of what information I know at the time. She responded that this was great and that I should see about getting this published. Eventually I contacted Borgo Press and they were interested. I began re working what I had into the format that Borgo Press wanted. Unfortunately during this process Borgo had to suspend operations in 1999.

Now here I am with Wildside Press/Borgo Press. It been a long strange road for this and I have been very fortunate over the years with all the help and interest.

One of the problems with doing a work like this is it never ends. Many times I have reached a point where I thought the book was done. Then I would visit a library or bookstore and find something more that I should add. But eventually one has to put a foot down and say done.

ACKNOWLEDGMENTS

Along the way I have had the help of many individuals who have probably forgotten that they ever talked to me. I've tried to list everyone, but if I've left anyone out, please forgive this feeble old mind and accept my thanks.

Here's the list of those whom I remember:

My two daughters Katherine and Olivia and my wife Kelly. She has taken care of the girls whilst I have traveled to locations to browse various libraries. The constant clutter of paper, books and other detrious of the research. The request to order more books ("But dear, I don't have this edition!"). She has invaluable in the proofreading of this book. With out her there would be a lot more errors in this book. She has even translated much of the French for me.

My mother Betty and father Bill, see something did come from all that Science Fiction.

My brother Carl and sister Sue who scoured bookstores across the country for me.

Mr. Jack Williamson who graciously wrote the wonderful introduction and answered my questions regarding events of years gone by.

Mr. Robert Reginald and all the people at Borgo Press who have answered my questions and been patient with all my delays.

Mr. Sean Wallace, Mr. John Betancourt, Wildside Press, and Cosmos Press for continuing on.

The designers, planners and maintainers of the Internet.

Mr. Bertil Falk.

Mr. Hans Pierson.

Mr. Rick Morrisey.

Mr. Ken Hammarstrom.

Mr. David Lisa.

My cousin Larry Schwartz, librarian supreme.

My cousin J.J. Gombert who searched through bookstores in Holland.

Mr. Gene Bundy, Head Librarian of the Jack Williamson Collection at Golden Library at Eastern New Mexico University and his staff.

Ms. Allison Scott, Head librarian at Bowling Green State University. Also to her staff.

Mrs. Mary Walker.

Forrest J. Ackerman, Sci-Fi fan extraordinaire.

Mr. Eb Moesch for translating from the Russian.

Father Bartz for translating from the Greek text for me.

And especially Mr. Edmond Hamilton for days and nights of thrilling entertainment.

Denis Guiotœ, secretary du Jury du Grand Prix de la SF Frangaise.

Lorna Toolisœ of the Spaced Out Library.

Also I would like to thank the following for invaluable assistance me in this endevour:

Isaac Asimov, for his Hugo Winners Series.

Charles N. Brown & his staff, for publishing *Locus*.

The SFWA, for the Nebula Awards & it's series.

Andrew I. Porter & his staff, for publishing *SF Chronicle*.

Suggested Reading List

Edmond Hamilton

The Best of Edmond Hamilton
Planets in Peril
Moskowitz, Sam. **Seekers of Tomorrow**. Cleveland, OH: World Publishing Co. 1966.
Various. **Batman in the Fifties**. New York, NY: DC Comics, 2002.
Various. **World's Finest Comics - Archives, Vol. 1**. New York, NY: DC Comics, 1991.
Various. **World's Finest Comics - Archives, Vol. 2**. New York, NY: DC Comics, 2002.

Devolution	1936	ss
Exile	1943	ss
The Inn Outside the World	1945	ss
Alien Earth	1949	nt
What's It Like Out There?	1952	nt
Requiem	1962	ss
The Pro	1964	ss

Pulps

Rogers, Alva. **A Requiem for Astounding**.
Weber, Ronald. **Hired Pens: Professional Writers in America's Golden Age of Print**.

Comics

Daniels, Les. **Batman: The Complete History**. San Francisco, CA: Chronicle Books, 1998.
Daniels, Les. **DC Comics: Sixty Years of the World's Favorite Comic Book Heroes**. New York, NY: Bulfinch Press Book; Little, Brown and Company, 1995.
Daniels, Les. **Superman: The Complete History**. San Francisco, CA: Chronicle Books, 1998.
Overstreet's Comic Price Guide
Schwartz, Julius & Brian M. Thomsen. **Man of Two Worlds**. New York, NY: Harper Collins Publishing Inc, 2000.

Science Fiction

Warner Jr. Harry. **All Our Yesterdays**.

Web Sites

Cosmos Books	http://www.cosmos-books.com/
Hamilton, Edmond	http://www.pulpgen.com/pulp/edmond_hamilton/
Wildside Press	http://www.wildsidepress.com/

BIBLIOGRAPHY

Ash, Brian. **Who's Who in Science Fiction**. New York, NY: Taplinger Publishing Co. Inc.

Ashley, Michael. **The History of Science Fiction Magazine: 1926-1935**. Chicago, IL: Henry Regnery, 1974.

Benton, Mike. **The Illustrated History Science Fiction Comics**. Dallas, TX: Taylor Publishing Co. 1992.

Bleiler, Everett F. **Science Fiction: The Early Years**. Kent, OH: The Kent State University Press, 1990.

Briney, Robert E. & Edward Wood. **SF Bibliographies**. Chicago, IL: Advent Press, 1972.Brown , Charles N. & William G. Contento. **The Locus Index to Science Fiction (1984-1998)**. 2003. http://www.locusmag.com/index/0start.html

Brown , Charles N. & William G. Contento. **The Locus Index to Science Fiction: 1999**. 2003. http://www.locusmag.com/index/yr1999/0start.html

Brown , Charles N. & William G. Contento. **The Locus Index to Science Fiction: 2000**. 2003. http://www.locusmag.com/index/yr2000/0start.html

Brown , Charles N. & William G. Contento. **The Locus Index to Science Fiction: 2001**. 2003. http://www.locusmag.com/index/yr2001/0start.html

Brown , Charles N. & William G. Contento. **The Locus Index to Science Fiction: 2002**. 2003. http://www.locusmag.com/index/yr2002/0start.html

Brown , Charles N. & William G. Contento. **The Locus Index to Science Fiction: 2003**. 2003. http://www.locusmag.com/index/yr2003/0start.html

Clarke, I. F. **Tales of the Future**. 3rd. Edition. London: The LibraryAssociation, 1978.

Cole, Walter R. **A Checklist of Science Fiction Anthologies**. New York, NY: Arno Press, 1975.

Cook, Michael L. & Stephen T. Miller. **Mystery, Detective Espionage Fiction: A Checklist of Fiction in U.S. Pulp Magazines, 1915-1974, Vol. 2.** New York, NY: Garland Publishing, Inc. 1988.

Daniels, Les. **Batman: The Complete History**. San Francisco, CA: Chronicle Books, 1998.

Daniels, Les. **DC Comics: Sixty Years of the World's Favorite Comic Book Heroes**. New York, NY: Bulfinch Press Book; Little, Brown and Company, 1995.

Daniels, Les. **Superman: The Complete History**.San Francisco, CA: Chronicle Books, 1998.

De Camp, L. Sprague. **Science Fiction Handbook**. _: Hermitage House, 1952.

Finlay, Virgil. **Far Beyond**. Lancaster, PA: Charles F. Miller, 1994.

Finlay, Virgil. **Strange Science**. Novato, CA: Underwood-Miller, 1992.

Finlay, Virgil. **Women of the Ages**. Novato, CA:. Underwood-Miller, 1992.

Fletcher, Marilyn P. **Science Fiction Story Index Second Edition: 1950-1979**. Chicago, IL: American Library Association, 1981.

Fletcher, Marilyn P. & James L. Thorson. **Readers Guide to 20th Century Science Fiction**. Chicago, IL: American Library Association, 1989. 673p.

Gallagher, Edward Joseph. **The Annotated Guide to Fantastic Adventures**. San Bernardino, CA: The Borgo Press, 1985.

Hall, H. W. **Science Fiction & Fantasy Reference Index 1878-1985**. Detroit, MI: Gale Research Co. 1987.

Horn, Maurice. **The World Encyclopedia of Comics Vol. 1 & Vol. 2**. New York, NY: Chelsea House Publishers, 1976. P. 117 & 642.

Itoh, T. **Edmond Hamilton Bibliography**. Unpublished.

Itoh, T. with Koichi Yamamoto. **Captain Future Reader**. Tokyo: Hachioji-shi, 1994.

Kaye, Marvin & Saralee Kaye. **The Magazine that Never Dies: Weird Tales**. Garden City, NY: Doubleday Book & Music Clubs, Inc. 1988.

Kupperberg, Paul & Robert Greenberger. **The Greatest Batman Stories Ever Told Volume 2**. New York, NY: Warner Books, Inc. 1992.

Korshak, Stephan D. **A Hannes Bok Treasury**. Novato, CA: Underwood-Miller, 1993.

McGhan, Barry. **Science Fiction and Fantasy Pseudonyms**. Dearborn, MI: Howard DeVore, 1971.

Magill, Frank N. **Survey of Science Fiction Literature**. 5 vols. Englewood Cliff, NJ: Salem Press Inc.

Marshall, Gene & Carl F Waedt. "Health Knowledge Magazines -- Author Index" in The Science-Fiction Collector. #3, 1977.

Moskowitz, Sam. **Seekers of Tomorrow**. Cleveland, OH: World Publishing Co. 1966.

Moskowitz, Sam. **Explorers of the Infinite**. Cleveland, OH: World Publishing Co. 1963.

Mossman, Jennifer [Editor]. **Pseudonyms & Nicknames Dictionary: Vol. 1 A-K**. Detroit, MI: Gale Research Co. 1987. 1138pp.

New England Science Fiction Association. **The N.E.S.F.A. Index: Science Fiction Magazines and Original Anthologies 1971-1972**. Cambridge, MA: Spaulding Corp. 1973.

Nichols, Peter. **The Encyclopedia of Science Fiction**. New York, NY: Doubleday, 1979.

Overstreet, Robert M. **The Overstreet Comic Book Price Guide, 29th Edition**.

New York, NY: Avon Books, 1999.
Parnell, Frank H. with Mike Ashley. **Monthly Terrors: An Index to the Weird Fantasy Magazines Published in the United States and Great Britain**. Westport, CT: Greenwood Press, 1985.
Person, Hans. **Index to Jules Verne Magazinet**. Sweden. Unpublished.
Preiss, Byron. **Weird Heroes**. New York, NY: Pyramid Books, 1977. Vol. 6.
Pringle, David. **The Ultimate Guide to Science Fiction**. _: Pharos Books, 1990.
Pohl, Frederik; Martin H. Greenberg & Joseph D. Olander. **Galaxy: Thirty Years of Innovative Science Fiction**. Chicago, IL: Playboy Press, 1980.
Rogers, Alva. **A Requiem for Astounding**. Chicago, IL.: Advent Publishers, 1964.
Schwartz, Julius & Brian M. Thomsen. **Man of Two Worlds**. New York, NY: Harper Collins Publishing Inc, 2000.
Thiessen, J. Grant. "Books of Associated Interest" in The Science-Fiction Collector. #2. 1976.
Tuck, Donald H. **The Encyclopedia of SF & F: Through 1968: Vol. 1: Who's Who, A-L**. Chicago, IL: Advent Publishers, Inc. 1974.
Tymn, Marshall B. [Ed.] **The Science Fiction Reference Book**. Mercer Island, WA: Starmont House, 1981.
Unknown. DC Database Project. http://dc.wikia.com/wiki/Main_Page
Unknown. Grand Comic Book Database. http://www.comics.org/
Ward, Murray R. **The Legion of Super-Heroes Index**. 5 vols. Guernville, CA: Independent Comics Group, 1987.
Wingrove, David. **The Science Fiction Source Book**. New York, NY: Von Nostrand Reinhold Co. 1984.

Contemporary Authors Vol. 1-4. First Revision.

_, Alain. Sf.netliberte.org. January 29, 1999. (http://sf.netliberte.org/index.htm).
_, Pascal. Captain Flam Le Site. (http://www.capitaineflam.free.fr/captainfuture.htm).

APPENDICES

Appendix A
Awards, Achievements & Guest

Executive Director of The Science Fiction League (Thrilling Wonder Stories June 1938).

The Jules Verne Award.

The First Fandom's "Hall of Fame" Award.

Proffessional Guest of Honor Pacificon II (22nd annual WorldCon), 4-7 September, 1964. Hotel Leamington, Oakland, CA.

Appendix B
Pseudonyms

This section lists stories written under the various pseudonyms used by Mr. Hamilton. The stories are listed under the names of the real authors when known. This information is based upon the work of Everett F. Blieler, Edward Joseph Gallager, H.W. Hall, Edmond Hamilton, Peter Nichols and myself. The references have been crossed checked wherever possible.

Edmond Moore Hamilton, 1904-1977

Mr. Hamilton is known to have used the following pseudonyms:

Blade, Alexander
Castle, Robert
Davidson, Hugh
Garth, Will
Sterling, Brett
Tenneshaw, S. M.
Wentworth, Robert

He was also referred by the following nicknames in the editorial and letter columns of the magazines he wrote for.

Hamilton, World Saver
World Destroyer
[The] World Wrecker

ALEXANDER BLADE [house pseudonym, Ziff-Davis]

by Roger R. Graham
"Brain Storm" in Fantastic Adventures. (December, 1948).
"Warrior Queen of Mars" in Fantastic Adventures. (September, 1949).

by Edmond Hamilton
"Battle for the Stars" in Imagination, (June, 1956). Cover: Malcolm Smith. [See A3]
"The Cosmic Kings" in Imaginative Tales, (November, 1956). Cover: Lloyd Rognan.
"The Cosmic Looters" in Imagination Science Fiction, (February, 1958).

"The Sinister Invasion" in Imagination Science Fiction, (June, 1957). Cover: Lloyd Rognan.
"The Tattooed Man" in Imaginative Tales, (March, 1957). Cover: Malcolm Smith.

by Herb Livingston
"Silver Medusa, The" in Fantastic Adventures. (February, 1948). Illustrator: Virgil Finlay.

by Bill Terry
"World is Dead, The" in Amazing Stories, (August, 1949): 96. Illustrator: Bill Terry.

by Don Wilcox
"Eye of the World, The" in Fantastic Adventures. (June, 1949).
"Eye of the World, The" in Fantastic Adventures. (July, 1949).

by Unknown
"3117 Half-credit Uncirculated" in Science Fiction Adventures. 2:6 (June, 1958): 94.
"Beyond the Veil of Science"[cxliii] in Amazing Stories. (January, 1949): 134.
"Blacksheep's Angel" in Flying Saucers From Other Worlds. (October, 1957).
"Case of the Living Mummy" in Mammoth Detective. 1:2.
"Come Into my Brain" in Imagination Science Fiction. (June, 1957). Pg 62.
"The Cosmic Destroyer" in Imaginative Tales. (September, 1957): 6. Cover: Lloyd Rognan.
"Curtain Call" in Mammoth Detective. 4:2.
"Death Wears a Rose" in Fantastic Adventures. (January, 1947).
"Diamond of Doom" in Fantastic Adventures. (July, 1945).

REPRINTS:

b as "Den bevinge de ormen" in Jules Verne-Magasinet. #42/1946 – #1/1947.

"Gambit on Ganymede" in Fantastic Adventures. (March, 1953).
"Is this the Night?" in Amazing Stories. (March, 1945) Page 102.
"Lamp of No Light" in Fantastic Adventures. (May, 1949).
"The Laughing Death" in Space Adventures, (Spring, 1971).
"Man Called Meteor, A" in Fantastic Adventures. (February, 1953).
"Man Outside, The" in Mammoth Mystery. 3:1.
"Man Who Hated Tuesday, The" in Fantastic Adventures. (February, 1951).
"Man Who Laughed at Time, The" in Fantastic Adventures. (August, 1949).
"Mermaid of Maracut Deep, The" in Fantastic Adventures. (March, 1949)
"Night Has a Thousand Eyes, The" in Mammoth Detective. 2:4
"Octopus of Space, The" in Fantastic Adventures. (October, 1949).
"Professor Cyclone" in Fantastic Adventures. (December, 1943).
"Queen City Murder Case, The" in Mammoth Mystery. 2:6.

"Return of a Demon" in Fantastic Adventures. (May, 1943).
"The Strange Adventure of Victor MacLiesh" in Amazing Stories. 15:5 (May, 1941).
"War of the Giant Apes" in Fantastic Adventures. (April, 1949).
"Wednesday Morning Sermon" in Imaginative Tales. (January, 1957): 114.
"Whip of Death, The" in Mammoth Detective. 2:1.
"Zero Hour" in Imagination Science Fiction. 7:2 (April, 1956):98-103.

ROBERT CASTLE

by Edmond Hamilton
"The Conqueror's Voice" in Science Fiction Stories, (March 1939): 34.
"Short-Wave Madness" in Science Fiction Stories, (June 1939): 57.

HUGH DAVIDSON

by Edmond Hamilton
"The House of the Evil Eye" in Weird Tales, (June 1936).
"Snake-Man" in Weird Tales. (January 1933).
"The Vampire Master" in Weird Tales. (October, 1939).
"The Vampire Master" Pt 2, in Weird Tales. (November, 1939).
"The Vampire Master" Pt 3, in Weird Tales. (December, 1939).
"The Vampire Master" con, in Weird Tales. (January, 1940).
"Vampire Village" in Weird Tales. (November, 1932).

WILL GARTH [house pseudonym]

by Otto Binder
"Rays of Blindness" in Thrilling Wonder, (April, 1938): 106.

by Edmond Hamilton
"Great Illusion, The" in Thrilling Wonder Stories, (June, 1938): 97. with Eando Binder, John Russell Fearn, Raymond Z. Gallun & Jack Williamson.

by Henry Kuttner
"Hands Across the Void" in Thrilling Wonder, (December, 1938): 15.

by Mort Weisinger
"Incident on Titan" in Thrilling Wonder. (June, 1941): 93.

REPRINTS:

b as "[ventyr p] titanus" in Jules Verne-Magasinet. #27/1942.

"Turnabout" in Startling Stories, (March, 1939): 117.

by Unknown
"Arab Interlude" in Thrilling Mystery. 11:3.
"Astral Newspaper" in Strange Stories. 4:2.
"Bloodless Peril, The" in Thrilling Wonder, (December, 1937): 100.
"Cellar of Skulls" in Thrilling Mystery. 14:3.
"Cross and Doublecross" in Thrilling Mystery. 12:1.
"Day of Debts, The" in Thrilling Mystery. 16:3.
"Dead Shall Rise Up, The" in Strange Stories. 4:1.
"Double Ring" in Strange Stories. 1:3.
"Fulfillment" in Strange Stories. 1:2.
"Hate's Handiwork" in Strange Stories. 5:1.
"House of the Griffin" in Strange Stories. 2:2.
Masked Rider. Harlequin #220. 1953.
"Memory Block" in Captain Future, (Spring 1941): 109.
"Men of Honor" in Captain Future, (Spring 1940): 115.
"Murder Dream" in The Masked Detective. 1:2.
"Murder in the Waxworks" in Thrilling Mystery. 11:2.
"Passing of Eric Holm" in Strange Stories. 2:3.
"Sea Vision" in Strange Stories. 2:1.
"Vengeful Ghost" in Thrilling Mystery. 10:1.

BRETT STERLING [house pseudonym, Standard magazines]

by Ray Bradbury
"Reverent" in Thrilling Wonder, (October 1948): 148.

by Edmond Hamilton
"Magic Moon" in Captain Future, (Winter 1944): 15. Illustrator: Orban.
"Red Sun of Danger" in Startling Stories, (Spring 1945): 11. Illustrator: Thomas. Cover: Earle Bergey. [See A25]
"The Star of Dread" in Captain Future, (Summer 1943): 13. Illustrator: Thomas. [See A48]

by Joseph Samachson
"Days of Creation" in Captain Future, (Spring 1944): 11.
"Worlds to Come" in Captain Future, (Spring 1943): 15.

S.M. TENNESHAW [house pseudonym, Ziff-Davis]

by Edmond Hamilton
"Last Call for Doomsday" in Imagination Science Fiction, (December, 1956).

by Unknown
"Frame Me in Oils" in Mammoth Detective. 6:3.
"The Friendly Killers" in Imagination. (June, 1958): 6.
"Kill Me if You Can" in Imagination Science Fiction. (June, 1957): 62.
"The Man Who Hated Noise" in Imaginative Tales. (March, 1957): 112.
"The Ultimate Weapon" in Imaginative Tales. (January, 1957): 6. Cover: Malcolm Smith.

ROBERT WENTWORTH

by Edmond Hamilton
"World Without Sex" in Marvel Science Stories, (May, 1940): 41.

Appendix C
Captain Future

Alphabetical Listing

"Birthplace of Creation" in Startling Stories, 23:2 (May, 1951): 120. Illustrator: Orban. See B204.

Reprints:

aa in Startling Stories, (August, 1952). [British]
b in Starwind: Science Fiction & Fantasy, 2:1 (Fall, 1976) Pg. 46. Illustrator: Michael Jones. Introduction: Gary Hoppenstand.
c in **Captain Future Handbook**. Edited by unknown. _: <publisher unknown> July 1983. [Japanese]
d in Thrilling Novels, No. 39 (1996).

"Calling Captain Future" in Captain Future Magazine, 1:2 (Spring 1940). Pg. 12. Illustrator: H. Wesso. See A10.

Reprints:

b as **Panik Im Kosmos**. Rastatt: <publisher unknown>, 1962. p. (U 311). Translator: M.F. Arnmann. [German]
c **Calling Captain Future**. New York, NY. Popular Library. 1967. 144 p. 18cm. paper. (60-2421).
d Tokyo: Hayakawa Publishing, Inc. 30 November 1971. Translator: Masahiro Noda. [Japanese]
d _: <publisher unknown> February 1973. (SF Bungaku Zenshu #18). Translator: Chikashi Uchida. [Japanese]
e as **Panik Im Kosmos**. _: Utopia, 1974. ? p. [German]
f as <unknown>. _: SF, 1977. ? p. [Korea]
g adapted into an animated television program in four parts[cxliv]. _: Toei Doga, 1978-79. [Japanese]
Note: This is available in Video, DVD, Video CD and in some cases LaserDISC in French, German, Italian, Japanese and Spanish.
h as **Kollisionsziel Erde**. Bergisch Gladbach: publisher unknown, 1981. (BSF 25002). Translator: Marcel Bieger. [German]
i in <unknown>. _: <publisher unknown> 1993. 336 p. [Russian]

Note : This is a collection containing: **Calling Captain Future**, **Captain Future's Challenge** and **Quest Beyond the Stars**.

j Tokyo: Hayakawa Publishing, Inc. March 1995. ? p. [Japanese]

k in <unknown>. _: <publisher unknown> 1993. 394 p. [Russian]

Note : This is a collection containing: Outlaw World, Calling Captain Future, Outlaws of the Moon.

l in <unknown>. _: <publisher unknown> 1998. 401 p. [Russian]

Note : This is a collection containing: Captain Future's Challenge, Calling Captain Future, and Quest Beyond the Stars.

m in **The Collected Captain Future, Volume One: Captain Future and the Space Emperor**. Edited by Stephen Haffner. Royal Oak, Michigan: Haffner Press. 1 July 2009, 648 p. Hardback. Introduction by Walter Jon Williams. Illustrated by Hugh Rankin. ISBN-10 1893887332; ISBN-13 97818938871336.

"*Captain Future and the Seven Space Stones*" in Captain Future Magazine, 2:2. (Winter 1941). p. 14. Illustrator: H. Wesso. See A14.

REPRINTS:

b as "Kapten Frank och de sju magiska stenarna." in Jules Verne Magasinet #10 - #25 (16 Parts): 1942. Pg. 25. [Swedish]

c as **Diamanten der Macht**. Rastatt: <publisher unknown> 1960. (UGB 151). Translator: Heinz Zwack. [German]

d as **Captain Future and the Seven Space Stones**. Tokyo: Hayakawa Publishing, Inc. 28 February 1966. Translator: Masahiro Noda. [Japanese]

e as **Diamanten der Macht**. _: Utopia, 1972 ? p. [German]

f Tokyo: Hayakawa Publishing, Inc. 31 March 1972. 202 p. Translator: Masahiro Noda. [Japanese]

g Tokyo: Hayakawa Publishing, Inc. 1974. ? p. [Japanese]

h adapted into an animated television program in four parts.[cxlv] _: Toei Doga, 1978-79. [Japanese]

Note: This is available in Video, DVD, Video CD and in some cases LaserDISC in French, German. Italian, Japanese and Spanish.

ca as **Diamanten der Macht**. Bergisch Gladbach: <publisher unknown> 1982. 171 p. (BSF 25005). Translator: Richard Bellinghausen. [German]

g Tokyo: Hayakawa Publishing, Inc. 1995. ? p. [Japanese]

"*Captain Future and the Space Emperor*" in Captain Future Magazine, 1:1 (Winter 1940). p. 12. Illustrator: Wesso. See A9.

REPRINTS:

b as **Captain Future and the Space Emperor**. New York, NY: Popular Library. 1967. 128 p. 18cm. paper (60-2457).

c as <unknown> _: <publisher unknown> 1969. [Greek]

d as <unknown> Hayakawa Publishing, Inc. 31 May 1974. 279 p. Translator: Masahiro Noda. [Japanese]

e as **Captain Future en de Keizer van het Heelal**. Rotterdam: Ridderhof. 1975. 195 p; 18cm. ISBN: 90.308.0215.4. (Science Fiction serie s No. 24).[cxlvi] Translator: Iskraa Bundels. [Dutch]

f in **The Collected Captain Future, Volume One: Captain Future and the Space Emperor**. Edited by Stephen Haffner. Royal Oak, Michigan: Haffner Press. 1 July 2009, 648 p. Hardback. Introduction by Walter Jon Williams. Illustrated by Hugh Rankin. ISBN-10 1893887332; ISBN-13 9781893887133 6.

g adapted into an animated television program in four parts[cxlvii]. _: Toei Doga, 1978-79. [Japanese]
Note: This is available in Video, DVD, Video CD and in some cases LaserDISC in English, French, German, Italian, Japanese and Spanish.

h as **Kapten Frank och rymdkejsaren.**[cxlviii] in Kapten Frank Rymdens Hjalte. Malmo: Pulp Press. 1980. 112 p. paper. Translator: Bertil Falk. ISBN: 91-86086-00-6. [Swedish]

i as **Die lebende Legende**. Bergisch Gladbach: <publisher unknown>, 1981. (BSF 25001). Translator: Marcel Bieger. [German]

j as **The Sombre Emperor**. Athens: Sympan/Lyhnari, 1989. Translated by Geni Mistraki. [Greek]

"Captian Future's Challenge" in Captain Future Magazine, 1:3 (Summer 1940). p. 14. Illustrator: H. W. Wesso. See A11.

REPRINTS:

b New York, NY: Popular Library. 1967. paper.

c as **Kampf Um Gravium**. Rastatt: <publisher unknown> 1961. (UGB 147). Translator: Heinz Zwack. [German]

d as **Kampf Um Gravium**. _: Utopia, 1971. p. [German]

e Tokyo: Hayakawa Publishing, Inc. 31 July 1971. 307 p. Translator: Masahiro Noda. [Japanese]

f adapted into an animated television program in four parts.[cxlix] _: Toei Doga, 1978-79. [Japanese]
Note: This is available in Video, DVD, Video CD and in some cases LaserDISC in English, French, German, Italian, Japanese and Spanish.

g as **Die Gravium Sabotage**. Bergisch Gladbach: <publisher unknown>

1982. 154 p. (BSF 25003). Translator: Richard Bellinghausen. [German]

h in <unknown>. _: <publisher unknown> 1993. 336 p. [Russian]
Note : This is a collection containing: Calling Captain Future, Captain Future's Challenge and Quest Beyond the Stars.

i Tokyo: Hayakawa Publishing, Inc. March 1995. ? p. [Japanese]

j in <unknown>. _: <publisher unknown> 1994. 475 p. [Russian]
Note : This is a collection containing: Captain Future's Challenge, Calling Captain Future, and Quest Beyond the Stars.

k in <unknown>. _: <publisher unknown> 1998. 402 p. [Russian]
Note : This is a collection containing: Captain Future's Challenge, Calling Captain Future, and Quest Beyond the Stars.

l in **The Collected Captain Future, Volume One: Captain Future and the Space Emperor**. Edited by Stephen Haffner. Royal Oak, Michigan: Haffner Press. 1 July 2009, 648 p. Hardback. Introduction by Walter Jon Williams. Illustrated by Hugh Rankin. ISBN-10 1893887332; ISBN-13 97818938871336.

"*Children of the Sun*" in Startling Stories, 21:2 (May, 1950) Pg. 98. Illustrator: Orban. See B199.

REPRINTS:

b in **Captain Future Handbook**. Edited by unknown. _: <publisher unknown> July 1983. [Japanese]

c as <unknown>. _: <publisher unknown> 1990. 256 p. [Russian]
Note: This is a collection containing: Pardon my Iron Nerves and Children of the Sun.

d as <unknown>. _: <publisher unknown> 1993. 512 p. [Russian]
Note: This is a collection containing: Pardon my Iron Nerves, Outlaw World and Children of the Sun.

e in Thrilling Novels, No. 39 (1996).

"*The Comet Kings*" in Captain Future Magazine, 4:2 (Summer 1942). p. 11. Illustrator: H. W. Wesso. See A20.

REPRINTS:

b **The Comet Kings**. _: Hayakawa. 1942. [Japanese]

c as "Kapten Frank och kometkungarna." serialized in Jules Verne Magasinet 51/1943 - 16/1944 (16 Parts). [Swedish]

d New York, NY: Popular Library. 1960. 127 p. paper.

e as **Im schatten der allus**. Rastatt: <publisher unknown> 1962. (U 349). [German]

da New York, NY: Popular Library. 1969. paper. (60-2407).
f as **Im schatten der allus**. _: Utopia, 1978? p. [German]
ba Tokyo: Hayakawa Publishing, Inc. 31 March 1978. 246 p. Translator: Masahiro Noda [Japanese]
g adapted into an animated television program in four parts.[cl] _: Toei Doga, 1978-79. [Japanese]
Note: This is available in Video, DVD, Video CD and in some cases LaserDISC in French, German. Italian, Japanese and Spanish.
ea as **Im schatten der allus**. _: Bastei Lhubbe. 1983. Translator: Horst Mayer. [German]
db as **Im schatten der allus**. Bergisch Gladbach: <publisher unknown> 1983. 155 p. (BSF 25011). Translator: Ralph Tegtmeier. [German]

"*Days of Creation*"[cli] in Captain Future Magazine, (Spring, 1944) Pg. 11.

REPRINTS:

b as **The Tenth Planet**. New York, NY: Popular Library, 1960.
C Tokyo: Hayakawa Publishing, Inc. April 1980. p. [Japanese]

"*Earthmen No More*" in Startling Stories, , 23:1 (March, 1951) _: <publisher unknown> , Pg. 76. Illustrator: Orban. See B203.

REPRINTS:

b in **Captain Future Handbook**. Edited by unknown. _: <publisher unknown> July 1983. [Japanese]
c in Thrilling Novels, No. 39 (1996).

"*The Face of The Deep*" in Captain Future Magazine, 5:1 (Winter 1943). p. 15. Illustrator: Orban. See A22.

REPRINTS:

b as **The Face of The Deep**. Tokyo: Hayakawa. 1943. [Japanese]
c as "Kapten Frank och fångtransparten," serialized in Jules Verne Magasinet 13/1943 - 16/1943 (14 Parts). Pg. 26. [Swedish]
d Tokyo: Hayakawa Publishing, Inc. 31 August 1973. 290 p. Translator: Masahiro Noda. [Japanese]
e adapted into an animated television program in four parts.[clii] _: Toei Doga, 1978-79. [Japanese]
Note: This is available in Video, DVD, Video CD and in some

cases LaserDISC in French, German, Italian, Japanese and Spanish.

f as **Planetoid des Todes**. : <publisher unknown> 1983. 158 p. (BSF 25013). Translator: Ralph Tegtmeier. [German]

"*The Harpers of Titan*" in Startling Stories, 22:1 (September, 1950) 96. Illustrator: Orban. See B200.

REPRINTS:

aa in Startling Stories, (September, 1950). [Canadian]

ab in Startling Stories, (September, 1950). [British]

b in **Worlds of Weird**. Edited by Leo Margulies. _: publisher unknown? <year>, paper.

c included with **Dr. Cyclops**. by Henry Kuttner. New York: Popular Library. 1967. paper.
Note: Includes "Too Late for Eternity" by Bryce Walton.

d as **Les Harpistes de Titan**. _: J'ai Lu, April 1977. p. [French]

e in SF. #8 (August 1977). [Japanese]

f in **Captain Future Handbook**. Edited by unknown. _: <publisher unknown> July 1983. [Japanese]

g as "Les Harpistes de Titan" in **Les meilleurs recits de startling stories**. Edited by Jacques Sadoul. __" editions J'ai lu. [French]

"*The Lost World of Time*" in Captain Future Magazine, 3:2. (Fall1941). p. 14. Illustrator: H. Wesso. See A17.

REPRINTS:

b as "Kapten Frank i en försvunnen värld" in Jules Verne Magasinet #5 - #18 (14 Parts): 1943. Pg 18. [Swedish]

c as **Im Zeitstrom verschollen**. Rastatt: 1961. (UGB 144). Translator: Heinz Zwack. [German]

d Tokyo: Hayakawa Publishing, Inc. 15 January 1967. 192 p. Translator: Masahiro Noda. [Japanese]

e as **Im Zeitstrom verschollen**. _: Utopia, 1972 p. [German]

f Tokyo: Hayakawa Publishing, Inc. 30 September 1972. 274 p. Translator: Masahiro Noda. [Japanese]

g as <unknown>. _: SF, 1975. p. [Korea]

h _: <publisher unknown> December 1978. p. (SF Kodomo Toshokan # 26). Translator: Masami Fukushima.
[Japanese]

i adapted into an animated television program in four parts.[cliii] _: Toei Doga, 1978-79. [Japanese]

Note: This is available in Video, DVD, Video CD and in some cases LaserDISC in English, French, German, Italian, Japanese and Spanish.

ca as **Im Zeitstrom verschollen**. Bergisch Gladbach: <publisher unknown> 1982. 155 p. (BSF 25008). Translator: Ralph Tegtmeier. [German]

"The Magician of Mars" in Captain Future Magazine, 3:1 (Summer 1941). p. 14. See A16.

Reprints:

b as **The Magician of Mars**. __:Hayakawa. 1941. [Japanese]

c as "Kapten Frank och trollkarten från Mars" serialized in Jules Verne Magasinet. 46/1941 - 6/1942. [Swedish]

d New York, NY: Popular Library. 1968. 128p. paper (60-2450).

e Tokyo: Hayakawa Publishing, Inc. 31 December 1970. 302 p. Translated by Masahiro Noda. [Japanese]

f _: Gemini, November 1977. (Editions Solaris). [Italian]

g adapted into an animated television program in four parts. [cliv] _: Toei Doga, 1978-79. [Japanese]
Note: This is available in Video, DVD, Video CD and in some cases LaserDISC in French, German. Italian, Japanese and Spanish.

h as **Der Marsmagier**. Bergisch Gladbach: <publisher unknown> 1982. 156 p. (BSF 25007). Translated by Ralph Tegtmeier. [German]

i in <unknown>. _: <publisher unknown> 1994. 475 p. [Russian]
Note : This is a collection containing: Captain Future's Challenge, Calling Captain Future, and Quest Beyond the Stars.

j Tokyo: Hayakawa Publishing, Inc. March 1995. p. [Japanese]

k in <unknown>. _: <publisher unknown> 1998. 472 p. [Russian]
Note : This is a collection containing: The Magician of Mars, Outlaws of the Moon, Outlaw World, and Quest Beyond the Stars.

Reviews:

D. Paskow. Luna Monthly 19:22. (December 1970)

"Magic Moon[clv]" in Captain Future Magazine, 6:1 (Winter 1944) p. 15. Illustrator: Orban. See A24.

Reprints:

b as "Den magiska mänen." in Jules Verne Magasinet #33, 1945. Pg. 45. [Swedish] c as **Magic Moon**. Tokyo: Hayakawa Publishing, Inc. 31 August 1974. Translator: Masahiro Noda. [Japanese]

d adapted into an animated television program in four parts.[clvi] _: Toei Doga, 1978-79. [Japanese]
Note: This is available in Video, DVD, Video CD and in some cases LaserDISC in French, German, Italian, Japanese and Spanish.

e as **Captain Future: Magic Moon**. _: publisher unknown. 1987.

"*Moon of the Unforgotten*" in Startling Stories, 22:3 (January, 1951) 118. Illustrator: Orban. See B202.

REPRINTS:

aa in Startling Stories, (January, 1951). [Canadian]

b in **Captain Future Handbook**. Edited by unknown. _: <publisher unknown> July 1983. [Japanese]

c in Thrilling Novels, No. 39 (1996).

d as **La Luna degli Eterni Ricordi**. _: Nova SF, August 2001. ? p. (Nova SF # 50). [Italian]

"*Outlaw World*" in Startling Stories, 13:1. (Winter 1946). p. 11. Illustrator: Orban. Cover: Earle Bergey. See A27

REPRINTS:

aa "Outlaw World." in Startling Stories, (Winter 1946). p. 11. Illustrator: Orban. Cover: Earle Bergey. [British]

ab "Outlaw World." in Startling Stories, (June 1949). p. 11. Illustrator: Orban. Cover: Earle Bergey. [Canadian]

b **Outlaw World**. New York: Popular Library. 1960.

c as **Die Radium Falle**. _: <publisher unknown> 1961. [German]

ca as **Die Radium Falle**. Rastatt: <publisher unknown> 1962. (U 354). Translator: Werner Eppelsheim. [German]

ba New York, NY: Popular Library. 1969. 126 p. paper. (60-2376).

d _: Gemini, September 1978. (Editions Solaris). [Italian]

e as **Die Radium Falle**. _: Utopia, 1982 ? p. [German]

f Tokyo: Hayakawa Publishing, Inc. 30 June 1982. 258 p. Translator: Masahiro Noda. [Japanese]

g as <unknown>. _: <publisher unknown> 1992. 352 p. [Russian]

h as <unknown>. _: <publisher unknown> 1993. 512 p. [Russian]
Note: This is a collection containing: Pardon my Iron Nerves, Outlaw World and Children of the Sun.

i as **Captain Future: Outlaw World**. _: . 1996.

j in <unknown>. _: <publisher unknown> 1993. 394 p. [Russian]
Note : This is a collection containing: Outlaw World, Calling Captain Future, Outlaws of the Moon.

k in <unknown>. _: <publisher unknown> 1998. 472 p. [Russian]
Note : This is a collection containing: **The Magician of Mars**, **Outlaws of the Moon**, **Outlaw World** and **Quest Beyond the Stars**.

"*Outlaws of the Moon*" in Captain Future Magazine, 4:1 (Spring 1942). p. 14. Illustrator: Orban. See A19.

REPRINTS:

a as "Kapten Frank och radiumkriget" serialized in Jules Verne Magasinet 1/1942 - 2/1943 (14 Parts). [Swedish]

b New York, NY: Popular Library. 1960.

ba New York, NY: Popular Library. 1969. 128p. paper. (60-2399).

c Tokyo: Hayakawa Publishing, Inc. 30 June 1980. 260p. Translator: Masahiro Noda [Japanese]

d as **Das Erbe der Lunarier**. _: publisher unknown ? 1983. 160 p. (Bd. 25010). [German]

e as **Captain Future: Outlaws of the Moon**. _: . 1997.

f in <unknown>. _: <publisher unknown> 1993. 394 p. [Russian]
Note : This is a collection containing: **Outlaw World**, **Calling Captain Future and Outlaws of the Moon**.

g in <unknown>. _: <publisher unknown> 1998. 472 p. [Russian]
Note : This is a collection containing: **The Magician of Mars**, **Outlaws of the Moon**, **Outlaw World** and **Quest Beyond the Stars**.

"*Pardon My Iron Nerves*" in Startling Stories, 22:2 (November, 1950): 78. Illustrator: Orban. See B201.

REPRINTS:

aa in Startling Stories, (November, 1950). [British]

b in SF. (August 1966). [Japanese]

c _: <publisher unknown> Feberuary 1972. ? p. (Space Opera Meisaku-sen #1). [Japanese]

d in **Captain Future Handbook**. Edited by unknown. _: <publisher unknown> July 1983. [Japanese]

e as <unknown>. _: <publisher unknown> 1990. 256 p. [Russian]
Note: This is a collection containing: "Pardon my Iron Nerves" and "Children of the Sun."

f as <unknown>. _: <publisher unknown> 1993. 512 p. [Russian]
Note: This is a collection containing: "Pardon my Iron Nerves," **Outlaw World** and **Children of the Sun**.

g in Thrilling Novels, No. 49 (1996).

"*Planets in Peril*" in Captain Future Magazine, 4:3 (Fall 1942). p. 13. Illustrator: Morey. See A21.

REPRINTS:

b as "Kapten Frank - nationalhjälten" in Jules Verne Magasinet. #39/1944 – 32/1945 (16 Parts). [Swedish]

c as **Planets in Peril**. New York: Popular Library. 1960. paper.

d as **Held der Sage**. Rastatt: <publisher unknown> 1962. (U 351). Translator: Horst Mayer. [German]

ca New York, NY: Popular Library. 1969. 128 p. paper. (60-2416).

e as **Held der Sage**. _: Utopia, 1978 p. [German]

f Tokyo: Hayakawa Publishing, Inc. 31 July 1978. 290 p. Translator: Masahiro Noda.

g adapted into an animated television program in four parts.[clvii] _: Toei Doga, 1978-79. [Japanese]
Note: This is available in Video, DVD, Video CD and in some cases LaserDISC in French, German, Italian, Japanese and Spanish.

h as **Held der Vergangenheit**. _: Bergisch Gladbach, 1983. 156 p. (BSF 25009). Translator: Richard Bellinghausen. [German]

"*Quest Beyond the Stars*" in Captain Future Magazine, 3:3 (Winter 1942) p. 15. Illustrator: Orban. See A18.

REPRINTS:

b as **Quest Beyond the Stars**. New York, NY: Popular Library. 1941. paper.

c as "Kapten Frank och de kosmiska strälarna," serialized in Jules Verne Magasinet 28/1943 - 40/1943 (13 Parts). Pg. 40. 1943. [Swedish]

ba New York, NY: Popular Library. 1960. 128 p. paper.

d as **Gefahr aus dem Kosmos**. Rastatt: <publisher unknown> 1961.p. (UGB 153). Translated by Heinz Zwack. [German]

bb New York, NY: Popular Library, 1969. 142 p. paper (60-2389).

e as **Gefahr aus dem Kosmos**. _: Utopia, 1973 p. [German]

f Tokyo: Hayakawa Publishing, Inc. 31 May 1973. 263 p. Translated by Masahiro Noda. [Japanese]

g as **Komisk Fara**, Stokholm: Bokforlaget Regal. 1975. 152 p. ISBN: 91-85048-53-4. paper. (#18 of Science Fiction-serien). Translator:

Bertil Falk. [Swedish]

h adapted into an animated television program in four parts.[clviii] _: Toei Doga, 1978-79. [Japanese]
Note: This is available in Video, DVD, Video CD and in some cases LaserDISC in French, German, Italian, Japanese and Spanish.

i as **Die Matariequelle**. Bergisch Gladbach: 1983. 157 p. (BSF 25009). Translated by Richard Bellinghausen. [German]

j as **I Metanastes ton Astron**. Athens: Sympan/Lynari. 1989. Translator: Anna Papadimtriou.

k in <unknown>. _: <publisher unknown> 1993. 336 p. [Russian]
Note : This is a collection containing: Calling Captain Future, Captain Future's Challenge and Quest Beyond the Stars.

l in <unknown>?. _: <publisher unknown> 1994. 475 p. [Russian]
Note : This is a collection containing: Captain Future's Challenge, Calling Captain Future, and Quest Beyond the Stars.

m in <unknown>. _: <publisher unknown> 1998. 402 p. [Russian]
Note : This is a collection containing: Captain Future's Challenge, Calling Captain Future, and Quest Beyond the Stars.

n in ?. _: <publisher unknown> 1998. 472 p. [Russian]
Note : This is a collection containing: The Magician of Mars, Outlaws of the Moon, Outlaw World, and Quest Beyond the Stars.

"Red Sun of Danger"[clix] in Startling Stories, 12:1 (Spring 1945). Pg. 11. Illustrator: Thomas. Cover: Earle Bergey. See A25

REPRINTS:

b as **Danger Planet**. New York, NY: Popular Library. 1968. mass market paperback.

c as **Danger Planet**. Tokyo: Hayakawa Publishing, Inc. 15 March 1981. Translator: Masahiro Noda. [Japanese]

d as **Die Krypta Der Kangas**. _: Utopia, 1981 p. [German]

e as **Die Krypta Der Kangas**. Rastatt: <publisher unknown> [U 305]. Translator: Heinz Zwack. [German]

"The Return of Captain Future" in Startling Stories, 20:3. (January, 1950): 94. Illustrator: Astarita. Cover:. See B198.

REPRINTS:

b in Startling Stories. (January, 1950). [Canadian]

c as "Kapten Franks Återkomst." : Jules Verne Magasinet #4. 1970. [Swedish] d in **Captain Future Handbook**. Edited by unknown. _: <publisher unknown> July 1983. [Japanese]

e as **Il Ritorno di Capitain Futuro**. _: Nova SF, May 2002. p. (Nova SF # 54). [Italian]

"The Solar Invasion"[clx] in Startling Stories, (Fall, 1946).

REPRINTS:

b New York, NY: Popular Library, 1968.

c as **Der geraube Mond**. _: Utopia, 1982 p. [German]

d Tokyo: Hayakawa Publishing, Inc. May 1982. p. [Japanese]

"The Star of Dread"[clxi] in Captain Future Magazine, 5:3 (Summer 1943). p. 13. Illustrator: Orban. Cover: Earle K. Bergey. See A23.

REPRINTS:

b as **Verrat Auf Titan**. Rastatt: <publisher unknown> 1962. (U 309). Translator: Horst Mayer. [German]

c as **Verrat Auf Titan**. _: Utopia, 1978 ? p. [German]

d Tokyo: Hayakawa Publishing, Inc. 30 November 1978. 263 p. Translator: Masahiro Noda. [Japanese]

e adapted into an animated television program in four parts.[clxii] _: Toei Doga, 1978-79. [Japanese]
Note: This is available in Video, DVD, Video CD and in some cases LaserDISC in French, German. Italian, Japanese and Spanish.

f as **Stern des Grauens**. Bergisch Glacbach: <publisher unknown> 1984. 158 p. (BSF 25015). Translator: Ralph Tegtmeier. [German]

"Star Trail to Glory" in Captain Future Magazine, 2:3 (Spring 1941). p. 14. Illustrator: H. W. Wesso. See A15.

REPRINTS:

b as "Kapten Frank och postränarna." Sweden: Jules Verne Magasinet #26 – #41 (16 Parts): 1942. Pg. 41. [Swedish]

c as **Star Trail to Glory**. Tokyo: Hayakawa Publishing, Inc. 31 July 1966. 178 p. Translator: Masahiro Noda.

d _: <publisher unknown> February, 1968. p. (SF Mesaku Series # 14). [Japanese] d Tokyo: Hayakawa Publishing, Inc. 31 May 1972. 260 p. Translator: Masahiro Noda. [Japanese]

e as **Sternstrasse zum Ruhm**. Bergisch Gladbach: <publisher unknown> 1982. 158 p. (BSF 25006). Translator: Ralph Tegtmeier. [German]

f _: Kaiseisha, . p. Translator: Masahiro Noda. [Jpanese]

g adapted into an animated movie.[clxiii] _: Ben J. Productions, 1989. Note: This is available in Video, DVD, in French.

h Tokyo: Hayakawa Publishing, Inc. September 1995. p. [Japanese]

"*The Triumph of Captain Future*" in <u>Captain Future Magazine</u>, 2:1 (Fall 1940). p. 14. Illustrator: H. W. Wesso. See A12

REPRINTS:

b as "Kapten Franks triumf" serialized in <u>Jules Verne Magasinet</u> 32/1941 – 43/1941 (12 Parts). [Swedish]

c as **Captain Zunkunft Greift Ein**. Rastatt: <publisher unknown> 1961. (UGB 142). Translator: Lothar Heinecke. [German]

d as **Galaxy Mission**. New York, Popular Library. 1967. 128p. 18cm. paper. (60-2437).

da as **Galaxy Mission**. New York, NY: Popular Library, 1969. paper. (60-2437).

e as **Captain Zunkunft Greift Ein**. _: Utopia, 1975. p. [German]

f Tokyo: Hayakawa Publishing, Inc. 31 May 1975. Translator: Masahiro Noda. [Japanese]

g adapted into an animated television program in four parts.[clxiv] _: Toei Doga, 1978-79. [Japanese]
Note: This is available in Video, DVD, Video CD and in some cases LaserDISC in French, German, Italian, Japanese and Spanish.

h as **Der Lebenslord**. Bergisch Gladbach: <publisher unknown> 1982. p. (BSF 25004). Translator: Ralph Tegtmeier. [German]

i in <unknown>. _: <publisher unknown> 1994. 475 p. [Russian]
Note : This is a collection containing: Captain Future's Challenge, Calling Captain Future, and Quest Beyond the Stars.

j in **The Collected Captain Future, Volume One: Captain Future and the Space Emperor**. Edited by Stephen Haffner. Royal Oak, Michigan: Haffner Press. 1 July 2009, 648 p. Hardback. Introduction by Walter Jon Williams. Illustrated by Hugh Rankin. ISBN-10 1893887332; ISBN-13 9781893887136.

"*Worlds To Come*"[clxv] in <u>Captain Future Magazine</u>, (Spring, 1943) Pg. 15.

REPRINTS:

b as **Uberfall aus Freunder Dimension**. _: Utopia, 1981. p. [German]

c Tokyo: Hayakawa Publishing, Inc. Agust 1981. p. [Japanese]

d in Thrilling Novels, No. 39 (1996).

The Collected Captain Future, Volume One: Captain Future and the Space Emperor. Edited by Stephen Haffner. Royal Oak, Michigan: Haffner Press. 1 July 2009, 648 p. Hardback. Introduction by Walter Jon Williams. Illustrated by Hugh Rankin. ISBN-10 1893887332; ISBN-13 97818938871336.

CONTENTS:

Introduction by ?
Original Magazine Editorial
Captain Future & the Space Emperor
Calling Captain Future
Captain Future's Challenge
The Triumph of Captain Future
"The Future of Captain Future"
Artwork Gallery

Captain Future Original Publication Chronology

Date	Title	Magazine
Winter 1940	Captain Future & the Space Emperor	Captain Future Magazine
Spring 1940	Calling Captain Future	Captain Future Magazine
Summer 1940	Captain Future's Challenge	Captain Future Magazine
Fall 1940	The Triumph of Captain Future	Captain Future Magazine
Winter 1941	Captain Future & the 7 Space Stones	Captain Future Magazine
Spring 1941	Star Trail to Glory	Captain Future Magazine
Summer 1941	The Magician of Mars	Captain Future Magazine
Fall 1941	The Lost World of Time	Captain Future Magazine
Winter 1942	The Quest Beyond the Stars	Captain Future Magazine
Spring 1942	Outlaws of the Moon	Captain Future Magazine
Summer 1942	The Comet Kings	Captain Future Magazine
Fall 1942	Planets in Peril	Captain Future Magazine
Winter 1943	Face of the Deep	Captain Future Magazine
Spring 1943	Worlds To Come[clxvi]	Captain Future Magazinee
Summer 1943	Star of Dread[clxvii]	Captain Future Magazinee
Winter 1944	Magic Moon*	Startling Stories
Spring 1944	Days of Creation[clxviii]	Startling Stories
Spring 1945	Red Sun of Danger[clxix]	Startling Stories
Winter 1946	Solar Invasion#	Startling Stories
Fall 1946	Outlaw World	Startling Stories
January 1950	The Return of Captain Future	Startling Stories
May 1950	Children of the Sun	Startling Stories
September 1950	The Harpers of Titan	Startling Stories
November 1950	Pardon My Iron Nerves	Startling Stories
January 1951	Moon of the Unforgotten	Startling Stories
March 1951	Earthmen No More	Startling Stories
May 1951	Birthplace of Creation	Startling Stories

*

Written by Manly Wade Wellman

About Captain Future:

Falk, Bertil. "Kapten Frank - stjarnviddernas centerpartist artikel" in Future Fan, #11. pp. 10-14.

Hamilton, Edmond. "An Inside Look at Captain Future" in PULP, #3. Pg. 3.

Itoh, T. and Koichi Yamamoto. **A Captain Future Reader**. Tokyo: Hachioji-shi, 1994, 847 p. [Japanese]

Unknown. **Captain Future Handbook**. _: <publisher unknown> July 1983. [Japanese]

The World of Captain Future Who's Who. _: Space Force, 1983.

In each issue of the Captain Future Magazine there were two articles: "Worlds of Tomorrow" and "Meet the Futuremen." The first of these was usually about two pages of detail with an illustration of at least one hemisphere of the world featured. The second article was an in depth look at the Futuremen. Ezra Gurney and Joan Randall were also profiled. The authors of these articles are unknown, but it is suspected, by this author, that it might have been the editor Oscar J. Friend.

The Futuremen

Captian Future - Curtis Newton

Curtis Newton is the son of Roger and Elaine Newton.

Roger Newton, a gifted scientist, fled to the moon with Dr. Simon Wright, his wife and young son.

He and Simon constructed a secret laboratory in Tycho crater so they could continue their research. Victor Corvo pursued them and killed Roger and Elaine in a brief confrontation. Having been orphaned at an early age, Curtis grew up with Simon, Grag and Otho as parents, teachers, and playmates. He became a scientist like his father and upon reaching adulthood he dedicated himself to ridding the Solar System of criminals.

Grag

Grag is a seven foot tall metal robot built by Roger Newton, Curt's father, and Simon Wright. His strength is unmatched within the Solar System. Grag has a bulbous metal head that swivels on a neck-joint. He has two bright photo-electric eyes.

Eek

Grag's pet, a dog-like life form, can live in the vacuum of space. He eats pure metals. He prefers copper and gold which will inebriate him.

Otho

Otho is the second creation by Roger Newton and Simon Wright. He is a synthetic man, an android.

He is super-humanly swift and deft. His eyes are slanted and green, and has no eyebrows or eye lashes. His skin is pure white and composed of a rubber-like synthetic substance which he can soften by applying certain chemicals. This enables him to be a master of disguise.

Oog

Otho's pet is a meteor mimic. An amorphous life form, in its natural state it looks like a blob of vanilla pudding. It is able to assume any shape it wishes.

The Brain - Dr. Simon Wright

Simon was once a normal human dying of an incurable illness. Roger Newton removed his brain and placed it in a transparent metal case. The brain is suspended in a life-sustaning serum. The case also houses pumps and purifiers which replace the functions of the heart, liver, etc. In the front of the case there are two flexible eye stalks with glass lened-eyes at the end. There is also a mechanical speech apparatus mounted on front. On each side there is mounted a microphonic "ear." At first, Simon was incapable of independant movement, but later on he was given movement by the use of projected rays of force.

The Comet

This is the Futuremen's ship. It is the fastest ship in the Solar System. Though small, within its hull there are marvels of minaturization allowing the Futuremen to take with them the equipment of a well stocked research facility.

Captain Future Character Index
Major Characters Other that the Futuremen

The stories abbreviations are listed at the end of this appendix.

Anders, Halk [CC,CK,OM,OW]
Commander of the Planetary Patrol.

Bonnel, North [CC,CK,OM]
President James Carthew's secretary.

Carthew, James [CC,OM]
President of the Solar System. He is killed in "Outlaws of the Moon".

Gurney, Marshal Ezra
[BC,CCF,CFC,CK,ENM,OM,OW]
In Calling Captain Future, he has been promoted to the of the division head quartered at Tartarus, Pluto because of his work in the Space Emperor case.

Randall, Joan
[CC,CFC,CK,OM,OW,PP]
The Planetary Patrol's top agent.

Other Characters

Those in italics are characters that have died.

Name		Story
Aggar	A captain of the Comatae Guard.	CK
Ahla	A young ancient earth woman who has a crush on Otho. She dies saving Otho.	LWT
Aj, Fwar	Leader of the Lunarians.	OM
Akk	A Uranian fisherman.	CFC
Arraj	A Martian gravium mine laborer.	CFC
Avam, Vasc	A Jovian, the boss of Neptunian Gravium Company's mine #1.	CFC
Brand, Carson	Superintendant for the Neptunian Gravium Company.	CFC

Name		Story
Brewer, Lucas	An inmate at the Cerebus prison. Curt put him there during the Space Emperor case.	CCF
Brower	First mate of the Arcturian.	CK
Burke	Captain of a starship.	ENM
Burq	Captain Future's Martian nom de plume.	LWT
Carew, Mark	One of the first explorers of space.	CFC, ENM
Carlin, Philip	He becomes a child of the Sun.	CS
Cary, John	He wakes up from a very long nap.	ENM
Chameleon Man	An associate of Quorn.	SS
Corvo, Victor	An unscrupulous schemer who killed Curt Netwon's parents.	SS
Darmur	A scientist of ancient Katain He sends a message through time.	LWT
Del, Ber	A withered old vegan space captain.	QBS
Delaporte, Etienne	A crewmember of the Victix.	ENM
Dordo	A Tarast.	PP
El, Kerk	Head of the Mercurian Gravium Company.	CFC
Fenner, Lane	A crewmember of the Victix.	ENM
Forbin	A member of Garrand's crew.	BC
Gaines, William	A crew member of the Victix	ENM
Garrand	A scientist	BC
Gatola	Astronomer-Director of the Syrtis Observatory. He almost disappears.	CCF
Gellimer, Henry	An astro-physicist who disappears	CCF
Gerdek	From another universe.	PP
Grako	An ancient Martian captain.	LWT
Groro	A Jovian fishing boat captain.	CFC
Gunn, Julius	President of the Neptunian Gravium Company.	CFC
Hab, Haro	A Plutonian member of the Wreckers gang.	CFC
Hearer	An associate of Quorn.	SS
Herrick	Garrand's pilot.	BC
Igir	The chairman of the Council of Suns.	PP
Illok, Ki	A Captain from Sagittarius.	QBS
Iri, Ki	A Venusian member of the Wreckers gang.	CFC
Jhulun	Darmur's son, he is found as a captive on Mars.	LWT
Johnson, Gorham	An old long-gone space explorer.	ENM

Name		Story
Jon, Robert	A Mercurian astronomer who disappears.	CCF
Jor, Hol	A giant space captain from Antares.	QBS
Kaffr	A legendary Tarast hero.	PP
Kah	A Vulcanian.	CS
Kal, Skur	A young Antarian.	QBS
Kallak	A member of Dr. Zarro's Legion of Doom.	CCF
Kane, Kansu	An Astro-physicist with the Venus Observatory who disappears.	CCF
Kardak, Ka	A Mercurian.	OM
Kel, Hok	The Jovain mine boss of King Planetary Metals Lunar radium mine.	OM
Khinkir	Captain of the Cometae King's Guard.	CK
King, Lauren	Head of King Planetary Metals.	OM
Kiri	Tharb's grandfather. An old Plutonian who Remembers.	CCF
Kor	An ancient Earth chieftan.	LWT
Krin, Victor	Fur-Magnate with settlements on Charon.	CCF
Kwolok	The King of Thruun.	QBS
Lacq	A Tarast prisoner of the Cold Ones.	PP
Lane, Rundall	Warden of the Interplanetary Prison on Cerebus. He has a secret that costs him his job.	CCF
Lartsan	The King of Kor.	QBS
Lester, Kenneth	An archeologist with the Institute of Interplanetary Science.	SS
Libro, Orr	Head of the Martian Gravium Company.	CFC
Limor	King of the Stygians.	CCF
Lockley	A specialist oninterplanetary jewels.	SS
Lowther	He's trying to get a monopoly on fuel.	ENM
LuLain	Queen of the Comatae.	CK
Lunn	Ancient King of Othar, Mars.	LWT
Lureen	Darmur's lovely daughter.	LWT
Melton, Brad	A young earth metor miner. He hears the call through time.	LWT
Mwwr	The leader of the Cold Ones.	PP
Nilga	A Martian scientist working with the meteor miners.	LWT
Njdd, Commander	A commader in the Cold Ones' forces.	PP
Norton	Young second mate of the Arcturian.	CK
N'rala	Quorns female Martian companion.	SS
Olor, Roh	From Deimos.	OM

Name		Story
Querdel	The Cometae King's trusted Advisor.	CK
Quirus	A spy for Zikal.	LWT
Qull, Quarus	Head of the Saturnian Gravium Company.	CFC
Quorn, Ul	Half Martian, quarter Earthman and quarter Venusian. A.K.A. the Magician of Mars.	SS
Roga, Fer	An ancient lord of Vulcan.	CS
Roj	A dwarf member of Dr. Zarro's Legion of Doom.	CCF
Romer, Cole	Chief Planetographer at Pluto and head of the Pluto Survey. He also has a secret.	CCF
Ruun	The Leader of the Allus.	CK
Sel, Reh	Lunarian Chieftan.	OM
Shiri	Gerdek's sister.	PP
Siql	An Allus.	CK
Slig	An ancient Martian conjurer.	LWT
Sparks	The Televisor Operator on board the Pallas.	CC
Sperry	A member of Garrand's crew.	BC
Strike, Gil	A. Wissler's pilot and aide.	OM
Tar, Taunus	A fat star-captain from Formalhaut.	QBS
Thabar, Than	A Mercurian chosen in the Lottery.	QBS
Thar, Tzan	A Martian. The head of the Jovopolis Maintanence Division of the Planetary Patrol.	CK
Tharb	A Plutonian guide for the Planetary Police. Guides C.F. to his grandfather Kiri and is very impressed by the feats of heroism he witnesses.	CCF
Thardis	He used to be Fer Roga's chief Physicist .	CS
Thoh, Lord	A tall ancient Martian, he captures Otho and Ahla.	LWT
Thoryx	King of the Cometae.	CK
Thrin, Tiko	A scientist from the Syrtis Labs.	CK, PP
Thuun, Thuro	An ancient Martian scientist.	SS
Thyria	A princess of Thruun.	QBS
Twih, Si	A Martian representative of "The Organization".	SS
Ullman, Jan	An Earth fisherman.	CFC
Uvan, Dhul	A Uranian fisherman captured by the Wrecker.	CFC
Vostol	A Tarast .	PP
Wenzi, Jan	An old long-gone space explorer.	ENM
Wissler, Albert	A scientist who discovers a secret of Captain Future's.	OM
Wrecker, The	A mysterious person out to destroy the Solar	CFC

Name		Story
	System's production of Gravium.	
Yale, Harrison	A rich collector. He has one of the space stones in hispossession.	SS
Zarro, Dr.	A strange scientist claiming to be able to save the Solar System.	CCF
Zikal	An ancient Katain with a horrible plan to save the Katainians and advance himself. He is outwitted by Captain Future.	LWT
Zirro, Zin	The owner of the Fisherman's Haven in Amphitrite.	CFC
Zuur	A Tarast scientist, he created the Cold Ones.	PP
Zuvalo	Head of the Uranian Gravium Company.	CFC

Ships

Name		Story
Arcturian	A Space-freighter	CK
Empress of Mars		ENM
Ferronia	A Planet Patrol Cruiser	CK
Morning Star		ENM
Pallas	A Space Liner	CCF
Royal Jove		ENM
Spray	Groro' fishing boat.	CFC
Star of Venus	A liner	ENM
Victrix	A long-ago lost exploration ship	ENM

Cities

Name		Story
Amphritite	Earth colony city on Neptune.	CFC
Bebemos	The capital city of the Tarast Empire. On Tatarsia	PP
Othar	An ancient Martian city	LWT
Vavona	Capital of the ancient planet of Katain	LWT

Planets & Satellites

Name		Story
Vulcan		
Mercury		
Venus		
Earth		
Moon		
Mars		

Name			Story
	Deimos		
	Phobos		
Katain		The ancient fifth planet between Mars and Jupiter.	LWT
	Yurga	Katain's only moon	LWT
Jupiter			
Saturn			
Uranus			
Neptune		Neptune has the Great Maelstrom, a large whirlpool that empties somewhere unknown.	
	Triton		
Pluto			
	Cerebus		
	Charon		
	Styx		
Kor		A world within the Dust cloud at the B.O.C.	QBS
Raskol		A world within the star cluster	PP
Tarasia		Capital planet of the Tarast Empire	PP
Thool		Supreme world of the Cold Ones	PP
Thruun		A world within the Dust cloud at the B.O.C.	QBS

Alien Words or Phrases

Word		Story
Koom	The ancient's name for Deneb	LWT

Creatures

Name		Story
Cave-tiger	A native creature of Venus.	CCF
Crawler	A native creature of Jupiter.	CCF

Dridur CFC

A myriapodal black bodied python-like creature that inhabits an unamed asteroid. Its head has too many faceted eyes and a wide jaw with cruel fangs.

Ice-tiger CCF

A large cat-like creature native to Pluto.

Korlat CCF

A large bear-like creature native to Charon. Similar in appearance to an Earth Grizzly, it has six legs. The front two

Name	Story
are used to grip and tear. Its over sizes head has very large fangs. It has long grey fur.	
Night Bat	QBS
A nocturnal creature native to Kor.	
Swallowers	CCF
A creature native to Neptune.	
Ursals	CCF
The biggest and most feared of Neptune's native fauna. It is large dinosaur-like creature with an enormous scaled body and small head.	

Races

Name	Story
Allus	CK
Antarians	QBS
Cold Ones	PP
They are humanoids. Their arms, legs and torsos are of human proportions but are of white bone. They are fleshless and have no nose their mouth is an opening between hinged jaws.	
Cometae	CK
Formalhautians	QBS
Rotund pink skinned humanoids.	
Korians	QBS
They are natives of the planet Kor, a planet of a Green sun within the dust cloud that surrounds the Birthplace of Creation.	
Lunarians	OM
The Lunarians are a humanoid race. They have short stocky bodies. Their unusually round heads sit necklessly on their shoulders. Their skin is white, but with a slight greenish pallor. The noses are merely gaping orfices, and their dark, large pupilled eyes have shutter-like lids above them. They are white haired. They have webbed hands and feet which are flat. Their clothing is a short garment of pale soft leather. They live in a primitive village and sustain themselves by hunting, fishing and farming. They live in a large cavern deep within the moon. This cavern holds the last remnant of the lunar atmosphere.	

Name	Story
There is a large radium-ore mountain surrounded by a sea in the center. The Lunarians live on the strip of land running between the sea and the cavern walls. The Northern coastal region is a marsh known as the Marsh of Monsters.
Sagittarians	QBS
Brown skinned Humanoids.
Stygians	CCF
The stygians are the semi-human race that inhabit Styx, the moon of Pluto. They have an advanced science and have hidden their world from the rest of the system by projecting a lanketing illusion of water. The Stygian race is covered from head to toe with a short white fur. Their feet are two-toed and they have two-fingered hands. They have flat heads with two large black pupil-less eyes.
Sun-Children	BC
These are will-o-wisp creatures of fire. They were created by a scientist of the long-ago Denebian Empire. The Vulcanese scientists changed themselves into sun-children originally to study the solar furnace, but found themselves in an environment too beautiful to leave. They are practically immortal.
Tarasts	PP
These are humanoids with a normal human appearence except for their marble-white skin and platinum hair.
Thruunians	QBS
These are natives of the Thruun, a planet of a Red star within the dust cloud surrounding the Birthplace of Creation.
Tritonians	CCF
They are native inhabitants of Triton, a moon of Neptune. They have small bodies with spider-like limbs. These bodies support an enormous head. Their main activity is to sit and think. They maintain a "thought field" around their city. In this field whatever a person thinks materializes instantly out of thin air. This is not a popular spot with most of the Systems inhabitants.
Vegans	QBS
This is a blue skinned humanoid race.

Materials

Name	Story
Gravium

Name | Story

This is a gray metal. If an electric current is sent through a coil of gravium it can increase or decrease the weight of any matter in the immediate area. The change in weight is proportional to the strength and polarity of the current. Gravium mines exist on: Mercury - The Hot side*; Mars*; Saturn*; Oberon - Moon of Uranus*; Neptune^

* Destroyed by the Wrecker. See CFC.
^ Mines #1 and #2 were destroyed by the Wrecker. See CFC.

Captain Future Equiptment List

Name	Story
Achronic Beam Projector This device was created by Darmur of Katain. It was used by Darmur to project his call for help across time.	LWT
Anti-Heater This device deflects heat. It is used by ships that are approaching to close to the Sun.	CS
Fluorovisor This is a boxlike apparatus with a broad, white lens at one end and an eyepiece at the other. It is designed to make it possible to see highly radioactive materials, even though they are embedded between other minerals. It is based on the principle of hypersensitivity to the gamma radiation of radioactive substances.	LWT
Gas Gun These were used by ancient Martians (Martians of 100,000,000 years ago). It shoots a highly concentrated cloud of very corrosive green gas.	LWT
Macerators These are used to pulverize metals into a fine powder which then can be used as fuel. The Comet carries one to pulverize copper to power its cyclotrons.	LWT
Matter-transmitter It was developed by Tiko Thrin from the equipment left by the Allus. It projects matter through time.	PP
Neutron Gun	LWT

Name	Story

This is a thin glass tube that is mounted on a metal stock. It projects a deadly neutron beam. It was used by the ancient Katainians.

Time Thruster — LWT

This device was created by Captain Future and Simon Wright. It allows travel in the time dimension. It does this by manipulating the orbital speed of the electron. Reverse the orbit, travel back in time.
Accelerate the orbit and travel forward in time.

Yugra Crypts — LWT

This is not a device per se, but a large group of caverns in the moon Yugra (of the planetKatain). Within these cypts, the people of Katain escaped the destruction of their planet by journeying to the star Sirrus. Each crypt consists of a metal bunk on which the people lie. From a disk placed above them, a blue force is projected which freezes (suspends) their organs. The force carefully balances the people between anabolism and catabolism. The crypt was then hermetically sealed.

Guide to Story Abbreviations

BC	Birthplace of Creation
CCF	Calling Captain Future
CFC	Captain Future's Challenge
CS	Children of the Sun
CK	The Comet Kings
ENM	Earthman No More
LWT	The Lost World of Time
MM	The Magician of Mars
OM	The Outlaws of the Moon
OW	Outlaw World
PI	Pardon My Iron Nerves
PP	Planets in Peril
QBS	Quest Beyond the Stars
RCF	The Return of Captain Future
SE	Captain Future and the Space Emperor
SS	Captain Future and the Seven Space Stones
TC	The Triumph of Captain Future

Captain Future Video

Voyage I **L'Empereur de l'Espace**
"Captain Future and the Space Emperor"

1) L'Empereur de l'Espace (The Emperor of Space)
2) La prison de la Mer de Feu (The Prison of the Ocean of Fire)
3) Prisonnier sur Mégara (Prisoner of Megara)
4) La bataille finale (The Final Battle)

Voyage II **Les cinq mines de gravium**
"Captain Future's Challenge"

5) Le complot de Wrackar
6) Prisonnier sous la mer (Prisoner under the Sea)
7) Les créatures aquatiques (The Aquatic Creatures)
8) Le secret de Wrackar (The Secret of the Wrecker)

Voyage III **Départ pour le passé** **"Lost World of Time"**

9) Départ pour le passé (Leaving for the passage)
10) Planète inconnue (Unrecognizable Planet)
11) La naissance du Système Solaire
(The Birthplace of the Solar System)
12) Un voyage de cinq millions d'années
(A Voyage of Five Million Years)

Voyage IV **Le Créateur Universel** **"Quest beyond the stars"**

13) La planète qui se meurt (The Planet that is Dead)
14) Le Créateur Universel
15) La loi ancestrale
16) L'arme absolue (The Absolute Army)

Voyage V **L'univers parallèle** **"The Magician of Mars"**

17) Le défi de Kahlon
18) La vallée des murmures
19) Le Capitaine Flam fend l'espace
20) Le fantôme de la planète transparente

Voyage VI **Le secret des 7 pierres**
"Captain Future & the Seven Space Stones"

21) Le sorcier de la Galaxie
22) Sous le plus grand chapiteau de l'univers
23) La mort du Capitaine Flam
24) Sauvetage d'un micro-univers

Voyage VII La planète noire "Calling Captain Future"

25) Le cimetière de l'espace
26) Le pays glacé
27) Le chasseur de Morsicus
28) La fin des illusions

Voyage VIII La révolte des prisonniers "Face of the Deep"

29) La révolte
30) Escapade hors de la galaxie
31) Impossible exploit (Impossible exploit)
32) La mort d'un héros

Voyage IX Silence, on tourne! "Magic Moon"

33) La doublure du Capitaine Flam
34) Tournage au fond des mers
35) La planète aux mirages
36) Les cendres sacrées

Voyage X La comète de Halley "The Comet Kings"

37) De mystèrieuses disparitions
38) Le maître de la Comète
39) Lumière sur les Luxoïdes
40) Cauchemar en quatre dimensions

Voyage XI La source de l'immortalité "The Triumph of Captain Future"

41) Les pourvoyeurs de l'immortalité
42) Le défi de l'Empereur d'Immortalité
43) Terreur dans la Vallée des Champignons
44) Combat dans la capitale éternelle

Voyage XII Les semeurs de givre "Planets in peril"

45) Sauvetage de la planète Tarust
46) Au secours de Grag
47) Le châtiment de l'âme abjecte
48) Kafoul, le héros

Voyage XIII La Caverne de Vie "Star of Dread"

49) Le mystère des ruines de l'espace
50) Le mystère des hommes animaux
51) La grande bataille
52) Au-delà des ténèbres

La course à travers le Système Solaire **"Star trail to Glory"**
1989 - Ben J Productions

Appendix D
The Hamilton-Brackett Memorial Awards

1977: 1st Edmond Hamilton Memorial Award

1: **Camber of Culdi** by Katherine Kurtz
Brothers of Earth by C.J. Cherryh
Children of Dune by Frank Herbert
The Triune Man by Richard A. Lupoff
Dragonsong by Anne McCaffrey

1978: 2nd Hamilton-Brackett Memorial Award

1: **The Forbidden Tower** by Marion Zimmer Bradley
A Little Knowledge by Michael Bishop
Time Storm by Gordon R. Dickson
Moonstar Odyssey by David Gerrold
"In the Hall of the Martian Kings" by John Varley

1979: 3rd Hamilton-Brackett Memorial Award

1: **Midnight at the Well of Souls** by Jack Chalker[clxx]
"Mikal's Songbird" by Orson Scott Card
"The Works of His Hand Made Manifest" Karen G. Jollie
Saint Camber by Katherine Kurtz
The White Dragon by Anne McCaffery

1980: 4th Hamilton-Brackett Memorial Award

1: **Titan** by John Varley
A Planet Called Treason by Orson Scot Card
The Fadec Sun: Kutach C.J. Cherryh
The Jesus Incident by Frank Herbert & Bill Ransom
Harpist in the Wind by Patricia A. McKillip

1982

1: "The Dust" by Somtow Sucharitkul

Note: The winner is the first book or story listed for each year. The others are runners up, listed in order. This award is sponsored by "The Spellbinders, Inc." and is given out at Octocon, if it is held. It is awarded to a work of any length with a publication date within the previous calendar year.The award is a brass plate inscribed "Hamilton-Brackett Memorial Award, honoring the memory of Edmond Hamilton and Leigh Brackett" followed by the date, author and work. This plate is attached to a redwood plaque.Originally it was the Edmond Hamilton Memorial Award. After the death of Leigh Brackett the year following its inception, it was decided to change the name to honor them both.

Appendix E
Character Index

Characters in bold type are the main character of the story.

Characters:

Name		Story
1	The supreme authority of the Martians.	de
40	A martian on a mission to Earth.	de
92	40's partner.	de
, Ala	one of the female guards.	wws
, Carl	One of Lisler's henchmen.	im2
, Ellen	Meets Sam Macklin when he arrives at Babylon.	bs
, Joseph	One of Lisler's henchmen.	im2
, Linni	one of the female guards.	wws
, Luse	one of the female guards.	wws
, Norua	one of the female guards.	wws
, Puddinghead	Court janitor.	km
, Teena	Ala & Rann Haddan's daughter.	wws
. Tiny	One of Stock Adam's men.	ff
, Todd	Responsible for security on Babylon.	Bs
Abel, North	One of J. Wilson's Men.	SoL
Abo, Brun	A Saturnian who tries to hire the free-lance of Space.	FlS
Abo, Brun	A Jovain pirate captain.	TP
Abul, Kan	King of Jotun.	DW
Adad	Lord of the Lightning.	SP
Adams, Garth	Plant superintendant.	dcg
Adams, Gary	A New York newspaper reporter on vacation.	AG
Adams, Lane	Associate geologist - aka the Watcher.	WA
Adams, Mrs.	C. Lane's Aunt	CWE
Adams, Stock	Public Enemy number 1.	ff
Adams, Val	Day generator operator on Bott's Island.	DB
Aegir	An Aesir.	TG
Aegir	The white-bearded Sea King.	YV
Akarau, Az	A Martian jeweler.	
Aiello, Sgt.	UNIS base 1's communications crew.	sh
Ailing, Darl		UWS
Al, Kark	A Martian salesman.	MV
Alascia, Concepcion	Dr. H. Alascia's daughter.	Mg

Name		Story
Alascia, Dr. Hermis		mg
Allen,	A survivor of the Invisible Masters' attack.	Im
Allen, Capt. John	Formerly of the Earth Colonial Service now a convict on Europa.	moe
Allen, Rake	The notorious free-lance.	FIS
Allen, Varn	Federation Sector Administrator.	CWE
Allison, Mart	crew of the Pioneer.	wsb
Alph, Doctor	A Venusian scientist that develops a new weapon.	MV
Alsop, Col. Willam J.	Commander of UNIS base 15 – Europa.	sh
Ambrosia	Fellow treasure hunter.	WoNm
Ames	A member of the Vulcan's crew.	HA
Ames, Col.	In command of the Space Mirror.	smr
An, Dasan	A Turkish guide for Dick Brent.	CW
Andrews, Sander	A mining engineer.	ed
Anders, Angus	The engineer of the Pioneer.	wsb
Anderson	P. Blaines gardener.	MM
Andersen, Nils	Nuclear chemist - melancholy Dane.	T
Andvar	The Alfing King.	YV
Antar, Zank	A red-skinned Martian chief engineer at the solar station.	dov
Anu	Lord of the Sky.	SP
Aral	A contemporary Ryn female.	HS
Arbulian	Wounded personnel of UNIS base 15.	sh
Ardic	Vega Queen's 2nd Pilot, Skerethian.	FotS, FSe
Argal, Neela		cq
Argal, Ran		cq
Arkol, Nald	A Martian prisoner at Lunar prison.	MM
Arkol, Nald	The head of the Martian Secret Service.	MV
Arnol, Jon	A Federation scientist.	CWE
Arrik	C. Baker's Martian remshi.	WoNM
Arrin	Vurna Supreme Commander.	CotSL
Arn, Jhal	Emperor of the Empire.	tBS
Arn, Zarth	A scientist, brother to Jhal.	KotS
Aryll	A beautiful women of Noh-E, one of Lords of the Morning.	LM
Asha	One of the Hairy ones.	VoC
Ashton, James	Hired the Mercs to find brother.	SW2
Ashton, Randall	Whom the Mercs are looking for.	SW2
Asoka	A Buddist Emperor, of the Brotherhood.	IOW
Atten, Garr	Outlaw Captain with big plans.	tSH
Atzala	An Aztec princess.	QT
Austin	Part of a previous expedition now lost.	hc
Av, Sual	a Venusian, and one of the three planeteers.	TP

Name		Story
Avila	A captain for Montezuma.	QT
Avul, Ark	Stephen Drew's Martian name.	STW
Awl, Stakan	Of the Jovian Secret Service.	FIS
Axayaca	Montezuma's father.	QT
Bacon, Francis	of the Brotherhood.	IOW
Baird, Farrel	Out to find his father's killer.	TW
Baird, John	F. Baird's Father, Baw's brother.	TW
Bal		CWE
Ballard, Jean	S. Ballard's daughter.	pp13
Ballard, Smith	The superintendent of Power Pit 13.	pp13
Barbour	L. Harvey's henchmen.	TM
Barin	Kree's Son.	VoC
Barker, Colin	On hunt for his remshi's killer.	WoNM
Barnett	Dr. Melford's houseman.	srm
Barsoff	A payclerk for the Etna Construction Company.	im
Barton		vv
Bascom, Dr.	The inventor of the Fear Neutralizer.	FN
Bascom, Helen	Dr. Bascom's lovely daughter.	FN
Baw	Bal's brother.	CWE
Belath		CK
Bellaver	Chief antagonist.	LoL
Berkt	A Starwwolf leader.	SW2, SW3
Berreau, Andre	A botonist in charge of the station.	AE
Berreau, Lys	Andre's sister.	AE
Biler, Mrs.	An inhabitant of Middletown.	CWE
Binetti,	Died during the mission for the survey.	S
Binetti,	a thin young navigator.	ntsm
Bixel	A mercenary.	SW1
Bladomir	King of Drylanders.	DW
Blaine	Last of the Strange Ones.	DJ
Blaine, Dr.	A close second to Dr. Carl Randall and guardian to his four children.	ct
Blaine, Farrel	The first man to land on Venus.	U
Blaine, Philip	Eric Rand's uncle.	MM
Blaine, Dr. Philip	a famous earth physocist.	TP
Blake, Edna	Jim Blake's wife.	de
Blake, Jim		de
Blaney	A policeman.	mkf
Blaun,	a German soldier.	pl
Bluedarn	A Tharinese Earth farmer.	NEI
Bogan, Dr. John	Dean of American Philologists.	HS
Bohn, Julius	An investment banker.	cp2
Bohn, Robert	Julius' brother and partner.	cp2

Name		Story
Boker	A blue Hlakran and old friend of J. Kettrick.	DS
Bollard	A mercenary.	SW1, SW2, SW3
Bombey, Mother	runs a shabby inn/bar in Saturnopolis.	TP
Booker	Wounded personnel of UNIS base 15.	sh
Borchard	Middletown's coal dealer.	CWE
Borrodale	The most famous teleaudio broadcaster.	R
Borrow, Wythe		wi
Bowers, Dr. Ernest	Dr. Graeme's partner.	ff
Bradford, Mark	an agent of the U.S. War Dept. on assignment in Brazil.	vim
Bradley	An instructor at the same college that Fessenden works at.	Fw
Bradley, Bill	Young assistant to Mark Stanton.	va
Bradley, James	accused of murder.	tg
Bragi	An Aesir.	TG
Bragi	Gentle looking Aesir with dreamy eyes.	YV
Brain, The	large superintelligent computer.	TLU
Braller, Dr. Luther	A brillant surgeon.	mc
Brancato	Fellow treasure hunter.	WoNm
Bran	a negative man.	ntsm
Brant,	Psychologist and former school mate of Rand Carr.	de
Braun, Dr. Richard	A Space-Rocket scientist of Berlin.	srm
Bray	A member of the expedition.	YV
Bray, Gen.	Murdered commander of the Space Mirror.	smr
Brazell	One of four SF authors that get together.	E
Bregg	Sakae.	SmB
Brent, Dick	An adventurer.	CW
Brewer, Bertta	Doc's daughter.	TM
Brewer, Doc	Head of the Carnival.	TM
Brilling	Dr. Walton's assistant.	EI
Brinley, Det. Sgt. Jim	A police detective.	dd
Britt, Capt.	Medical officer of the Space Mirror.	smr
Bronic of Linar	An ancient VanRyn.	HS
Bros	An Arkuuin.	SW2
Brusul, But	A squat warrior.	DW
Bryant, Hugh	Scout pilot who tries to get Feltri back to the Federation.	CK
Buford, Lt.	A crewmen of the R-404.	HS
Bugeyes	G. Crane's Venusian servant.	LtoM
Burdeau	Commander of UNIS base 13.	sh
Burdine, Lucas	The Head of Synthesubstances.	STW
Burgin,	A meteor-miner.	ma
Burke	A member of Dead Legs' gang.	dl
Burmer, Bemo	A Jovain secret agent.	Dov

Name		Story
Burnham, Hall	Advances to Colonel.	CTW
Burns	The Courier's man.	in
Burr	Missouri's tribesman.	CotSL
Burrel, Hull	Antaran pilot.	tBS
Burrel, Ivan	A former employee, a chemist	dcg
Burris		T
Caesar, Julius	Of the Brotherhood.	IOW
Cain, Commander	Head of the Earth-Guard.	eeg
Cain, Gov. Daniel	The Governor of Europa colony.	moe
Cain, Martin	A pirate and the only man to land and return from Erebus.	TP
Cain, Lefty		cp2
Cain, Lana	Martin Cain's daughter and leader of the pirates.	TP
Cain, Nura	The Governor's daughter and finacé of Carse Lasser.	moe
Caird, Dr. Jonas	From the Foundation of Extraterrestrial Sciences,	SW2
Calden,	Pilot of Earth-Guard Rocket #28.	eeg
Caravella	A Tharinese Earth farmer.	NEI
Cardell	A member of the Vulcan's crew.	HA
Carew	English, Zaria's assistant.	T
Carew	Outer Planets Bureau Personell.	TW
Carlin, D.A. Andy		cp2
Carlin, Donald	Henry Carlin's son.	he
Carlin, Henry	Vice President of Taurstion National Bank and Donald's father.	he
Carlin, Laird	A Cosmic Engineer (Chief Surveyor) forced to take a vacation on Earth.	FW
Carlson	J. Shane's aide/worker.	STW
Carnaby, Rick	Pilot - lost one year ago.	KS
Carr, Rand	Jim Blake's boss at Federated Elecric.	de
Carrick	One of four SF authors that get together.	E
Carrul, Dr. John	Chief of the expedition.	YV
Carson	Office manager where Henry works.	DW
Carson, Dr. Robert	A surgeon, one of the best.	Dl
Carter, James	Dr. L. Kindler's college.	km
Carton	A newspaperman.	mc
Carton, Charlie		im
Carvello	The Warden/Keeper.	DB
Cay, Ranl	Chairman of the Venusian Congress.	dov
Chai	A Tchell servant of J. Kettrick.	DS
Chane, Morgan	A different Earthman.	SW1, SW2, SW3
Chane, Thomas	A Earth Missionary to Varna.	SW3
Chattan, Joe	A spaceman that gets into more than he should.	TM
Chaves, Hernando de	A Spanish conquistador from out of the	LM

Name		Story
	past.	
Cheerly, Jenk	A pirate captian from Uranus.	TP
Cheers, Mjr. Walter	Personeel of UNIS base 1.	sh
Chell	A Chorann.	FotS, Fse
Chi, Capt. Yuan	Chinese officer.	lcb
Chowdhury, Mr.	Babylon's coordinator.	bs
Christensen, Nils	Chief of the Lunar Project.	HS
Christina	A Lazurite leader.	LoL
Chroll	A Starwolf friend of M. Chane.	SW2, SW3
Clark, Mrs.	She runs a rooming house.	bh
Clark, Nick	A pilot.	QT
Claus	A Patrolman.	mc
Clede	One of the Fourth men.	SoL
Cline	Fellow treasure hunter.	WoNm
Clymer, Jim	Died of martian sickness.	WLOT
Collard, Dr. John	A biologist.	im2
Collins	A policeman.	im
Cooper	Part of a previous expedition now lost.	hc
Cord, Det. Sgt.		
Corr, Mr.	The chief bookkeeper.	MM
Cortez, Don Hernando	Leader of the Spanish expedition.	QT
Crail, Jean	Finds Kimball Drew, a biology student at Los Angeles Universtiy.	ep
Crail, Police-Capt.	Investigating Dr. Melford's death.	srm
Crain, Capt.	Captain of the Pallas.	SS
Crain, John	Philip's amnesic father.	TLU
Crain, Philip	An Engineer.	TLU
Cralley	A farmer on the edge of the swamp.	S-m
Crane, Gareth	Archeaologist.	LtoM
Crane, Jimmy	He becomes a General.	CTW
Crane, Rab	An agent of the Terrestrial Secret Service.	MV, smr
Cray, Arline	Wilson Cray's daughter.	dov
Cray, Wilson	A Venusian scientist.	dov
Crellys, Peter	A lieutenant in the R.A.F.	vim
Crisci	The youngest of the Industrial Research Lab Staff.	CWE
Croft		vv
Croy. 'old'	Pilot captian of the Farhope.	Sfl
Cryver, Cyn	Count of the Marches of Outer Space.	KotS, tBS
Cubbison, Dr. Walter	Director of the station.	T
Cucia	A policeman.	mkf
Cuitlahua	Montezuma's brother.	QT
Cyra	A forbidden daughter of Phaon.	CK
Daedalus	Sorcerer-scientist, builder of the Labyrinth.	Pl

Name		Story
Daigh, Col.	Personnel of UNIS base 15.	sh
Daigh, Harker	One of the Superintendents of the King Munitions Works and husband to Eve.	mkf
Dain Kenneth	An astronaut.	GI
Dale, Dr. John	Henry Carlin goes to him for help.	He, vm
Dall, 'Dead Legs'	Wheelchair bound leader of a crime gang.	im
Dalton, Hugh	An old college pal of Dr. J. Pollard.	MwE
Daly, John	Dr. Rand's assistant.	tg
Dandor	A Baran scientist.	TLU
Dane, Jimmy	The Vulcan's radio operator.	HA
Darnow, Dr.	The leader of the mission. From the Historical Bureau.	R
Dart, Doremus	Steve Dart's father.	DM
Dart, Lina	Steve Dart's sister.	DM
Dart, Steve	A Pleb worker.	DM
Dawes, Curtis	John Woodford's best friend.	MwR
Dawkes, Wilson	A world-famous cytologist.	MSD
Dec, Lalla	A Venusian college student.	MV
de Alvarado, Pedro	Second in command of the Spanish.	QT
De Ferdey	Head of expedition, an elderly scholar.	SP
De Guzman	Leader of the party to capture Noh-Ek.	LM
De Lane,	A Hollywood movie star.	tg
de Leon	A young red-bearded Spaniard.	QT
de Montejo	A cheerful Spaniard.	QT
Denman	Federation agent.	FSe
de Oli	A ferocious and reckless Spaniard.	QT
de Olmedo, Father Bartolome	The Spanish chaplan.	QT
de Ordas, Diego	A Spaniard.	QT
de Sandoval, Gonsalo	Don Pedro Lopez's comrade.	QT
Detmold	A professor of Electro-chemistry at Juson University.	MG
DeWitt, Glenn	In charge of Special Research.	HS
Diaz, Sgt. Bernal	A Spaniard.	QT
Diaz, Manuel	A Spanish soldier who captures Aryll.	LM
Dillon	A policeman.	mkf
Dilullo, John	Head of the Mercenaries.	SW1, SW2, SW3
Din, Jhul	Lieutenant of the Interstellar Patrol.	OU
Diri, Zin	Thin twitching fellow from Argo.	tSH
Doll, Obd	Captain of the command ship sent to pick up the Qhallas.	tBS
Donahue, Old	A mercenary from J. Dilullo's past.	SW2
Dong,	State's attourney.	tg
Donsel, Ellen	AKA Lalu, she's come to find Yann.	C

Name		Story
Dordemos	A pirate captain.	MM
Drake, Anson	Gillen's assistant in the 1stattempt to conquer Mars.	CTW
Drew, Jesse	Owner of Drew Tranium Mines	STW
Drew, Stephen	Son of Jesse Drew.	STW
Drummond, Frank	Narrator .	T
Dubman	A waspish archeologist.	YV
Drew, Kimball		ep
Drick	A member of the Vulcan's crew.	HA
Drinn, Slih	The proprietor of the Dream Palace.	dov
Duff, Josephine	Gilson's Secretary.	STW
Dunn, Ruth	A nurse with the American Hospital Unit.	lcb
Durak, Tanya	A Russian refugee of some sort.	wi
Durand, Prof. Ernest		MSD
Durin	A Skerethian.	Fse
Dwerris, Mayor	The mayor of Central City.	tg
Ebbut, Sec. Sheldon	Secretary of UNIS.	sh
Eckhard	Leader of the Scoundrels.	AA
Edam, Quel	The Venusian ambassador.	dov
Edwards, Jean	Fellow treasure hunter.	LToM
Egir	Khal Kan's uncle, Kan Abul's brother, a traitor.	DW
Eglin, Piers	A Federation historian.	CWE
Ei	Leader of the Winged Ones.	VoC
Elena	Hyrst's wife.	LoL
Ellerman, Berk	Venusian Minister of Justice.	dov
Ellsworth, Dr. Calvin	President of American University.	im
Emrys, Ryll	Orion scientist with a big secret.	tSH
Enlil	Lord of the Wind.	SP
Ennel, Berk	a fellow prisoner.	wws
Ennimer, Donn	A drunken Earthman.	MV
Erlik, Dark	Lord of the Shadows, older than Earth.	KS
Eron	The ruler of Rith.	SW3
Escoba, Col.	Jailor.	mg
Etain	Ulios' wife.	AA
Evens, Lewis	A citizen of Carnarvon, Wales.	SW2
Evans, Hobe		WLOT
Evans, Capt. Wright	Captain of Earth-Guard Rocket #28.	eeg
Evers, Vance	Pilot	CotS
Ewan	Skerethian, opposition member.	FotS, FSe
Fairlie, Chann	A new outlaw from Lyra.	tSH
Fairlie, Dr. Robert	Professor of Linguistics at Massachusettes University.	HS
Fallon, John	Narrator - searching for friend.	KS
Farah	A shopkeeper on thieves' world.	TM

Name		Story
Farley	A Patrolman.	mc
Farley	Cemetery caretaker.	vm
Farquhar	A Tharinese Earth farmer.	NEI
Farrel, John	Captain of the Space Ship Thetis.	ntsm
Farrel, Ross	The hero.	SfI
Farris	A fellow researcher with E. Martin.	LM
Farris, Hugh	A teak hunter.	AE
Fawcett, Col.		WA
Fayaman of Draco	An outlaw Captain & B. Holl's enemy.	tSH
Fellowes	The new telegraph operator.	vm
Felton, Gregg	A former student of Dr. Robbie's.	cp
Felton, Ned		bowm
Feltri	The most important man in the star frontier.	TM
Fennelin of the Dark World	An ancient VanRyn.	HS
Fenris	One of Loki's pets.	TG
Fenson, Dr. Raymond	Dr. Grant's assistant.	wa
Fenris	One of Loki's pets.	YV
Fersen	Under-Secretary for Interstellar Trade: represents Earth in the Hyades Cluster.	DS
Fessenden, Arnold	The greatest scientist of Earth.	fw
Fife	Leader of the escaped slaves.	FotS, FSe
Finchley, Clyde	Perfected the practicable cycloton-turbine.	nwe
Finetti	A crewman on SC-1419.	tSH
Firmin	Outer Planets Bureau personell.	TW
Ficher,	A southwestern Senator.	sh
Flandrin, Geoffrey	A vice president for the bank.	sm
Floring , Ross	The Control Council Earth representative.	FW
Follansbee	Associate geologist.	WA
Forney, Pvt.	Personnel of UNIS base 1.	sh
Forseti	A sober young Aesir.	YV
Foster	Detmold's assumed name.	MG
Franklin, Ben	Of the Brotherhood.	IOW
Frey	An Aesir and Freya's kinsman.	YV
Freya	A lovely Aesir maiden.	YV
Freya	Freya's grandmother.	YV
Frigga	Odin's wife.	YV
Froisland,	Deceased personnel of UNIS Base 15.	sh
Fulton, Scott	A Pilot.	TLU
Fuor	Of the Korlu.	vim
Gaines, John	A lanky mining Engineer.	wi
Gann, Galos	The last man of all.	IWD
Garces	Brigidier commanding the Division.	SmB

Name		Story
Garcia, Dr. Martin	From the Cuernavaca School of Extraterrestrial Anthopology.	SW2
Garret	Part if a previous expedition now lost.	hc
Garonia	A translator.	wa
Garris, Mayor	The Mayor of Middletown.	CWE
Garrison	Survivor of a ship-wreck.	IS
Geary, Dr. Thomas		DD
Geer	Burly trail bosses.	WA
Geisert, Gerritt	The Vampire master.	vm
Gerda	Frey's lovely wife .	YV
Gersemi	Freya's mother, daughter of Freya.	YV
Gilbert, Dr. Howard	The world's greatest authority on certain branches of electrical science.	mm
Gillen, Ross	An scientist who conquers space.	CTW
Gilson, Johnny	Runs the boat-livery on Bott's Island.	DB
Gilson, Walter	Drew's Earth agent.	STW
Glevan	An old Engineer from Pittan.	DS
Golden Wings	Dryland princess, Bladomir's daughter.	DW
Gomez	A mercenary.	SW1
Gordon, John	Main character.	KotS, tBS
Gorley,	Federated's aggressive president.	de
Gorley, Red	A big, red-headed, Irish first mate.	ntsm
Gormon, Holl	The spokesperson for the Third Men.	SoL
Gorrel, Dr. John	Developer of a machine that can listen to minds.	swm
Graal	A Starwolf female.	SW3
Graff, Jacob	A rocket engineer for the Central Empire.	lmg
Grach Chai	Leader of the Varkonids.	CK
Graeme, Dr. Robert	Noted Plastic Surgeon.	ff
Graham, Dr. Harlan	Chair of Astro-Physics at American University in New York City.	dt
Graham, Ilse	Fiancee to Jim Clymer.	WLOT
Grahan	A contemporary Ryn male.	HS
Grant, Dr. Howard	Head of the Biology department of Manhatten University.	wa
Grann, Willis	A friend of John Woodfords.	MwR
Grantham, Dr. Howard	The Super-physcisist at American Universtiy.	im
Grassia, Mrs.	Henry Carlin's housekeeper.	he
Gresznik, Lt. Col. George Casimir	Personnel of UNIS base 15.	sh
Gray	Grantham's assistant.	im
Gray, Chan	An exploerer of Erebus.	TP
Grih	One of the Clawed Ones.	VoC
Grih, Sin	A Mercurian prisoner at lunar prison.	MM
Gron	Captain of the warriors of Yamaya.	Lcb

Name		Story
Groro	The King of Krim.	vim
Grugo	A Uranian prisoner at the lunar prison.	MM
Guatemozin	Montezuma's nephew.	QT
Guinard, Carlus	One of the four most important people postwar Europe.	IOW
Gurth, Roger	A Pleb worker, laboring for the Patricos.	DM
Guru, Sessun	The Vice-President of Venus.	dov
Gwaath		SW3
Haddan, Rann	found guilty of rebelling against the ruling council.	wws
Hadden, Mr.	Father to Frank Hadden.	WLOT
Hadden, Sgt. Frank	Narrator.	WLOT
Haddon, John	The great space pirate.	ma
Haddon, Thorn	Prisoner in a Brazilian jail.	mg
Hagulian	A crew member.	HS
Hahl	Of the Hairy clan.	DJ
Haines, Pinky	A grey-faced, squinty crook.	cp2
Haj, Serk	Chief of the Council of Suns for Federated Suns.	OU
Halfrich, John	From the Survey.	S
Halkett, Mart	He becomes a traitor.	CTW
Hall, Ruth	Marries David Rand.	HHW
Hall, Wilson	Ruth's father.	HHW
Hallos, Mihai	The Headman of Weislant.	vv
Haly, John	Commander of the Pioneer.	wsb
Hammond, Kirk	Twentieth century space explorer.	SoL
Haney, Frederick	Tom's twin brother.	bh
Haney, Det. Tom	One of the best men on the force.	bh
Hanson, Dr. Leon		MSD
Hara,	Boss of the Island.	IU
Harben, Ross	A fellow lab scientist.	im2
Haring, Doc	The doctor on Bott's Island.	DB
Harkann	A Starwolf raid leader.	SW3
Harker, Dr. Allan	President of Manhatten University.	wa
Harkness	The teller at the Vance National Bank.	im
Harmon	Partners in an expedition to Arabia.	hc
Harmon, Edward	Olivia Ralton's beau.	vm
Harriman, Dr.	Brings David Rand into the world and cares for him.	HHW
Harris, Lt. Alex	A member of the R.A.F.	lcb
Harron, Stephen	Dr. Graham' lab assistant.	
Hartley,	Earth-Guard rocket #28's 3rd officer.	eeg
Harvey, Laurence	Head of Interstellar Research.	TM
Hatha	Leader of the Hoofed Ones.	VoC
Haug, Sgt.		bh
Hausman, Col.	Second in command of personnel, UNRC.	SmB

Name		Story
Hawk	A space pirate.	eeg
Hayerman	Dead.	Sfl
Hayes, Dr. William	The Australian scientist.	srm
Hazen,	The architect, he became a taxi driver.	de
Heimdall	An Aesir.	TG
Heimdall	Warder of the Asgard gate.	YV
Hel	A Jotun princess.	YV
Hela	An Aesir.	TG
Helmer	An Arkuuin.	SW2
Hemmerick, Dr. John	Of Yates University and Eastern Zoological Museum.	S-m
Henderson, Dr. William	Comes to Dr. Dale with a request.	vm
Hermod	One of Odin's sons.	YV
Hill	Head of Morrow base security.	HS
Hirota, Major	A major with the Imperial Japanese Army.	lcb
Hnoss	Freya's aunt.	YV
Hof	A Starwolf council member.	SW3
Hogrim, Joseph	A renowned spy-chief.	vim
Holk	A bear-like warrior of Anshan.	VoC
Holl, Brond	Former officer of a Hercules Baron .	tSH
Holl, Gorr	A Capellan outlaw. H. Mason assumes his identity.	CWE
Hollis	The butler.	mkf
Holmes, Dr. John	Trying to get to the moon.	hf
Holmes, Mr. Morris	The secondary partner in Narberth & Holmes Toy Importers.	dd
Holt, Daniel	A business man.	wi
Holt, Steve	Burgin's partner.	ma
Homer, Dr. Jackson	He has perfected the treatment.	MXE
Hoom, Gabriel	The fatest law officer.	dcg
Horger, Mr.	A vice president for the bank.	sm
Horne, Jim	Vega Queen's pilot accused of causing the wreck.	FotS, FSe
Horruf	A Jovian pirate captain.	MM
Horva, Horva	Captain of Lianna's Starship.	KotS
Hoskins, Richard	Chairman of the Earth government.	TP
Houston	The Vulcan's Second Officer.	HA
Hoxie	An old outlaw captain.	tSH
Hubble	Head of Industrial Research Labs.	CWE
Hull, Juss	A fellow prisoner.	wws
Hungerford, Dr. Cyrus	A Space-rocket scientist.	srm
Hunter	Partners in an expedition to Arabia.	hc
Hurriman	A politician.	pp
Hurg	Council member from Venus.	tw
Hurth	A blue Hlakran.	DS
Hyrst	Wrongly convicted of murder, he wakes up 50 years	LoL

Name		Story
	into his future.	
Ibir	A Yamayan noble.	lcb
Icarus	Deceased son of Daedalus.	pl
Idwal, Norman	An importer from Earth.	MV
Idun	Bragi's noble-featured wife.	YV
Ikhnaton	King of Egypt 14th Century BCE of the Brotherhood.	IOW
Iormungandr	One of Loki's pets.	TG
Irrun	A Starwolf council member.	SW3
Ivan, Kim	A fellow prisoner.	wws
Ivers, Rik	A Mercurian superintendant at the solar station.	dov
Jackson	First Officer of the Vulcan.	HA
Jackson	Did not survive the Invisible Masters' attack.	Im
Jackson, Dr.	Treating Alice Wilsey.	vm
Jackson, Dr. Lewis	A brillant surgeon that assists Dr. Braller.	mc
Jackson, Dr. Lloyd	A superior of Dr. Melford.	srm
James	Dr. Braller's butler.	mc
Jameson,	The chauffer.	sm
Jandron, Wald	One of the leaders of the survivors of the Martian Queen.	SS
Janissar	King-Sovereign of Orion.	tHS
Janney	One of P.C. Crail's men.	srm
Janson	A policeman.	im
Janssen	A mercenary pilot.	SW2, SW3
Jere	A member of Project Freewill.	DB
Jergen, Breck	Sgt of the squad - died in mutiny.	WLOT
Jergen, Mr.	Father to Breck Jergen – carpenter.	WLOT
Jergen, Mrs.	Mother to Breck Jergen – talker.	WLOT
Jhanon	Holk's brother.	VoC
Johnson	An electrician that lives at the edge of Middletown.	CWE
Jones, Hayden	A citizen of Carnarvon, Wales.	SW2
Julud	Council member from Saturn.	tw
Juss	A Captain in the army of Groro.	vim
Kallant	Weislant's innkeeper.	vv
Kan, Avul	A Martian.	STW
Kan, Khal	Son of the King of Jotan.	DW
Kan, Korus	Lieutenant of the Interstellar Patrol.	OU
Kan, Shorr	Lord of the Dark Worlds.	tBS
Kann, Mar	A third man.	SoL
Karnath	Assistant guardian of the Force.	AA
Kasman, 'old'		DM
Kaubos	J. Edward's guide, a Jovian.	LToM
Kau-ta-leh	Ancient Martian King of Rylik.	LToM

Name		Story
Keene, Stilicho	an old norotius pirate captain.	TP
Kechnie	A member of the Vulcan's crew.	HA
Kellard, Hugh	Space Cadet.	S
Keller, Police Chief		cp2
Kellon, Capt.	Captain of a survey ship.	R
Kells,	A stocky second-mate.	moe
Kells, Fred	Public Enemy No. 1.	DD
Kenniston, John	A resident of Middletown.	CWE
Kent, Rance	First officer of the Pallas.	SS
Keogh	John Gordon's psychiatrist.	KotS
Kerr, Fred		wi
Kerr, Janice	Fred's wife.	wi
Kerth, Jan	A Micro-man.	DM
Kettrick, John	A Trader banned from the Hyades Cluster.	DS
Khan, Fizar	A Persian official.	va
Khephr	A Starwolf council member.	SW3
Khitu	A Tchell servant of Seri.	DS
Kiernan, Reed	Scientist, UNRC, Ohio.	SmB
Kimer	Chief of Middletown's Police.	CWE
Kimmel	The mercenary ships captain.	SW2
Kincaid, Martin	Started to Proxy Project.	pp
Kindler, Dr. Lewis	Psycho-physiologist researcher at Gotham University.	km
King, Alfred	Cyrus' third son.	
King, Mr. Cyrus	The great Munitions Lord.	mkf
King, Eve	Cyrus' daughter.	mkf
King, Jean	A member of the Earth Diplomatic Service.	FlS
King, Kinnel	a pirate captian from Earth.	TP
King, Robert	Cyrus' second son.	mkf
King, Shelly	Secretary to Dr. J. Collard .	im2
King, Theodore	Cyrus' son.	mkf
King, Virgina	Paul Randall's fiancée.	ct
Kingston	A representative of New York City's government.	im
Kinner	Outer Planets Bureau personell.	TW
Kirtland	Partners in an expedition to Arabia.	hc
Klaber of Ryn	An ancient VanRyn hero.	HS
Klain, Kendall	Venusian war mMinister.	dov
Klimmer, Joe	Night generator operator on Bott's Island.	DB
Kor, Dri	Demonstrates Martian hypnotic hunting in an earth circus.	STW
Kor, Kol	Dri Kor's brother, does the same.	STW
Korkhann	A Kren, Liann's minister of Non-Human Affairs.	KotS
Krasny	A reasearcher in Budapest	srm
Kraus, Patrolman	The officer on the beat	dd

Name		Story
Kree	Leader of the Brotherhood	VoC
Krell	One of the leaders of the survivors of the Martian Queen.	SS
Kribo	A Saturnian slith hunter.	TP
Kro	Dandor's robot.	TLU
Kuluun	King of Amaya.	
Kurdley, Halk	A fellow convict..	moe
Kwolek, Capt.	Pilot of an R-409.	HS
Labdibdin	A Vhollan scientist.	SW1
Laird	Of the homicide squad.	im2
Laird, Capt. Thomas	A retired veteran of the planetary patrol and a neighbor of P. Baline.	MM
Laird, Moira	Captain T. Lairds' daughter.	MM
Lal'lor	A large grey Miran.	CWE
Land, Gramp	Johnny Lands' grandfather.	FW
Land, Harb	Jahnny Lands' brother.	FW
Land, Johnny	A Earthman cosmic engineer.	FW
Land, Marn	Johnny Lands' sister.	FW
Landon, Clark	A geologist/adventurer.	EB
Lane, Carol	J. Kenniston's fiance.	CWE
Lane, Lois	John Daly's fiancé.	tg
Lane, Wilson	John Daly's fiancé's father.	tg
Laneeh	A Vhollan woman.	SW1
Lang,	Deceased personnel of UNIS base 15.	sh
Lanham, Jerry	Prisoner in a Brazilian jail.	mg
Lanham, Ray	David Winn's editor.	MXE
Lanier, Gilbert	An instructor at J.U. & Detmold's friend.	MG
Lansin, Fred	One of Stock Adam's men.	ff
Lanu	Philip's half-brother & King of Bara.	TLU
Lao-Tsu	Chinese Philosopher, of the Brotherhood.	IOW
Lanson, Lt.	A Martian post commander.	CTW
Larson, Cpl.	Personnel of UNIS base 15.	sh
Larus, Lacq	Chief of the Interstellar Patrol.	OU
Las, Lan	A fellow prisoner.	wws
Lassen	Died in his bunk.	WLOT
Lasser, Carse	John Allen's former subordinate on Venus.	moe
Lauber	A resident of Middletown.	CWE
Laughlin	Eric's best friend and employer.	TG
Laurent, Marie	F. Drummond's love interest.	T
Laryl	A member of Project Freewill.	DB
Laver, Lt.	Crew of the Space Mirror.	smr
Leach	No. 2 badguy.	Sfl
Lecayo, Mr.	Of Babylon.	Bs

Name		Story
Lee, Lorri	A woman teleaudio broadcaster.	R
Leigh, Cmdr.	Commands the Inner Planet Alliance squadron.	TP
Leigh, Francis	A.K.A. Rake Allen.	FlS
Leigh, Thaddus	Older, graying scientist from Gotham University.	nwe
Leigh, Theron	David Madden's assistant.	lmg
Leighton, Mark	A former engineer now working as a supply-clerk at power pit 13.	pp13
Lemmiken, Getrude	Ohio college student.	SmB
Leslie, Ben	C. Narberth's clerk.	dd
Lester, Francis		bowm
Lester, Ruth	Frank Lester's sisters and Ned Felton's girlfriend.	bowm
Lewis, Griff	A citizen of Carnarvon, Wales.	SW2
Lex Val	Vel Quen's son & Zarth Ars' lab assistant.	KotS
Lianna	Princess of the Fomalhaut Kingdom.	KotS
Liggett	Second Officer of the Pallas.	SS
Ligor	Surp's son.	TLU
Li Kin	A small Chinese major.	VoC, tBS
Liline	Last of the Watchers.	lmg
Limbar, Val	A Micro-man.	DM
Lindeman, Eric	Scientist .	CotS
Linna	Specialist in Earth Cultures, Sect 7-y Social Technics.	CotSL
Lisetti	Another linguist.	HS
Lisler, Frederick	A war criminal with big plans.	im2
Lita	An unreasonable woman.	IU
L'lan, Lin	J. Drew's servant.	STW
Loesser	Helps Johnny Land with his plans.	FW
Loki	The Archdevil & old foe of the Aesir.	TG
Loki	The traitor, a great scientist.	YV
Lonnat	Council member from Mercury.	tw
Lopez, Don Pedro	Nick Clark's past identity.	QT
Lor, Lun	Aged Chief Counsillor.	cq
Lora	The child of the Winds.	CW
Lorgor	A member of the Jovian Secret Service.	FlS
Loring, John	25th century space explorer, of the Brotherhood.	IOW
Lorron, President Jon	President of Venus.	dov
Louis,	Wounded personnel of UNIS base 15.	sh
Lovering, Carl	A space captain.	MM
Lua	A beautiful Lyran.	tSH
Lua	Of the Korlu, invisible people.	vim
Luane	Daughter of Daedalus and priestess of the labyrinth.	pl
Lugach	A large tattooed idiot.	TM
Lund, Gurth	One of J. Wilson's men.	SoL
Lund, Norden	Federation Sector Deputy administrator.	CWE

Name		Story
Lurgh	A Gargoyle-like alien former slave.	FotS, FSe
Lute	A small furry Capellan.	TM
MacDonald	The man Hyrst was supposed to have killed.	LoL
Machris	A mercenary.	SW1
Macklin, Hobie	Sam's son and afraid to be smart.	bs
Macklin, Hugh	30 year old archeologist.	SP
Macklin, Joanie Ann	Hobie's sister.	bs
Macklin, Ma	Hobie's mother.	bs
Macklin, Sam	An alarming rabble-rouser .	bs
Madden, David	A rocket engineer.	lmg
Madison	One of four SF authors that get together.	E
Madison, Dr, John	A physicist experimenting in Mexico.	QT
Madison, Kay	Nick Clark's fiancee.	Qt
Magro	A white furred Spican.	CWE
Mallen, Marta	The lone female survivor of the Martian Queen.	SS
Mann, Allan	SN#2473R6 charged with a breech of reason.	IU
Manning, Ray	A young official of the electical company. that Dr. H. Gilbert used to work for.	mm
Manrique	A Spanish soldier.	LM
Mara	One of the Ephemerae.	ep
Mara	A Baran princess.	TLU
Marden, Thayn	A beautiful Vramen.	SoL
Marduk	Ancient hero-king.	SP
Marina	Cortez's mistress.	QT
Marker	A policeman.	dcg
Markolin	A Vhollan general.	SW1
Marlin, Brad	An american fighter pilot.	pl
Marston, James	Owner of the hotel.	wi
Martilette	Old French missionary in Khotan.	KS
Martin, Bud	Owner of Bud's Garage Middletown.	CWE
Martin, Edward	An archeologist researching Mayan ruins.	LM
Martin, Dr. John	A geologist.	TLU
Martin, Kay	Philip's friend and daughter of Dr. J. Martin's.	TLU
Martabalne	Starwolf council member.	SW3
Marty	The lame time keeper.	pp13
Mason, Carse	Detective sargent .	mkf
Mason, Hugh	A Terran Empire agent.	tSH
Masters, Kieth	A physicist.	YV
Mathers		T
Mathis	Federation co-ordinator.	CWE
Matlock, Dave	Ship's pilot.	SW2
Mattison	Dr. Robine's helper.	bowm
Maxson, Jay	A rising politician in the Federation congress.	R

Name		Story
McCloskey	One of P. C. Crail's men.	srm
McGoun, Jewett	An interstellar trader.	SW2
McIntyre	A policeman.	mc
McLachlan, Angus	A. Scotts second engineer.	va
McLain	Manager of a trucking company in Middletown.	CWE
Melford, Arthur	Dr. Melford's nephew, and an instructor in Physics at Manhattan University.	srm
Melford, Dr. Ferdinand	Chemistry professor at the Philadelphia School of Science.	srm
Merriam, Prof.	A fellow researcher with Dr. Thorne.	ed
Mertaud, Henri	A late French rocket-experimenter.	srm
Mesa	The Spanish gunner.	QT
Meeva	An escaped alien slave.	FotS, FSe
Meherbal	Leader of Noh-Ek and the Lords of the Morning.	LM
Meister, Warden	Hyrst's warden.	LoL
Meloni	UNRC Commanding Captain.	SmB
Merridew, Dr.	The attending physician when Hyrst wakes up.	LoL
Merrill	A U.S. Lt. assigned to guard Guinard.	IOW
Metzger	A Tharinese Earth farmer.	NEI
Mica	A Skerethian.	FSe
Midgard Serpent	One of Loki's pets.	YV
Millera, Domenic	Issues a warning.	he
Millera, Julia	Stricken by the evil eye.	he
Millis, Mr.	Father to Walter Millis.	WLOT
Millis, Walter	Shot during mutiny.	WLOT
Milner	A mercenary.	SW2
Minos	King of Crete.	pl
Mione, Joseph	Father to Rose.	he
Mione, Peter	Rose's grandfather.	he
Mione, Rose	Donald Carlin's love interest.	he
Mitchell	Companion to the narrator.	MGoM
Moheen	Leader of the Grass people.	NEI
Molokoff, L.		srm
Montezuma	The Aztec Emperor.	QT
Mordaunt, Lane	The Roadhouse owner.	wi
Moreau, Etienne	From France.	vim
Moretti	A wholesale produce merchant in Middletown.	CWE
Morgan	A Srockton, WV farmer.	MG
Morivenn	Skerethian leader of the opposition.	FotS, FSe
Morris	A friend of C. Landon.	EB
Morris, Dick	A Seattle bond salesman.	wi
Morris, Dr.	A college of Dr. Harriman.	HHW
Morrow, Mjr.	Second in command of the Space Mirror.	smr
Moorow, Felix	An Englishman.	Srm

Name		Story
Morse	Died during the mission for the Survey.	S
Moss, Albert	A canidate for gevernor.	tg
Most Ancient, The	Leader of the Nagas.	lcb
Mother-wind	A kind gentle wind.	CW
Muirhead	A crewmember.	HS
Muller, Julius	A toy store owner.	dd
Munn	A Starwolf council member.	SW3
Murdat	Council member from Uranus.	tw
Murnik	Martian servant of H. Skene.	WoNM
Mursul	Wizened oldest of the four Kirghiz.	KS
Myra	One of the last Strange Ones.	DJ
Myrrha	Lovely girl about 17 years old.	IS
Nal, Dur	Captain of squadron 598-77 of the Interstellar Patrol.	OU
Naramore	Outer Planets Bureau Chief Medical Officer.	TW
Narath Teyn	Lianna's cousin, ruler of Teyn.	KotS
Narberth, Charles	Senior partner in Narberth & Holmes Toy Importers.	dd
Narth, Nim	A Martian secret agent.	dov
Nash, Dr.		mkf
Natal, Than	Venusian Foreign Minister.	dov
Nebo, Mr. Peter	A mysterious visitor.	srm
Nelson, Capt. Eric	The mercenary officer.	VoC
Newton, Arthur	Another victim of the Vampire Master.	vm
Nila	Laird Carlins' significant other.	FW
Nichols,	Former head of UNIS.	sh
Nilga, Kin	A Saturnian rocket engineer.	MV
Nimurun	A Starwolf leader.	SW2
Niord	A squat, jovial, bald Aesir of middle age.	YV
Nison, Clymer	Visted Uranus, Neptune and Pluto.	TP
Noll	Council member from Neptune.	tw
Norris, Doug	A Proxy operator.	pp
Norse, Howard	John Woodford's boss.	MwR
Noskat	An eskimo guide.	EB
Noston, Don	A fellow prisoner..	wws
Nsharra		VoC
Nshurra	A Starwolf female.	SW3
Nunez, Father		mg
Nunez, Pelao	Husband of Tina.	mg
Nunez, Tina	Wife of Pelao.	mg
Nuro, Duun	An undersecretary in the North Venus Department.	ov
Nurth	Chief elder of the Korlu, and Lua's father.	vim
Odenjaa	A Kharali, brought the Mercs a job.	SW1
Odin	King of the Aesir.	TG, YV

Name		Story
Odur	Freya's grandfather.	YV
Oga, Gorm		UWS
Oliphant	H. Mason's superior.	TSH
Or, Dirk	fellow prisoner.	wws
Orlie, 'Mink'	Duke Warner's Lieutenant.	Bh
Orlu	A martian trying to save his race.	hf
Ormond, Ross	A young scientist .	ep
Ormond, Ross	An astronaut.	GI
Orr, Thol	A physicist imprisoned on Kuum.	SoL
O'Shannaig	A mercenary.	SW1
Otku, Seri	J. Kettrick's old partner.	DS
Owen, Harley	Dr. Dale's assistant.	vm
Owen, Stuart	A young physician and friend of Dr. Walton's.	EI
Owin, Harley	Dr. Dale's assistant.	he
Oyumi	A Japanese researcher.	srm
Pablo	A worker.	ed
Pasiphne	Wife of Minos.	pl
Pateo, Thomaz	Dr. H. Alascia's superintendent.	mg
Peters, Dr. Ferdinand	Of the Manhattan University Observatory.	AG
Peterson	An operator at the New York Power Station.	pp
Phaon	Father of Cyra and Belath.	CK
Phardon	Elder Martian holy/wise man.	WoNM
Piang	Farris' Laotian guide.	AE
Poe, Edgar Allen	A.K.A. Yann, a man from the future.	C
Pollard, Dr. John	A biologist.	MwE
Pollock, Dr. John	Eminent geologist.	WA
Preek	A plump butter-coloured Mintakan.	TM
Preyder, Lt.	A young German leiutenant.	Pl.
Price	20th century man transported 60 years into the future.	CotSL
Purdy, Harry	Helen's brother.	km
Purdy, Helen	Pete Purdy's wife.	km
Purdy, Percival	Helen & Pete's son.	km
Purdy, Pete		km
Quayle, Roy	A young fashion designer	R
Quard, M	A large Sirian; head of Sect. 6 of the Spaceman's Federation.	TM
Quinn	A member of Dead Legs' gang	dl
Quobba, Rab	A Vegan member of J. Wilson's men	SoL
Quorr	Leader of the Clawed Ones.	VoC
Raab	A physicist.	HS
Rabelais, Francois	Of the Brotherhood.	IOW

Name		Story
Ralls, William	Missing President of the largest bank in the nearby town.	sm
Ralston, Daved	Son of William Ralston.	dcg
Ralston, Mortn	David's cousin and treasurer of the Ralston Chemical Company.	dcg
Ralsotn, William	President of the Ralston Chemical Company.	Dcg
Ralton, Allene	The Vampire Master's first victim.	vm
Ralton, James	Worried for his daughter.	vm
Ralton, Olivia	First daughter of James and Allene.	vm
Ralton, Virginia	Second daughter of James and Allene.	vm
Rand, David	He that hath wings.	HHW
Rand, Eric	A young bookkeeper and son of John Randall.	MM
Rand, Dr. Jason	Inventor of the Truth gas.	tg
Randall, Dr, Carl	The greatest embryologist in the world.	ct
Randall, John	A famous space pirate.	MM
Randall, Leigh	Fourth child of Dr. Carl Randall.	ct
Randaal, Martha	Third child of Dr. Carl Randall.	ct
Randall, Paul	Eldest child of Dr. Carl Randall.	ct
Randall, Roger	Second child of Dr. Carl Randall.	ct
Ransome, Arthur	A witness.	swm
Ransome, Dr, Harlod	A brillant surgeon that assists Dr. Braller.	mc
Rasper, Mrs.	Neighbor from across the street.	bh
Rath, Dal	A Venusian lineman at the solar station.	dov
Ratzler	Runs a fur store.	bh
Raul	An Arkuuin member of the Open Worlds party.	SW2
Rawl	One of the Lords of the Morning, betrothed to Aryll.	LM
Rawling, Capt.	Captain of the Vulcan.	HA
Rawling, Frank	Corala's rising young lawyer.	s-m
Ray, Jim	A witness.	swm
Ray, Paula	A dark woman, 30, psychologist.	SmB
Ray, Marta	David Winn's fiancee.	MXE
Raymond, Arthur	From the Deptartment of Prosecutions.	DS
Reicher	The doctor.	HS
Reiman	Outer Planets Bureau Personell.	TW
Rendell	Secretary of Defense U.S.	HS
Reno, Pvt. Orrin	Personnel of UNIS base 15.	sh
Rewer, Dr. Lewis	President of the foundation.	im2
Rider, Ethel	Dr. Rider's daughter & assistant.	wsb
Rider, Dr. Thomas	A scientist on board the Pioneer.	wsb
Rillard, Hugh	Virgina Ralton's beau.	vm
Rimil	A pirate captian from Jupiter.	TP
Riney, Mr.	The second officer.	R

Name		Story
Riskin, Vincent	First Vice President of Transmutation, Inc.	STW
Roberts, Capt. Ray	A terrier-like Detective Captain.	dcg
Robbie, Dr. Thomas	An astrophysicist.	cp
Robine, Dr.	One of the most brillant biologists alive.	bowm
Robinson, Mr.	Mayor of Harmonville.	WLOT
Rodemos	Ancient Atlantian, founder of the Brotherhood.	IOW
Rogers	A policeman.	mc
Rogers, President	President of Manhatten University.	wa
Roos, Jan	Dutch artist.	SP
Roper	A member of Dead Legs' gang.	dl
Roth, Robert	Made the first space flight in 1996.	TP
Ruchs	A Krimian jailor.	vim
Ruiz, Arnolfo	Firebrand revolutionary, Mexican exile.	CotSL
Runnal	Council member from Earth.	tw
Ruric	Ardic's Father, leader of the Vellae.	FotS
Russ, Michael	A fellow worker with A. Mann.	IU
Rutledge	A mercenary.	SW1
Ryan, Phil	Assistant in the Cytology Lab.	im2
Rymer	One of the first Vramen.	SoL
Sabah, Hasan	The Old man of the Mountain.	va
Safetta, widow		he
Safetta, Felix	Stricken by the Evil Eye.	he
Sandihir	A Tharinese friend of John's.	NEI
Sanetti	Did not survive the Invisible Masters' attack.	Im
Sanders, Ross	Corala's deputy sheriff.	s-m
Sandra	J. Ketrick's companion.	DS
Sands	A southwestern Senator.	sh
Sattargh, S	A scientist from Arcturus III.	SW2
Saulton, Roscoe	A candidate for Governor.	MXE
Sawyer	Chief of the Missouris.	CotSL
Schuyler	Owner of Schuyler Metals.	CotS
Seaworth, Franics	An interplanetary agent.	eeg
Sekkinen	A mercenary.	SW1, SW3
Sekma, Mr.		DS
Senn, Steve	A fellow convict.	moe
Shan Kar	A Humanite leader for L'lan.	VoC
Shane, Gloria	Beautiful daughter of Jared Shane.	STW
Shane, Jared	President of Transmutation, Inc.	STW
Shaner	Outer Planets Bureau Squad Leader.	TW
Sharr	A Valloan girl.	CotS
Shay	Navigator for the 2nd mission.	S
Shearing	A Lazurite.	LoL
Shemsi	A superman from a heavy world of Betelgeuse.	TM

Name		Story
Sherriff, Elda	M. Sherriff's daughter.	TW
Sherriff, Marriden	Head of the Outer Planets Bureau.	TW
Shoba Ruk	A Thirbarian expert in comparative cultures.	TM
Shota	A Japanese researcher.	srm
Sigri	John Terrell's Burmese servant.	lcb
Simms	Part of a previous expedition now lost.	hc
Skan	An eskimo guide.	DJ
Skeel, Herbert	One of C. Landon's fellow adventurers.	EB
Skene, Howard	Leader of renegade colony at Kirruk.	WoNM
Skuro	A Baran soldier & former Electrae.	TLU
Slavin	Burly trail boss .	WA
Sleeper		IS
Sloan, Nick	A mercenary.	VoC
Smith	A young flight-technician.	HS
Smith	A Tharinese Earth farmer.	NEI
Smith, Dr. Hayden	An astrophysicist	Ds
Snedeker, Maj. Frederick	Personnel of UNIS base 15.	sh
Socrates	Of the Brotherhood.	IOW
Somtum	A Starwolf council member.	SW3
Spafford, Louis	A worker on a burn crew.	u
Speer. Dr. James	Proffessor of Linguistics at Pacific University.	HS
Sinetti	A member of Dead Legs' gang.	dl
Spinoza	Dutch Philosopher, of the Brotherhood.	IOW
S'San	Of the Clawed clan.	DJ
Ssarn	A Starwolf.	SW2
Sserk	A Gerrn, Local leader, 2nd under Narath Teyn.	KotS
Stack	Captain of scout SC-1419.	tSH
Staines	L. Burdines's young aide.	STW
Stanton, Clark	A secret agent for the secret service division of the Earth government.	dov
Stanton, Mark	American chief engineer in Iran for the Trans-Iranian Railroad.	va
Steppling, Mr.	The cashier at the bank.	sm
Stevens, Emma	Henry's wife.	DW
Stevens, Henry	30 year old insurance official.	DW
Sthan	Ulios' servant.	SS
Stinson, Victor	Aggressive mine promotor.	WA
Strang, David	A geologist working with Dr. Thorne.	ed
Strann	Leader of the Wind people.	NEI
Straw, John		CotS
Stuart, John	A young insurance agent.	FN
Surp	A Baran noble with designs on the throne.	TLU
Su Suum	The last man, of the Brotherhood.	IOW

Name		Story
Su, Dr, Quil	A Martian biologist.	FlS
Sullivan	A policeman.	dcg
Susurr	A H'harn.	tBS
Sutur	Lord of Muspelheim.	TG
Sweetbriar	Old leathery chief.	CotSL
Sweigert, Jay	J. Edward's large Earthman guide.	LToM
Takinu, Dr.	Chief of Astrophysical research at the Bureau of Astronomy, Tananaru.	DS
Tammas, Shau	A Mizarian member of J. Wilson's men.	SoL
Tark	Leader of the Hairy Ones.	VoC
Tatichin	A Vhollan general.	SW1
Taylor	A payclerk at the Etna Construction company.	im
Tepper, Alan	John's older brother.	NEI
Tepper, John	A Terran farmer on Tharin.	NEI
Tepper, Larry	John's nephew.	NEI
Tepper, Nancy	John's niece.	NEI
Terrell, John	An agent on a mission.	lcb
Thal	A martian trying to save his race.	hf
Thanl	Master of the cold fire.	WA
Tharkol	Philip Cranes's father's Baran name.	TLU
Theramos of Korsh	An ancient VanRyn.	HS
Thoh	A mechanized man, servant to N. Arkol.	MV
Thomason	An engineer.	HS
Thor	Of The Hammer; son of Odin.	TG, YV
Thorn, John	A dark headed earthman and a planeteer.	TP
Thorn, Dr. Willis	Psychoanalyst	DW
Thorne, Christa	Dr. Thorne's daughter.	ed
Thorne, Dr. Ferdinand	A geologist working in the hills of New Mexico.	ed
Thorneycroft, Mrs.	The most formidable matron in the suburb.	de
Thorneycroft, Wibur	The banker, husband of Mrs. Thorneycroft	de
Thorpe	An operator at the New York Power Station.	pp
Thorpe		SP
Thrandirin	A Vhollan.	SW1
Thrayn	A contemporary VanRyn male.	HS
Th'Rulu	A Martian inn keeper in Little Mars.	STW
Tiamat	Evil serpent goddess – princess.	SP
Tiberius/Caligula	A Roman emperor.	AA
Tinnis, Bert	A fellow prisoner.	wws
Todd, Peter	Deputy Sheriff.	sm
Tolarg	Council member from Pluto.	tw
Tolti	Martian girl.	SfI
Townsend, Francis	Dr. H. Gilbert's assistant.	Mm

Name		Story
Trask, Francis	An over-daring American prospector.	Vim
Trask, Haskell	Dictator of the League of Cold Planets.	TP
Trask, Luther	Corporate counsel of the King company.	mkf
Travis	One of C. Landon's fellow adventurers.	EB
Trondor	Leader of the Hoofed clan.	DJ
Tula	Liline's sister.	lmg
Twist	Missouris tribesman.	CotSL
Tyr	Of the Sword. An Aesir master Swordsman, a Berserk.	TG, YV
Ulios	The Guardian of the Force .	AA
Ullman, Burke	Dr. J. Madison's assistant.	QT
Urmson	A member of the Vulcan's crew.	HA
Utgar	The Jotun King.	YV
Usk, Jurk	A Jovian shipping-magnate.	MV
Vail, Vagros	Outer Planets Bureau Personel.	TW
Vaillant	Human.	SmB
Valain	Female of the First Race.	KS
Valdes	Chief of the Terran Empire Intellegence Organization.	tSH
Valinez, Joe	Firstt casualty - died in transit.	WLOT
Valinez, Martin	Father to Joe Valinez .	WLOT
Vali	One of Odin's sons.	YV
Vallely,	Dr. Darnow's assistant.	R
Van Duyck	Did not survive the invisible Masters' attack.	im
Van Fleet	One of L. Harvey's henchmen.	TM
Van Fossen	A mercenary.	SW2, SW3
Van hijnn, Willwm	A Dutch engineer.	srm
Van Voss, Peit	A Dutch mercenary.	VoC
Vare, Joel	Owns a drugstore on Bott's Island.	DB
Vaughn,	Mjr. Cheers relief operator.	sh
Veblen,	The sociologist who comes up with the theory of conspicous consumption.	de
Venetti,	A policeman.	mc
Vengant	A Starwolf.	SW2, SW3
Vernon	Bellaver's No.1 henchman.	LoL
Vickers, Howard	Chief of Solar System Security.	DS
Victor	R. Farrel's friend and shipmate.	SfI
Vidar	One of Odin's sons.	YV
Vinson	The Vega Queen's second pilot.	FSe
Vinson, Lt.		SmB
Viresson, Mr.	A member of the survey ship's crew.	R
Vito	Helps with Johnny Lands' plans.	FW
Von Der Ahe	Fellow treasure hunter.	WoNm

Name		Story
Von Gersten, Dr. Herman	from Berlin.	srm
Vonn	A Starwolf Council member.	SW3
Voss, Roscoe	A fat promoter.	nwe
V'rann	An Orion intelligence agent.	tSH
Vrenn	Martian bartender.	WoNM
Vreya	An Arkuuin member of the Open Worlds party.	SW2
Vurll	John's Tharinese forman.	NEI
Wade, Marshal	H. Vicker's aide.	DS
Wade, Sgt.		mc
Wade, Sgt.	A police inspector.	Im
Wall,	Of the UNIS.	sh
Wall, Capt.		WLOT
Wallace	Bryants co-pilot and astrogator.	CK
Wally, Uncle	Corala's conjure man.	s-m
Walters,	The attorney.	de
Walters, Chad	Tall, haggard, blond, young scientist at Gotham University.	nwe
Walton, Dr.	A scientist.	EI
Wandek, Lt. Charles	UNRC, Detroit.	SmB
Warner, Duke	A gangster that runs a night club.	bh
Wasek	Captain of the Vega Queen.	Se
Weathering, Richard	Leader of the 2nd Mars expedition.	CTW
Webber	Human.	SmB
Weiler, Major		WLOT
Weiler, Gen. Bert	Comander of UNIS base 1.	sh
Weiler, Lucy	Wife of General Bert Weiler.	sh
Welk, Gunner	A huge mercurian and a planetter.	TP
Wentworth, Ann	John Wentworth's daughter.	HA
Wentworth, John	Owner of Wentworth Mines.	HA
White, Dr.	He performs the surgery.	HHW
White Dr. Norbert	He thinks he's solved death.	MSD
Whitmer	No. 1 bad guy.	SfI
Wilets, Miss Christine	A.K.A. Jean King.	FlS
Wilkes	One of P.C. Crail's men.	srm
Wilkes, Bodie	The Mayor of Bott's Island.	DB
Williams, John	A farmer on the edge of the swamp.	s-m
Williams, William	A citizen of Carnarvon, Wales.	SW2
Willingdon, James	Owner of Willingdon and company.	MXE
Willis	Outer Planets Bureau Ganymede commander.	TW
Wilsoff, Serge	Of the Soviet Moscow laboratories.	srm
Wilsey, Alice	Arthur Newton's fiancee.	vm
Wilsey, Mrs.	Alice's concerned mother.	vm
Wilson	A policeman.	Mc

Name		Story
Wilson	A fellow worker with Eric Rand.	MM
Wilson, Iva	Jon's Daughter.	SoL
Wilson, Jon	Leader of a group trying to get to Althar.	SoL
Wilson, Mr.	John Stuart's boss.	FN
Wilson, Shay		cp2
Wimer	A burn crew worker who saw two Vennies.	U
Winn, David	A young newspaper reporter.	MXE
Winn, Dr. harris	Of the Detroit Scientific College.	srm
Winstedt	A biologist.	HS
Winster, Lefty	A cockney mercenary.	VoC
Winters	An office clerk at the Proxy Project.	pp
Withers. Mr.	The sponsor of the non-tonal music.	de
Withers, Owen	A representative of the Smithsonian.	HS
Winton, Peter	The local representative of the automobile industry.	s-m
Witter, Mike	A watchman.	CWE
Wolverson, Eric	A man with a lost past..	TG
Woodford, Dorothy	Jack Woodford's wife.	MwR
Woodford, Jack	John Woodford's son.	MwR
Woodford, John	Suffers from cataleptic sleeps.	MwR
Wolley,	A middle-aged clerk in a NY office.	mm
Wright, Arthur	An old college pal of Dr. J. Pollard.	MwE
Yanez, Pedro	A Spanish soldier recovering from a coma.	LM
Yarr	A Starwolf council member.	SW3
Ylleen	a negative woman from Mars.	ntsm
Ylva	Martian woman.	WoNM
Yorolin	A Vhollan.	SW1
Yu Chi	A minor Chinese warlord fighting the Communists.	VoC
Yso	Morivenn's daughter.	FotS, FSe
Zarias	Brilliant physicist, irreverent Greek.	T
Zoor	Wizened third member with Khal and But.	DW
Zyskyn	A 31st century physist, of the Brotherhood.	IOW

Cities:

Name		Planet	Story
Annamar	Bryant's secret city.	Midway	CK
Angkor	A dead city.	Earth	WA
Anshan	Humanite town of L'lan.	Earth	VoC
Ardmore, PA	Home of Hugh Macklin.	Earth	SP
Asgard	Home of the Aesir.	Earth	TG
Basra		Earth	SP
Chelorne	Mythical.	Mars	WoNM
Chicago, IL	Home of Millis.	Earth	WLOT
Cuffington, NE	Home of Graham.	Earth	WLOT

Name			Story
Copan	Ancient Mayan city.	Earth	LM
Ganymede Colony		Ganymede	DB
Harmonville, OH	Home of Hadden.	Earth	WLOT
Ingomar	Baran Capital.	Bara (Mars)	TLU
Khartach	Ancient ruins.	Mars	SfI
Khlun	Last City on Earth.	Earth	cq
Khotan			KS
Kirruk	Martian/Human.	Mars	WoNM
Kothamr	Ancient City.	Midway	CK
Kranzak	Hungarian village.	Earth	va
Linnabar		Lyra	tSH
L'lan	A hidden valley.	Earth	VoC
L'lon	An abandoned city.	Bara (Mars)	TLU
Llona	Martian.	Mars	WoNM
Lluegos	Cuban port.	Earth	EI
M'lann	Ancient ruins.	Akruu	SW2
Noh-Ek	Ancient Venusian colony.	Earth	LM
Quroon City		Quroon	tSH
Rillah		Skereth	FotS
Rurooma		Earth	SoL
Rylik	Ancient ruins.	Mars	LToM
San Gabriel, CA	Home of Valinez family.	Earth	WLOT
Santahar	City of shadows.	Earth	KS
Saturnopolis	the capital of Saturn.		TP
Sharanna	Vramen fortress.	Althar	SoL
Stortfors	Norwegian village.	Earth	TG
Syrtis City	Human colony.	Mars	LoL, LToM
Terraopolis		Earth	NEI
Uranopolis	A city.	Uranus	FlS
Ushtu	Ancient ruins.	Mars	LToM
Vonn	The 3rd Men's City.	Althar	SoL
Vosek	A Jovian city.		TP
Vruun	Brotherhood town of L'lan.	Earth	VoC
Weislant	Hungarian village.	Earth	va
Yarr	City.	Akruu	SW2
Yen Shi	A Chinese frontier town.	Earth	VoC
Yurgan	A village in Turkey.	Earth	CW
Zor	The last city.	Earth	AE

Places:

Name		Story
Aarn	A land of the far future.	C
Altai		KS

Name		Story
Dragal Mountains	On Thar.	DW
Galoon	On Thar.	DW
Jotanland	Coastal Country.	DW
Kizil Kum		KS
Krim	Land where the Shining God resides.	vim
Kaubos	On Thar.	DW
Transuranice Station	On the face of the moon.	T
UNRC Space Lab #5	A.K.A. Wheel Five, a space station.	SmB
Yamaya	The fabled land where the flame of life is supposed to be.	lcb
Zambrian Sea	On Thar.	DW
Zair	A river in Aarn.	C

Ships:

Name		Story
Algol	A transport Ship.	STW
Alice N.	A wrecked freighter.	HA
Cauphal	A pirate ship.	TP
Draco	A passenger ship.	FlS
Earth-Guard Rocket 28		eeg
Expedition One		WLOT
Expedition Two		WLOT
Expedition Three		WLOT
Expedition Four		WLOT
Farhope		Sfl
Gargol	A Saturnian Cruiser.	TP
Grellah	Boker's Ship.	DS
Gull	Flagship of the Ineer Planet Alliance fleet.	TP
Happy Dream		LoL
Jackson N. Willings	A wrecked freighter.	HA
Larkoom	Old second-rate starship.	FW
Lightning	A pirate ship.	TP
Martian Queen	A passenger ship.	SS
Martin P. Green	Earth Ato-Freighter.	TW
Mary Andrew	Doc Brewer's Carnival Ship.	TM
Moonflower II	David Maddeen's project.	lmg
Pallas	A one man rocket.	eeg
Pallas	A transport Ship.	STW
Pallas	A freighter.	SS
Peter Saul	An auxilary Ice-breaker.	YV
Phoebus	J.C.'s Ship.	TM
Phoenix		CotS
Pioneer		wsb

Name		Story
Rantal	An alliance cruiser.	TP
Spacehawk	John Randall's ship.	MM
Starbird	Seri Otku's ship.	DS
Thanis	A Federation ship.	CWE
Tharine	An alliance cruiser.	TP
Thetis		ntsm
Vega Queen	A Federation packet.	FotS
Vulcan	A big space-liner.	MV, HA
Y-90	Experimental cruiser.	S

Planets:

Name		Story
Akruu		SW2
Algol 1		TM
Altair Two		SmB
Altair 4		FW
Althar	The mysterious Vramen World.	SoL
Bara	Baran for Mars.	TLU
Canopus 2		FW
Cholu	Baran for Earth.	TLU
Chorann	A planet out on the Rim.	FotS
Erebus	The tenth planet.	TP
Gurra	A planet of the Hyades Cluster.	DS
Hathyr	Capital of the Fomalhaut Kingdom.	tBS
Heartworld	The birthplace of all humans.	TM
Kabu	Baran for a Martian moon.	TLU
Kirnanoc	A Planet of the Hyades Cluster.	DS
Kuum	The Prison Planet.	SoL
Midway	A barely habitable planet on the Rim.	CK
Mrunn		SW3
Noru	Baran for a Martian moon.	TLU
Polaris 1		FW
Qui	A moon of Thar .	DW
Quilus	A moon of Thar.	DW
Quroon	Chief World of the Marches.	tSH
Rigel II		TM
Rith		SW3
Rutha	Baran for Venus.	TLU
Ryn	Home of the Vanryn (Altarir III).	HS
Sako		SmB
Sirius 5		TM
Shandor 5		SW1
Skereth		FotS

Name		Story
Tananaru	Capital of the Hyades Cluster.	DS
Teyn	Nareth Teyn's World.	KotS
Thallarna	Capital of the Dark Worlds.	tBS
Thar		DW
Thirbar		TM
Tharin	A Human colony with two native races.	NEI
Throon	Capital of the Empire.	tBS
Thwayn	A planet of the Hyades Cluster.	DS
Trace	A planet of the Hyades Cluster.	DS
Turkoon	The pirate asteroid.	TP
Varkon	Somewhere in the Megellanic Cloud.	CK
Varna	Home world of the Starwolves.	SW1
Vega 4	Capital of the Federation.	CWE
Vhol	A world bent on conquering it's neighbor, Kharal.	SW1

Stars:

Name		Story
Aar		tBS
Allamar		FSe
Altair		HS, SmB
Binnoth		FSe
Marral	Teyn.	KotS
Quroon	Quroon.	HS, tSH
Sirius	Home of the Aliens.	KS
Vira		FSe

Races:

Name — Story

Altor — GI

Each being is a soft, bulbous white mass about eighteen inches across that is both the head and body. They have eight long, thin, white tendrils. They do not use these tendrils to stand or walk, but they float in the air trailing the tendrils beneath them.

Andromedans — OU

Beings of this race are tall (six feet) columns of green gas. Each side of the column projects two smaller "arms." Their bodies are solid like flesh. They move by gliding through the air.

Antarian — OU

Name	Story

This race has a metal shell replacing what would be human skin. They have three arms and three legs and stand upright. They have a ball-like upper brain chamber with a triangle of three eyes. This race is immune to fatigue.

Antolians tw

These are the inhabitants of the four worlds of the star Antol. They are a race of liquid beings. Their bodies are a pool of thick viscous black fluid. They have two eyes that float within the pool. They can expand pseudopod limbs in any direction and at any time.

Beetle-men dt

They are from the Fifth Dimension. The are out to conquer the earth for its' mineral wealth.

Bunts DW

This is a tribe to the south of Jotan. They are barbarian green men and are enemies of Jotan.

Chorann FotS

Each is a furry, dark green spheroid being about four feet in diameter that half floats in the air and half walks on 4 or 5 long red tentacles. They are from a planet with gravity greater than the Earth's. They have no head, eyes or face.

Children of the Stars S

They look like flakes of flame. They possess extreme telepathic powers.

Ei CotSL

They are taller than men and they have cowls and draperies edged in thin translucent gray that is their substance, quivering, shifting, gliding around some unguessable central core being. It is not known if there are faces and eyes under the black folds.

Felshi NEI

This is a race of humaniods that live exclusively on top of the scarps of Tharin. They have highly developed telepathic powers.

First Race KS

These are shadow people.

Name	Story
Fourth Men	SoL

Gerrn — KotS

This is a felinoid centaur-like race. The largest are able to carry an adult male as a rider. They have large slanted eyes.

H'harn — tBS

Hoomen — SoL

These are humans 1000 years in the future.

K'harn — CotS

Krens — KotS

They are about 5 feet tall and feathered. Their wings terminate with a long clawed hand. This species is flightless.

L'lorn — HS

These are bipedal humanoids with short thick arms, legs and bodies. They have dark hairless skins and no perceptible sex organs. Their heads are broad and neckless with wide mouths and nostril-openings. Their eyes have no pupils. With some technological device, they are able to cloak themselves in shadows.

Mineral-Fleshed Men — pp13

This race is a silicon based life form that lives in the depths of the Earth. Their semi-human bodies are grey and rough. Their faces are blank and eyeless possessing only a mouth. They project fire from their mouths and from any puncture wound. Their digestive system work using fire.

Moon Men — mm

This race is about as tall as humans. They are plump and dark, oily skinned. Thick round projections of arms and legs end in flipper like hands and feet. They are small, round heads without noses or ears. Their mouth is a narrow horizontal slit and the eyes are tiny and closed set, white in color without pupils.

Nagas — lcb

This race is human sized, and us an ophidian character of mankind. They have greyish-green bodies. Their legs and arms are more like tentacles. Their heads are snakelike, blunted and

Name	Story

browless. They have wide, white-lipped mouths and lidless eyes. Their skin shines with a faint iridescent luminosity.

Octopus-men hc

These biengs look like a sphere of black flesh roughly a foot in diameter. The have two black-pupilled eyes and a narrow mouth opening. They have innumerable 5-6 foot tenteceles in every direction.

Qhalla tBS

These are stubby-winged reptilian avian bipeds. They are much bigger than the Krens. They have no feathers instead their skin is grey or tan and leather-like. They have bulging eyes above a long toothed beak. Their wings serve as arms and end in claw-like hands.

Raddies pp

These inhabitants of Mercury are little clouds of radon gas with a denser core of an unknown radium compound. The core is a crystalized gaseous neuron structure that has evolv into a neuronic structure that is able to recieve and remember stimuli. The body consists of radon gas that is emanated from the core. Since the half-life of radon is the same as its emission from the radium, the creature exists in equlibrium.

The race is of high intelligence and pursues purely intellectual ideals. They do possess great knowledge about radioactivity.

Rheans MM

This race is native to Rhea, the moon of Saturn. They are a gaseous life form. They look like small clouds of coiling black vapor. They enter a human body through the mouth and nose and are able to posses that person.

Sakae SmB

These are inhabitants of Sako. They are bipedal lizardoids of high intelligence and they are an advanced civilization.

Serpent People OU

This race is from an unknown small dark galaxy close to the Andromeda galaxy.They have long, slender snake-like shapes of wriggling pale flesh. They are about ten feet long with both ends being flat. One end has a pair of bulging many-lensed eyes and a small black opening below.

Name	Story
Spician	OU

This is a Crustacean race whose shell is a glossy black. They have short, thick and stiff erect bodies with two upper arms and two legs. Their head is conical with two protruding round eyes.

Tharinese — NEI

This is a humanoid race of Tharin.

Third Men — SoL

Valloan — CotS

Vanryn — HS

These humans native to the the planet Ryn, are identical to humans from Earth. Thirty thousand years ago, these are abandoned colonists began a terran civilization and culture.

Varkonides — CK

Lean Olive-green skinned Human warriors. They usually wear a fancy harness when on a raiding mission.

Vennies — U

These are the native Venusian life-form. They are big and appear to be the muddy beginnings of men. They have coarse-grained gray skin.

Venusians — srm

They have green-skinned bodies in a basic human shape. They seem to have no skeleton. Their legs and arms are great tentacles that taper down to semi-human fingers and toes.This race developed in the oceans of Venus.

Vramen — SoL

They are normal humans except that they live forever, barring physical injury.

Vurna — CotSL

This race is from Vrain 4. They are tall and well-formed and they looked much like Earthmen. They are bronzed and their hair is silver.

? — FotS

Name Story

These are small grey skinned humanoid beings about 5 feet tall. They are accented with beautiful shadings of electric blue banded with fine lines of black and yellow on their breast, back and along their limbs. Their eyes are yellow.

? FotS

This race appears to be humanoid up to the neck. Their heads have pointed ears.

Creatures:

Hunati

These are humans drugged such that they live at the same metabolism rate of plants.

Moon Dogs

These small gray-scaled, massive beasts have six short legs and large blunt heads. They have wide jaws with enormous fangs.

Pimul Birds

This is a species of bird native to Mars.

Pyam

This is a small yellow furred mannequin-like, turnip shaped native of Vhol. It has two small legs, two eyes, and a small mouth. It has the ability to read the minds of anyone it can see. It has enough language ability to repeat this.

Slith

A bulbous, oily gray monster that is native to Saturn. It is ten feet high. It has a dumpy shapeless body with thick little legs. It has two bright eyes in front of it's faceless body. It has a white fanged mouth.

Space-dog

Stand about 3 feet high at the shoulder. The body si dusty mineraline gray flesh that has and inoganic look to it. It's four legs end in heavy digging pawes. It's mouht is furnished with great grinding tusks. It has no nostrils because it does not need to breathe.

Vardak

A furry martian critter.

Story Abbreviations

Capitalized abgreviations indicate longer works and lowercase for shorter works.

AA The Avenger from Atlantis (The Vengence of Ulios)
AE Alien Earth
AG The Accursed Galaxy
bh A Brother to Him
bs Babylon in the Sky
bowm Beasts that Once Were Men
C Castaway
CK *The Cosmic Kings as Alexander Blade*
CotS Corridor of the Suns
CotSL Citadel of the Star Lords
cp The Cosmic Pantograph
cp2 Copper Proof
cq Cosmic Quest
ct Children of Terror
CTW A Conquest of Two Worlds
CW Child of the Winds
CWE City at Worlds End
DB The Dark Backward
dcg Death Comes in Glass
dd Death Dolls
DD Dweller in Darkness
de The Deconventionalizers
DJ Day of Judgement
dl Dead Legs
DM Day of the Micro-men
dov Doom Over Venus
DS Doomstar
dt The Dimension Terror
DW Dreamers Worlds
E Exile
EB The Earth Brain
ed The Earth Dwellers
eeg Evans of the Earth-Guard
EI Evolution Island
EP The Ephemarae
ff Face to Face
FlS The Free-Lance of Space
FN The Fear Neutralizer
FotS Fugitive of the Stars
FSe Fugitive of the Stars (expanded)
fw Fessenden's Worlds
FW Forgotten World
GI *Great Illusion As Will Garth*
HA The Horror on the Asteroid
hc The Horror City
he The House of the Evil Eye
hf Holmes' Folly
HHW He that Hath Wings
HS Haunted Stars, The
im The Invisible Master
im2 Indestructable Man
IOW The Inn Outside the Universe
IS The Isle of the Sleeper
IU The Island of Unreason
IWD In the World's Dusk
km The Knowledge Machine
KotS Kingdom of the Stars
KS The King of Shadows
lcb The Lost City of Burma
LM Lords of the Morning
lmg Lilene, the Moon Girl
LoL Legion of Lazarus
LToM Lost Treasure of Mars
ma Murder Asteroid
mc The Murder in the Clinic
MG The Metal Giants
mg Master of Genes
MGoM The Monster-God of Mamurth
mkf Murder in the King Family
MM Mystery Moon
mm The Moon Menace

moe Mutiny on Europa
MSD The Man Who Solved Death
MV Murder in the Void
MwE The Man who Evolved
MwR The Man Who Returned
MXE The Man with X-Ray Eyes
NEI No Earthman I
ntsm Never the Twain Shall Meet
nwe The Night the World Ended
OU Outside the Universe
pl Priestess of the Labyrinth
pp Proxy Planeteers
pp13 Power Pit 13
QT The Quest in Time
R Requiem
S Sunfire
sh Sacrifice Hit
SfI The Ship From Infinity
s-m Snake-Man
sm Sea Murder
SmB The Stars, My Brothers
smr Space Mirror
SoL The Star of Life
SP Serpent Princess
srm Space-Rocket Murders
SS The Sargasso of Space
STW Son of Two Worlds
SW1 Starwolf #1: The Weapon from Beyond
SW2 Starwolf #2: The Closed Worlds
SW3 Starwolf #3: The World of the Starwolves
swm Short-Wave Madness
T Transuranic
tBS The Broken Stars
TG Twilight of the Gods
tg The Truth Gas
TLU Tharkol Lord of the Unknown
TM *The Tattooed Man As Alexander Blade*
TP The Three Planeteers
tSH The Star Hunter
TW Thunder World
tw Thundering Worlds
U The Unforgiven
UWS Under the White Star
va The Valley of the Assassins
vim Valley of Invisible Men
vm The Vampire Master
VoC The Valley of Creation
vv Vampire Village
WA The Watcher of Ages
wa World Atavism
wi Woman From the Ice
WLOT What's It Like Out There
WoNM World of Never-Men
wsb When Space Burst
wws World Without Sex
YV A Yank at Valhalla

Appendix F
Story Classification

Novels

A Yank at Valhalla
Across Space
Calling Captain Future
Captain Future and the Seven Space Stones
Captain Future and the Space Emperor
Captain Future's Challenge
Citadel of the Starlords
Cities in the Air
City at World's End
Comet Kings, The
Crashing Suns
Face of the Deep
Fire Princess, The
Forgotten World
Hidden World
Lake of Life
Legend of Lazarus, The
Legion of Lazarus, The
Lords of the Morning
Lost World of Time, The
Magic Moon - Brett Sterling
Magician of Mars, The
Other Side of the Moon, The
Outlaw World
Outlaws of the Moon, The
Outside the Universe
Planets in Peril
Red Sun of Danger-Brett Sterling
Quest beyond the Stars, The
Quest In Time, The
Ship From Infinity, The
Star Hunter, The
Star Kings, The
Star of Dread, The - Brett Sterling
Star of Life, The
Star Trail to Glory
Starman Come Home
Thunder World
Time Raider
Triumph of Captain Future, The
Universe Wreckers, The
Valley of Creation, The
Vampire Master, The -Hugh Davidson
World of Never-Men

Novelets

A Conquest of Two Worlds
Alien Earth
Birthplace of Creation
Children of the Sun
Comet Doom, The
Corsairs of the Cosmos
Death Lord, The
Dictators of Creation
Dimension Terror, The
Dogs of Dr. Dwann, The
Doom Over Venus
Earthman No More
Gift From the Stars
Great Brain of Kaldar, The
Invisible Master, The
Kingdom of the Stars
Lilene, The Moon Girl
Lost Treasure of Mars, The
Man who Lived Twice, The
Monsters of Mars
Murder in the Clinic, The
Mystery Moon

Never the Twain Shall Meet - Brett Sterling
Pardon My Iron Nerves
Polar Doom, The
Return of Captain Future, The
Revolt on the Tenth World, The
Sea Horror, The
Sea Terror, The
Serpent Princess
Son of Two Worlds
Ten Million Years Ahead
Valley of Invisible Men
World with a Thousand Moons, The

Short Stories

Accursed Galaxy, The
After A Judgement Day
Alien Earth
Armies of the Past
Atomic Conquerors, The
Avenger From Atlantis, The
Castaway
Child of the Winds
Comet Drivers, The
Comrades of Time
Conqueror's Voice - Robert Castle
Cosmic Cloud, The
Cosmic Pantograph, The
Cosmic Quest
Cosmos End
Day of Judgement
Dead Legs
Dreamers Worlds
Earth Brain, The
Earth-Owners, The
Easy Money
Emphemerae, The
Eternal Cycle
Evens of the Earth Guard
Exile
Fessenden's Worlds
Fire Creatures, The
Free-Lance of Space, The
Great Illusion, The - Will Garth
He That Hath Wings
Horror City, The
Horror on the Asteroid
In the Worlds Dusk
Inn Outside the World, The
Invaders from the Monster World
Island of Unreason, The
Ilse of the Sleeper, The
Kaldar, World of Antares
King of Shadows, The
Life Masters, The
Locked Worlds
Man Who Conquered Age, The
Man Who Evolved, The
Man Who Returned, The
Man Who Saw the Future, The
Man Who Solved Death, The
Man With X-Ray Eyes, The
Master of Genes
Metal Giants, The
Might-Have-Been, The
Mind-Master, The
Monster-God of Mamurth, The
Moon Menace, The
Murder in the Void
Murder in the Grave
Never the Twain Shall Meet - Brett Sterling
Pigmy Island
Plant Revolt, The
Pro, The
Reign of the Robots, The
Requiem
Sargasso of Space, The
Second Satellite, The
Seeds From Outside, The
Serpent Princess
Shot From Saturn, The
Short-Wave Madness - Robert

Series

<u>Captain Future</u>
See Appendix C
<u>Charlie Carton</u>
"The Invisible Master"
"Murder in the Clinic"
<u>Rab Crane</u>
"Space Mirror"
"Murder in the Void"
<u>Brian Cullan</u>
"The Shining Land"
Lost Elysium"
<u>Doctor Dale</u>
"The Vampire Master"
"House of the Evile Eye"
<u>Ethan Drew</u>
"Comrades of Time"
"Armies of the Past"
<u>Gabriel Hoom</u>
"Ball Bearing Death"
"Death Comes in Glass"
<u>The Interstellar Patrol</u>
"The Star Stealers"
"Within the Nebula"
"The Crashing Suns"
"The Comet Drivers"
- collected into **Crashing Suns**
"Outside the Universe"
"The Sun People"
"Corsairs of the Cosmos"
- collected into **Outside the Universe**"The Sun People"
<u>Stuart Merrick</u>
"Kaldar, World of Antares"
"Snake-Men of Kaldar"
"Great Brain of Kaldar"
<u>Star Kings or John Gordan</u>
The Star Kings
"The Broken Stars"
"The Kingdom of the Stars"
"The Shores of Infinity"
"The Horror From the Magellanic"
- collected into **Return to the Stars**
<u>Starwolf or Morgan Chane</u>
The Weapon From Beyond
The Closed Worlds
World of the Starwolves
- collected into **Starwolf**

Translations

"A Conquest of Two Worlds
Die Eroberung Zweier Welten
"A Yank at Valhalla"
En Yankee Far Till Vahall
Unternehmen Walhalla
"After a Judgement Day"
Nach Einem Gerichstag
"Alien Earth"
Fremde Erde
"Accursed Galaxy"
Die Verflichte Galaxis
"Babylon in the Sky"
Die Stadt am Himmel
"Battle for the Stars"
Die Gestirn der Ahen
Die Heimat der Astronauten
La Spedizione della V Flotta
La Spedizione della Quinta Flotta
"Calling Captain Future"
Panik Im Kosmos
Kollisionsziel Erde
"Captain Future & the Space Emperor"

Diamanten der Macht
Captain Future en de Keizer van het Hedal
Die lebende Legende
Kaoten Frank och rymdkejsaren
"Captain Future's Challenge"
Kampf Um Gravium
Die Gravium Sabotage
"Castaway"
Ein Ausgetossner
"Child of the Winds"
Das Kind Der Winde
"City at World's End"
SOS, die Erde erkaltet
Ville Sous Glode
Agonia della Terra
"The Closed Worlds"
Todesschranke um Allubane
Morgan Chane, Il Lupo dei Cieli
Les Monde Interdits
"The Comet Doom"
Der grune Komet
Kosmisches Schauspiel
"The Comet Kings"
Im schatten der allus
"Crashing Suns"
Patrulha Interstellar
"Danger Planet"
Die Krypta der Kangas
"Day of Judgement"
Tag Des Gerichts
"Devolution"
Die Degenerierten
"Easy Money"
Leichtverientes Geld
"Face of the Deep"
Planetoid des Todes
"Fessenden's Worlds"
Fessendes Welten
"Fugitve of the Stars"
Fluchtling der Randwelten
"The Haunted Stars"
Das Gestirn der Ahnen
Gli Incappucciati d'ombre
"He That Hath Wings"
Der Mann, Der Flugel Hatte
"In the Worlds Dusk"
Der Letzte Mensch
Welt im Damerlicht
"The Island of Unreason"
Die Insel Der Umvernunft
"Kingdom of the Stars"
Konigreich Der Sterne
Die Sternenkonigreiche
"The Lost World of Time"
Im Zeitstrom verschollen
"The Magician of Mars"
Der Marsmagier
"The Man Who Evolved'
Der Mann, Der Sich Entwickete
"The Man Who Returned"
Der Mann, Der Zuruckkehrte
"The Monster-God of Mamurth"
Der Monster-Gott Von Mamurth
"Outlaw World"
Die Radium Falle
"Outlaws of the Moon"
Das Erbe der Lunarier
"Outside the Universe"
Luta Inter-galactica
L'invasione della Galassia
Hors de l'univers & Les voleurs d'etoiles
"Planets in Peril"
Held der Sage
Held der Vergangenheit
"The Pro"
Der Profit
"Quest Beyond the Stars"
Komisk Fara
Gefahr aus dem Kosmos
Die Matariequelle
"Return to the Stars"
Le retour aux etoiles
Ihre Heimat sind die Sterne
Regresso Aos Ceus
"The Seed from Outside"
Dir Saat Aus Dem All
"The Shores of Infinity"
An den fern der Unendlichkeit

"The Star Kings"
Les Rois des Etoiles
Herrscher im Weltraum: 200,000 Jarhe Spater
Guerra nella galassia
Los reyes de las estrellas
Dir Sternenkonige
"Star of Dread"
Verrat Auf Titan
Stern des Grauens
"The Star of Life"
Das Gestirn des Lebens
La stella dellavita
L'Astre de Vie
"Star Trail to Glory"
Sternstrasse zum Ruhm
"Starman Come Home"
Im Banne der Cergangenheit
"The Stars, My Brothers"
Meine Bruder Sind Die
"Sterne Sunfire"
Kinder der Sonne
Sonnefeuer
"The Sun Smasher"
Im Banne der Vergangenheit
Die Macht der Valkan
"Thunder World"
In Den Klauen Jupiters
"The Triumph of Captain Future"
Captain Zunkunft Greift Ein
Der Lebenslord
"Twilight of the Gods"
Gotterdammerung
"The Valley of Assassins"
Das Tal Der Assassinen
"The Valley of Creation"
Das Tal der Schoepfung
Les Vallee Magique
La Vallee Magique
O Vale Da Criacao
"The Watcher of Ages"
Wachter Der Zeiten
"The Weapon from Beyond"
Arma do Alben
Der Sternwolf
Il lupo dei Cieli
Les Loups des etoiles
L'Arme de Nulle Part
"What's It Like Out There?"
Wie Ist Es Dort Draussen
Godensctemering
Wie Ist Es Da Ohen
"World of the Starwolves"
Die Singenden Sonnen
Le Planete des Loups

Notes

[i.] Best guess from signature.

[ii.] This edition possibly includes a reprint of "Island of Unreason." Unconfirmed.

[iii.] See A4.

[iv.] According to I.F. Clarke in "Tales of the Future," this book had only 70 pages. However, according to the British Library card catalog it has 256 pages.

[v.] From the Royal Library the Hague, Netherlands card catalog.

[vi] Please visit http://www.capitaineflam.free.fr/ for more information on media format and what languages.

[vii.] This is part of a series of which no more were published. This looks much like a magazine. It advertises a part two "Kapten Frank och spokstjarnan," and also contains two short articles, one on Grag and one aboutJupiter. The article on Grag is a reprint from Captain Future Magazine.

[viii] Please visit http://www.capitaineflam.free.fr/ for more information on what formats are available in what languages.

[ix] Please visit http://www.capitaineflam.free.fr/ for more information on what formats are available in what languages.

[x] Please visit http://www.capitaineflam.free.fr/ for more information on what formats are available in what languages.

[xi] Please visit http://www.capitaineflam.free.fr/ for more information on what formats are available in what languages.

[xii] Please visit http://www.capitaineflam.free.fr/ for more information on what formats are available in what languages.

[xiii] Please visit http://www.capitaineflam.free.fr/ for more information on what formats are available in what languages.

[xiv] Please visit http://www.capitaineflam.free.fr/ for more information on what formats are available in what languages.

[xv] Please visit http://www.capitaineflam.free.fr/ for more information on what formats are available in what languages.

[xvi] Please visit http://www.capitaineflam.free.fr/ for more information on what formats are available in what languages.

[xvii]. This story was originally titled "Dead Universe," but changed at the editor's request. In a letter from Oscar J. Friend dated 27 Feb. 1942.

[xviii] Please visit http://www.capitaineflam.free.fr/ for more information on what formats are available in what languages.

[xix] Please visit http://www.capitaineflam.free.fr/ for more information on what formats are available in what languages.

[xx]. Originally published under the pseudonym of Brett Sterling.

[xxi] Please visit http://www.capitaineflam.free.fr/ for more information on what formats are available in what languages.

[xxii]. Originally published under the pseudonym of Brett Sterling.

[xxiii] Please visit http://www.capitaineflam.free.fr/ for more information on what formats are available in what languages.

[xxiv]. Originally published under the pseudonym of Brett Sterling.

[xxv]. Originally published under the pseudonym of Brett Sterling. Cover, title and date is from Curry. Also contains "Magician" by E. Hoffman Price, p. 26-33. Printed in Erie.

[xxvi]. This only contains an exerpt of the original story.

[xxvii]. This story was serialized, at least twice, by King Feature. It is unknown where the serializations appeared or when, other than they were started prior to Oct 1959. From a letter from Leo Margulies dated 15 Oct. 1959.

[xxviii]. A letter from Helen M. Herman of New American Library dated 20 Sept 1950 states that "Beyond the Moon's" publication date will be 22 September 1950.

[xxix]. A letter from Oscar J. Friend dated 23 September states that reprint rights have been given to Malcom Reiss for reprinting in Planet Stories. It is not known when or if this story actually appeared in that magazine.

[xxx]. Taken from a royalty statement from Frederick Fell, Inc. dated 23 November

1951.

xxxi. From a letter from Wayne Da Metz dated 26 November 1951 requesting permission to make a dramatic presentation of "**Beyond The Moon**." It is unknown when or if the production went on.

xxxii. TTB stands for Terra-Taschenbuch.

xxxiii. Also found listing as Munchen. Perhaps publisher exists (existed) in both cities.

xxxiv. There were at least two printings of this edition, one in 1961 and the other in 1964.

xxxv. __: Crest, . 1960 p. (P-2625).

xxxvi. Originally published under the pseudonym of Alexander Blade.

xxxvii. This novellet was enlarged and released under Mr. Hamilton's own name.

xxxviii. This story was expanded and then reprinted.

xxxix. This book has 142 pages according to I.F. Clarke in "Tales of the Future."

xl. This is a collection of shorter stories edited together to make a novel.

xli. The last two stories "The Broken Stars," and "The Horror From the Magellanic" were written by Mr. Hamilton at the request of the French publisher. Those stories had not appeared in English publications prior to the publication of the French edition.

xlii. This edition contains a bilbliograh of Mr. Hamilton by Pierr Versins.

xliii The Starwolf trilogy is recommend by the Science Fiction Museum and Hall of Fame as an example for the category of Space Opera. http://www.sfhomeworld.org/make_contact/details.asp?display=sfmRec&list=spaceopera

xliv. Part #14 of the Lindquists LP pocket series.

xlv. The title story originally appeared in Amazing Stories 39:4 (September 1964) Pg. 6. The second story "The Shores of Infinity" originally appeared in Amazing Stories (April 1965)

xlvi. The title story originally appeared in Amazing Stories (September 1962). The story "The Comet Doom" originally appeared in Amazing Stories (June 1928). The story "Babylon in the Sky" originally appeared in Amazing Stories (March 1963). The story "Devolution" originally appeared in Amazing Stories (December 1936).

xlvii. The title story originally appeared in Thrilling Wonder Stories (December 1952) p. 66.

xlviii. From the Royal Library the Hague, Netherlands card catalog.

xlix Volume one of a planned 14 volume series from Haffner Press.

l Volume two of a planned 14 volume series from Haffner Press.

li Volume one of a planned 6 volume series from Haffner Press.
Also check Appendix C for more information on Captain Future.

lii. Letter from Farnsworth Wright (Weird Tales) dated 26 Mar. 1926. This story was Mr. Hamilton's first publication. It was originally titled "Beyond the Unseen Wall," but Mr. Wright did not think that that was a good title, letters dated 1 Feb. 1926 & 9 Feb 1926.

liii. Letter from Farnsworth Wright (Weird Tales) dated 18 May 1926.

liv. This stands for Hugh Rankin

lv. In a letter dated 25 Jan. 1937 Farnsworth Wright (Weird Tales) gives the publication date as "Coronation time".

lvi. A letter from Farnsworth Wright (Weird Tales) dated 7 March 1933 states that "The Master of Minds" will be given early broadcast. It is unknown if this was ever recorded and broadcast.

lvii. In letters from Oscar J. Friend (28 July 1949 & 8 Oct. 1949) this anthology is supposed to be a Hall-of-fame anthology.

lviii. The cover this month for this story was by an unknown artist.

lix. Reprinted as a "Hall of Fame Classic".

lx. A letter from Farnsworth Wright (Weird Tales) dated 7 March 1937 states that this was recorded for broadcast in April of 1937. The cast was: Wm.

Darnum; Priscilla Dean; Frank Glendon; Robert Hoover; John Ince; Pat O'Mally; Bert Roach. It is unknown if and when this broadcast took place.

[lxi]. Originally published under the pseudonym of Hugh Davidson.

[lxii]. A letter from Farnsworth Wright (Weird Tales) dated 7 March 1933 states that this story will be given early broadcast. It is unknown if this was ever recorded and broadcast.

[lxiii]. Originally published under the pseudonym of Hugh Davidson.

[lxiv]. This story is possibly included in the 1946 Utopia Press repirint of the anthology **Murder in the Clinic**.

[lxv] The story has an introduction that starts on page 153.

[lxvi]. Written under the pseudonym of Hugh Davidson.

[lxvii]. The cover depicted this story. The artist is unknown.

[lxviii]. This story was purchased for the movies. However, RogerCorman's movie of the same name is not based upon this. Thestory was purchased to forstall any potential legaldifficulties afterwards.

[lxix]. Reprinted as a "Hall of Fame Classic."

[lxx]. This signature was hard to read. It is believed to be"Marchism"

[lxxi]. This anthology is a derivative anthology of the previous entry. It was plit by Sphere into two Volumes, **Weird Tales** and **More Weird Tales**.

[lxxii]. From a letter from Farnsworth Wright (Weird Tales) dated 31March 1934.

[lxxiii]. This story was chapter 17 of the collaberative effort "Cosmos".

[lxxiv].This 7,000 word story was the first submission to Solar Sales Service. An Author agent service started by Mort Weissinger and Julius Schwartz while still in there teens.

Schwartz, Julius & Brian M. Thomsen. **Man of Two Worlds**. New York, NY: Harper Collins Publishing Inc, 2000. Page 25.

[lxxv]. From a letter by Charles D. Horning (Wonder Stories) dated 8 February 1935.

[lxxvi] One of Julius Schwartz's high points as an agent for Solar Sales service was when he was able to sell this story to Astounding, a magazine Mr. Hamilton had not been able to crack.

Schwartz, Julius & Brian M. Thomsen. **Man of Two Worlds**. New York, NY: Harper Collins Publishing Inc, 2000.

[lxxvii] From a letter by Doone Burkes of the Fiction Digest Co. dated16 Oct. 1936. It is unknown what issue this appeared in. <u>30 Thrilling Tales</u> was a <u>Reader's Digest</u> like magazine that reprinted abridged versions of stories from other magazines.They did not pay the author, nor ask his permission. This letter basically states that this has been done.

[lxxviii] Originally published under the pseudonym of Hugh Davidson.

[lxxix] The last name of the artist is difficult to make out. It might be "Deloy."

[lxxx] From a letter by Farnsworth Wright (<u>Weird Tales</u>) dated 7 July1936.

[lxxxi] This story is on the NESFA Core Reading List of Fantasy and Science Fiction. http://www.nesfa.org/reading.htm

[lxxxii] This story is one of Mr. Hamilton's most popular stories in India.

[lxxxiii] Originally published under the pseudonym of Robert Castle.

[lxxxiv] This story was voted the Most Popular Story of the Month forthe April 1938 appearance in Thrilling Wonder Stories.

[lxxxv] From the Royal Library the Hague, Netherlands card catalog.

[lxxxvi] The artist's signature is difficult to make out. It could beMarchio."

[lxxxvii] Originally published under the pseudonym of Robert Castle.

[lxxxviii] This cover was done by Hannes Bok though Virgil Finaly wasoriginally slated to do it. From two letters by Farnsworth Wright (<u>Weird Tales</u>) dated 11 December 1939 & 29 January 1940.

[lxxxix] Originally published under the pseudonym of Robert Wentworth.

[xc] From the Royal Library the Hague, Netherlands card catalog.

[xci] This story is on the NESFA Core Reading List of Fantasy and Science Fiction. http://www.nesfa.org/reading.htm

[xcii] This story is on the NESFA Core Reading List of Fantasy and Science Fiction. http://www.nesfa.org/reading.htm

[xciii.] There was a Mexican edition of this book that did contain atranslation of this story.

[xciv.] From the Royal Library the Hague, Netherlands card catalog.

[xcv.] In another letter from Oscar J. Friend (24 August 1950) it states that this story ill appear in **Ten Short Science Fiction Novels** edited by Leo Margulies & Oscar J. Friend, to be published by Merlin Press. This could be **Giant Book of Science Fiction**.

[xcvi.] Two letters from Oscar J. Friend, one not dated and the other 19 April 1959, mention a Pelligrini & Cudahy collection by Augie Derleth (possibly published by Arkham House). It is unknown whether or not that proposed anthology became this one.

[xcvii.] From the Royal Library the Hague, Netherlands card catalog.

[xcviii.] From the Royal Library the Hague, Netherlands card catalog.

[xcix.] From the Royal Library the Hague, Netherlands card catalog.

[c.] A letter from Drayton S. Haff dated 5 August 1948 mentions this story going to be an anthology by Mr. Furman of Lantern Press.It is unknown what ever became of this.

[ci.] From the Royal Library the Hague, Netherlands card catalog.

[cii.] This ws being turned into a play in Tulsa, Oklahoma. From Mr. Forrest J. Ackerman.

[ciii.] From the Royal Library the Hague, Netherlands card catalog.

[civ.] Possibly 1981. Rastatt/Baden: Pabel. 1961. Translation: Horst Hoffmann

[cv] This story is on the NESFA Core Reading List of Fantasy and Science Fiction. http://www.nesfa.org/reading.htm.
This story is also mentioned in the article "Educational Program about Wildland Fire Integrates Plant Science into Curriculum" in Plant Science

Bulletin. 43:7 (2001) ISSN 0032-0919. Pg. 86. Published quarterly by Botanical Society of America, Inc. 1735 Neil Ave. Columbus, OH 43210. http://www.botany.org/bsa/psb/2001/psb47-3.html

cvi This story is on the NESFA Core Reading List of Fantasy and Science Fiction. http://www.nesfa.org/reading.htm

cvii. This information came from two letters from Pierre Versins, one dated 8 August 20,960 and the other 2 May 1961. Exact date of broadcast is unknown.

cviii. From the Royal Library the Hague, Netherlands card catalog.

cix. Originally published under the pseudonym of Alexander Blade.

cx. Originally published under the pseudonym of Alexander Blade.

cxi. Originally published under the pseudonym of Alexander Blade.

cxii. Originally published under the pseudonym of S. M. Tenneshaw.

cxiii. Originally published under the pseudonym of Alexander Blade.

cxiv. This is listed as starting on page 8 in the contents of the magazine.

cxv. From the Royal Library the Hague, Netherlands card catalog.

cxvi. This story was incorporated into “Return to the Stars”.

cxvii This story is on the NESFA Core Reading List of Fantasy and Science Fiction. http://www.nesfa.org/reading.htm

cxviii. From the Royal Library the Hague, Netherlands card catalog.

cxix. This is the only known collaberation between Mr. Hamilton andhis wife, Leigh Brackett.

cxx. Found in the Jack Williamson Collection at Easter New Mexico University, Portales, NM as item H2 W956.

cxxi. Found in the Jack Williamson Collection at Easter New Mexico University, Portales, NM as item H2 F721. Suspected to be in ___.

[cxxii.] Found in the Jack Williamson Collection at Easter New Mexico University, Portales, NM as item H2 T328.

[cxxiii.] Found in the Jack Williamson Collection at Easter New Mexico University, Portales, NM as item H2 T583.

[cxxiv.] Found in the Jack Williamson Collection at Easter New Mexico University, Portales, NM.

[cxxv.] No reference to this series can be found. It is believed that this series was never aired. In the Hamilton papers at Golden Library - Eastern New Mexico University, there is also a copy of the authors background and "Munsey's Proton's" by Martin Stern. (This is referred to as 5901). This script is registered 1959, by Pine-Key Productions, Inc.

[cxxvi.] Horn, Maurice. **The World Encyclopedia of Comics Vol.1 & Vol. 2**. New York, NY: Chelsea House Publishers. 1976. Pg. 117. Benton, Mike. **Superheroes Comics of the Golden Age**. Dallas, TX. Taylor Publishing Co.

This is questionable as this is earlier that the correspondence between Mr. Hamilton and Mr. Weisinger where Mr. Weisinger treis to woo Mr. Hamilton to scripting comics.

[cxxvii.] From Mort Weisinger.

[cxxviii.] From **Batman: The Complete History**, by Les Daniels. San Francisco, Callifornia: Chronicle Books. 1999. 209 p.

[cxxix.] Schwartz, Julius & Brian M. Thomsen. **Man of Two Worlds**. New York, NY: Harper Collins Publishing Inc, 2000. Page 114.

[cxxx.] **Schwartz, Julius & Brian M. Thomsen. Man of Two Worlds**. New York, NY: Harper Collins Publishing Inc, 2000. Page 114.

[cxxxi] In the DC series 52 Grant Morrison made reference to this story. As explained in the notes to 52 "a wink and nod to silver age planet Lexor."

[cxxxii.] This script is H2 B334 in the Special Collections at Golden Library of Eastern New Mexico University. There is a letter referring to this script being sent back to Edmond Hamilton. The note states that the changes are all the editor's fault, and the story is good for his first comic story.

[cxxxiii.] This script is H2 G797 in the Special Collections at Golden Library of Eastern

New Mexico University. This script is incomplete.

[cxxxiv.] This is Curt Swans favorite Superman story.
Daniels, Les. **Superman: The Complete History**.San Francisco, CA: Chronicle Books, 1998.

[cxxxv.] This script is H2 S959 in the Special Collections at Golden Library of Eastern New Mexico University. This is part two of the story begun in "The World that was Krypton's Twin!." On the cover of the script is a note stating that it was sent May 26, 1957.

[cxxxvi.] This script is H2 S959 in the Special Collections at Golden Library of Eastern New Mexico University. "The World that was Krypton's Twin!" is part one of a story that concludes in "The Substitute Superman!." On the cover of the script is a note stating that it was sent May 22, 1957.

[cxxxvii.] A reference to this article was found in one of the other Future Fan's in the Jack Williamson collection. The fanzine is in swedish so only part of it is known to the compiler.

[cxxxviii.] The title of this article is unknown.

[cxxxix.] This article is from the Edmond hamilton Collection at Eastern New Mexico University's Golden Library. The clipping, however, did not contaion the name, date or even page number of the newspaper it was taken from.

[cxl.] This entry is the only one that is not a World Wide Web page. This is a text document that can be downloaded. Entering this URL into the Web browser should begin the transfer of this file.

[cxli.] The letter I sent to this address came back "Addressee Unknown - Return to Sender"

[cxlii.] Please see Appendix B - Pseudonyms for more on the pseudonyms used by Mr. Hamilton.

[cxliii.] This is a non-fiction article.

[cxliv] Please visit http://www.capitaineflam.free.fr/ for more information on what formats are available in what languages.

[cxlv] Please visit http://www.capitaineflam.free.fr/ for more information on what formats are available in what languages.

[cxlvi.] From the Royal Library the Hague, Netherlands card catalog.

[cxlvii] Please visit http://www.capitaineflam.free.fr/ for more information on what formats are available in what languages.

[cxlviii.] This is part of a series of which no more were published. This looks much like a magazine. It advertises a part two "Kapten Frank och spokstjarnan," and also contains two short articles, one on Grag and one about Jupiter. The article on Grag is a reprint from Captain Future Magazine.

[cxlix] Please visit http://www.capitaineflam.free.fr/ for more information on what formats are available in what languages.

[cl] Please visit http://www.capitaineflam.free.fr/ for more information on what formats are available in what languages.

[cli.] Written by Joseph Samachson writing as Brett Sterling.

[clii] Please visit http://www.capitaineflam.free.fr/ for more information on what formats are available in what languages.

[cliii] Please visit http://www.capitaineflam.free.fr/ for more information on what formats are available in what languages.

[cliv] Please visit http://www.capitaineflam.free.fr/ for more information on what formats are available in what languages.

[clv.] Written by Edmond Hamilton writing as Brett Sterling.

[clvi] Please visit http://www.capitaineflam.free.fr/ for more information on what formats are available in what languages.

[clvii] Please visit http://www.capitaineflam.free.fr/ for more information on what formats are available in what languages.

[clviii] Please visit http://www.capitaineflam.free.fr/ for more information on what formats are available in what languages.

[clix.] Written by Edmond Hamilton writing as Brett Sterling.

[clx.] Written by Manly Wade Wellman.

[clxi.] Written by Edmond Hamilton writing as Brett Sterling.

[clxii] Please visit http://www.capitaineflam.free.fr/ for more information on what formats are available in what languages.

[clxiii] Please visit http://www.capitaineflam.free.fr/ for more information on what formats are available in what languages.

[clxiv] Please visit http://www.capitaineflam.free.fr/ for more information on what formats are available in what languages.

[clxv.] Written by Joseph Samachson writing as Brett Sterling.

[clxvi.] Written by J. Samachson as Brett Sterling.

[clxvii.] Written by Edmond Hamilton as Brett Sterling.

[clxviii.] Written by J. Samachson as Brett Sterling

[clxix.] Written by Edmond Hamilton as Brett Sterling.

[clxx.] A vote for any book in this series was counted as a vote for this book.

Made in the USA